THE CRITICAL RESPONSE
TO TILLIE OLSEN

**Recent Titles in
Critical Responses in Arts and Letters**

THE CRITICAL RESPONSE TO TILLIE OLSEN

Edited by
KAY HOYLE NELSON
and
NANCY HUSE

Critical Responses in Arts and Letters, Number 10
Cameron Northouse, Series Adviser

GREENWOOD PRESS
Westport, Connecticut • London

Library of Congress Cataloging-in-Publication Data

The Critical response to Tillie Olsen / edited by Kay Hoyle Nelson and
  Nancy Huse.
    p. cm.—(Critical responses in arts and letters, ISSN
  1057-0993 ; no. 10)
   Includes bibliographical references and index.
   ISBN 0-313-28714-7 (alk. paper)
   1. Olsen, Tillie—Criticism and interpretation. I. Nelson, Kay
Hoyle. II. Huse, Nancy Lyman. III. Series.
PS3565.L82Z615 1994
813'.54—dc20   93-41228

British Library Cataloguing in Publication Data is available.

Library of Congress Catalog Card Number: 93-41228
ISBN: 0-313-28714-7
ISSN: 1057-0993

First published in 1994

Greenwood Press, 88 Post Road West, Westport, CT 06881
An imprint of Greenwood Publishing Group, Inc.

Printed in the United States of America

The paper used in this book complies with the
Permanent Paper Standard issued by the National
Information Standards Organization (Z39.48-1984).

10 9 8 7 6 5 4 3 2

Copyright Acknowledgments

The editors and publisher gratefully acknowledge the following for permission to use copyrighted materials:

Peter Ackroyd. "The Living Image." *Spectator* 14 December 1974: 767-68. Excerpt reprinted with the kind permission of Spectator Ltd.

Margaret Atwood. "Obstacle Course." *New York Times Book Review* 30 July 1978: 1, 17. Copyright © 1978 by The New York Times Company. Reprinted by permission.

Joanne Trautmann Banks. "Death Labors." *Literature and Medicine* 9 (1990): 162-71. Reprinted with permission of The John Hopkins University Press.

Selma Burkom and Margaret Williams. "De-Riddling Tillie Olsen's Writings." *San Jose Studies* 2.1 (February 1976): 65-83. Reprinted with the kind permission of *San Jose Studies* and authors.

Robert Cantwell. "The Literary Life in California." *New Republic* 22 August 1934: 49.

Constance Coiner. "'No One's Private Ground': A Bakhtinian Reading of Tillie Olsen's *Tell Me a Riddle.*" This article (with revisions) is reprinted from *Feminist Studies*, Volume 18, number 2 (Summer 1992): 257-81, by permission of the publisher, *Feminist Studies, Inc.*, c/o Women's Studies Program, University of Maryland, College Park, MD 20742.

Richard M. Elman. "The Many Forms Which Loss Can Take." *Commonweal* 8 December 1961: 295-96. Copyright © 1961 *Commonweal*. Reprinted by permission.

permission of Tillie Olsen and Delacorte Press/Seymour Lawrence, a Division of Bantam, Doubleday, Dell Publishing. Copyright 1956; "Tillie Olsen Says," *People's World* April 18-June 11, 1946. Passages quoted extensively with the kind permission of the author; *Yonnondio: From the Thirties.* Passages quoted by the contributors. Reprinted by permission of Tillie Olsen and Delacorte Press/Seymour Lawrence, a Division of Bantam, Doubleday, Dell Publishing. Copyright 1974.

Linda Park-Fuller. "Voices: Bakhtin's Heteroglossia and Polyphony, and the Performance of Narrative Literature." *Literature in Performance: A Journal of Literary and Performing Art* 7.1 (November 1986): 1-12. Reprinted with the kind permission of the author.

Adrienne Rich. The lines from "Diving into the Wreck" are reprinted from *The Fact of a Doorframe, Poems Selected and New, 1950-1984,* by Adrienne Rich, by permission of the author and W. W. Norton & Company, Inc. Copyright © 1984 by Adrienne Rich. Copyright © 1975, 1978 by W. W. Norton & Company, Inc. Copyright © 1981 by Adrienne Rich.

Ellen Cronan Rose. "Limning: Or Why Tillie Writes." *The Hollins Critic* April 1976: 1-9, 11, 13. Reprinted with the kind permission of *The Hollins Critic* as holder of Copyright.

Deborah Rosenfelt. "From the Thirties: Tillie Olsen and the Radical Tradition." This article is reprinted from *Feminist Studies,* Volume 7, number 3 (Fall 1981): 371-406, by permission of the publisher, *Feminist Studies, Inc.,* c/o Women's Studies Program, University of Maryland, College Park, MD 20742.

Catharine R. Stimpson. "Three Woman Work It Out." *The Nation* 30 November 1974: 565-66. This excerpt is reprinted from *The Nation* magazine. © 1974 The Nation Company, Inc.

Valerie Trueblood. "Books: Tillie Olsen. *Silences."American Poetry Review* May-June 1979: 18-19. Reprinted with the kind permission of World Poetry, Inc., Philadelphia, Pennsylvania.

Scott Turow. "Tillie Olsen's *Yonnondio." Ploughshares* 2.2 (1974): 113-17. Reprinted with the kind permission of the author.

Contents

The 1970s-1990s: Mentorings through Word & Deed

Series Foreword

Critical Responses in Arts and Letters is designed to present a documentary history of highlights in the critical reception to the body of work of writers and artists and to individual works that are generally considered to be of major importance. The focus of each volume in this series is basically historical. The introductions to each volume are themselves brief histories of the critical response an author, artist, or individual work has received. This response is then further illustrated by reprinting a strong representation of the major critical reviews and articles that have collectively produced the author's, artist's, or work's critical reputation.

The scope of *Critical Responses in Arts and Letters* knows no chronological or geographical boundaries. Volumes under preparation include studies of individuals from around the world and in both contemporary and historical periods.

Each volume is the work of an individual editor (in this case with assistance from a co-editor), who surveys the entire body of criticism on a single author, artist, or work. The editor then selects the best material to depict the critical response received by an author or artist over his/her entire career. Documents produced by the author or artist may also be included when the editor finds that they are necessary to a full understanding of the materials at hand. In circumstances where previous, isolated volumes of criticism on a particular individual or work exist, the editor carefully selects material that better reflects the nature and directions of the critical response over time.

In addition to the introduction and the documentary section, the editor of each volume is free to solicit new essays on areas that may not have been adequately dealt with in previous criticism. Also, for volumes on living writers and artists, new interviews may be included, again at the discretion of the volume's editor. The volumes also provide a supplementary bibliography and are fully indexed.

While each volume in *Critical Responses in Arts and Letters* is unique, it is also hoped that in combination they form a useful, documentary history of the critical response to the arts, and one that can be easily and profitably employed by students and scholars.

Cameron Northouse

Acknowledgments

This project began long before we knew how it might be accomplished.

Upon first encountering Tillie Olsen's work in an NEH Seminar on Jewish American Writing Since 1945, I was perplexed by a pattern—a couple of early poems and articles, a long period of silence, then a few short stories followed by more silence, finally a collection of talks and essays engaging the concept of literary silence. My friend and colleague Nancy Huse responded to my queries about this woman's life and art by proposing that we collaborate on a collection that would bring Olsen more of the recognition she richly deserves yet respond to the critical questions raised so often by teachers like ourselves and students.

Locating the reviews, articles, and essays seemed a daunting task, scattered as they were in popular magazines and newspapers, in periodicals devoted to poetry and fiction, in journals conversant with literary and feminist theory, in publications both foreign and domestic. Later Tillie Olsen would prove an ally in recalling some of the rarer pieces. She readily agreed to meet and talk when she learned of my long-standing friendship with Dale Huse, who still revels in the time he squired her about the Illinois-Iowa Quad Cities during a week-long symposium there in her honor.

When the time arrived for retrieval of so many items contained in this book, or mentioned in the bibliography, Kay Culhane, the librarian for Interlibrary Loans at Aurora University, seemed to make it a personal quest; she managed to gather an impressive number by locating even the most arcane sources. Then our inclusion in the series *Critical Responses in Arts and Letters* gave us an orientation and prompted our respective academic institutions to help. The Augustana College Faculty Research Committee, chaired by Bea Jacobson, provided funding for manuscript preparation. The Aurora Faculty Development Committee contributed toward the cost of supplies as well as secretarial assistance. Their generous support was more than matched by the efforts of our word processing expert from Augustana, for without Susan Granet this collection would still be a project under consideration.

Special thanks are due to Dale Huse for lending his proofreading skills, to Lois Roney for reminding me of reader expectations, and to Sara Frasher for agreeing to a painstaking review of the introduction to this volume.

Many others have applauded and encouraged this undertaking, and we hope that they will find the collection itself a gesture of our appreciation.

Kay Hoyle Nelson

Chronology

1912   Tillie is born January 14 on a Mead, Nebraska, tenant farm, the
or   second child of Samuel and Ida Lerner, Russian Jews who first
1913   met in the Minsk Bund, left their homeland after the failed 1905
        revolution, emigrated to New York, then settled in Nebraska.

1917   Moves with family to Omaha where her father finds employ-
        ment as a painter, paper-hanger, and packinghouse worker
        while her mother raises the children. Her father, who actively
        supports American workers beginning to organize in agriculture,
        mining, and industry, joins the Socialist Party in Nebraska. Her
        parents participate in social and cultural organizations promot-
        ing secular Jewish activities—these laying the foundation for her
        Yiddishkeit.

1918 - Assists with the care of five siblings and attends elementary
1924   school. Childhood illnesses provide the major time for reading.
        Because of stuttering, she speaks little but listens attentively to
        the many who frequent her home—socialist orators, packing
        house workers, immigrants, Afro-American neighbors, sodders,
        even cowboys. All speech—including that of librarians, teachers,
        and peers—fascinates her.

1925 - Attends Central High, the only public college preparatory school
1929   in Omaha, reading classic writers such as Shakespeare, Browne,
        and DeQuincy as well as contemporary poets like Sandburg. She
        produces a humor column for the school paper. During this
        period, she must work—shelling almonds, acting as a mother's

helper, assisting in a grocery store. Nevertheless, reading becomes a passion. Because she has only the school hour for this activity she develops speed—planning to read all the fiction and biography in the public library. In a bookstore stall, she discovers *Atlantic Monthly* issues with the unsigned *Life in the Iron Mills*; it confirms her desire to write of the voiceless working class. She begins keeping journals. She joins the Young People's Socialist League and writes skits and musicals for the group.

1929 - Leaves school after the 11th grade. With the onset of the
1930   Depression, she embarks on a decades-long employment odyssey of low-paying jobs. She moves to Stockton, California. Her early poetry develops as she discovers the modern poets.

1931   Relocates to the Kansas-Missouri area, joins the Young Communist League, and attends the Party school. She is jailed for distributing leaflets to packing-house workers. Later she will leave the YCL.

1932   Starts writing a novel after moving to Faribault, Minnesota, to recover from incipient tuberculosis contracted in jail. Her first daughter Karla is born in Minneapolis.

1933   Returns to California, a working mother surviving on a diet of cheap and plentiful artichokes. Employment at San Francisco's luxury St. Francis Hotel means promotion from cleaning rooms to checking supplies. She meets YCL associate Jack Olsen, a waterfront warehouseman, union organizer, and educator who shares her commitment to struggle for justice for the working class.

1934   Contributes to waterfront organizing by mimeographing, typing, and writing leaflets. After the clashes which result in "Bloody Thursday," she joins the General Strike; she is jailed for "vagrancy" along with hundreds of strikers, activists and individuals from the general populace. She publishes the two poems "I Want You Women Up North to Know" and "There Is a Lesson," the short story "The Iron Throat," and the two pieces of reportage, "Thousand-Dollar Vagrant" and "The Strike."

1935   Attends American Writers Congress in New York along with such contemporaries as Mike Gold, James Farrell, and Nelson Algren.

1936   Establishes life-long relationship with Jack Olsen. She holds various jobs to maintain the household income.

1938   Gives birth to second daughter Julie and writes occasional pieces for *People's World*, a communist newspaper.

1939 - Helps with warehouse unions and war relief through the
1942   Congress of Industrial Organization. She becomes the California Director of the CIO and President of its Women's Auxiliary; she works for the War Relief and the Serviceman's Committee.

1943 - Gives birth to third daughter Katherin and marries Jack Olsen.
1944   Jack Olsen is drafted, and Tillie works with the canteen and family services. She helps establish the first child care center in San Francisco and becomes President of the PTA.

1946   Writes a column for *People's World*. From time to time, her membership in Communist Party lapses.

1948 - Gives birth to fourth daughter Lauri. Her activism focuses on
1953   better schools and libraries. During the McCarthy era, both Jack and Tillie Olsen are targeted as subversives—he is barred from sensitive waterfront employment and must begin a new career as a printer's apprentice; she is tracked by the FBI and is forced to move from job to job. In response to the Cold War, she begins anti-nuclear activities.

1954   Enrolls in, but does not complete, a creative writing course at San Francisco State.

1955 - Publishes the story "Help Her to Believe" which is later re-
1956   printed as "I Stand Here Ironing." She receives a Stanford University Creative Writing Center Fellowship.

1957   Publishes "Hey Sailor, What Ship?" and then "Baptism" which is reprinted later as "O Yes."

1959   Receives Ford Foundation Grant in Literature.

1960   Publishes the novella "Tell Me a Riddle" which wins the O.
            Henry Award for Best Story of the Year.

1962 -   Collects the four stories in *Tell Me a Riddle*. She accepts a two-
1964   year fellowship for Independent Study at Radcliffe Institute.

1965   Publishes in *Harper's Magazine* "Silences—When Writers Don't
            Write," an edited version of the speech delivered at the 1963
            Radcliffe Institute.

1967   Receives National Endowment for the Arts, Grant in Literature.

1969 -   Becomes Professor and Writer-in-Residence at Amherst College.
1970   She publishes "Requa-I."

1971 -   Takes a position as Visiting Lecturer at Stanford University
1972   Writing Center Seminar and gives a course on women and
            literature; she constructs the first reading list for women's
            studies. The speech "Women Who are Writers in Our Century"
            is later edited for *College English*. She puts together the
            manuscript for *Yonnondio*.

1972   Writes as grantee at MacDowell Colony in New Hampshire and
            publishes "A Biographical Interpretation," the afterword to *Life
            in the Iron Mills* by Rebecca Harding Davis.

1973 -   Lectures as Writer-in-Residence at Massachusetts Institute of
1974   Technology. She becomes Distinguished Visiting Professor at
            University of Massachusetts at Boston. Later at University of
            California, Santa Cruz, she lectures: her subjects include The
            Real Life Shakespeare Sisters (Dorothy Wordsworth, Alice
            James, Sophia Thoreau, Mary Moody Emerson); Eclipsed or
            Forgotten: Women Writers We Should Know; Women's Jour-
            nals and Letters; Women Writers and the Reality of Mad-
            ness/Suicide Mystique.

1974   Publishes the novel *Yonnondio: From the Thirties*. The original,
            recovered manuscripts, owned by the Berg Collection of the New
            York Public Library, are exhibited.

1975 -   Receives a Guggenheim Fellowship. She is cited for distinguished
1976   contribution to American Literature by the American Academy
         & National Institute of Arts and Letters.

1978   Publishes *Silences*, the collected talks and essays on the
         relationship of circumstances to creativity and what one does in
         the world. She teaches as the Board of Regents Visiting Lecturer
         at the University of California, San Diego.

1979   Accepts an honorary Doctor of Arts & Letters from University
         of Nebraska. She records "Reading: Selected Passages from the
         Novel *Yonnondio: From the Thirties,* 'I Stand Here Ironing,'
         'Tell Me a Riddle,' and Interview with Tillie Olsen."

1980   Travels as International Visiting Scholar for Norwegian Univer-
         sities at Trondheim, Bergen, Oslo, Tromosö. She speaks as the
         William James Synoptic Lecturer at Grand Valley College and
         as Radcliffe Centennial Visitor and Lecturer. More honors
         accrue in the annual "Ministry to Women" award from the
         Unitarian Women's Federation. With the worldwide issuance of
         stamps commemorating Emily Bronte, Charlotte Bronte, George
         Eliot, and Elizabeth Gaskell, the British Post Office and
         Business and Professional Women co-sponsor a special award for
         "the American woman writer best exemplifying in our time their
         ideals and literary excellence"; the award is presented to Olsen
         in Omaha. A film version of "Tell Me a Riddle" appears.

1981   Is honored by the San Francisco Mayor and Board of Supervi-
         sors who proclaim May 18 as "Tillie Olsen Day." She records
         "Tillie Olsen Interview with Kay Bonetti."

1982   Accepts an honorary degree as Doctor of Literature from Knox
         College. Her novel *Yonnondio: From the Thirties* is dramatized
         at the Twentieth Ozarks Arts Interpretation Festival.

1983 -   Is distinguished speaker, respondent and guest at the Tillie
1984   Olsen Week: The Writer and Society, March 21-26, a symposium
         sponsored by five colleges in the Quad Cities of Illinois and Iowa
         under direction of The Visiting Artist Series, Davenport, IA. She
         receives a Senior Fellowship from the National Endowment for
         the Humanities. An essay on her mother appears as "Dream-
         Vision" in *Mother to Daughter: Daughter to Mother: Mothers on*

Mothering: A Daybook and Reader. She accepts an honorary Doctor of Arts and Letters from Hobart and William Smith.

1985   Receives an honorary degree from Clark University.

1986   Contributes the Foreword to *Black Women Writers at Work.* She records "Tillie Olsen Reads 'I Stand Here Ironing' (Short Story) and Excerpts from *Yonnondio* and 'O Yes.'" She receives an honorary degree from Albright and becomes Hill Visiting Professor at the University of Minnesota.

1987   Co-authors with daughter Julie Olsen Edwards the prefatory essay "Mothers and Daughters" in *Mothers and Daughters: That Special Quality: An Exploration in Photography.* As Regents Lecturer, she teaches at University of California, Los Angeles.

1989   Her long-time partner Jack Olsen dies.

1991   Accepts the Mari Sandoz Award from the Nebraska Library Association in Omaha. She is recipient of an honorary degree from Wooster College.

1992 -   Continues reading and speaking engagements at conferences,
1993   works on writing at MacDowell Colony.

Introduction

In late April 1935, Tillie Olsen was one of thirty-six women among the four thousand people who attended the first Congress of American Writers in New York. She had the distinction of being the youngest of two hundred delegates gathered to organize the League of American Writers which would affiliate with The International Union of Revolutionary Writers. The following week, the leftist publication *New Masses* reported on the conference and included three papers addressing the values, benefits, and traditions of the movement. The papers and report were accompanied by a two-page spread of caricatures. Profiles of Malcolm Cowley, Edward Dahlberg, James Farrell, and Josephine Herbst, among others, were identified; the young Tillie Lerner was visible among the luminaries.[1]

This event along with its record acknowledged the activism and art of a promising new writer. As a keynote for *The Critical Response to Tillie Olsen*, this early recognition is a defining moment.

Those who know Olsen realize that she has achieved a foremost position on the American literary scene even though she has produced only a modest body of work. The offerings can be easily tallied: two early protest poems and two reportorial essays, the unfinished novel *Yonnondio: From the Thirties*, the four stories collected in *Tell Me a Riddle* plus "Requa," selected talks and notes on the circumstances of writing gathered in *Silences*, and a few prefatory essays and extraliterary publications. Those who have followed Olsen's career also realize that this working class woman writer without the advantages (or disadvantages) of a formal college education has earned substantial recognition in the academy. Her fiction appears on literature and creative writing syllabi; her nonfiction prose has become basic reading for women's studies courses. Moreover, with each reissued work, anthologized piece, and foreign language translation, she gains a wider hearing.

Her work has had broadest appeal to women and those concerned with the affairs of women. The reasons for the popularity are quite straightforward. Primarily, Olsen has gained attention because she has placed women at the center of her art as the stalwarts of class and gender struggle. She has crystallized the charge that twentieth-century American society has failed to understand and cultivate the full potential of its underclasses, particularly its working class women. In addition to fixing this perspective on women, she has fastened on the centrality of mothering, a role generally ignored in the literature. Furthermore, she has extended her sphere of concern to the circumstances which proscribe or preclude creative activity, mindful of the irony for mothers who find conditions for artistic productivity most elusive.

By her own struggle to develop a craft, and with a small but successful body of creative work, Olsen herself exemplifies a vital and under-appreciated source of creative potential. Her life and art demonstrate why the working class majority rarely speaks and why it leaves little evidence of its presence or part in the historical and literary record. More importantly, her life and art illustrate not only what can be lost when circumstances hinder creative expression but also what might be gained if encouragement is given.

The reviews and essays, which comprise the documentary section of this volume, will confirm the energy and resilience required for this achievement. For even by her early twenties, the political activist and aspiring writer Tillie Lerner, born to Russian Jewish immigrant parents and raised in the Nebraska heartland, had already left high school without receiving her diploma, embarked on a succession of blue-collar jobs, joined the Young Communist League, protested the intolerable factory conditions in Kansas City, and then relocated to California where she supported striking longshore and warehouse workers. Her poetry, fiction, and reportage took shape in a 1930s Marxist milieu which did not discriminate against feminist leanings. Two poems appeared early in 1934: "I Want You Women Up North to Know," based on a letter to the editors of *New Masses*, decried San Antonio sweatshop conditions, and it sought redress from other women by suggesting that the department store consumer purchased not only a lovely hand-embroidered child's dress but the lifeblood of its Mexican American seamstress; "There Is a Lesson" warned of the toll of a rising Nazism which had closed Austrian schools. Six months later, this young woman assessed the costs of a dual posture as writer and activist in two essays: "The Strike" exposed the wrenching dilemma of the activist-writer whose report comes at the price of withdrawal from the front lines; the "Thousand-Dollar Vagrant" recounted her arrest for associating with communists and mocked a justice system that levied a $1,000 bail with a vagrancy charge. During this period, Tillie Lerner also started the novel which tracked an American family from Wyoming coal mine to Dakota tenant farm to Nebraska slaughter house—with the plight of the country's working class men, women, and children an indictment of the capitalist system and the family's near-heroic struggles to withstand and survive widespread oppression a tribute to the human spirit. The first chapter only reached print in 1934.

Activism on behalf of community and country plus the increasing responsibilities of marriage and motherhood left little time for literary creation although Olsen did identify herself as a writer—she held positions as a staff writer for the *Western Worker* in the 1930s and as a columnist for the *People's World* in the 1940s. When World War II took men to serve and left women to shoulder the weight of industry, household, and child-rearing, like so many of her generation she felt deeply the economic, social, and political pressures which drain away the spirit. In the mid-1950s when her four daughters were nearly grown and her family duties were somewhat relaxed, she began the fiction which depicted these pressures. The stories subsequently collected and published in *Tell Me a Riddle* in 1961, along with "Requa" written a decade later, reveal her abiding theme—the struggle and survival of individuals cut off from the exercise of their full potential. Two exceptionally poignant working class female figures have become classic representations of the wrenching battle and the latent power: in "I Stand Here Ironing," the mother reflects on the life of her daughter which cannot be separated from her own, lamenting yet braced against the pressures that shape and misshape their lives; in "Tell Me a Riddle" an old woman at the end of her life battles more openly—her body racked by the spreading cancer and her spirit besieged by claims from husband, children, and grandchildren, all to be withstood if she is to reclaim her own early life-supporting vision of revolutionary idealism and hope. These especially powerful demonstrations of an oral/aural experience out of the printed word have had an influence beyond what might be anticipated for two short stories. Their importance rests in the new angle of vision on the mothering or mentoring role: they re-adjust the angle so that a new line of literary investigation opens.

The orientation toward mothering and mentoring also emerges as a literary midwifery. In the mid-1960s, Olsen had initiated an inquiry into the circumstances of writers, like herself, who had been silenced, or nearly so. Then in 1972, she watched over the reissue of *Life in the Iron*

Mills by Rebecca Harding Davis, the story she had discovered as a young writer which was the first art outside of socialist literature to show her the possibility of speaking for a silenced working class. This retrieval of the work of her literary foremother Davis afforded an opportunity to reengage with the literature of the past—to retrieve it and redeliver it. Olsen then undertook a similar but more complicated project with her own manuscript. Painstakingly, she pieced together and published in 1974 the unfinished *Yonnondio: From the Thirties.* This manuscript worked on during the mid-1930s, then laid aside as the weight of activism, employment, and motherhood grew heavier, surfaced and gave her, as she has said, an opportunity to partner with herself as the young author—*not* to complete the novel or to rewrite or revise, but to mentor, to bring that young writer of the 1930s to her own growing audience of the 1970s. Another form of mentoring came with the 1978 publication of *Silences.* This history of the circumstances of writing, the struggles and achievements, drew its examples from Olsen's experience and from others kept from writing. The first part included commentary familiar from earlier publications: "Silences in Literature—1962" and "One Out Twelve: Women Who Are Writers in Our Century—1971"; it concluded with the afterword she had written for the Davis story. The second part, a collage of notes and commentary, marked a return to poetry and reportage as a vehicle for communication.

At this time, Olsen also began cultivating a more immediate relationship with her audience. In conjunction with college lecturing, she began a daunting schedule of speaking engagements and literary readings. She refashioned an oral tradition nearly lost to the twentieth century. This favoring of the spoken word over the written word disappointed the many waiting for more stunning fiction or additional biographical outpourings. Yet for those who listened, Olsen's turn to the oral art simply confirmed her life-long love of the living language. Each appearance became a gift and a model for action.

Although admirers wondered about a retreat from writing as they saw years of creative opportunity slip away, their speculations rarely emerge as a discernible thread in the critical record. Rather, the studies retrace the major writing periods and accent, in varying degrees, the activism, the art, and the mentoring. The articles collected in this volume demonstrate, in addition, the reach of this author—with reviews and essays drawn from newspapers and popular magazines as well as literary and scholarly journals, with audiences comprised of novice readers and professional writers, high school students as well as university teachers.

Most of the responses in this collection focus on Olsen's place as a major working class feminist writer, although several assess her art within other literary traditions. To supplement the existing information, interpretations, and evaluations, new essays have been commissioned; they provide specific details from Olsen's Omaha milieu, facts about her newspaper columns, additional perspectives on the less frequently discussed stories, and fuller disclosures of the impact of this author's writing and speaking.

In keeping with the design of the series, *The Critical Response to Tillie Olsen* surveys the reception of her work, but this volume can serve too as a casebook and a companion to the other full-length studies. The representative reviews and landmark essays have been arranged in keeping with the primary writing periods, even though the resulting three-part structure may be as prone to misrepresentation as a straight chronology which would ignore the unusual publication history. Because space constraints have made it impossible to reprint many influential reactions, the following review of the critical reception quotes selected responses which merit special notice but do not appear in this collection. In acknowledging the reviews and essays which do appear, the commentary directs the reader to salient points or to the primary rationale for inclusion.

The 1930s-1940s: Radical Writings Discovered & Recovered

During the early period, Olsen's love of language, storytelling, and historical accuracy took form in poetry, fiction, and the reportorial essay. Although only the fiction has elicited sustained critical attention, it has always been appreciated as an art which exhibits the grace of poetic expression coupled with an excruciating realism. The first mention came in mid-1934 when author Robert Cantwell surveyed the country's burgeoning literary scene in "The Little Magazines." In the course of explaining the phenomenal appearance of dozens of literary magazines, he emphasized a cultural setting unwelcoming to disparate views—authors with specific social, political, and artistic agendas were establishing their own vehicles in order to reach wider audiences. His subsequent identification and classification of these magazines generated less excitement, however, than his discovery of "one fragment (by Tillie Lerner) so fresh and imaginative that even a cautious critic can call it a work of early genius."[2] In closing, he returned to this new writer and made her work even more appealing by declaring that "the imagery, the metaphors distilled out of common speech, are startling in their brilliance." He compared the young Tillie Lerner with the established Elizabeth Madox Roberts, finding the young writer's prose "firm where that of the older writer is soft and nostalgic, and poignant and tender where that of the older writer is sentimental and blurred" (297).

The next month in "The Literary Life in California," Cantwell felt compelled to update his readers since his praise had prompted Random House publishers to ask his help in locating her. In the process of relating a problem in tracking the young woman, he once more laid out the political climate and repressive circumstances that typified the straits for the country's 1930s radicals who sometimes just *"disappeared"*—some hiding, others missing, and a few, like Tillie Lerner, jailed. Although this first glimpse of a promising new writer initiated a search and eventual contact, efforts failed to induce the young working mother to publish further.

The piece that had so captured Cantwell's attention in 1934 was "The Iron Throat," the first chapter of the novel that follows a poor, working class family across the midwestern plains. Forty years later, in 1974, when the manuscript fragments were reassembled and published as *Yonnondio: From the Thirties,* reviewers seemed as impressed with the retrieval as with the fiction itself. Two of the three reviews reprinted in this volume elaborate on this reaction. In "Three Women Work It Out," feminist Catharine Stimpson heralds the novel as an historical witness saved from erasure, applauding as well this saga of disheartening life in the American heartland, a story which challenges once again the prevailing myth of a jazz-age America in the 1920s. In "The Living Image," a commentary appearing in the British *Spectator,* Peter Ackroyd commends the vibrancy of a language which raises the telling above a sentimental recounting of the American Depression but evinces little interest in the remarkable history of the narrative.[3] On the other hand, Scott Turow, a writer close to Olsen who saw the original manuscript, vividly recalls those fragments—his description of the brittle, yellowed sheets reminding his readers of the miracle of the transforming imagination.

Turow's appreciation of the language in *Yonnondio* as passionate, impressionistic, lyrical, compact, and concrete was echoed by other reviewers. For some, the aural appeals, evident in all Olsen writings, reverberated with a wider and deeper history. In "A Writer's Sounds and Silences," Annie Gottlieb elaborated on the novel's ability to reach into the past; she felt "it should be read aloud by firelight, that it was something very close, for immigrant America, to the myths of origin and wandering that carried the whole inner history of American Indian tribes."[4] Equally impressed by the pioneering spirit, Bell Gale Chevigny, in the *Village Voice,* spoke on behalf of Olsen's feminist positioning and her acute sense of her audience: "Tillie Olsen is miner, archeologist, and museum-curator for a special and growing collection. Special because in it she disdains her role of culture-bearer, of preserving man's culture, and salvages instead the work, the thought, the dream nearly buried beneath it because it belongs to the poor and forgotten, especially women." [5]

Yonnondio documented part of American history in the recovered writings of a young radical writer of the 1930s,[6] but it also shed new light on the working class woman who had gained substantial recognition in the 1950s for the four short stories collected in *Tell Me a Riddle*. In response to these revelations, Selma Burkom and Margaret Williams wrote an influential review essay in 1976. It reprinted the two early poems in their entirety and quoted from the essays to give readers immediate access to the writer; it also included details from Olsen's Nebraska upbringing as well as her California life with waterfront unionizing and violent city-wide strike actions. This study, included here, broadens the perspective on Olsen by setting her concern with the lives of women and children within a humanism that is tied to Marx and indebted to Whitman.

A second major contribution, one which elucidates the early problems faced by this working class woman, arrived in 1981 with Deborah Rosenfelt's essay "From the Thirties: Tillie Olsen and the Radical Tradition." Rosenfelt builds on the Burkom and Williams presentation, supplying more details from the formative years. She also draws on the unpublished journals and letters in Olsen's files, setting forth the dilemmas that come with a social commitment to political action and a personal dedication to the literary arts. Equally important, her discussion lays the groundwork for an unacknowledged socialist feminist literary tradition, a tradition that connects Olsen with her forerunners Gilman and Glaspell; her peers LeSueur, Slesinger, and Herbst; and her contemporaries Piercy, Paley, and Alice Walker.[7] For Olsen and this line of writers, Rosenfelt raises the complex questions rooted in the crossing of the political ideology that promotes literature in the service of politics and the literary tradition that prizes individuality and innovation over community and conformity.

Linda Park-Fuller reconciles the conflicting artistic and political goals, perhaps indirectly, by approaching the novel *Yonnondio* as performance art. In her 1986 essay "Voices: Bakhtin's Heteroglossia and Polyphony, and the Performance of Narrative Literature," reprinted here, Park-Fuller examines a collaboration between the novel's literary discourse, which widens a reader's perspective, and its oral speech, which cultivates a more intimate association between speaker and listener. She proposes a novel working on three levels: the first, taking a Marxist position in the political debates of the 1930s; the second, calling into question formal aesthetic theories; and the third, illustrating the vitality of narrative multivocality. For Park-Fuller, the third is the most important. Her essay demonstrates how a language theory can clarify the exchange between performance and text, and then it shows how performance of the Olsen text opens up this narrative to new interpretations.[8]

Although these and other reviewers and critics have treated the poetry, fiction, and essays of the 1930s quite extensively, no one has addressed the newspaper columns Olsen did write on occasion in the 1940s. Michael Staub, long interested in the influence of the Communist press on her writing, undertook a special assignment for this collection, locating some of the articles occasionally mentioned but never quoted. In a brief review entitled "Labor Activism and the Post-War Politics of Motherhood: Tillie Olsen in the *People's World*," he ponders the significance of the short history of the column "Tillie Olsen Says," adding yet one more perspective on the affairs of the woman-activist-writer.

The 1950s-1970s: Fictions of Struggle & Survival

While many critics have been attentive to the art of the 1930s, others claim the fiction of the 1950s constitutes Olsen's primary contribution to American literature. One early review of the 1961 collection *Tell Me a Riddle* captured the tone for much of the acclaim that ensued. In his "Dilemmas of Day-to-Day Living," William Peden appreciated the writing "with a feeling and understanding so deep as to be often literally painful, with at times an almost miraculous rendering of the interrupted rhythms of thought and speech patterns, with expert economy, with effective counter-pointing of past and present, with judicious use of traditional and contemporary narrative methods or devices."[9] Not all concurred. A few reviewers were exceedingly uneasy with the intensity. William Wiegand entitled his commentary "Tormented Alienation Dramas." He seemed wary of "a raw and jagged expressiveness that comes partly from the terrible vulnerability of the consciousness which presides over each story, and partly from the 'conscience' that moves startled and frightened along the way."[10] A reaction from England, pointedly entitled "Dressed to Kill," found the collection too "emotionally exhausting," too wearing.[11] The passion did not turn away Dorothy Parker, however. She only complained that not enough attention was being paid to the stories that "are more powerfully moving, dig deeper in the memory than do the reams of exercises in lyrical style that clutter the bookshops."[12]

The reviews reprinted in this collection suggest how perceptions of Olsen's working class background and feminist orientation have been as basic to the critical assessment as the style and subject matter. In "Stories: New, Old and Sometimes Good," Irving Howe sounded a first, almost reluctant appreciation. After a grudging reflection on the story writing trend in the middle class which saw housewives participating, he admits as remarkable Olsen's final story "Tell Me a Riddle." Richard M. Elman was equally impressed but more welcoming. In "The Many Forms Which Loss Can Take," he spots an unevenness in the four stories but willingly forgives any shortcomings in light of the writer's compassion, authentic renderings, and poetic compression. Hailing the feminist perspective as a vital contribution, the effusive Elizabeth Fisher, in "The Passion of Tillie Olsen," calls Olsen's consciousness of human mortality and pain essential to the quest for intensity of experience.

With Olsen touching such deep emotional chords, there were various efforts to reach a larger audience. In the late 1970s, "I Stand Here Ironing" became a favorite for adaptation by theatre workshops, women's ensembles, and church groups. "Tell Me a Riddle," read and performed in university theaters in Minnesota and Iowa, found its way to smaller theaters in large cities. The New York production, as a "Brechtian parable" at the Modern Times Theatre, received an appreciative review because the performance imported some of the original dialogue and raised fond memories of the original version.[13] Another rendition at the Caravan Theatre in Boston worked as a tone poem; it pleased with its good direction and occasional fine acting but drew criticism of its jungle gym stage set, a too youthful casting of the children, and an actor's poor imitation of David's Jewishness.[14] Overall, the live productions boasted some success, but a similar attempt to turn the stories into films has been deemed generally unsatisfactory. In 1982, Mordecai Newman reviewed the film version of *Tell Me a Riddle* in "Do Jewish Filmmakers Have Enough to Say?" with a firm negative because at the end it shifted the emphasis from the old woman's revolutionary stance to a relationship with her granddaughter. Carolyn Sutten Owen, for a 1988 master's thesis entitled "Tillie Olsen: A Comparative Study of Two Works of Fiction and Their Film Adaptations," found the new versions of "Tell Me a Riddle" and "I Stand Here Ironing" pale beside the originals.

Sustained inquiry from readers with diverse orientations has generated a broad spectrum of comparisons over the decades. A 1963 essay in *Studies in Short Fiction*, "The Short Stories of Tillie Olsen" by William Van O'Connor, likened her style to Thornton Wilder, Dylan Thomas, Thomas Hardy, and William Faulkner.[15] In 1975, a *Midstream* article, "The Riddle of Tillie Olsen" by Elenore Lester, associated her issues with those of Erica Jong, Iris Owens, Sylvia Plath, Anais Nin, Doris Lessing, Jean Rhys, and Joan Didion.[16] At the same time, a *New Republic* review, "Reconsideration" by educator and child psychiatrist Robert Coles, found this author spiritually akin to George Eliot in that Olsen portrayed the unfulfilled lives of women and the "meanness of opportunity."[17] In 1990, Julia Connolly and Joanne Trautmann Banks, writing for *Literature and Medicine*, paired "Tell Me a Riddle" with Tolstoy's "The Death of Ivan Ilych."[18]

The most persistent issue raised in scholarly response, however, has been the relevance of the feminist positioning. Ellen Cronan Rose lays out the problem in the 1976 essay reprinted in this volume. In "Limning: Or Why Tillie Writes," she contends that the temptation to treat the stories as feminist documents limits their scope. Rose believes that the reader learns more from tracing the influence of Rebecca Harding Davis on Olsen.[19] Her brief references to the Davis novel *Margaret Howth* and her longer analysis of *Life in the Iron Mills* are a studied attempt to open up the conversation on Olsen's artistic talents. While this critic admits that the stories of *Tell Me a Riddle* exemplify a feminist aesthetic, she redirects readers to classic aesthetics. Definitions of observation and insight, distinctions between the aesthetic eye which abstracts and the visionary or creative eye which pierces to the interior—these frame pertinent inquiry. For Rose, the "trespass vision"—that line of sight and degree of comprehension peculiar to women and others not permitted into the larger world—links Olsen with the aesthetics of Hawthorne and the sympathies of Whitman and places her in a familiar American literary tradition.

As if in response to warnings against feminist readings, Joanne Frye is quick to defend the feminist orientation. And she is even quicker to remind readers of the victory for women, and all writers, in Olsen's focus on women and particularly in her wresting of the symbol of motherhood from those writers who use it expressly as a metaphor for art, where the work becomes the offspring of the artist. In "'I Stand Here Ironing': Motherhood as Experience and Metaphor," published in 1981 and reprinted here, Frye emphasizes the fusion of experience and metaphor as instrumental in the introduction of a new literary theme. She discusses the short, frequently anthologized "I Stand Here Ironing" as a classic depiction of the complexities of motherhood and the economic, social, and psychological factors which affect mother and daughter.

Many critics working from a feminist perspective have elaborated on the mother-daughter issues Olsen raises. Judith Kegan Gardiner has recognized "Tell Me a Riddle" as a representation of the spirited life that can be drained by love and duty, but she has been more intrigued by another problem which lies embedded within its structure. In "A Wake for Mother: The Maternal Deathbed in Women's Fiction," Gardiner speculates on the story as a silent witness to a hidden matrophobia within the contemporary culture, an issue, she believes, Olsen raises then sidesteps through a shift to the relationship between the grandmother Eva and granddaughter Jeannie at the story's conclusion. In "'A child of anxious, not proud, love': Mother and Daughter in Tillie Olsen's 'I Stand Here Ironing,'" Helen Pike Bauer also pursues the ambivalence; she recounts the inherent dangers when a mother becomes an unwitting and unwilling model for her daughter.

When the theme of the lost mother ties into motifs of reclamation and survival, as in Olsen's fifth and last fiction, the narrator may strike a new pose. Elaine Orr suggests this possibility in an essay written expressly for this collection. In "Rethinking the Father: Maternal Recursions in Tillie Olsen's 'Requa,'" she uses contemporary theories of the narrative death of the mother to support her proposal of a maternal narration. Orr believes that as a performance of the maternal voice in the fiction Olsen's thematic and linguistic experiment may well illustrate a transfer of the practice of maternal caring into the lives of men.

The response to Olsen from women who have not seen their lives fully represented in literature frequently occurs in the unrecorded events of the classroom. More recently, with the increasing credibility and acceptance of reader response criticism, these moments have begun to enter the public record. The story "O Yes" has encouraged teachers to speak of Olsen's power to establish an intimacy, especially with female readers. This story of a young white girl attending the baptism services of her young black girl friend crosses into the sensitive area of race relations. During the service, it is the young white girl who is initiated, at the church and later at home, into the racism which has so successfully segregated a society if not the feelings of people. By projecting the social barriers into worship services and family discussions where they startle, and by using imagery wide open to interpretation, this story simultaneously initiates the reader. In the short 1986 note reprinted here, "Olsen's 'O Yes': Alva's Vision as Childbirth Account," Naomi Jacobs explains how her women students grapple with the strange dream-vision sequence as if it were an extension of their own experience. Nancy Huse has written another essay for this collection which develops along similar lines. But her "Re-reading Tillie Olsen's 'O Yes'" turns to questions of mothering and sistering. Using her students' and her own readings and misreadings, Huse provides an exemplary model of the learning invited by a reader response approach. She confirms, in the process, Olsen's interweaving of race, gender, and class which evokes wonder, curiosity, understanding, grief, and fear.

Critics have also recognized that, as a master of narrative spaces which require an attentiveness comparable to that needed while reading poetry, Olsen inspires an ongoing involvement in the literary experience. But they have been equally tantalized by her reliance on traditional strategies of engagement as well. Small bits of esoteric information pose little puzzles while the broad situations tell the larger riddles of the human condition. Two essays in this collection illustrate these orientations in "Tell Me a Riddle." The brief reference to Thuban, a pole star for ancient Egypt, might be brushed aside by those intent on tracking Eva's journey into the Russian revolutionary past, but for Edward Niehus and Teresa Jackson it stands as a challenge: Thuban becomes a reference to locate, a sign to explicate, a meaning to share. Their findings in "Polar Stars, Pyramids, and 'Tell Me a Riddle'" not only clarify the allusion but also explain how Eva might have such knowledge and why it surfaces as she faces death. The approach to death might seem almost too commonplace for the critic like Joanne Trautmann Banks who comes to literature from the health care profession. However, Eva's painstaking journey back to her Olshana youth in search of a nearly buried vision of revolutionary hope upsets Banks's expectations. Its mysterious path prompts a closer look and leads Banks, in "Death Labors," to an unexpected birthing.[20]

For critics who situate their analyses within the social or cultural context, Olsen's Jewish heritage has had an important bearing on the response to her subject matter and philosophical orientation. In 1978, Jacqueline Mintz cast Olsen into the company of Jewish American women writers. In "The Myth of the Jewish Mother in Three Jewish, American, Female Writers," she placed Olsen in a line that begins with the earlier Anzia Yezierska and continues with Susan Fromberg-Schaeffer. Olsen has acknowledged her *Yiddishkeit*, the Eastern European Jewish cultural heritage, as a prime shaper of her convictions and commitments. In a 1983 interview with Naomi Rubin entitled "A Riddle of History for the Future," Olsen speaks of its celebration in "Tell Me a Riddle," the story she dedicated to the Jewish Russian revolutionaries who, like her mother and Eva, have been the models for her own life.

The Jewish social and cultural heritage proposes another tradition for Olsen. In the 1980s, various critics explored this dimension. Helge Normann Nilsen, in "Tillie Olsens's [*sic*] 'Tell Me a Riddle': The Political Theme," discussed this writer's insistence on a human perfectibility and its roots in the radical Jewish humanistic tradition. John Clayton worked in a similar vein in "Grace Paley and Tillie Olsen: Radical Jewish Humanists." A longer treatment reprinted in this volume is "Tillie Olsen: The Writer as a Jewish Woman." Bonnie Lyons documents the secular Jewish influence at every point—in political and social ideals, in mother and child relationships, in the physical, emotional, intellectual and spiritual hungers, and in the lyric voice. In addition, a new essay by Linda Ray Pratt extends this perspective on the cultural and social milieu but also maps out the concrete details of place. In "The Circumstances of Silence: Literary Representations and Tillie Olsen's Omaha Past," Pratt identifies specific landmarks and builds support for an autobiographical rereading of the fiction. Her essay clearly links the storyteller and the stories told.

Even when the critical responses utilize different theoretical approaches, the question of the relation between art and politics always returns. Deborah Rosenfelt, whose assessment of *Yonnondio: From the Thirties* centered on the activist as writer, has recently reread *Tell Me a Riddle* to "consider what happens textually when the revolutionary consciousness that has informed the literature of a radical social movement survives into a nonrevolutionary era." After re-reading Olsen in the political climate of the Reagan-Bush years, an era comparable to the 1950s when the works were written, Rosenfelt reassesses her earlier views. From the later vantage point, she detects a "prevailing mood of alienation" which would move Olsen's fiction into the company of Ralph Ellison's *Invisible Man* and Clancy Sigal's *Going Away*. Rosenfelt concludes that Olsen's ability to work "against and with the age" provides further evidence of the power and endurability of this art.[21]

Constance Coiner has approached *Tell Me a Riddle* with a similar interest in the crossing of politics and art. But rather than focus on the activist as writer, Coiner shows the writer as activist. Her 1992 essay "'No One's Private Ground': A Bakhtinian Reading of Tillie Olsen's *Tell Me a Riddle*," reprinted and slightly expanded in this collection, shows how Olsen crafts her fiction as a democratizing force, a democratizing force cultivated through the cacophony of marginalized voices. Coiner analyzes Olsen's narrative and political strategies. She finds a narrative strategy designed to record the heteroglossia (the language force which resists unity, conformity, and domination yet recognizes the existence of another); she sees a political strategy calculated to establish a common ground wherein the writer, text, and reader collaborate. For Coiner, these actions are undeniably powerful political acts.

In an earlier study of Olsen's frequently ignored short fiction from 1970, Blanche Gelfant had understood a similar orientation but proposed it as a model and enactment of reader participation. In the 1984 essay "After Long Silence: Tillie Olsen's 'Requa,'" reprinted here, Gelfant addresses the strategies in this story of a young Depression era boy who after losing his mother is taken in by his uncle. After periods of restorative sleep, the boy helps his uncle sort miscellaneous items in a junkyard. These periods of work and rest represent therapeutic stages in the boy's recovery. The wasteland motifs along with the themes of memory and love set within a fragmented narrative, all reminiscent of T. S. Eliot, convince Gelfant that Olsen intentionally draws her reader into the composing process, showing how broken worlds can be made whole and giving the reader an opportunity to practice this art.

The 1970s-1990s: Mentorings through Word & Deed

With the 1978 publication of *Silences,* the critical response to Olsen grew more divisive, primarily in reaction to a form that seemed a patchwork of autobiographical notes, historical retrospectives, and poetic lamentations on the circumstances of the silenced writer. Few reviewers were as openly hostile as Isa Kapp who charged a succession of faults, from a moralizing posture to a disorganized text. In "A Literary Life," he weighed the argument and found it lightweight: "about 100 pages (out of 289), incredibly jumbled and chopped up, are devoted to appendices and miscellanies that house a formidable litany of feminist grievances."[22]

Kapp was not alone. Others reviewers vacillated because of an apparent split within the work itself. In "The Lament for Lost Art," Joan Peters epitomized this view: "As a lament for lost art and for the struggles of artists, *Silences* is powerful but as an argument it is weak."[23] In contrast, women who felt betrayed by a tradition sympathetic to men rallied behind its message and its form. Iris Tillman Hill voiced the sentiments of those who saw Olsen at the forefront of a feminist fervor for change. She hailed the writings as "sacred texts to be examined and commented upon . . . a scripture without inspiration, full of frustration and anguish."[24]

Joyce Carol Oates and Margaret Atwood sharpened the on-going debate over the intersection of aesthetics and politics, a debate which erupts whenever Olsen writes. Their reviews, reprinted in this volume, delineate the sides. An open admirer of the earlier fiction, Oates rejects *Silences* as a new offering. She finds it unsatisfying in its failure to disclose more of the author's own experiences, disappointing in its dearth of discussion, and frustrating in its lack of coherence. The opposing argument stands in Atwood's "Obstacle Course." Her impressive front page essay in the *New York Times Book Review* detects in the documentation of silencing and crippling a moving tribute to the spirit of survival. Atwood highlights the "reverence" of the audience for a writer who is both witness and "biblical messenger"; her language, like Hill's, resonates with imagery appropriate for Olsen as an icon for the women's movement.

Despite antagonistic postures, critics did agree that *Silences* revitalized interest in Olsen. Two additional reprinted reviews sketch that reacquaintance. Nolan Miller finds the history a casebook providing a strong incentive to reread the earlier works; he urges readers to return to the writing with a renewed appreciation of its very existence. Valerie Trueblood concurs. She explains how the introduction to the circumstances which inhibited Olsen's productivity pressed her to return, rediscover, and reconfirm Olsen's contributions.

As these commentaries illustrate, most of the positive reaction to *Silences* responded to its message. Negative criticism generally aimed at its form. However, in a 1990 essay in *Literary Journalism in the Twentieth Century*, Shelley Fisher Fishkin took up, in earnest, a line other readers had intimated but had not developed; she analyzed the text and declared it an innovative literary form. She clarified strategies that Olsen had "designed to teach her readers to allow voices previously faint or silent . . . to be heard."[25] Looking at the text as one looks at a poem in print, this critic scans the visual representations of print on the page for a meaningful message; she ventures that Olsen "dramatizes the theme of 'silence' with peculiar immediacy and intensity by confronting the reader with the 'visual silence' of blankness of the page" (154). Fishkin, thus, rationalizes the order and structuring of sections along with the visual dimension. She sees *Silences* as a model for writing, one that will make a space for a speaking and a hearing for the self and others.

An example of the process Fishkin envisions may be occurring in the review of *Silences* by writer Alix Kates Shulman. The long essay that appeared in the *Harvard Education Review* in 1979 demonstrates the full range of Olsen's compelling art, as Shulman interweaves commentary on *Silences* with an exploration of her relationship to her own writing students. At first, Shulman only assesses the text: "More than a collection, this book is an eloquent argument presented in a fluid, unorthodox form. It is a case carefully documented and substantiated by testimony from writers spanning time, gender, race and class, which grows increasingly powerful as the evidence accumulates from topic to topic."[26] A little later, Shulman addresses its emotional effect: "To me, reading *Silences* is rather like sitting in a circle with a group of trusted fellow writers for mutual encouragement and support, so much of the experience described is recognizable. Our circle spans generations" (533). Finally, Shulman discloses the motivational power of the writing as she too takes up the mantle of the mentor: "We are sitting in a circle, sharing our experience and ideas, reading and discussing each other's work, searching for a common truth, growing stronger and more confident and more determined through our mutual support and inspiration. Let us continue to expand the circle" (533).

Over the decades the critical response to Olsen has moved from descriptive to celebratory to analytical. This pattern also characterizes the full-length studies. In 1984, Abigail Martin wrote a short monograph as part of the Western Writers Series. Her informative *Tillie Olsen* includes a short biography, a publication history, story summaries and brief analyses, a bibliography of reviews and criticism, plus extensive lists of readings, lectures, talks, fellowships and honors. In 1987, Elaine Orr launched a longer study and appreciation in *Tillie Olsen and a Feminist Spiritual Vision*. With perspectives grounded in religious studies and feminist orientation, Orr finds a unified writing with transcending vision and moral comprehension, a canon exploring themes of revolution, rebuilding, nurturance, and encouragement. She believes that Olsen writes out of a secular Jewish humanism and socialism and out of "a largely unacclaimed working class American tradition of discovery and invention through necessity."[27] For this critic, Olsen's background accounts for her transformation of history into fiction and politics into poetry, and it prompts the spirituality and didacticism that surface in quest motif, struggle for empowerment, and affirming vision.

In 1991, Mickey Pearlman and Abby H. P. Werlock collaborated on *Tillie Olsen*, a volume in the Twayne United States Authors Series. Armed with interviews, chronology, biographical sketch, critical analyses, and an updated, annotated bibliography, they sought an objectivity that would counter a too adulatory criticism. They quote early unpublished manuscripts housed in the Berg Collection of the New York Public Library to show an artist who "found at age 18 the major themes and metaphors of her lifetime."[28] References to published reviews, essays, and full-length studies of Olsen enrich the explications. A challenge to earlier critics, this examination takes issue with Olsen's fragmentary texts, and it takes exception to the sympathy accorded this style by feminist critics like Orr. It calls for a closer scrutiny by American literature scholars who can place Olsen within a broader literary tradition where she rightfully belongs.

The latest full-length examination, while not specifically addressing Olsen's place in an American literary tradition, does advance literary analysis. In *Protest and Possibility in the Writing of Tillie Olsen*, Mara Faulkner outlines her own theoretical approach as one of a multiple vision and organic feminist criticsm, perspectives in accord with a central Olsen paradigm of "blight, fruit, and possibility." Faulkner takes up the primary themes—motherhood as a source of creativity and change; patriarchy as cause of separations between men and women and between the family unity and society; the individual's competing responsibilities to self and to others; and the erasures and distortions which come from silence and language as well.[29] In a final chapter on language and silence, this critic does raise the question of Olsen's silence in later years, then proposes tentative answers in the unbreakable habits of a lifetime, the consequences of the 1950s political censorship, and the weight of stories the writer cannot bring herself to tell (139-141).

Although these studies confirm Olsen's place in the literary record, the profound influence she has had will be hard to fully measure by simply reading the reviews, essays, books, and ever-growing numbers of doctoral dissertations.[30] Another, generally unrecorded dimension has developed in the teaching and speaking engagements which also take Olsen to professional meetings, campus lectures, and literary readings with ethnic and working class women writers. These time-consuming and taxing undertakings have become an essential part of an agenda which keeps this writer in touch with the audience she loves and enables her to promote the oral tradition she values. Although in the later years Olsen has published a couple of short prefatory essays, including a remarkable tribute to her mother in "Dream-Vision," most of her words have not found their way into print.[31] Only a few of her many formal and informal interviews have been published, and even fewer recordings of interviews and readings have been made available commercially.

Just as the words go unrecorded so too does the impact of this integral part of her legacy. Sometimes recognition of the mentoring does surface, as in the recent biography of Anne Sexton which briefly recounts a summer meeting and friendship then credits Olsen with inspiring a change in Sexton's views.[32] On occasion, simple tributes grace the beginnings of critical projects: a review by Sandy Boucher, an interview with Kenneth Turan, the essay by Burkom and Williams. But the personal gesture, like that woven into the fabric of the long review essay by Shulman, is rare.

Personal testimonies come forth gingerly from the professional community, even though *Silences* dramatizes and validates such witnessing. An obvious explanation lies in the simple lack of opportunity. The many touched by Olsen, whether through reading or listening, usually have little chance to reach beyond their intimate circle of friends. Nevertheless, a more deep-seated barrier may reside in a self-compromising disclosure. One individual who has agreed to share the hesitancies, ambiguities, ambivalences, and pride in such moments is essayist Carol Lauhon. For this collection, she has undertaken a two-fold task: reading Dorothy Bryant's 1981 murder mystery *Killing Wonder*, loosely based on the life and work of Tillie Olsen, as another form of critical response, but interpreting this response in light of her own experience with Olsen. Thus, the concluding entry in this collection, "Lessons in Killing Wonder," follows the thread of the mystery story and simultaneously traces the deeper mysteries of life and art exemplified by Tillie Olsen, allowing us to detect the way in which one spirit opens to another and touches, and how that touch remains.

Kay Hoyle Nelson

NOTES

1. The demographics of the delegation were reported in the May 7, 1935, issue of *New Masses*. The article "The League of American Writers" mentioned 64 delegates attending from 24 states other than New York, 36 women including both delegates and guests, 21 black writers, four delegates sent from Mexico, one representative each for Cuban and Jewish writers, and a German delegate who brought greetings from revolutionary writers interned by the Nazis. Of the thirty papers delivered, three were condensed and printed in this issue. The caricatures of seventeen delegates included three women—Olsen, Herbst and the Cuban writer and editor Lola de La Torriente (16-17).

To give her readers some sense of Olsen with her contemporaries, Janet Jacobsen's "Study Guide for *Tell Me a Riddle* reprints four sketches (2).

2. Robert Cantwell, "Little Magazines," *New Republic* 25 July 1934: 295. Subsequent reference will be parenthetical.

3. The novel had great potential for sentimentality, and the finished product might have developed in that direction. In "Coming of Age in the Thirties: A Portrait of Tillie Olsen," Erika Duncan outlines Olsen's plans for the completed novel: a strike, Jim abandoning the family, pregnant Anna seeking an abortion and later dying, Maizie taking a job and being sexually abused, Ben dying, Baby Bess sent to an orphanage, homeless Maizie and Will joining the Communist Party and moving to California (219).

4. Annie Gottlieb, "A Writer's Sounds and Silences," *New York Times Book Review* 31 Mar. 1974: 5.

5. Bell Gale Chevigny, "Review of *Yonnondio: From the Thirties*." *Village Voice* 23 May 1974: 38.

6. Because this work documented women's issues so sensitive that they went undiscussed, the art has served an evidential purpose. In "Violence Against Women in Literature of the Western Family," Melody Graulich uses *Yonnondio: From the Thirties* (along with novels by Mari Sandoz, Agnes Smedley, Meridel LeSueur) to reveal the violence which has been ignored until the latter part of the twentieth century.

7. Deborah Rosenfelt elaborates on these issues in "Divided Against Herself."

8. Park-Fuller's earlier production record and Olsen interview are listed in the bibliography.

9. William Peden, "Dilemmas of Day-to Living," *New York Times Book Review* 12 Nov. 1961: 54.

10. William Wiegand, "Tormented Alienation Dramas," *New Leader* 5 Feb. 1962: 29.

11. "Dressed to Kill." *Times Literary Supplement* 6 Feb. 1964: 101.

12. Dorothy Parker, "Book Reviews," *Esquire* June 1962: 66.

13. Mel Gussow, "Stage: Prize Story Takes New Form," *New York Times,* 22 Feb. 1978: C18.

14. Kevin Kelly, "'Riddle' Makes an Eloquent Statement," *Boston Globe,* 20 May 1977: 16.

15. William Van O'Connor, "The Short Stories of Tillie Olsen," *Studies in Short Fiction* 1 (Fall 1963): 24.

16. Elenore Lester, "The Riddle of Tillie Olsen," *Midstream* Jan. 1975: 75-76.

17. Robert Coles, "Reconsideration," *New Republic* 6 Dec. 1975: 29.

18. The Connolly essay, "The Whole Story," considers the value of storytelling in the physician-patient relationship and compares the old couple in *Tell Me a Riddle* with Connolly's patients. The Banks essay is reprinted in this volume.

19. For another brief comparison of *Life in the Iron Mills* and *Yonnondio: From the Thirties,* see Frances M. Malpezzi's "Sisters in Protest: Rebecca Harding Davis and Tillie Olsen"; for a longer analysis see Rose Kamel's discussion in "Literary Foremothers and Writers' Silences: Tillie Olsen's Autobiographical Fiction" in *MELUS,* later revised and included as "Riddles and Silences: Tillie Olsen's Autobiographical Fiction" in *Aggravating the Conscience: Jewish American Literary Mothers in the Promised Land.*

20. For another reading of the journey, as it relates to Robert Butler's "life review" and Erik Erikson's "integrity," see Gerald F. Manning's "Fiction and Aging: 'Ripeness is All.'" Social Work professor Vicki L. Sommer in "The Writings of Tillie Olsen: A Social Work Perspective" uses Sonja L. Rhodes' developmental family life cycle to assess the relationship of the pair facing the death of one partner.

21. Quoted from the currently unpublished manuscript of Rosenfelt's new essay "Rereading *Tell Me a Riddle* in the Age of Deconstruction." Rosenfelt is currently working on a casebook for "Tell Me a Riddle."

22. Isa Kapp, "A Literary Life," *New Leader* 22 May 1978: 5.

23. Joan Peters, "The Lament for Lost Art," *Nation* 23 Sept. 1978: 281.

24. Iris Tillman Hill, "Book Reviews: Silences. By Tillie Olsen." *Georgia Review* 33.4 (Winter 1979): 960.

25. Shelley Fisher Fishkin, "The Borderlands of Culture: Writing by W. E. B. DuBois, James Agee, Tillie Olsen, and Gloria Anzaldùa," *Literary Journalism in the Twentieth Century,* ed. Norman Sims (New York: Oxford U P, 1990) 153.

26. Alix Kates Shulman, "Overcoming Silences: Teaching Writing for Women," *Harvard Educational Review* 49.4 (Nov. 1979): 529. Subsequent references will be parenthetical.

27. Elaine Orr, *Tillie Olsen and a Feminist Spiritual Vision* (Jackson: U P of Mississippi, 1987) 35.

28. Mickey Pearlman and Abby H. P. Werlock, *Tillie Olsen* (Boston: Twayne, 1991) 15.

29. Mara Faulkner, *Protest and Possibility in the Writing of Tillie Olsen* (Charlottesville: U P of Virginia, 1993) 32.

30. Each year one or two dissertations appear—from fields of Modern Literature, American Literature, American Studies, Women's Studies, Theology, Cultural Studies Comparative Literature, or Education.

31. Olsen's extraliterary projects, the daybook and the photograph collection listed in the bibliography, have been admired and reviewed but not studied as part of her professional contributions to arts and letters.

32. Diane Wood Middlebrook, *Anne Sexton* (Boston: Houghton Mifflin, 1991) 195-98.

THE 1930s-1940s:
RADICAL WRITINGS
DISCOVERED & RECOVERED

The Literary Life in California[*]

Robert Cantwell

Sir: Readers of The New Republic may be interested in a footnote to my article on the little magazines in your issue of July 25. In that article I referred to a story by Tillie Lerner as being the outstanding contribution among the two-hundred-odd stories found in all the magazines being reviewed.

Immediately after the article appeared, the editors of two publishing houses wired me asking for my aid in locating Tillie Lerner; they had read the story when it first appeared in The Partisan Review and had tried to locate the author, but their letters and telegrams had been returned. Since I did not know Tillie Lerner, I relayed this message to two individuals in Northern California, where, it seemed, she had been living. Unfortunately, just at this time General Hugh Johnson was frothing around California, calling on the local patriots to clean up the Reds—drive them out like rats, was his mischievous phrase. One of the messengers, I have been told, was captured in Sacramento, and has been in jail ever since. The other has simply disappeared. A lot of people have disappeared out here, Communists and others. The newspapers explain these disappearances by saying that all the radicals are "in hiding." The

[*] Reprinted from The New Republic 22 August 1934: 49.

fact is that they have *disappeared,* and until the repression is broken there will be no way of telling whether they managed to escape or what has happened to them.

There was, however, a good reason why the publishers who wanted to see Tillie Lerner's unfinished novel had trouble reaching her. She was in jail. She happened to be visiting some friends during that period when Johnson's patriots were running loose in the streets. Police raided the house. They beat up four young men they found there, and carried the six occupants off to jail—the four boys, Tillie Lerner (Theresa [*sic*] Landale) and another girl, Marion Chandler. They were suspected of being radicals. They were charged with vagrancy, with bail set at $1,000.

Meanwhile two more publishers and a literary agent were trying to locate her in order to see about publishing her novel. Perhaps, I ought to say that the author is twenty-one years old, married, the mother of a baby girl, and that the story that aroused so much interest was her first published work. She had been delayed in writing her novel because of illness—incipient tuberculosis—and had been rewriting the last part when the police interrupted her.

I mention this because I now feel that in my article I minimized the difficulties that impede the progress of the young writers. To the difficulties of finding hospitable publishers must now be added the problems of dodging the police and General Johnson's patriots if writers are to get their novels finished. In addition, I feel that this little episode regarding the treatment of writers in this country ought to be called to the attention of those critics, such as Max Eastman and J. Donald Adams, who have lately been beefing so much about the humiliation of Boris Pilynak, and the literary framing of Eugene Zamyatin.

Three Women Work It Out[*]

Catharine R. Stimpson

Suppose that we could recover the literary texts that have been lost, censored, and suppressed. Suppose, too, that we could figure out why they had been erased from consciousness while other texts had come down to us as cultural legacies. Our discoveries might add up to a new literary and social history, an analogy to the way in which the concept of the black hole has given astrophysicists the premise for a new cosmology.

Tillie Olsen's novel, *Yonnondio*, is a recovered text. She began the book in 1932. She was then 19 years old. A chapter was published and praised in 1934. Two or three years later she abandoned the project and, for a long time, writing itself. Her silence was less the result of a romantic rendezvous with the abyss at the edge of language than of acute self-doubt, the responsibilities of raising four children, the need to hold a full-time job, the demands of community tasks, and the moral pressure of radical politics. Such a constellation of causes is more apt to affect the writer who is a woman than the writer who is a man.

Nearly forty years later, her reputation as a writer finally established through a collection of stories, *Tell Me a Riddle*, Olsen was going through some old papers. Among them she found the chaotic, disheveled, unfinished manuscript that she had thought she had lost and that she has now reconstructed.

Ostensibly, the action of *Yonnondio* occurs in the early 1920s. It concerns the Holbrook family: Jim, the physically powerful father; Anna, the once energetic and idealistic mother; the five children they have, within eight years, conceived in genuine passion and she has borne in some pain. The Holbrooks represent the people from whose toil a Tom Buchanan profits sufficiently to buy a Daisy a string of pearls and himself a string of polo ponies. Jim works in a mine, on a tenant farm, on a sewer construction crew, in a hellish meat-packing plant. Anna struggles with the children in the houses in which Jim settles them. When she can, she takes in laundry.

The Holbrooks are vital and decent. Their children, for whom they are ambitious, justify their struggle to realize the American dream. Capable of love in the present, they wish to exercise that love for the sake of the future. Like Whitman at his most cheerful, Olsen believes that human nature, if permitted to express itself freely and spontaneously, will be

[*] Excerpt reprinted from *Nation* 30 Nov. 1974: 565-66.

good. (She takes her novel's title from a Whitman poem.) Physical nature is the most fertile setting for such expression, although moments of human community, a family singing or a picnic, can suggest a harmonious balance among people, animals, plants, earth, water, fire, air. The Holbrooks are happiest on the farm, which they lose. The industries Olsen despises most—mining, early agri-business, slaughterhouses—spoil both human and physical nature for financial gain.

The "overwhelming, hostile forces" of modern capitalism bar the Holbrooks from their Eden. The modesty, the simplicity of their hopes help to make their failure poignantly grievous. Anna wants nothing more than:

> School for the kids, Jim working near her, on the earth, lovely things to keep, brass lamps, bright tablecloths, vines over the doors, and roses twining.

Eventually, an angry, frustrated Jim will brutalize his wife and children; an exhausted Anna will also turn on the children, will lapse into a psychic coma; a sensitive little girl will escape from an urban slum into a memory of the farm so enveloping that she veers toward schizophrenia. Anna, who has nearly died during a pregnancy terminated by a miscarriage, weeps on the back porch of a rickety house, which the stink of garbage and packing plants commands:

> The children. What's going to happen with them?. How we going to look out for them in this damn world? Oh Jim, the children. Seems like we cant [sic] do nothing for them.

As Jim comforts her, he silently makes "old vows again, vows that life will never let him keep."

Olsen's compelling gift is her ability to render lyrically the rhythms of consciousness of victims. Imaginative, affectionate, they are also alert to the sensual promise of their surroundings. Harsh familial, social, political and economic conditions first cramp, then maim, and then seek to destroy them. The fevers of poverty, dread and futility inflame their sensibilities. They risk reduction to defensive fantasy, pain, madness or cruelty. They remain, if in shadow, heroes and heroic.

Olsen assumes that such victims cannot often speak for themselves. Their dumbness is no fault of their own. Her self-imposed task is to become their voice as well as their witness, their text as well as their mourner. She signifies her respect for their dignity in the exactitude and scrupulous effort of her work. She sardonically tells her reader that the received categories of culture, such as classicism and romanticism, also fit the citizens of a Wyoming town as they wait to hear how many men have died in a mine explosion that official cowardice, incompetence and corruption have caused. If she were to take part in that theological quarrel over whether an artist's primary commitment is to craft or to social change, she might say that an artist can work for change through writing about the oppressed with all the craft and tools at hand. She also comments on the economic basis of high culture. She writes of an adolescent boy forced into the mines:

> Earth take your dreams that a few may languidly lie on couches and trill "How exquisite" to paid dreamers.

Olsen's politics and anger are a part of a particular decade: her subtitle, "From the Thirties," is seriously meant. She notes that *Yonnondio* "bespeaks the consciousness and roots of that decade, if not its events." An anachronism or two betrays the gap between narrative setting and actual reference. Despite her nostalgia for rural ritual, she refuses to offer an exclusive vision of bucolic joy. She wants unions and solidarity among all workers, no matter what their race or ethnic heritage In an apostrophe to a rebellious young worker which approaches polemic, she writes:

> I'm sorry . . . as hell we weren't stronger and could get to you in time and show you that kind of individual revolt was no good, kid, no good at all, you had to bide your time and take it till there were enough of you to fight it all together on the job . . . till the day millions of fists clamped in yours, and you could wipe out the whole thing, the whole goddam thing, and a human could be a human for the first time on earth.

The Living Image[*]

Peter Ackroyd

A great many Americans novels have concerned themselves with poverty and the Depression, but most of them have been very quickly smothered in that sentimental form known as 'documentary.' *Yonnondio* is written by a young girl who could never have heard of such a thing, since the book has that quality of innocence which comes from wonder rather than from knowledge: "'I am Maizie Holbrook,' she said softly, 'I am a knowen thing, [*sic*] I can diaper a baby. I can tell ghost stories. I know words and words'." Maizie is the child of one of those families which were slowly beaten into shape during the 'thirties when "words and words" were the merest palliative in the struggle to live. But Maizie's mother, a beautifully achieved character known as Anna, wants an "edjication" for her children and the whole family go on a long desolate wandering through America: they become tenant-farmers until their debts overtake them, and then they move into one of those restless American cities which were at that moment testing their strength. It is here that Tillie Olsen leaves them, to a fate which was not worth having.

It is a conventional story, as stories go, but the plot is in fact the least important element of the novel. This is not because it is incomplete (the book has only recently been recovered in a less than perfect form), but because the narrative is consumed by the effects of Miss Olsen's prose. A pattern of images is cast over the writing from the opening chapters, and there is a characteristic attention to description rather than analysis—it is a matter of dialogue rather than character, of situations rather than incidents. *Yonnondio* is a romantic novel, in the sense that Man and Nature are seen in a close and often destructive relationship, and its language becomes the space between them—instinctive with life, both mortal and at the same time capable of expressing certain permanent truths.

It is out of the mouths of children that this will come most naturally and there are some marvellously childish moments in this book. A young girl dreams of things which will not come:

> Luxuriously on her rug, pretend silk slinking and slithering on her body, turbanned, puffing her long pretend cigarette: Say vamp me, vamp me. I'm Nazimova. Take me to the roadhouse, I want to make whoopee. Hotcha.

[*] Excerpt reprinted from *Spectator* 14 Dec. 1974: 767-68.

Never never never. O my gigolo, my gigolo. A moment of ecstacy, a lifetime
of regret.

And the spell is broken by younger children who sing of things which
certainly will come:

Mother, Mother I am sick
Call the doctor quick, quick, quick.
Doctor, Doctor, will I die?
Yes. You will. And so shall I.

Yonnondio is one of the most powerful statements to have emerged
from the American 'thirties; a young woman has pulled out of that
uneasy time a living document which is full of the wear and tear of the
period, and she has done so without doctrinaire blues, and without falling
into the trap of a sentimentality which is, at bottom, self-pity.

Review of *Yonnondio: From the Thirties*[*]

Scott Turow

The publication of Tillie Olsen's *Yonnondio* is to me a personal event because Tillie Olsen herself has had such large effect upon me—as teacher, as friend, as a writer reverenced long before I met her—and these remarks do not pretend to be either objective or dispassionate. Rather, they are meant in frank appreciation of the older writer who has been such a generous guide to a younger one still struggling with his craft and of the splendid talent, the genius, already manifest in this early book, wrought when its author was still engaged in that struggle herself, albeit more successfully.

Yonnondio has been forty years in waiting for a public life. Tillie Olsen was nineteen when this novel was begun in 1932. Born Tillie Lerner, she had been raised in Omaha, the daughter of immigrant parents, revolutionaries who had fled Tzarist Russia after the revolt of 1905. By her mid-teens she had left home. Most of her education had been undertaken in public libraries,[1] and she was already a feminist-humanist and a revolutionary in her own right, one of an American variety, her ideology drawn as much from Whitman as from Marx. And already a writer at work. In 1934 an early chapter of *Yonnondio* appeared in the newly-established *Partisan Review*. It was hailed there as an "unmistakable work of early genius," attracting widespread attention, and when Tillie was jailed for her participation that year in the San Francisco General Strike a small legion of New York publishers arrived to bail her out. Yet by 1937 the book had been set aside. There was a family, and the immediate human obligations entailed—not only the work of motherhood, but everyday jobs, participation in neighborhood urgencies and causes, even presidency of the grade-school P.T.A.—all precluded writing, attention to herself. For twenty years she was silent, but during the McCarthyist fifties, when her children were older, when the organization of a neighborhood childcare coop permitted a change of jobs, when later the youngest child was in school, what had been "beginnings of writing . . . struggled toward endings,"[2] though it was far from a time unburdened and unhindered. In 1956, however, she received a Creative Writing Fellowship at Stanford and "snatches of time" became eight month's writing time: "I did not have to go out on a job. I had continuity, three full days, sometimes more . . ." The long story she began that year, "Tell Me A Riddle," is an unequivocal masterpiece—"It will be read," Julian

[*] Reprinted from *Ploughshares* 2.2 (1974): 113-17.

Moynihan has said, "as long as the American language lasts"—and it won
for her the O'Henry Prize, opened the way to fellowships and grants,
teaching jobs, and, at last, the opportunity to devote her time more fully
to literature. A volume of four stories, *Tell Me A Riddle,* appeared in
1962, and two novels have been in the works since then. A piece of one,
Requa, was printed in *Best American Short Stories 1971.*

In 1971, in searching through old papers, the manuscript that is now
called *Yonnondio* was rediscovered. I saw a section of it then, typed and
handwritten on greenish sheets, the paper so brittle with age that the
edges flaked cleanly like chips of paint when touched: the few chapters
were bound together with an old, curliqued paperclip, a kind that I had
never seen, and I recall that somehow that clip became symbolic to me of
the entire manuscript, a human design, useful, ingenious, forgotten. I
read through those pages with great excitement, but it seemed inconceiv-
able to me that the book could possibly be made whole. The pages were
discontinuous, passages were incomplete, the many marginal notations
seemed often indecipherable or obscure. Nevertheless, with time at the
MacDowell Colony in 1972, Tillie set about the job of trying to put the
novel back together. Nothing was rewritten. The first four chapters are
intact, published as they were written in the thirties, the rest pieced
together, as Tillie has said, "in arduous partnership" of the older writer
with the young one, from old makings, choosing between drafts, notes,
scribbles.

Unfinished, it is nonetheless a remarkable, towering work. *Yonnondio*
deals with the Holbrooks, Anna and Jim, and their five children—Mazie,
Will, Ben, Jimmie and Bess—and their participation in the primeval
American quest in search of a better life, moving from a gritty, Wyoming
coal-mining town, to a profitless tenant farm in South Dakota, then onto
the back of the stockyards squalor of an unnamed prairie city. In all
quarters theirs is a life of unvarnished misery, of poverty, illness,
demeaning labor, of cramped desire, and of an existence so absorbed in
the small mechanics of survival that any sense of greater human purpose
lies obliterated, obscured, a distant aching, a knowledge too remote to be
recognized or named. Without apology, this is a proletarian novel, didactic
in intent. The brutal working conditions, the stockyard smells, the
gouging bankers, the shabby homes, the yoke of mindless, female toil are
all recorded with a vividness sprung from an infinite outrage and
compassion. Early in the novel, there is even an angry address to the
owners of the coal mines from the author:

> Dear Company. Your men are imprisoned in a tomb of hunger, of death
> wages. Your men are strangling for breath—the walls of your company town

have clamped out the air of freedom. Please issue a statement. Quick, or they
start to batter through with the fists of strike, with the pickax of revolution.

Yet *Yonnondio* does not suffer from the facile pretense which marred
so much proletarian literature of the thirties—*The Grapes of Wrath* comes
most immediately to mind—in which noble, dauntless working people
moved between crushing travails without loss of spirit. "The maiming
power of circumstance," the dust jacket says in describing the novel's
theme and I can think of no better description of my own. The Holbrooks
and their five children are unable to prevent material conditions from
deforming them and their best hopes, and the greatness of *Yonnondio*
rests on its portrayal of the relationship between poverty and the acts of
an embattled spirit, evoking it as a true human process, inevitable and
complex, rather than the kind of small-minded arithmetic which that
relationship became in the liberal sociology of the sixties. Jim drinks
hard, occasionally beating his wife and children out of frustration, reviling
Anna for not being able to always make a dollar "stretch like rubber," and
she, in turn, curses him for his failure to earn, sinking on her own at
times into a reclusive dreaminess, remote from the endless duties of her
household. Mazie, still longing for country freedoms, fails in school and
is forced by her mother, in need of aid, into the same homebound female
realm. And Will, recognizing somehow that his only future is the hard life
of his parents, becomes surly, rebellious, headed for a losing mismatch
against the world. The small triumphs of spirit—warm moments with the
family united, the children's avid education of themselves, Anna's brief
sensation of "happiness, farness, selfness" experienced as she is picking
greens for her family's supper in an overgrown suburban lot—are never
sufficient to overcome the crippling effects of deprivation.
  The telling of all of this is in the Tillie Olsen style, high-flown, lyrical,
impressionistic. One disdains, for obvious reasons, an academic discussion
of technique, and yet, of course, an author's style represents not simply
a technical know-how, but a way of seeing, the manner in which one
consciousness apprehends experience, and it is remarkable that forty
years ago a style unique to all our literature had already taken shape,
that this young writer was so much in touch with herself. All of the
hallmarks of Tillie Olsen's narrative manner are present: the tender
frugality with words, the passionate description of sensation, the stripped
compression of individual scenes, and the remarkable choral effect of a
voice which somehow, like Faulkner's sweeps from recitation of the stray
thoughts of a child passed on the street to direct address of the reader.
Like God, the authorial personna [*sic*] in Tillie Olsen's work knows all,
and like a God men have not dreamed of in centuries, she knows it with

a compassion which requires articulation for those too tormented to speak for themselves, the transformation of all human feeling into the majestical, the poetical, the eternal. Consider, for instance, the luminous moment that is made of the random banging of a pot lid by the infant Bess.

> She releases, grabs, releases, grabs. I can do. Bang! I can do. I! A Neanderthal look of concentration is on her face. That noise! In triumphant astounded joy she clashes the lid down. Bang, slam, whack. Release, grab, slam, bang, bang. Centuries of human drive work in her; human ecstacy [*sic*] of achievement, satisfaction deep and fundamental as sex: *I achieve, I use my powers; I! I!*

And yet that same atmosphere of grand purpose which animates the narrative and which gives *Yonnondio* its rolling, incantatory power at times becomes overbearingly sentimental and romantic; that is probably the novel's only significant fault, that ordinary gestures and events are so often attributed enormous meaning. Even a spell of miserable, oppressive heat which falls upon that prairie city is treated as if it were part of an active conspiracy against the working poor. The mute, small appreciation of day to day affairs with which we all make do—the rhythm of labor, the relief of trivial irony, coarse humor, uninspired companionship, those long periods of time for which the most adequate verb is neither "want", nor "dream", nor even "suffer", but simply "is"—is to some extent unacknowledged in *Yonnondio,* and with those moments underrepresented, the novel occasionally seems distorted, unfairly intense, almost gothic in the texture of its reality. And there are smaller flaws as well, a tendency throughout toward melodramatic contrivance of events—at one point an almost extra-sensory urge causes Mazie to dash across the broken cornfields in South Dakota to receive deathbed advice from an old man who's shown her kindness—and the children, Mazie especially, are to my taste cloyingly precious compared to the children who appeared in Tillie Olsen's later fiction, which had been enriched by twenty years of motherhood.

But that is the point of course, that the faults of *Yonnondio* are directly attributable to its author's youth, a point which goes to one of the great values of this book beyond the immediate realm of art. So many of our writers of stature suppress, *hide* the books which were the very touchstones for discovery of their talent, the first books which went unread, unpublished. Where is the novel for which Mailer could not find a publisher when he left Harvard, the three books Walker Percy wrote then condemned to the drawer before he finished *The Moviegoer*? Though a public now exists which would read these books with interest, they are turned aside as bastard children, unworthy of their author's current reputation; in consequence, we are too often left with the impression that important writers spring like Minerva, from the head of Jupiter, full-grown, replete with wisdom and skill. Tillie Olsen would no longer write a book flawed in the ways of *Yonnondio* but she has sent it forth, and it stands as a frank encouragement to younger writers to see, to learn, to know that even great talent is not always perfect in its inclination, in its shape, and that what inspires those imperfect efforts is not of itself less worthy than what will be said later with greater finesse.

There is, then, even beyond its intrinsic richness and force, the potent feel of History always attached to *Yonnondio*—the history of one young writer journeying to herself, and also the history of lives that have been largely unrecorded in our literature. The subtitle, "From the Thirties," is somewhat misleading, for although that is when the novel was written, *Yonnondio* actually addresses the 1920's, an era we are now inclined to recall primarily in terms of the grim, glittery life portrayed by Fitzgerald, and the romantic expatriotism of Hemingway, and the intellectual despair of Eliot. *Yonnondio* preserves for us the other lives of that period, lived, even before the hard times of the thirties, in destitute migration and anguished powerlessness until the Labor movement won for many a small hold on an easier existence. And in both regards—the author and the times—though the degree and nature of the triumph is different, we are able to take from *Yonnondio* the sole comfort of History, evidence of the old and noble glory of human progress and development.

NOTES

1. Reading outside academic strictures, she was the discoverer and maker of her own literary tradition. In old volumes of the *Atlantic Monthly* from 1861—purchased for a dime in an Omaha junkshop—she first read *Life In The Iron Mills* by Rebecca Harding Davis, a brief novel dealing with the life of the working poor in mid-nineteenth century America. Both in its subject matter and as the work of a gifted female artist whose talent was eventually crushed and squandered, it has been a long inspiration to Tillie, and partly at her suggestion, The Feminist Press last year re-issued *Life* which had been for a century virtually unread. Tillie provided a lengthy afterword, a biographical interpretation of the life of Rebecca Harding Davis.

2. "Silences: When Writers Don't Write," *Harper's*, October 1965.

De-Riddling Tillie Olsen's Writings[*]

Selma Burkom and Margaret Williams

A burst of applause, then the audience in the Kresge College Auditorium grew quiet. The striking woman with clipped gray hair and piercing blue eyes, sitting before the microphone, began. It was the second day of the Virginia Woolf Symposium. Yesterday, critical papers were read and this morning, the California writer Tillie Olsen was addressing us. Her voice was soft. She began by saying how pleased she was to be at the University of California, Santa Cruz sharing in the discussions about Virgina Woolf, whom she had long known and loved. Her words, as she continued, were only to be "personal remarks" since she lacked the formal academic training of the other speakers. The apology was unnecessary. Her "remarks" constituted not only a cogent intellectual analysis but also created the emotionally felt reality of the British writer. As she sifted and selected among the many fragments which were her notes, she seemed to be randomly touching first one topic, then another. The structure was not linear, but gradually a coherent whole emerged. A superb technician herself, Olsen honored Woolf's craftsmanship. A member of the working class, she praised Woolf (nearly an aristocrat) for her awareness of the difficult and destructive reality of working-women's lives. As a feminist, Olsen applauded her earlier sister's political consciousness. Finally, as a woman she sympathized and sorrowed at the loss of Woolf's sanity. A masterful evocation of the "human" Virginia Woolf, the talk revealed equally the breadth and depth of Tillie Olsen's humanism.

Olsen's humanism not only informs her speaking and writing, it is embodied in her daily life. She takes great pride in the San Francisco co-op, Saint Francis Square, where she has lived since its inception. Built on land cleared for urban renewal, just above the Mission district, the group of apartments constituting the cooperative escapes the grim facelessness of much inner city architecture. All the apartments face in, onto grassy squares. There are trees, birds, children's jungle gyms. Originally sponsored by the Longshoremen's Pension fund, the group is no longer linked to the Union. It is an independent unit, open to anyone within a limited income range who wishes to live in a multi-racial, multi-ethnic, self-governing community. Olsen does not believe that the Square is the "ideal" community come to fulfillment in the "real" world. Her notion of the relation between "ideal" and the "real" is more complex. But, she points out with satisfaction, Saint Francis Square is a coherent commun-

[*] Reprinted from *San Jose Studies* 2.1 (Feb. 1976): 65-83.

ity, it has endured, it reveals that brotherhood *can* be lived if men choose to do so.

Olsen at Santa Cruz, Olsen in Saint Francis Square. Both descriptions indicate characteristics important to her writing. She is a consummate artist, a working class writer, a feminist. Olsen is importantly connected with both women's and proletariat literature; to read her entire canon is to recognize that she is neither sexist nor leftist but a passionately committed humanist. Ultimately her point of view is not simplistically polemical, but as complex as humanity is broad. De-mystifying Olsen's works means lining out her paradoxical vision and indicating the patterns and motifs which come to characterize her work. As the bibliography of her publications indicates, her writing falls into three periods: the first centers on the years 1933-34; the second, 1953-56; the third, 1959 to the present.[1]

Born in 1913, the second of seven children of Samuel and Ida Lerner, she grew up in Wyoming and Nebraska. Her parents were revolutionaries who had fled from Russia after the failed 1905 rebellion. Despite being both Russian and Jewish, despite laboring long hours as farmer, packinghouse worker, painter, and paperhanger, Samuel Lerner became State Secretary of the Nebraska Socialist Party. The economic pressures which drove him from job to job in the attempt to support his family affected his daughter as well. Forced to leave high school before graduating, Olsen experienced the laborer's life as trimmer in a slaughterhouse, power press operator, hash slinger, mayonnaise-jar capper in a food processing plant, and checker in a warehouse. Sharing her parents' commitment to bettering the lives of working people, she was an active member of the Young Communist League. Her attempt at organizing warehouse workers ended by her being jailed in Kansas City. She became ill with pleurisy which, without adequate medical care in prison, worsened into incipient tuberculosis. She began her first novel at age 19, bore her first daughter at 20, and by 1933 had moved from the midwest to California (Stockton, San Francisco, Venice) which was to be her home thereafter.[2] Since Olsen was innately one on whom, in Henry James' words, "nothing is lost," she brought the reality of these experiences—the experiences of the majority of mankind in its struggle for life—to her writings.

Compared to her later pieces, the writing of Olsen's first period was overtly political. Most of her works appeared in periodicals sponsored by the John Reed Clubs or other Communist Party affiliates. Her first publication grew out of an indictment made by a Texas woman, Felipe Ibarro, against capitalists who sweated Chicanas to death in the clothing industry. Ibarro's charges were loaded with specifics—names, ages, salaries. Two months later, many of her "facts" were repeated in Olsen's poem published in *The Partisan* (March 1934). This devotion to concrete data is a continuing characteristic of Olsen's writing and illustrates the grounding of her fiction in the day-to-day facts of people's lives:

I Want You Women Up North To Know
(Based on a Letter by Felipe Ibarro in *New Masses*, Jan. 9th, 1934.)

i want you women up north to know
how those dainty children's dresses you buy
    at macy's, wanamakers, gimbels, marshall fields,
are dyed in blood, are stitched in wasting flesh,
down in San Antonio, "where sunshine spends the winter."

I want you women up north to see
the obsequious smile, the salesladies trill
    "exquisite work, madame, exquisite pleats"
vanish into a bloated face, ordering more dresses,
    gouging the wages down,
dissolve into maria, ambrosa, catalina,
    stitching these dresses from dawn to night,
    in blood, in wasting flesh.

Catalina Rodriguez, 24,
    body shrivelled to a child's at twelve,
catalina rodrigruez [*sic*], last stages of consumption,
    works for three dollars a week from dawn to midnight.
A fog of pain thickens over her skull, the parching heat
    breaks over her body.[*sic*]
and the bright red blood embroiders the floor of her room.
    White rain stitching the night, the bourgeois poet would say,
    white gulls of hands, darting, veering,
    white lightning, threading the clouds,
this is the exquisite dance of her hands over the cloth,
and her cough, gay, quick, staccato,
    like skeleton's bones clattering,
is appropriate accompaniment for the esthetic dance
    of her fingers,
and the tremolo, tremolo when the hands tremble with pain.
Three dollars a week,
two fifty-five,
seventy cents a week,
no wonder two thousands [*sic*] eight hundred ladies of joy
are spending the winter with the sun after he goes down—

for five cents (who said this was a rich man's world?) you can
    get all the lovin you want

"clap and syph aint much worse than sore fingers, blind eyes, and
    t. b."

Maria Vasquez, spinster,
    for fifteen cents a dozen stitches garments for children she has never
    had,
Catalina Torres, mother of four,
    to keep the starved body starving, embroiders from dawn to
    night.
Mother of four, what does she think of,
    as the needle pocked fingers shift over the silk —
    of the stubble-coarse rags that stretch on her own brood,
    and jut with the bony ridge that marks hunger's landscape
    of fat little prairie-roll bodies that will bulge in the
    silk she needles?
(Be not envious, Catalina Torres, look!
    on your own children's clothing, embroider,
    more intricate than any a thousand hands could fashion,
    there where the cloth is ravelled, or darned,
    designs, multitudinous, complex and handmade by Poverty
    herself.)

Ambrosa Espinoza trusts in god,
    "Todos es de dios, everything is from god,"
    through the dwindling night, the waxing day, she bolsters herself up
    with it —
but the pennies to keep god incarnate, from ambrosa,
and the pennies to keep the priest in wine, from ambrosa,
ambrosa clothes god and priest with hand-made children's dresses.

Her brother lies on an iron cot, all day and watches,
on a mattress of rags he lies.
For twenty-five years he worked for the railroad, then they laid him off.
    (racked days, searching for work; rebuffs; suspicious eyes of policemen.)
    goodbye ambrosa, mebbe in dallas I find work; desperate swing for a
    freight,
    surprised hands, clutching air, and the wheel goes over a
    leg.
    the railroad cuts it off, as it cut off twenty-five years of his life).
She says that he prays and dreams of another world, as he lies there, a
    heaven (which he does not know was brought to earth in 1917 in Russia,
    by workers like him).

Women up north, I want you to know
when you finger the exquisite hand made dresses
what it means, this working from dawn to midnight,
on what strange feet the feverish dawn must come
          to maria, catalina, ambrosa,
how the malignant fingers twitching over the pallid faces jerk them to work,
and the sun and the fever mounts with the day—
          long plodding hours, the eyes burn like coals, heat jellies the flying fingers,
down comes the night like blindness.
          long hours more with the dim eye of the lamp, the breaking back,
          weariness crawls in the flesh like worms, gigantic like earth's in winter.
And for Catalina Rodrigruez comes the night sweat and the blood
          embroidering the darkness.
          for Catalina Torres the pinched faces of four huddled
          children,
          the naked bodies of four bony children,
          the chant of their chorale of hunger.
And for twenty eight hundred ladies of joy the grotesque act gone over—
          the wink—the grimace—the "feeling like it baby?"
And for Maria Vasquez, spinster, emptiness, emptiness,
          flaming with dresses for children she can never fondle.
And for Ambrosa Espinoza—the skeleton body of her brother on his mattress
of rags, boring twin holes in the dark with his eyes to the image of christ,
remembering a leg, twenty five years cut off from his life by the railroad.

Women up north, I want you to know,
I tell you this can't last forever.

I swear it won't.

While underscoring the depth of Olsen's politicization, the work also
reveals genuine poetic skill. The central metaphor transforms the women
themselves (maria, ambrosa, catalina) into the clothing they embroider—*they* become the product of their labor. Ideologically bound to Marx,
Olsen's debt to Whitman is obvious in the repetition of individual words
and phrases, and in the free verse form. Horrible as the human reality of
these lives is, simplistic as the political analysis may be, Olsen clearly
reveals that she can elevate polemical outrage into the realm of art.

Beneath the propagandistic assertions, Olsen voices what will be her
lasting concern—the suffering of humanity, particularly the anguish of
women and children. Her plea to women in the mainstream from those
of the Third World repeatedly returns to images of deprivation—"body
shrivelled," "skeleton's bones," "starved body starving," "bony children,"
"skeleton body." Being a skeleton child—and mothering such a child—are

two of Olsen's most important motifs. Later, such human waste will be Olsen's total focus; here it shares center stage with the political explanation which is its cause.

The following month she published another political poem in *The Partisan* (April 1934):

There is a Lesson

"All Austrian schools, meanwhile, were closed for an indefinite period under a government decree issued to keep children off the hazardous streets." (Feb. 15, S. F. Chronicle)

Keep the children off the streets,
    Dollfuss,
there is an alphabet written in blood
    for them to learn,
there is a lesson thundered by collapsed
    books of bodies.

They might be riddled by the bullets
    of knowledge,
The deadly gas of revolution might
    enter their lungs,
in the streets, the hazardous streets.

In a week, in a month, let them out
    of their corners,
it will be safe then . . . (safe Dollfuss?
    safe Bauer and Seitz?
there is a volume written with three
    thousand bodies that can never
    be hidden,
there is sentence spelled by the
    grim faces of bereaved women,
there is a message, inescapable, that
    vibrates the air with voices of
    heroes who shouted it to the last:
"Down with Fascism!
Down with Social Democracy!
Long Live our Soviets")

Keep them off the streets, Dollfuss,
It will quiver your fat heart with terror

> The alphabet written in blood out there
>   that children are learning.

The brilliant transformation of abstractions (alphabets and lessons) into concrete forms (blood and bodies) is a technique which remains characteristic even in her prose. At one level a simple polemic, at another the poem reveals some recognition of the negative side of the reality teaching the lesson necessary for revolution: of the "deadly gas," of the horror of "three thousand bodies," of "the grim faces of bereaved women." Even the most virtuous ends entail dire means. Here we see a dim foreshadowing of the use of apparent opposites which becomes a landmark of Olsen's later works.

Four weeks later, Olsen's first short story appeared in the *Partisan Review*. The genesis of this early fiction is revealed in Olsen's notes to the 1972 re-issue of the Rebecca Harding Davis classic, *Life in the Iron Mills*. Olsen tells us she first read the Davis novella at age 15, "in an edition [I] bought for ten cents in an Omaha junkshop." *Life in the Iron Mills* seemed to say to her, "literature can be made out of the lives of despised people"; "you too must write." Subsequently, Olsen began the novel we now know as *Yonnondio,* the first section of which was printed in 1934 as "The Iron Throat."

That story opens as the Holbrook family is awakened by the metal whistle (the iron throat) of the coal mine. As the tale proceeds, the *details* of the day-by-day lives of Jim and Anna Holbrook and their children Mazie, Will, Ben and Jimmy are defined by dismal economic conditions, physical suffering, a desire for education and wasted creative urges. Olsen's attitude toward her characters reflects passionate indignation at the waste of human potential.

Stylistically, the story looks back to the earlier poetry. There is an echoing of imagery—the coal costs the miner's blood—and of phrases —"skeletons of starved children," "fat bellies." Repetition of phrases weaves the whole together: an immigrant neighbor, Mrs. Kvaternick, speaks of the mine as "da bowels of the earth" at the tale's beginning; later this phrase "trembles" into Mazie's mind. Peculiar to the girl's self-examination is the phrase "I am a-knowen"; in its positive and negative forms, it is repeated eight times in a single paragraph.

The story looks forward, too, in the double movement of its conclusion. Alone in the dusk, 6½ year old Mazie is frightened by the flames which dart up one side of the culm. Imaginatively she transforms them into "purty tongues"; then "gently, gently hard swollen [her] lump of tears [melts] into a swell of wonder and awe." The emotional movement here is like that expressed in the epithet at the close of "Tell Me a Riddle":

"Death deepens the wonder." Characteristically, Olsen links the tragic and the marvelous.

In substance, much of "The Iron Throat" is leftist polemic. The protagonists are proletariat and the "message" is Marxist. One-third of the whole is an address by an omniscient narrator to a thirteen year old boy as he goes into the mines for the first time. The voice details his fate: the "bowels of earth" have now "claimed" him; never again will he know fresh air, a starlit sky, or "sweet rain." As his father before him lost *his* dreams of "freedom and light and cheering throngs and happiness," so will he. He will lose the "heritage of man" so that "a few fat bellies can grow fatter." Here follows a prophecy of rebellion: "someday strong fists [will] batter the fat bellies, and skeletons of starved children batter the fat bellies."

The attitude toward experience in the concluding lines of "The Iron Throat" is typical of Olsen: "Bits of coal dust" striking Mazie "somehow reminded her of the rough hand of her father when he caressed her, hurting her, but not knowing it, hurting with a pleasant hurt." This double vision—here we would call it the "pleasure-pain principle"—rings through the later prose.

In an era unwilling to accept non-chauvinist and non-capitalist experience as meaningful, Olsen's story elicited at least one glowing response. In *The New Republic* (July 25, 1934), Robert Cantwell described "The Iron Throat" as "a work of early genius." He went on to say that Olsen's metaphors . . . are startling in their brilliance" and to praise the "21 year old girl" for being a stronger writer than Elizabeth Maddox [*sic*] Roberts. And in a letter Cantwell published in *The New Republic* on August 22, 1934, he says that four editors and a literary agent wish to contact Olsen about publication. Unfortunately none could reach her, for in the summer of '34 she had submerged herself in San Francisco Maritime Strike politics.

In the 1920's, management in San Francisco had formed an Industrial Association which attempted to lock national unions out of the waterfront. Initially successful, the Industrial Association was challenged in May, 1934 by a local of the International Longshoreman's Association which sought national recognition. When the employers resisted, the longshoremen went out on strike. Picket lines were thrown up along the Embarcadero; scabs were recruited; the sides clashed. On Thursday, July 5th, a strike-breaking attempt erupted into a pitched battle which left several strikers dead and many injured on both sides. A week after "Bloody Thursday," in a show of solidarity, the Teamsters struck the whole of San Francisco. On July 16th, the first general strike since 1919 began in America. The unions found themselves indicted as "Commie" front organizations in the Hearst press. While Harry Bridges, the head of the I.L.A., was a Communist Party member, the number of Communists in his union and others was small. Still, a highly efficient "Red Terror" campaign frightened liberal unionists, and broke the General Strike.

Olsen published two essays chronicling her involvement in this event. "Thousand-Dollar Vagrant" appeared in *The New Republic* one week after Cantwell's letter. Prefaced by the statement that "it was Lincoln Steffens who commanded me to write this story," Olsen's first person narrative outlines how she was rounded up along with "Billy, Jack and Dave" by five "bulls" who beat up the men, slandered the Communist Party and ultimately took her to jail. There, she gave a false name—Teresa Landale—and address to protect her family. On discovering the phony address, the police booked her on a vagrancy charge and set bail at $1000.

"Thousand-Dollar Vagrant" demonstrates Olsen's attitude. The pose she strikes is that of the wronged innocent, one merely "guilty by association." She asserts that no evidence was adduced proving that she was a Communist Party member and tells the judge that she had no leanings toward Communism until she was arrested. (Of course, she had long been a member of the Young Communist League.) "The Strike," Olsen's second essay on the San Francisco labor scene, appeared in the September/October issue of *Partisan Review*. It is at once more political and more poetic than "Thousand-Dollar Vagrant." The bulk of the text summarizes, from the worker's viewpoint, the events leading to the General Strike on July 16th. After a dramatic opening, "Do not ask me to write of the strike and the terror; I am on a battlefield," the essay chronicles the happenings. Ultimately, Olsen reveals that she is *not* "down . . . by the battlefield" but sitting "up in headquarters, typing *accounts* of the events," because "this is all I can do, because that is what I am supposed to do." Olsen was both participant and observer.

"The Strike" describes an equally paradoxical fact: economic deprivation and police brutality call forth total brotherhood. "That night . . . we League kids came to the meeting in a group, . . . we felt ourselves a flame . . . . Spirits of song flaming up from downstairs, answered by us, echoed across the gallery, solidarity weaving us all into one being." Suffering creates a coherent human community.

As in her second poem, knowledge is gained by "trying to read *the lesson* the morning's bodies underneath were writing . . . . " And as in "The Iron Throat," the capitalists are "fat bellies." The essay is imbued with the agony of common men's lives and with a burning zeal for political reform. The following sentence with its chant-like quality typifies Olsen's poetic form and highly political content:

And the story was the story of any worker's life, of the thousand small deprivations and frustrations suffered, of the courage forged out of the coldness and darkness of poverty, of the determination welded out of the helpless anger scalding the heart, the plodding hours of labor and weariness, of the life, given simply, as it had lived, the things which he had suffered should not be, must not be . . . . " [Ellipsis in original.]

"The Strike" is a passionately realized account of labor history. Olsen is pulled toward the communal, political world and equally toward the self-absorbed, solitary artist's life:

If I could go away for a while, if there were time and quiet, perhaps I could do it. All that has happened might resolve into order and sequence, fall into neat patterns of words. I could stumble back into the past and slowly, painfully rear the structure in all its towering magnificence, so that the beauty and heroism, the terror and significance of those days, would enter your heart and sear it forever with the vision.

After repeating the desire to flee from the action, Olsen closes the essay with an apology not unlike that she will offer for her art decades hence:

Forgive me that the words are feverish and blurred. You see, If I had time, If I could go away. But I write this on a battlefield.

The rest, the General Strike, the terror, arrests and jail, the songs in the night, must be written some other time, must be written later . . . . But there is so much happening now . . . . " [Ellipsis in original.]

The conclusion aptly predicts her later subject matter, for "the terror, arrests and jail, the songs in the night" are the topics she *will* transform into the searing vision of "Tell Me a Riddle." And her point of view, there, will have been pre-figured in the beginning of this essay—an almost Yeatsian view in which beauty and terror occur simultaneously.

"The Strike" was the last publication of Olsen's first period. The October/November 1935 issue of *The Anvil: The Proletariat Fiction Magazine* carried an announcement that "Skeleton Children," a novelette by Tillie Lerner, will appear in the next edition. But there was no next edition; *The Anvil* merged with *Partisan Review* and "Skeleton Children" never appeared (except perhaps as the first part of Chapter Five of the later *Yonnondio*).

In 1936, Tillie Lerner married Jack Olsen. Her "occupation" for the next sixteen or seventeen years was, in her own words, "children and helping to support them." To that end she gave birth to three daughters and re-entered the world of the "common" laborer as waitress, shaker in a laundry, secretary, transcriber in a dairy equipment company, and Kelly "Girl."

Her literary silence was broken between late 1953 and early 1957. In 1954, when her youngest child entered school, she enrolled in a Creative Writing course taught by Arthur Foff at San Francisco State. She was 41; this was the first time she could avail herself of the "privilege" of higher public education. Her partially finished manuscript of "Help Her to Believe" aided her in winning a Stanford University Creative Writing Fellowship for eight months in 1955-56. This award relieved her of the economic necessity of holding down jobs other than running her household and writing. The resultant freedom seems to have triggered the burst of creativity which is evidenced by her writing and publishing "I Stand Here Ironing," "Baptism," "Hey Sailor What Ship [sic]" and starting "Tell Me a Riddle." By early 1957, her expressive urges were dammed up again when she had to return to "regular" employment. Another silence closed in; luckily it was broken within two years when in 1959 she was granted a Ford Foundation Grant. This allowed her to finish and publish "Tell Me a Riddle"—and then to collect it, along with the other three stories she had written in the '50's as *Tell Me a Riddle.*

Each time Olsen reprinted a story, she reworked it. Here the typography differs; there, words and word orders are switched; elsewhere, entire lines or sections are deleted in one version and reenter in another. That she is a consummate craftsman is confirmed by Richard Scowcroft's comment in the "Preface" to *Stanford Short Stories* (1960): "I remember Tillie Olsen pouring not months but years into an anguished and constant reshaping, reappraising of any story . . . . Mr. X, Mrs. Y. and Mrs. Olsen are Egyptian slaves lashed into subjection to a concept; one wrong stone and they find themselves with a cube instead of a pyramid."

The stories of the second period demonstrate Olsen's maturation. The concerns, the vision of the first period, do not vanish but the emphasis shifts slightly as the author's consciousness becomes increasingly more complex and more correspondingly humane. The monstrous machines of Capitalism—mines, police forces—the "fat bellies" which devour "skeleton children"—no longer loom so large. The dream of brotherhood is tempered by the sense of betrayal and loss, the knowledge that while the ideals of freedom and brotherhood can never by fully realized they do not vanish but continue to live on informing daily existence. Understanding that the human condition is thus paradoxical—riddling— becomes central.

Olsen shifts her gaze from the outer, the public, to the inner, the private sphere. It is in the family that individual growth—physical and intellectual—occurs. Paradoxically, the family both creates and destroys. Endurance, and caring for others so they can endure, becomes significant.

The last three stories in *Riddle* focus on the life of one family. In "Sailor," Lennie and Helen are the parents of three daughters: Jeannie, who is just graduating from junior high; Carol, who is ten; and Allie, who is in first grade. The family lives in San Francisco, a setting that recurs in "Oh Yes," [*sic*] in which the children are several years older (Jeannie is seventeen; Carol, twelve). "Riddle" is set in Los Angeles after Jeannie has become a social worker and focuses on her grandparents, Eva and David.

In all the stories, poverty, hunger, and large families define existence. The struggle for survival is reality for these groups. Each of the first three stories centers around a relationship involving one "despised" person, a minority group member. The first is a mother who believes she emotionally abandoned her daughter; the second is an ageing alcoholic; the third is a black adolescent. Each tale teaches some new paradox of the human condition. Despite her abandonment, the child whom the mother grieves over has "come through." Although the middle-aged drunkard has thrown away his own life, he has heroically saved those of his friends. Regardless of the impossibility of interracial friendship in our divided culture, whites must continue to "care" about blacks. All three stories reiterate Olsen's awareness that the ideal human community is never achieved, but neither is the dream of it destroyed. Affirmation comes in the comprehension of this enigma. The life of the individual and of the race become one. Life is a riddle and understanding this fact is man's only solution; accepting it, he must love.

At the more simple level, the story "Tell Me A Riddle" chronicles the lives of the Jewish immigrant couple, David and Eva. As she dies of cancer in her seventies, we travel back across their 47 years of marriage, to their youth. The tale opens with the quarrel which has knotted them together for nearly half a century. It is the archetypal Male/Female fight. David has worked hard to maintain his family and now, in his old age, he wishes to retire to his Circle's Haven, where "success [is] not measured by accumulation," where he can be expansive, gregarious. Eva wants "never again to be forced to move to the rhythm of others." Having adapted her life to that of her children, now that they are grown she wishes to do the things *she* chooses. He has lived in the outer, the social world and wishes to continue to do so. She has lived in the isolated world of the home, is not socially adept, and does not wish now to become so. Bitter over her antisocial, unself-fulfilled life, it is symbolically appropriate that she be riddled with cancer.

She wants to die in her own home; he takes her on the cross-country trip *he* has always wanted, and her end comes in one of the cheap "dwelling places of the cast-off old." Yet her death is no defeat. Her energy "rages" against "the passing of the light." She resists going to a hospital and, in the end, has made the rented place a home by having "something of [her] own around her"—a cookie made in the likeness of a little Mexican girl who has just died. With fitting irony, Eva cherishes the *Pan del Muerto,* the "Bread of the Dead," as if it were the staff of life. Silent in life, as she lies dying Eva becomes a "babbler." David, who has always wanted her to be more outgoing, feels betrayed when she speaks now, for there is "nothing of him, of the children, of their intimate life together"—only the public world, "every song, every melody, every word read, heard, and spoken . . . . "

It is precisely in the larger sphere that even greater ironies are compounded. As Eva dies, she begins to repeat those "ideals" of her youth, ideals for which she was imprisoned in Siberia when a girl. She believed in "reason," "justice," "freedom," "the light of humankind," "life-worthy capacities." To this end, she and David left the "world of their youth—dark, ignorant, terrible with hate and disease" and came to America. Here, their children's lives *were* better: they were not hungry, cold, ill, or uneducated. But material improvement coincides with spiritual loss. They lack the "joyous certainty . . . of being one and indivisible with the great of the past, with all that freed [and] ennobled man." It is the old Olsen paradox: the ideal of brotherhood gleams brightest when physical life is at its lowest ebb.

Certainly, Eva's fate is characteristic of many minority persons in this country. In the shtetl, the Jewish village where Eva grew up, woman's place was lower than that of her man's. As Orthodoxy had it, even "in Paradise woman . . . will be the footstool of [her] husband . . . . " Ironically, Eva's position is no better in America; at least in the coherent culture of the shtetl, woman *did* have a respected place; Judaism valued her contributions. In America, Eva goes without the support of a community which shares her values; nor is she allowed to fulfill her individual needs. Freedom from a religious culture does not bring sexual equality any less human egalitarianism.

At every level, all have betrayed and been betrayed. Lisa, the highborn Tolstoyan who taught Eva to read, abandons her faith in non-violence by trying to kill the traitor who has had her imprisoned; she is executed. Eva's own ideal—to "spill no drop of blood"—has been violated, for her son, Davy, kills and is killed in World War II. More narrowly, she has failed her children: Clara, the eldest daughter, whose place in her heart was usurped by the younger ones; Lennie, whose creativity, like her own, might never come to fruition.

David has betrayed Eva's desire for knowledge, for selfhood. He has coaxed her away from books when she tried to read, and even paraded "the queerness of her for laughter" before the others. When he tries to put her in the hospital when she is near her death, she calls him out: "Weakling . . . betrayer. All your life you have run." The climactic moment of the story comes as David realizes the extent of his betrayal—and "with it the monstrous shapes of what had actually happened in the century."

He suddenly sees the ideal—"the flame of freedom . . . and light of knowledge . . ." juxtaposed against the reality of our century's "78,000" dead "in one minute." Here the story turns: up to this moment, hers have been the words out of the past; his, the cynical syllables of the present. Now, as he begs for the "stone" of the idealist's faith, she gives him "day-old bread"—muttering words out of the reality which she has endured. Recognizing the existence of her dream in the world in which they have lived—understanding the paradox of the ideal and the real bound together—David does not betray her further in death.

He neither asks the doctor to stop her medication, nor asks Jeannie to come sit with her. Instead, he lies down in the bed next to hers and takes her hand. The quarrel is over. The "monstrous shapes" of life and death are thus transformed through understanding, through love. As Eva's "poor body" suffers the agony of her final day, Jeannie tells David that her grandmother has gone back "to when she first heard music, a little girl on the road of the village where she was born." "It is a wedding and they dance." This is the last image of the tale. The urge to life appears even in death.

Olsen won the O'Henry Award for *Riddle* in 1961. Hereafter, she "worked" more and more inside academe. She was a fellow at the Radcliffe Institute from 1962-64. She was awarded a grant by the National Endowment for the Arts in 1967. She taught at Amherst in 1969-70; at the University of Massachusetts (Boston) in 1970-71; at Stanford in 1972. She was a grantee at the McDowell [*sic*] Colony, a New England retreat for artists, in 1972-73. In 1973 she was the Writer in Residence at M.I.T., and she returned to the University of Massachusetts as Distinguished Visiting Professor in 1973-74.

Although she abandoned neither the family as topic nor paradox as point of view, Olsen's primary interest in her third period may be labeled "reclamation." The two essays she published attempt to explain why artistic talent does not come to fruition—why creativity is "lost." The novella, "Requa I," treats the rebirth of an adolescent boy after his mother's death. The reissue of Rebecca Harding Davis' *Life in the Iron Mills* attempted to redeem that work from the neglect into which it had fallen, and her "Biographical Interpretation" of Davis' life was a similar act of restitution. Finally, with the publication of *Yonnondio*, she salvaged the novel she began in 1932.

Both essays explore the same topic—the relationship obtaining among creativity, sex and class. "Silences: When Writers Don't Write" examines those "enforced and unnatural silences that are so much a part of the creative life." Olsen deals not with the failure of creativity but (using an image from "Ironing") with its being "clogged and clotted." The natural metaphors reveal her concept of artistic creativity as organic: "the seed strikes stone"; "the soil will not sustain." After examining such periods of abortion among "the very great"—Hardy, Melville, Rimbaud, and Hopkins—she explains her own twenty years' silence. To understand rationally is to reclaim the past.

Among the "very great," she identifies most closely with Melville. Her twenty-year hiatus is surpassed by his "thirty-year night." Her desire for withdrawal is paralleled by Melville's confession to Hawthorne: "the silent grass growing moods in which a man ought always to compose . . . can seldom be mine." The final similarity is that both are wage earners. Melville's cry, "dollars damn me," might equally well have been Olsen's. Lucre is never more filthy than in its relation to creativity. Olsen explains that during the years she did not write, the "world of [her] job" was to blame. Having to be, as she put it, "part-time" artist was destructive. The young Communist would have pointed a message here. The moral is now left implicit—economic freedom connected, in our society, with class is the single element *most* crucial to creativity. She further explains what is needed for creativity: "wholly surrendered and dedicated lives; time as needed for the work; totality of self." The "part-time" artist must do work *other* than creating.

Important to her feminism is Olsen's insistence that her involvement in a "full extended family life" did not fracture her selfhood. On the contrary, being female and an artist were complementary, not contradictory. Her life fed her art. As a feminist, she explicitly rejects the argument that women's life experience is antithetic to art.

In the final sections of the essay, she discussed two groups for whom both class or sex *have* generally obviated creativity. She describes the proletariat as "mute inglorious Miltons" whose "working hours" are "*all* struggle for existence." So dire are the economic conditions of their lives that most never become literate, can never "come to writing." The facts of the lives of the majority of women are almost as defeating. Unless they are rich enough to have servants, they must "serve" to keep the "daily flow of life" going. Here again is the economic determinant. Further, cultural programming—to "place others' needs first, to feel these needs as their own" robs most women of the totality of selfhood necessary for artistic creativity.

If it seems that Olsen disclaims her similarity with other women and identifies only with men, in the essay's conclusion she allies herself with the woman writer who has been her model since she was a teenager —Rebecca Harding Davis. The diction with which she describes herself and Davis reveals that the older woman is almost her alter ego: "myself so nearly remaining mute . . . "; "herself . . . so close to remaining mute." Over all, Olsen has it both ways: she identifies with Melville, and equally with Davis. Creativity, she insists, subsumes sexuality.

In "Women Who are Writers in our Century: One out of Twelve," Olsen goes even further. Here, humanism entails feminism. Olsen's concept of the "part-self" is connected to Virginia Woolf's notion of the "angel in the house"—that creature who sacrifices her being to the needs of others. Parallel with this figure, Olsen creates that of the "essential angel," the woman who accepts "the physical responsibility for daily living, for the maintenance of life." This provider of sustenance must be a "part-time" writer. Generally, women are the essential angels *and* the angels in the house, part-time, part-self beings; clearly they cannot write.

The women who do write are "survivors." Here Olsen's individual identity as a "despised" person—the pariah who "makes it" *despite* her culture—merges with that of all women. The preeminence she holds rests partially on her being a double underdog (so to speak), damned by her class as well as her sex. Her double endurance further validates her claim that she is not a lesser but an equal artist.

Much of the essay repudiates the concept that subject matter is sex-appropriate. She insists that the traditional distinction between "men's and women's spheres" forces women into "one dimension"; in truth, women are as varied as men. Nor will she buy the idea that woman's "natural subject" is her biological sexuality. This reduction is "false to reality," for it denies those experiences of women's lives which occur "once they get out of bed and up from the childbed." Most importantly, casting women as no more that the "other half" denies them the "capacity to live the whole of human life." This is a crucial step, for Olsen insists that part of women's biological endowment as "human" is the capacity for creativity.

Olsen reconciles feminism and art by insisting that the reality rendered in fiction must mirror the whole of human experience. Proletariat existence is appropriately presented, since it brings "other *human* dimensions, realms" to light. Literature "signifies" because it teaches the complexity of reality. While this is a version of "realism," it is not narrowly "social" but broadly humanistic.

"Requa I," the novella begun in 1962, reflects a similar concern for reclamation. Its primary emphasis falls on "stealthily, secretly, reclaiming . . . broken existences that yet continue" and on the difficult, day-to-day endurances necessary in "having to hold up." The person to be "reclaimed" is an adolescent boy, Stevie, who withdraws from life when his mother dies. His Uncle Wes, who works in a junkyard salvaging usable items, must restore the boy's will to live. With infinite patience, Wes' "caring" slowly redeems the boy. Ultimately, he will not only endure but also "master" his world.

After this story, Olsen attempts the restitution of Rebecca Harding Davis' reputation. Her "Biographical Interpretation," printed in the reissue of *Life in the Iron Mills*, reveals that at sixty she still cherishes what she first found at fifteen. She describes Davis' writing "in absolute identification with 'thwarted wasted lives . . . mighty hungers . . . unawakened power,'" "despised love," "circumstances that denied use of capacities; imperfect, self tutored art that could have only odd moments for its doing . . . . "

In her notes, where she justifies the method she uses in the essay, Olsen points out how her life has altered her view: "I have brought to [Davis'] life and work my understanding as writer, as avid reader, as feminist-humanist, as woman." Olsen pictures Davis as torn between the desire for a full sexual and emotional life *and* a full creative intellectual life. We learn that on her visit to New England, the Boston Brahmins found her "intellectually impressive" and "shockingly full-blooded and direct for she observed that 'women feel physical desire for men just as men do for women!'" Davis is neither head nor heart—but both.

Olsen tells us that Davis was also torn by her own need to write as opposed to the needs first of her father, then of her husband and family. Davis' "The Wife's Story" is summarized as "the working [out] of woman's conflict between commitment to other human beings and the need to carry on serious work." Olsen further delineates Davis as "a part-time, part-self" being: "Often there were only exhausted tag ends of herself in tag ends of time left over after the house, Clarke [her husband], the babies, for a book that demanded all her powers, all her concentration."

Davis ultimately "lost her place in the literary world" because she made a conventional marriage and became both the essential angel and the angel in the house. Still, Olsen honors her art, because Davis tried to teach about the working class, tried to record the lives of those human beings "who did the necessary industrial work in the last century."

What is the most significant about the "Biographical Interpretation" is not that it reflects the experiences of one woman—Davis, Olsen—but that it renders the reality of many. "Nothing one says is ever merely personal," writes Doris Lessing. The "real" lives of most women in our time still fit the pattern lined out by this ancestral sister. "Time past *is* time present." Olsen's act of reclamation increases our knowledge of the here-and-now.

Yonnondio: From the Thirties is the latest of Olsen's published works. In "A Note About This Book," Olsen explains this is the novel begun in 1932 and put aside in 1936-37. She claims the book was completely written then—that this version contains "no re-writing, no new writing." Thus the novel's subtitle. What "the older" writer has done is to sift, select and order the hundreds of fragments left by "that long ago young writer." The book assures that the lives of the poor in the '20's will not be forgotten. The title, the epigram, come from Whitman: "Yonnondio! Yonnondio!—unlimned they disappear;/ . . . A muffled sonorous sound, a wailing word is bourn/through the air for a moment,/Then blank and gone and still, and utterly lost." The novel teaches us to see the history of the pre-Depression decade as more than that of Fitzgerald's flappers. It covers two-and-one-half years in the lives of the Holbrook family: Anna and Jim, and their children, Mazie, Will, Jimmie, Ben and finally Baby Bess.

Yonnondio flies off in many directions, not all of which are equally developed or coalesce with the others. To a degree, the book is a *Bildungsroman* trying to trace Mazie's psychosexual growth between 6½ and 9. At moments, it is a polemic for rebellion. But its most successful strain is its realistic depiction of the squalid conditions in which the unknown of America's working class miraculously endure.

Whether *Yonnondio* is viewed as her earliest or her latest completed work, it fully embodies Olsen's vision. The smallest, but the basic political unit—the family—is its focus. There are many children, since poverty breeds ignorance and vetoes medical intervention. People cannot "settle down" but must move in pursuit of their daily bread. Denied education themselves, the parents struggle so that the children may be enlightened. The young suffer limitless mental, emotional and physical privation. Few will know lives less grim than their parents. In the midst of such unrelenting horror, there is a bond of brotherhood. The dream of a day when "a human being [can] be human . . . " is sustained despite man's inhumanity to man. The violent, dirty urban landscape is transformed so that "streets shimmer and are diamond: . . . lamps [are] rayed and haloed." Endurance is changed into affirmation, affirmation lived in acts of love.

Formally, substantively, Olsen's later writing far outdistances the earlier. The dedication of the 1971 volume of *Best American Short Stories* to Olsen gives some indication of the esteem properly awarded her artistry. "Requa I" is appropriately republished in this collection. In the passage from it quoted below, Olsen's typical matter and manner coalesce. Echoing Shakespeare—in *his* most riddling play, "Hamlet"—the 20th-century humanist sums up all she is about better than we could:

But the known is reaching to him, stealthily, secretly, reclaiming.
Sharp wind breath, fresh from the sea. Skies that are all seasons in one day.
Fog rain. *Known weather of his former life.*
　　Disorder twining with order. The discarded, the broken, the torn from the whole: weathereaten weatherbeaten; mouldering, or waiting for use-need. *Broken existences that yet continue.*

Hasps	switches	screws	plugs	tubings	drills
Valves	pistons	shears	planes	punchers	sheaves
Clamps	sprockets	coils	bits	braces	dies

How many shapes and sizes; how various, how cunning in application. Human mastery, human skill. Hard, defined, enduring, they pass through his hands—link to his city life of the manmade marvel.
　　Wes: taking a towed-in car, one hundred pieces out of what had been one. Singing—unconscious, forceful—to match the motor as he machines a new edge, rethreads a pipe. Capable, fumbling; exasperated, patient; demanding, easy; uncomprehending, quick, harsh, gentle: *concerned* with him. *The recognizable human bond.*
　　The habitable known, stealthily, secretly reclaiming.
　　The dead things, pulling him into attention, consciousness.
　　The tasks: coaxing him with trustiworthiness, pliancy, doing as he bids.

having to hold up.

"Requa," p. 252

NOTES

1. The following bibliography of Tillie Olsen's publications includes different versions of the same work so that the interested reader may compare them. Abbreviated forms of these titles are used in the body of the essay. The first five entries are signed "T. Lerner."

"I Want You Women Up North to Know." *The Partisan,* 1 (March 1934), 4. [Poem.]

"There is a Lesson." *The Partisan,* 1 (April 1934), 4. [Poem.]

"The Iron Throat." *Partisan Review,* 1 (April-May 1934), 3-9. This is part of the first chapter of the novel *Yonnondio;* the story ends on page 14 of the novel with the words "swell and wonder and awe."

"Thousand-Dollar Vagrant." *New Republic,* 80 (29 August 1934), 67-69. [Autobiographic essay.]

"The Strike." *Partisan Review,* 1 (September-October 1934),3-9. [Expository essay.] Reprinted in *Years of Protest: A Collection of American Writings of the 1930's,* ed. Leon [sic] Salzman, New York: Pegasus, 1967, pp. 138-144.

"Help Her to Believe." *Pacific Spectator,* 10 (Winter 1956), 55-63. [Short story.] Reprinted in *Stanford Short Stories,* ed. W. Stegner and R. Scowcroft. Stanford, California: Stanford University Press, 1956, pp. 34-42. Reprinted as "I Stand Here Ironing" in *Best American Short Stories,* ed. Martha Foley. Boston: Houghton Mifflin Company, 1957, pp. 264-271. Reprinted as "I Stand Here Ironing" in *Tell Me a Riddle* (see below).

"Hey Sailor, What Ship." *New Campus Writing No. 2,* ed. Nowland [sic] Miller. New York: G. P. Putnam's Sons, 1957, pp. 199-213. [Short story.] Reprinted in *Stanford Short Stories,* ed. Stegner and Scowcroft. Stanford, California: Stanford University Press, 1957, pp. 1-21. Reprinted in *Tell Me a Riddle.*

"Baptism," *Prairie Schooner,* 31 (Spring 1957), 70-80. [Short story.] Reprinted as "O Yes" in *Tell Me a Riddle.*

Tell Me a Riddle." New World Writing 16, ed. Stewart Richardson & Corlies M. Smith. Philadelphia: J. B. Lippincott, 1960, pp. 11-57. [Novella.] Reprinted in *Stanford Short Stories,* ed. Stegner and Scowcroft. Stanford, California: Stanford University Press, 1960, pp. 82-122. Reprinted in *Tell Me a Riddle.*

Tell Me a Riddle. Philadelphia: J. B. Lippincott, 1961. This volume includes "I Stand Here Ironing," Hey Sailor, What Ship," "O Yes," and "Tell Me a Riddle." It appears also as a Delta paperback (New York: Dell Publishing Co., 1961). All references in this essay are to this paperback edition.

"Silences: When Writers Don't Write." *Harper's,* 231 (October 1965), 153-161. [Essay. Adapted from a talk, "Death of the Creative Process," presented at the Radcliffe Institute for Independent Study, 1962.]

"Requa" *Iowa Review* 1 (Summer 1970), 54-74. [Novella.] Reprinted as "Requa I" in *Best American Short Stories,* ed. Foley and Burnett. Boston: Houghton Mifflin Company, 1971, pp. 237-265.

"Women Who are Writers in Our Century: One Out of Twelve." *College English,* 34 (October 1972), 6-17. [Essay. Previously presented as a talk under the same title at a M. L. A. Forum on Women Writers in the Twentieth Century (December 28, 1971).]

"A Biographical Interpretation." *Life in the Iron Mills,* by Rebecca Harding Davis. New York: Feminist Press, 1972, pp. 69-174. [Biographic essay about Davis.]

Yonnondio: from [sic] *the Thirties.* New York: Delacorte Press/Seymour Lawrence, 1974. [Novel.]

2. Much of the factual information in this essay has been generously shared by Tillie Olsen; any erroneous interpretation of the facts is solely our responsibility.

From the Thirties: Tillie Olsen and the Radical Tradition[*]

Deborah Rosenfelt

PREFACE

This paper focuses on Tillie Olsen's experience as a woman, a writer, and an activist in the Old Left of the 1930s. It grew out of my view of Olsen's life and art as an important link between that earlier radical tradition and contemporary feminist culture. This perspective, of course, is only one lens through which to look at her life and art, magnifying certain details and diminishing others. In dwelling on Olsen's political activities and in placing her work in the context of a "socialist feminist" literary tradition, I have, as Olsen herself has pointed out to me, given insufficient weight to two poles of her life and art. On the one hand, there was the dailiness of her life, characterized most of the time less by political activism or participation in the leftist literary milieu than by the day-to-day struggles of a first-generation, working-class mother simply to raise and support a family—the kind of silencing that takes priority in all of her own writings. On the other hand, there was her sense of affinity as an artist with traditions of American and world literature that lie outside the "socialist feminist" literary tradition as I have defined it.

The latter point, especially, needs clarification. Obviously, literary traditions are not demarcated by clear boundaries. Some works of literature, by virtue of their art and scope, transcend the immediate filiations of their authors to become part of a "great tradition" of their own—not in an idealistic sense, but as models which inspire and challenge later writers, regardless of their political commitments. Olsen's work is part of this "great tradition," both in its sources and in its craft. Then too, in some eras of intense political activity, such as the thirties or the sixties, writers whose essential concerns are not explicitly political or whose work takes other directions when the era has ended may be temporarily drawn into a leftist political milieu. Edna St. Vincent Millay, Katherine Anne Porter, Mary McCarthy, and Dorothy Parker were among the women writers associated, in the thirties, with the Left; in our own era, writers like Adrienne Rich and Susan Griffin—close to Olsen both as friends and as artists—initially shared connections and visions with the New Left, subsequently articulating values and world views partly in opposition to it.

[*] Reprinted from *Feminist Studies* 7.3 (Fall 1981): 371-406.

Yet the definition of a "socialist feminist" tradition is, I think, legitimate and useful, for it does identify writers who, like Olsen, shared a certain kind of consciousness, an engagement with the political issues of their day, and an involvement in a progressive political and cultural movement. It also enables us to examine the connections between the radical cultural traditions of the past and those our own era is creating, questioning that earlier heritage when necessary, but acknowledging also the extent to which we as contemporary feminists are its heirs.[1]

I could not have written this paper without Tillie Olsen's assistance, although its emphasis, its structure, and any errors in fact and interpretation are my responsibility. Over the past two years, Olsen has granted me access to some of her personal papers—journals, letters, and unpublished manuscripts. Both she and her husband, Jack Olsen, have been generous in sharing their recollections of life in the thirties. In fall 1980, Olsen responded with a detailed critique to an earlier version of this paper.[2] Some of her comments called for a simple correction of factual inaccuracies; some questioned my interpretations of her experience. The paper in its present form incorporated many, although not all, of her suggestions for revision.

This paper, then, is part of an ongoing dialogue about issues that matter very much to both Tillie Olsen and myself: the relationship of writing to political commitment; the "circumstances"—a favorite Olsen word—of class and sex and their effect on sustained creative activity, literary or political; and the strengths and weaknesses of the radical cultural tradition in this country.

Tillie Olsen's fiction and essays have been widely acknowledged as major contributions to American literature and criticism. Her work has been particularly valued by contemporary feminists, for it has contributed significantly to the task of reclaiming women's achievements and interpreting their lives. In 1961, she published the collection of four stories, *Tell Me a Riddle* (Philadelphia: J. B. Lippincott), each story focusing on the relationships between family members or friends; each revealing the injuries inflicted by poverty, racism, and the patriarchal order; each celebrating the endurance of human love and will. In 1974, she published *Yonnondio: From the Thirties* (New York: Delacorte Press/Seymour Lawrence), the first section of a novel about a working-class family, told mostly from the point of view of the daughter, Mazie. Begun in the thirties, then put away, this novel was finally revised forty years later "in arduous partnership" with "that long ago young writer."[3] In 1978, she published her collected essays in *Silences* (New York: Delacorte Press/Seymour Lawrence), a sustained prose poem about the silences that befall writers and those who would be writers—especially, although not exclusively, women; especially, although not exclusively, those who must also struggle for sheer survival. In addition to being a gifted writer and critic, Olsen is also a teacher who has helped to democratize the literary canon by calling attention to the works of Third World writers, working-class writers, and women.

Olsen's importance to contemporary women who read and write or who write about literature is widely acknowledged. Yet although her work has been vital for feminists today, and although one article does discuss her background in some depth,[4] few of Olsen's contemporary admirers realize the extent to which her consciousness, vision, and choice of subject are rooted in an earlier heritage of social struggle—the communist Old Left of the thirties and the tradition of radical political thought and action, mostly socialist and anarchist, that dominated the left in the teens and twenties. Not that we can explain the eloquence of her work in terms of its sociopolitical origins, not even that left-wing politics and culture were the single most important influences on it, but that its informing consciousness, its profound understanding of class and sex and race as shaping influences on people's lives, owes much to that earlier tradition. Olsen's work, in fact, may be seen as part of a literary lineage so far unacknowledged by most contemporary critics: a socialist feminist literary tradition.

Critics such as Ellen Moers and Elaine Showalter have identified a literary tradition of women writers who read one another's work, corresponded with one another about everything from domestic irritations to the major issues of the day, and looked to one another for strength, encouragement, and insight.[5] Literary historians like Walter Rideout and Daniel Aaron have traced the outlines of a radical literary tradition in America, composed of two waves of twentieth-century writers influenced by socialism in the early years, by communism in the thirties, who had in common "an attempt to express a predominantly Marxist view toward society."[6] At the intersections of these larger traditions is a line of women writers, associated with the American Left, who unite a class consciousness and a feminist consciousness in their lives and creative work, who are concerned with the material circumstances of people's lives, who articulate the experiences and grievances of women and of other oppressed groups—workers, national minorities, the colonized and the exploited—and who speak out of a defining commitment to social change.

In fiction this tradition extends from turn of the century socialists like Charlotte Perkins Gilman, Vida Scudder, and Susan Glaspell, through such thirties Old Left women, as Meridel LeSueur, Tess Slesinger, Josephine Herbst, Grace Lumpkin, and Ruth McKenney, to contemporary writers with early ties to the civil rights and antiwar movements and the New Left: Marge Piercy, Grace Paley, Alice Walker, and others. Although the specific political affiliations of these writers have varied from era to era and from individual to individual, the questions they raise have been surprisingly consistent. These range from basic questions about how to survive economically to more complex ones, such as how to understand the connections and contradictions between women's struggles and those struggles based on other categories and issues, or how to find a measure of emotional and sexual fulfillment in a world where egalitarian relationships are more ideal than real. Sometimes, as in Gilman's *Herland*, published serially in *The Forerunner* in the midteens, or Piercy's *Woman on the Edge of Time*, these writers try to imagine socialist feminist utopias. More often, as with the women writers associated with the Left, especially the Communist party, in the 1930s, their work constitutes a sharp critique of the present. Sometimes, as in Agnes Smedley's *Daughter of Earth*, Slesinger's *The Unpossessed*, Piercy's *Small Changes*, much of Alice Walker's fiction, and implicitly Olsen's *Tell Me a Riddle*, that critique includes a sharp look from a woman's point of view at the sexual politics of daily life in the political milieus with which these authors were associated.

Olsen's relationship to her political milieu in the 1930s most concerns me here, for this paper is not so much a literary analysis of Olsen's work as it is a study of her experience in the Left in the years when she first began to write for publication. I will first give a brief overview of Olsen's background and life in those years, focusing on the roots of both her political commitment and her creative work, and then identify a series of central contradictions inherent in her experience. In thus imposing a paradigmatic order on Olsen's individual experience, I have tried, not always successfully, to maintain a balance between fidelity to the idiosyncrasies of the individual life and the identification of patterns applicable to the experience of other women artists in leftist movements then and now.

Tillie Olsen's parents, Samuel and Ida Lerner, were involved in the 1905 revolution in Russia, fleeing to the United States when it failed and settling in Nebraska. Her father, in addition to working at a variety of jobs, including farming, paperhanging, and packing house work, became state secretary of the Nebraska Socialist Party, running in the midtwenties as the socialist candidate for the state representative from his district. Tillie Lerner, second oldest of six children in this depression-poor family, dropped out of high school in Omaha after the eleventh grade to go to work—although, as she is careful to remind people who today take their degrees for granted, this means that she went further in school than most of the women of her generation. Given the radical political climate of her home, it is not surprising that she too would have become active, first writing skits and musicals for the Young People's Socialist League, and subsequently, at seventeen, joining the Young Communist League, (YCL), the youth organization of the Communist party. During most of her mid and late teens, she worked at a variety of jobs, took increasing responsibility as a political organizer, and continued to lead an ardent inner literary and intellectual life, in spite of the interruption of her formal schooling. In the draft of a letter to Philip Rahv, editor of the *Partisan Review*, apparently in response to his request for biographical information, she later drew a swift self-portrait:

> Father state secretary Socialist party for years.
> Education, old revolutionary pamphlets, laying around house,
> (including liberators), and YCL.
> Jailbird—"violating handbill ordinance" [a reference to her arrest and imprisonment in the Argentine Jail in Kansas City for her work in organizing a strike in the packing houses.]
> Occupations: Tie presser, hack writer . . . , model, housemaid, ice cream packer, book clerk.

To this catalogue of occupations she might have added packing house work, waitressing, and working as a punch-press operator.

Although essentially accurate, this self-portrait does reflect some irony, some self-consciousness in the delineation of the pure working-class artist educated only in revolutionary literature and the "school of life." In fact, even as a young woman, Olsen was an eager reader, regularly visiting the public library and second-hand bookstores in Omaha. She recalls today that she was determined to read everything in the fiction category in the library, making it almost through the M's. She also borrowed books from the socialist doctor who took care of the family and from the Radcliffe graduate for whom she worked for several months as a mother's helper. Olsen's earliest journal, written when she was sixteen, in addition to recording the more predictable emotions, events, and relationships of adolescence, shows a familiarity with an extraordinary variety of literature—popular fiction, the nineteenth-century romantics, contemporary poets ranging from Carl Sandberg [sic] to Edna St. Vincent Millay. Although remarkably eclectic, her reading was predisposed toward what she calls "the larger tradition of social concern"—American populists like Walt Whitman; European social critics like Ibsen, Hugo, the early Lawrence, and especially Katherine Mansfield; black writers like W. E. B.

DuBois and Langston Hughes; American women realists like Elizabeth Madox Roberts, Willa Cather, and Ellen Glasgow; as well as leftists like Upton Sinclair, John Dos Passos, Mike Gold, Guy Endore; and socialist feminists like Olive Schreiner, whose *Story of An African Farm* she refers to in the journal as "incredibly *my* book," and Agnes Smedley, whose *Daughter of Earth* she would later bring to the attention of the Feminist Press and a new generation of readers.

As she explains in her Notes to The Feminist Press edition of Rebecca Harding Davis's *Life in the Iron Mills* (1972), she first read that work in a volume of bound *Atlantic Monthly's* bought in an Omaha junkshop when she was fifteen. Davis's work, she writes, on pages 157 and 158, said to her: "Literature can be made out of the lives of despised people," and "You, too, must write." Olsen's journals indicate that from a very early age, perhaps even before she read *Life in the Iron Mills*, she consciously and carefully apprenticed herself to the craft of writing. Her early journal is filled with resolutions for a future as a writer, expressions of despair at her own inarticulateness, and frequent humorous deprecations of her own attempts at poetic prose: "Phooey—I was just being literary."

Several passages show her grappling too with the critical and social issues raised by the journals of the Left:

> I read the *Modern Quarterly* today, and all the while
> I was thinking—Christ, how ignorant, how stupid I am.
> Paragraphs I had to read over, names as unknown to
> me as Uranus to man; ideas that were untrodden, undiscovered
> roads to me; words that might have been Hindu, so unintelligible they
> seemed . . . . But there was an article substantiating my what I thought
> insane conclusions about the future of art.

She does not elaborate on her "insane conclusions" but the *Modern Quarterly* at the time was a nonsectarian Marxist journal with a manifesto that, in Daniel Aaron's words, "denied the distinction between intellectual and worker and between pure art and propaganda and committed the magazine to Socialism." Its editor, V. G. Calverton, boasted that he printed "almost every left wing liberal and radical who had artistic aspirations";[7] the several references to the magazine scattered through Olsen's journal indicate that she was a regular reader, as she had been even earlier of *The Liberator*, the eclectically socialist journal of art and politics edited by Max Eastman. In another passage, the sixteen-year-old Olsen urges herself to take a stand on an almost comical array of global issues—issues, however that would continue to occupy her throughout her life:

> Have been reading Nietszche & *Modern Quarterly*. I must write out,
> clearly and concisely, my ideas on things. I vacillate so easily. And
> I am so-so sloppy in my mental thinking. What are my *true* opinions,
> for instance, on socialism, what life should be, the future of literature,
> true art, the relation between the sexes, where are we going . . . .
> Yes, I must write it out, simply so I will *know,* not flounder around
> like a flying fish, neither in air or in water.
>
> Later: That's quite simple to say, but there are so few things
> one can be sure and definite about —so often I am pulled
> both ways—& I can't have a single clear cut opinion. There are
> so few things I have deep, unalterable convictions about.

The clear opinions and deep convictions would come a year later through her disciplined work and study in the Young Communist League. Her own writings before that time—some stories and many poems—are not on the whole political. The poems I examined, some interspersed in her journals, some typed drafts, tend to be romantic, lyrical, full of the pain of lost or unrequited love, the anguish of loneliness, and the mysteries of nature, especially the winds and snows of the Nebraska winters. Several express deep love and affection for a female friend, and one describes a bond with her younger sister. Olsen says that there were other poems, now lost, on political themes like the execution of Sacco and Vanzetti in 1927. Mostly, though, these early poems are the effusions of an intense, imaginative young woman as influenced by the romantic traditions of nineteenth-century poetry and its twentieth-century practitioners like Millay as by the "larger tradition of social conern."

Olsen's decision to join the YCL in 1931 was a turning point; for the next year and a half she dedicated much of her energy to political work. She was sent from Omaha to Kansas City, where she attended the party school for several weeks, formed close ties to political comrades like the working-class women Fern Pierce and "Red" Allen, whom she helped to support by working in a tie factory, and became involved in an unhappy relationship with a party organizer. It was during this time that she was sent to the Argentine Jail for passing out leaflets to packing house workers. She was already sick at the time, having contracted pleurisy from working in front of an open window at the tie factory with a steam radiator in front of it; in jail, she became extremely ill and in 1932 was sent back to Omaha.

During this time, her poems begin to acquire different subjects, a different quality. They still focus on personal experience and emotion, including the anguish of an abortion or miscarriage and the bitterness of misplaced or betrayed love. But now she sometimes interweaves political metaphors to express emotional states. One such poem begins with the speaker sitting "hunched by the window,/watching the snow trail down without lightness." The poem goes on:

> The branches of trees writhe like wounded animals,
> like small frightened bears the buds curve their backs to
>   the white onslaught,
> and I think of what a Wobbly told me of his third degree,
> no violent tortures, but exquisitely, civilized,
> a gloved palm lightly striking his cheek,
> in a few minutes it was a hammer of wind pounding nails of
>   hail,
> in fifteen a sledge, in twenty, mountains rearing against
>   his cheek . . . .
> Somehow, seeing the constant minute blows of the snow
>   on the branches,
> and their shudder, this story falters into my mind,
> with some deeper, untranslatable meaning behind it,
> something I can not learn.

The untranslatable meaning finally has something to do with the

> wisdom
> of covering the dead, the decaying,
> the swell and stir of the past, the leaves of old hope,
>   with inexorable snow,
> Of stripping bare and essential the illusions of leaves,
> leaves that were moved by any wind.

This poem uses the landscape in a traditional way as a mirror for the speaker's state of mind, bleak but resolute, from which she can draw a lesson for living, but it complicates the natural imagery by attributing to a snowfall the implacable, impersonal characteristics of the professional interrogator—an analogy accessible only to someone with a certain kind of political experience and sympathy. The analogy doesn't quite work, because ultimately the inexorable snow has something redeeming in it, as the political interrogation does not; yet the parallel between the speaker and the Wobbly, both of whom must remain firm under onslaught, gives the poem a social as well as a natural dimension and suggests that its writer was struggling for both personal and political reasons to discipline the chaos of her emotions.

During this period of intense political organizing, Olsen began to have the "deep, unalterable convictions" she had earlier wished for, and she took herself to task for the relative absence of a political dimension in most of her earlier work:

> The rich things I could have said are unsaid, what I did write
> anyone could have written. There is no Great God Dough,
> terrible and harassing, in my poems, nothing of the common
> hysteria of 300 girls every 4:30 in the factory, none of the
> bitter humiliation of scorching a tie; the fear of being late,
> of ironing a wrinkle in, the nightmare of the kids at home to
> be fed and clothed, the rebelliousness, the tiptoe expectation and
> searching, the bodily nausea and weariness . . . . yet this was my
> youth.[8]

Late in 1932, Olsen moved to Faribault, Minnesota, a period of retreat from political and survival work to allow her recovery time from the illness that by now had become incipient tuberculosis. It was there at nineteen that she began to write *Yonnondio*, the novel that for the first time would give full expression to "the rich things" in her own and her family's experience. She became pregnant in the same month that she started writing, and bore a daughter before her twentieth birthday. In 1933, she moved to California, continuing her connection with the YCL in Stockton, Los Angeles, and San Francisco. She also continued to write—poems and reportage and more of the novel that would become *Yonnondio*. In 1936 she began to live with her comrade in the YCL, Jack Olsen, whom she eventually married; in the years that followed, she bore three more daughters and worked at a variety of jobs to help support them. Gradually she stopped writing fiction, concentrating on raising the children and working, but remained an activist into the forties, organizing work related to war relief for the Congress of Industrial Organizations (CIO), serving as president of the California CIO's Women's Auxiliary, writing a column for *People's World*, and working in nonleftist and nonunion organizations related to childcare and education, including the Parent-Teacher Association. During the late forties and fifties, she and her family endured the soul-destroying harassment typically directed at leftists and thousands of suspected leftists during that period. It was not until the midfifties that Olsen began writing again, her style less polemic, more controlled, her vision deepened by the years, her consciousness still profoundly political. In the years that followed, she produced the works which most of us know her for today: the stories in *Tell Me a Riddle;* *Yonnondio,* finally published in 1974, polished and organized, but not substantially rewritten; and the essays gathered and expanded in *Silences.*

As Elinor Langer has remarked, when Olsen began to write again in the fifties, it was not as a woman who had lived her life as an artist but as an artist who had lived her life as a women [*sic*].[9] Yet in those turbulent years of the early to midthirties, Olsen lived fully as artist, as activist, as worker, and as woman/wife/mother, though often suffering from the conflicting demands, always having to give primacy to one part of her being at the expense of another.[10] In examining the political contexts of Olsen's life in the Left in the thirties, I will consider the ways her participation both limited and nurtured her as a woman and an artist. I will focus on three basic contradictions confronting her as an activist, a writer and a woman in the Left in those years.

First, the Left required great commitments of time and energy for political work, on the whole valuing action over thought, deed over word; yet it also validated the study and production of literature and art, providing a first exposure to literature for many working-class people, fostering an appreciation of a wide range of socially conscious literature, and offering important outlets for publication and literary exchange. Second, although much left-wing criticism, especially by Communist Party writers, was narrowly prescriptive about the kind of literature contemporary writers should be producing, it also inspired—along with the times themselves—a social consciousness in writers that deepened their art. Third, for a woman in the thirties, the Left was a profoundly masculinist world in many of its human relationships, in the orientation of its literature, and even in the language used to articulate its cultural criticism; simultaneously, the Left gave serious attention to women's issues, valued women's contributions to public as well as to private life, and generated an important body of theory on the Woman Question.

The first contradiction, of course, affected both male and female writer-activists on the Left. Then as now, the central problem for an activist trying to be a writer was simply finding the time to write. In the section of *Silences* called "Silences—its Varieties," Olsen has a brief entry on page 9 labeled *Involvement* under the larger heading, "Political Silences":

When political involvement takes priority, though the need and love for writing go on. Every freedom movement has, and

has had, its roll of writers participating at the price of their
writing.

Olsen has spoken little of these silences compared with the fullness of her
analysis of other kinds of silences—not those freely chosen, but those
imposed by the burdens of poverty, racial discrimination, female roles.
Partly this disproportion exists because, in her own life, and the lives of
so many others, the compelling necessity to work for pay—the circumstance of class, and the all-consuming responsibilities of homemaking and
motherhood—the circumstance of gender, clearly *have* been the major
silencers, and if I do not speak of them at length here, it is because Olsen
herself has done so, fully and eloquently. Partly also, I suspect, she has
not wanted to be misread as encouraging a withdrawal from political
activism for the sake of "art" or self-fulfillment. Yet this little passage
could well allude to her own dilemma in the thirties.

The dilemma, as she points out now, was sharper for her as a working-
class woman and a "grass roots" activist involved in daily workplace
struggles than for those professionals who were already recognized as
writers, who participated in the movement primarily supported by
federally funded projects like the Works Projects Administration. Except
for the interlude in 1932 in Faribault and another withdrawal from
political activity in Los Angeles in 1935, another "good writing year,"
Olsen's political work came first throughout the early and midthirties—along with the burdens of survival work and, increasingly,
domestic work; and it required the expenditure of time and energy such
work always demands. As a member of the YCL in the Midwest, she
wrote and distributed leaflets in the packing houses, helped organize
demonstrations, walked in picket lines, attended classes and meetings,
and wrote and directed political plays and skits. In high school, she had
written a prize-winning humor column called "Squeaks"; in the YCL, she
recalls, she was able to use her particular kind of humor and punning to
great effect with the living audiences who came to the league's performances.

The nature of Olsen's commitment in the early thirties emerges with
particular clarity in a letter she received from a fellow YCL organizer and
close friend, as she recuperated from her illness in Omaha, ostensibly on
leave for two months from league duties. The letter praises her growth
as an organizer, but reprimands her for being "too introspective." It is full
of friendly advice and firm pressure:

Read. Read things that will really be of some help to you.
The Daily Worker every day . . . . the Young Worker. All the new

pamphlets . . . . and really constructive books . . . . You'll have time to now, and you've got to write skits and plays for the League. This you can do for the League, and it will be a great help . . . . have only one thing in mind—recovery, and work in the League, and if you pull thru, and are working in the League again in a few months, I will say that as a Communist you have had your test.

The letter concludes by asking her how the play is coming, and urging her to rush it as soon as possible, then adds a postscript: "How about a song for the song-writing contest?"

Reflecting on this letter in her journal, Olsen attributes to its author "full understanding of what it means to me to leave now." She goes on to condemn herself for "the paths I have worn of inefficiency, procrastination, idle planning, lack of perseverance," adding, "Only in my League work did these disappear, I have that to thank for my reconditioning." She expresses her wish to write in a more disciplined way but adds: "I must abolish word victories . . . . let me feel nothing till I have had action—without action feeling and thot [sic] are disease . . . . " The point is not, then, that insensitive and rigid communist bureaucrats imposed unreasonable demands on party members, but rather that rank-and-file communists made these demands on themselves, because they believed so deeply in the liberating possibilities of socialism; the necessity for disciplined, organized action; and the reality of the revolutionary process, in which their participation was essential. The times themselves instilled a sense of urgency and possibility: a depression at home, with all its concomitant anguishes of hunger, poverty, unemployment; the rise of fascism in Europe with its threat of world war; the example of a successful revolution in the Soviet Union and the feeling of connection with the revolutionary movements there and in other countries, such as China. Like many progressive people, Olsen felt herself to be part of a valid, necessary, and global movement to remake the world on a more just and humane model. If the Left in those year, especially the circles in which Olsen moved, tended to value action over thought, deed over word, there were good reasons.

Olsen's comments today about the author of this letter and her other movement friends suggest both the depth of her commitment to them and the feelings of difference she sometimes experienced as an aspiring writer. What becomes clear in her comments is that for her, political work with such women was a matter of class loyalty. She could not, then or later, leave the "ordinary" people to lead a "literary" life.

They were my dearest friends, but how could they know what
so much of my writing self was about? They thought of writing in the
terms in which they knew it. They had become readers, like so many
working class kids in the movement, but there was so much that
fed me as far as my medium was concerned that was closed to them.
They read the way women read today coming into the women's movement
who don't have literary background —reading for what it says about their
lives, or what it doesn't say. And they loved certain writings because of
truths, understandings, affirmations, that they found in them . . . .
It was not a time that my writing self could be first . . . . We believed
that we were going to change the world, and it looked as if it was
possible. It was just after Hindenberg turned over power to Hitler—and
the enormity of the struggle demanded to stop what might result
from that was just beginning to be evident . . . . And I did so love
my comrades. They were all blossoming so. These were the same kind
of people I'd gone to school with, who had quit, as was common in
my generation, around the eighth grade . . . . whose development
had seemed stopped, though I had known such inherent capacity
in them. Now I was seeing that evidence, verification of what
was latent in the working class. It's hard to leave something like that.

For Olsen, then, the relationship between the intellectual and the
working class was far more than an academic question, for she herself
belonged to one world by birth and commitment and was drawn to the
other by her gift and love for language and literature. Both the "intellectual" activities of reading and writing and the struggles of working people
to improve the quality of their lives were essential to her. The problem
was how to combine them. "These next months," she wrote in her
Faribault journal, at last with some free time before her,

I shall only care about my sick body—to be a good Bolshevik
I need health first. Let my mind stagnate further, let my
heart swell with neurotic emotions that lie clawing inside like a
splinter—afterwards, the movement will clean that out. First,
a strong body . . . . I don't know what it is in me, but I
must write too. It is like creating white hot irons in me & then
pulling them out . . . . so slowly, oh so slowly.

In beginning to write *Yonnondio*, Olsen hoped to link her writing and
her political commitment. But the chaotic years that followed—the moving
back and forth, the caring and working for her family, and the political
tasks—gave her little opportunity for sustained literary work. Her most
intense political involvement during these years centered around the San
Francisco Maritime strike of 1934, which spread from San Francisco up

and down the Western Seaboard to become the first important general strike of the era. She helped put out the Longshoremen's publication, the *Waterfront Worker,* did errands and relief work, and got arrested for "vagrancy" while visiting the apartment of some of the YCL members involved in the strike, going to jail for the second time.

Passages from her journal in these years include frustration at the amount of time required for housework and political work, agonized self-criticisms at not being able to write regularly in a more disciplined way, sometimes anger at the necessity to write specifically pieces on demand, often guilt because no matter what the choice of labor, something is always left undone:

> Struggled all day on the Labor Defender article. Tore it up
> in disgust. It is the end for me of things like that to write—I can't
> do it—it kills me . . . . Why should I loathe myself—why the guilt . . .

All the writing that Olsen did publish in the 30s came out in 1934. That year two poems were published in the *Daily Worker* and reprinted in *The Partisan.* One was based on a letter in the *New Masses* by a Mexican-American woman from Texas, detailing the horrors of work in the garment industry sweatshops of the Southwest, and the other celebrated the spirit of the Austrian socialists killed by the Dollfus government.[11] "The Iron Throat," the first chapter of *Yonnondio,* was published the same year in *The Partisan Review,*[12] as were "The Strike" and "Thousand-Dollar Vagrant," two essays based on her involvement in the San Francisco dock strike.[13] In "The Strike," one of the best pieces of reportage in an era noted for excellence in that genre, the conflict between her "writer self" and her activist self emerges strongly, here transformed into rhetorical strategy. The essay, in the published version, begins:

> Do not ask me to write of the strike and the terror. I am not on
> a battlefield, and the increasing stench and smoke sting the
> eyes so it is impossible to turn them back into the past. You leave
> me only this night to drop the bloody garment of Todays, to
> cleave through the gigantic events that have crashed one upon the
> other, to the first beginning. If I could go away for a while, if there
> were time and quiet, perhaps I could do it. All that has happened
> might resolve into order and sequence, fall into neat patterns of
> words. I could stumble back into the past and slowly, painfully rear
> the structure in all its towering magnificence, so that the beauty
> and heroism, the terror and significance of those days, would enter
> your heart and sear it forever with the vision.[14]

Toward the end of the essay, the writer explains that she was not on the literal battlefield herself, but in headquarters, typing, "making a metallic little pattern of sound in the air, because that is all I can do, because that is all I am supposed to do."The conclusion is another apology for her incapacity to do justice to the magnitude of the strike:

> Forgive me that the words are feverish and blurred.
> You see, if I had time I could go away. But I write this
> on a battlefield. The rest, the General Strike, the terror,
> arrests and jail, the songs in the night, must be written
> some other time, must be written later . . . . But
> there is so much happening now . . . .[15]

The conflict here is partly between her role as a writer, in this case a reporter doing her job, and her guilt at not being on the real battlefield herself—between the word and the deed. But more important is the conflict between two kinds of writing: the quick, fervent, impressionistic report from the arena of struggle, and the leisured, carefully structured and sustained rendering of the "beauty and heroism, the terror and significance" of those days—a rendering that, ironically, would require for its full development a withdrawal from the struggle.

For a committed leftist in the thirties, political action, with all its demands on time and energy, had to take priority over intellectual work, yet the atmosphere on the Left did value and nurture literature in a variety of ways. Olsen would have been a reader in any case, but her friends in the YCL in Kansas City were among the many working-class people inspired by the movement to read broadly for the first time. And Olsen's own reading, eclectic though it was, was to some extent guided, extended, and informed by left-wing intellectual mentors such as the critics of *The Liberator*, the *New Masses*, and the *Modern Quarterly*. She recalls today that the Left

> was enriching in the sense that . . . . in the movement people were
> reading like mad. There was as in any movement a looking for your
> ancestors, your predecessors . . . .
>
> There was a burst of black writers . . . . I knew about W. E. B. DuBois
> before, but because the movement was so conscious of race, of color,
> we were reading all the black writers, books like Arna Bontemps'
> *Black Thunder;* Langston Hughes. We read Ting Ling, we read Lu Hsun,
> we read the literature of protest that was beginning to be written
> in English out of South Africa; we read B. Traven; writers from every
> country. The thirties was a rich, an international period . . . .

And from whatever country or color this was considered to be part
of our literature.

Being part of the Left milieu, then, gave Olsen, a working-class woman
from Omaha, a sense of belonging to an international intellectual as well
as political community.

The literary establishment of the Left was receptive to and supportive
of the efforts of new, young writers like Olsen. The Communist party
sponsored the development of cultural associations called the John Reed
Clubs, established specifically to encourage young, unknown writers and
artists.[16] And there were outlets for publication like the *New Masses* and
the various organs of the local John Reed Clubs, including the *Partisan
Review* in New York and *The Partisan* in San Francisco, in both of which
Olsen published. Her work was well received and much admired. Joseph
North, a respected Left critic, compared her ability to portray working-
class life in "The Iron Throat" favorably to Tess Slesinger's rendering of
the East Coast intelligentsia in her first novel, *The Unpossessed*
(1934).[17] Robert Cantwell praised "The Iron Throat" in *The New Republic* as "a work of early genius."[18] A number of editors and publishers
sought her out after its publication, and eventually she made arrangements with Bennett Cerf at Random House for the publication of
Yonnondio on its completion, although at the time she could not be
reached because she was in jail for her participation in the dock strike,
becoming something of a cause célebre [*sic*]. In New York, Heywood
Broun chaired a protest meeting over her arrest, irritating her and her
jailed comrades who had not published anything and were therefore not
getting all this national attention.

After her release from jail, she visited Lincoln Steffens and Ella Winter,
who had invited her to their home in Carmel, California. This was her
first experience, she recalls now, with that kind of urbane, sophisticated
literary atmosphere. Steffens encouraged her to write the other essay
associated with the strike, "Thousand-Dollar Vagrant," which describes
her arrest in deliberately tough, colloquial language. The following year,
she was invited to attend the American Writers Congress in New York,
where she marched in a parade side by side with critics Mike Gold and
James Farrell, novelists Nelson Algren and Richard Wright, and
playwright Albert Bine, and where she was one of a very few women to
address the assembly, which included most of the major writers of the
day.[19] A drawing of her, a cartooned profile of a lean, intense young
woman, was one of a very few portraits of American women writers to
appear among the myriad renderings of male literary personages in the
May 7, 1935, issue of *New Masses* that reported on the congress.[20]

Clearly, though Olsen's involvement in the Left as an activist, coupled with the other demands on her worker-mother life, took time, energy, and commitment that might in another milieu and another era have gone into her writing, and although her closest friends in the midwestern movement did not always understand her literary aspirations, the atmosphere of the Left as a whole did encourage her. The Left provided networks and organs for intellectual and literary exchange, gave her a sense of being part of an international community of writers and activists engaged in the same revolutionary endeavor, and recognized and valued her talent.

The second contradiction I will consider is closely related to the first and third; in using it as a bridge between them, I will turn first to the way in which Left critical theory validated and supported Olsen's subject and vision before suggesting how some of its tenets ran counter to and perhaps impeded the development of her particular artistic gift.

Literary criticism flourished on the Left in the thirties, and writers like Mike Gold, editor of the *New Masses* and one of the most influential of Communist party critics, and James Farrell, a leading critic and writer for the increasingly independent *Partisan Review*, hotly debated such issues as the role of the artist in revolutionary struggle, the applications of Marxist thought to American literature, and the proper nature and functions of literature in a revolutionary movement.[21] As Olsen's early journals indicate, she followed such discussions with intense interest. There was much in the spirit even of the more dogmatic, party-oriented criticism to encourage her own writing.

Left critical theory accorded an honored place to the committed writer, the writer capable of expressing the struggles and aspirations of working-class people or of recording the decline of capitalism. Critical debates often centered on the best literary modes for accomplishing this purpose. The dominant critical theory on the Communist Left in the early thirties was proletarian realism, a theory which even nonsectarian leftists eventually viewed as far too limited. Nevertheless, its basic premise—that fiction should show the sufferings and struggles and essential dignity of working-class people under capitalism and allow readers to see the details of their lives and work—encouraged young working-class writers like Olsen to write of their own experiences and confirmed her early perception that art can be based on the lives of "despised people." This theory told writers that their own writing could and should be a form of action in itself; art was to be a weapon in the class struggle.[22]

All of Olsen's published writing during the early thirties is consistent with this view of the functions of literature. Her developing craft now had an explicitly political content which grew out of her own experience and was confirmed by major voices in the Left literary milieu. All of it expresses outrage at the exploitation of the working class and a fierce faith in the transformative power of the coming revolution. One need only compare the poem, "I Want You Women up North to Know,"[23] with the passage from her poetry cited earlier to see that the growing clarity of her literary and political convictions gave her work a scope and an assuredness that it had lacked earlier.

This poem juxtaposes the desperate situation of Mexican-American women workers and the families they struggle unsuccessfully to support with that of the "women up north" who consume the products of their labor. As Selma Burkom and Margaret Williams have noted, the poem faithfully constructs the details of their daily lives while its central metaphor "transforms the women themselves . . . . into the clothing they embroider—*they* become the product of their labor."[24] The poem is artful as well as polemical; its free-verse form is deliberately experimental, its subtler ironies woven into the fabric of diction and metaphor, its structure tight, its portraits clearly individuated. On one level, it is metapoetry, that is, poetry *about* art, for it specifically contrasts its own purpose and vision—to document the realities of these women's lives and to offer a Marxist interpretation of the causes of and solutions to their suffering —with the consciousness of the "bourgeois poet" who would find in the movement of their hands *only* a source of aesthetic pleasure.

On the other hand, the polemicism of the poem, especially the didactic interpolations of the speaker, represented a kind of writing that Olsen herself gradually rejected. The same issues arise in her work on *Yonnondio*, her most important literary effort during the thirties. In the rest of this paper I will focus on that novel, for its evolution reveals with special clarity the contradictory nature of Olsen's experience in the Left.

Olsen's earliest journals, before she joined the YCL, speak of her wish to write about her family and people like them. After her year and a half of intense involvement, she begins to do so in a serious, disciplined way, writing in her Faribault journal as she works on the early chapters: "O Mazie & Will & Ben. At last I write out all that has festered in me so long—the horror of being a working-class child—& the heroism, all the respect they deserve." Familiarity with the political and critical theory of the Left combined with and applied to her own experience gave her the coherent world view, the depth of consciousness, and the faith in her working-class subject essential to a sustained work of fiction.

Set in the 1920s, the novel's lyrical prose traces the Holbrook family's desperate struggle for survival over a two-and-a-half-year period, first in a Wyoming mining town, then on a farm in the Dakotas, finally in a

Midwest city—Omaha, perhaps—reeking with the smell of the slaughter-houses.   In *Yonnondio*, as in Olsen's later work, the most powerful theme is the tension between human capacity and creativity—the drive to know, to assert, to create, which Olsen sees as innate in human life—and the social forces and institutions that repress and distort that capacity. Olsen's understanding of those social forces and institutions clearly owes a great deal to her tutelage in the left. The struggles of her central characters dramatize the ravages of capitalism on the lives of working people—miners, small farmers, packing house workers, and their families—who barely make enough to survive no matter how hard they work, and who have not yet learned to seek control over the conditions of their workplaces or the quality of their lives.

Unfortunately for all of us, she never finished the novel. Its title, taken from the title of a Whitman poem, is a Native American word meaning "lament for the lost"; it is an elegy, I think, not only for the Holbrooks but also for Olsen's own words lost between the midthirties and late fifties, for the incompleteness of the novel itself. The demands on Olsen already discussed would have been reason enough for her not having completed the novel in those hectic years; what she wrote, after all, she wrote before she was twenty-five, in the interstices of her activist-worker-mother life. Yet I suspect that she was wrestling with at least one other problem that made completion difficult. For although Olsen's immersion in the theory and political practice of the Marxist Left and her exposure to its literature and criticism gave her a sense of the importance of her subject and strengthened the novel's social analysis, the dominant tenets of proletari-an realism also required a structure, scope, resolution, and political explicitness in some ways at odds with the particular nature of her developing craft.

What we have today is only the beginning of the novel that was to have been. In Olsen's initial plan, Jim Holbrook was to have become involved in a strike in the packing houses, a strike that would draw out the inner strength and courage of his wife Anna, politicize the older children as well, and involve some of the women in the packing plant as strike leaders in this essential collective action. Embittered by the length of the strike and its lack of clear initial success, humiliated by his inability to support his family, Jim Holbrook was finally to have abandoned them. Anna was to die trying to give herself an abortion. Will and Mazie were to go West to the Imperial Valley in California, where they would themselves become organizers. Mazie was to grow up to become an artist, a writer who could tell the experiences of her people, her mother especially living in her memory. In Mazie's achievement, political consciousness and personal creativity were to coalesce.

The original design for the novel would have incorporated most of the major themes of radical fiction at that time. Walter Rideout's study, *The Radical Novel in the United States, 1900-1954,* classifies proletarian novels of the thirties into four types: the strike novel, the novel of conversion to communism, the bottom dog novel, and the novel documenting the decay of the middle class. He also mentions certain typical subthemes: anti-Semitism, black-and-white relationships, episodes in American history, and the life of the communist organizer.[25] *Yonnondio* would have been both a strike novel and a novel of political conversion, and it would have touched on relationships between whites and people of color and on the life of the communist organizer. It would have fulfilled also a major tenet of proletarian realism—that proletarian fiction should demonstrate revolutionary optimism, including elements predicting the inevitable fall of capitalism and the rise of the working class to power.

Proletarian fiction, in other words, was supposed to show not only the sufferings of working-class people, but also their triumphs. When Meridel LeSueur, for example, published an account of the helpless sufferings of poor women in 1932, she was attacked by Whittaker Chambers in the *New Masses,* in a note appended to LeSueur's article, for her "defeatist attitude" and "non-revolutionary spirit."[26] "There *is* horror and drabness in the Worker's life, and we will portray it," wrote Mike Gold in the *New Masses* in 1930, in an article defining proletarian realism, "but we know this is not the last word; we know . . . . that not pessimism, but revolutionary elan will sweep this mess out of the world forever."[27]

Olsen, too, wanted to incorporate this optimism; indeed, it was central to her initial conception of the novel.

> Characters [she writes in her journal when she was beginning
> *Yonnondio*]. Wonderful characters. Hard, bitter, & strong.
> O communism—how you come to those of whom I will write
> is more incredible [*sic*] beautiful than manna. You wipe the sweat from
> us, you fill our bellies, you let us walk and think like humans.

She immediately cautions herself, "Not to be so rhetorical or figurative or whatever it is"—a struggle against didactic rhetoric that would characterize her work on the novel itself. Olsen maintained throughout her work on *Yonnondio* in the thirties her commitment to show the transformative power of Communism—her commitment, that is, to "revolutionary optimism," but as her craft developed she felt less and less satisfied with *telling* about the coming revolution—and more and more concerned with *showing* how people come to class consciousness in "an earned way, a bone way." She gradually rejected the political explicitness that alone was enough to win praise for literary work in the more sectarian Left criticism, but she had a hard time incorporating the essential vision of systematic social change in other ways.

The "revolutionary elan" in the opening chapters of *Yonnondio* still partakes of the didacticism she ultimately rejected. It comes less through the events or characterizations than from the voice of the omniscient narrator, who in the first five chapters provides both political analysis and revolutionary prophecy. In the first chapter, this voice comments on the life of thirteen-year-old Andy Kvaternick, on his first day in the mines:

> Breathe and lift your face to the night, Andy Kvaternick. Trying so
> vainly . . . . to purge your bosom of the coal dust. Your father had
> dreams. You too, like all boys, had dreams—vague dreams of freedom
> and light . . . . The earth will take those too . . . .
> old tired dreams, swell and break, and strong fists batter the fat
> bellies, and skeletons of starved children batter them . . . . [P. 14]

In the second chapter, the voice becomes ironic as it comments on a scene where women wait at the mouth of a mine for word of their men after an accident. Like "I Want the Women up North to Know," this passage attacks the modernist aesthetic, which elevates a concern for form over a concern for subject, yet it also argues that Olsen's subject itself is worthy of the transformations of enduring art.

> And could you not make a cameo of this and pin it onto your
> aesthetic hearts? So sharp it is, so clear, so classic. The shattered dusk,
> the mountain of culm, the tipple; clean line, bare beauty . . . .
>
>   Surely it is classical enough for you—the Greek marble of the women,
> the simple, flowing lines of sorrow, carved so rigid and eternal. [P. 30]

And the voice goes on to prophesy revolution against the companies and the system they represent: "Please issue a statement: quick, or they start to batter through with the fists of strike, with the pickax of revolution" (p. 31).

In chapter 5, we hear the voice of the revolutionary prophet twice. The first passage comments on the life of young Jim Tracy, Jim Holbrook's codigger in a sewer, who quits when the contractor insists that two men must do the amount of digging previously done by several. Here, the voice is at first scathingly satiric, pointing out how Tracy will be victimized by his own naive belief in the shibboleths of American culture—"the bull about freedomofopportunity," and predicting Tracy's inevitable descent into the hell of unemployment, hunger, cold, vagrancy, prison, death;

damned forever for his apostasy to "God Job." The passage concludes with an apology to Jim, in which the narrator speaks with the collective "we" of the revolutionists:

> I'm sorry, Jim Tracy, sorry as hell we weren't stronger and could
> get to you in time and show you that kind of individual revolt was
> no good, kid, no good at all, you had to bide your time and take it till
> there were enough of you to fight it all together on the job, and bide
> your time, and take it till the day millions of fists clamped in yours,
> and you could wipe out the whole thing, and a human could be
> a human for the first time on earth. [P. 79]

This is the voice that concludes the chapter, too, as Jim Holbrook sits in the kitchen holding his daughter Mazie after Anna has had a miscarriage, bitterly condemning himself for not seeing her illness, bitterly aware that he has no access to the food and medicine and care the doctor has prescribed for Anna and Baby Bess:

> No, he could speak no more. And as he sat there in the kitchen
> with Mazie against his heart . . . . the things in his mind so vast and
> formless, so terrible and bitter, cannot be spoken, will never be
> spoken—till the day that hands will find a way to speak this: hands. [P. 95]

In these interpolations, Olsen was deliberately experimenting with the form of the novel, not unlike Dos Passos, whom she had earlier read. Rachel Blau DuPlessis suggests that Olsen has appropriated certain modernist techniques here to turn dialectically against modernism.[28] On the other hand, the prophetic irony of these passages, the imagery of hands and fists uniting in revolution, characterize much of the writing of the leftists during this period; this is the tone and imagery that appear at the conclusion of Olsen's two published poems and that predominate in "The Strike." In any case, these passages add a dimension of "revolutionary elan" not present in the early events of the novel itself. The narrator sees more, knows more, than the characters, about the causes of and remedies for their suffering, and the voice is the device used to incorporate that knowledge into the novel.

Olsen's correspondence indicates that she was aware of a disjunction between that voice and the increasingly more lyric, less didactic tone and texture of the whole. In March 1935, John Strachey, whom she had met in Carmel and to whom she had sent the first three chapters of *Yonnondio* for evaluation and advice, wrote to her in Venice, California: "As to advice, personally I like both your styles of writing, and I am in favor of having the interpolations in the book. "Their "agit-prop" quality was increasingly at odds with the direction in which Olsen's art was growing. It was developing gradually away from the didacticism that made the incorporation of "revolutionary elan" relatively easy and toward a more lyrical, less explicit mode, at its best when lingering on the details of daily life and work, exploring the interactions between individual growth, personality, and social environment, and laying bare the ruptures and reconciliations of family life. As the novel progressed, as the characters acquired a life and being of their own, Olsen, I think, found herself unable to document the political vision of social revolution as authentically and nonrhetorically as she was able to portray the ravages of circumstance on families and individuals and the redeeming moments between them. She did not want to write didactically. She wanted to write a politically informed novel that would also be great art. The problem is that the subtlety and painstaking craft of her evolving style did not lend themselves readily to a work of epic scope, and she was increasingly unwilling to rely on shortcuts like the narrative interpolations to tell rather than extending the novel in its intended direction. In a note on its progress from sometime in the midthirties, she writes: "Now it seems to me the whole revolutionary part belongs in another novel . . . . and I can't put out one of those 800 page tomes."

I think that there was a tension, too, between two themes: the awakening class consciousness that was the central drama of her time, and her other essential theme, the portrait of the artist as a young girl—not an inevitable conflict based on inconsistent possibilities, for Olsen's own experience embraced both processes, but a writing tension, based on the difficulty of merging the two themes in a cohesive fictive structure. Yet the more "individualistic," subjective, and domestic concerns —the intellectual and psychological development of the young girl, the complicated familial relationships, the lyrical vision of regeneration through love between mother and child—would not have been acceptable to Olsen or the critical establishment of the Left without the projected Marxian resolution that showed working-class people taking power collectively over their own lives. In other words, Olsen had so fully internalized the Left's vision of what proletarian literature could and should do to show the coming of a new society that she did not even consider then the possibility of a less epic and for her, more feasible structure. Nor could she be content simply to accord centrality to the familial interactions and the stubborn growth of human potential in that unpromising soil, leaving the tensions between human aspiration and social oppression unresolved. So *Yonnondio* remained unfinished, but the struggle to write fiction at once political and nonpolemical was an essential apprenticeship for the writer who in her maturity produced *Tell Me a Riddle.*

The concerns I have called, for lack of better terms, more "subjective" and "domestic," grew to a great extent out of Olsen's experience as a woman and a mother. Thus, my second and third contradictions overlap, for as we shall see there was little in Left literary criticism that would have validated the centrality of these concerns, except insofar as they touched on class rather than gender. The rest of this paper, then, will be concerned with the third contradiction: between the fact that the world of the Left, like the larger society it both challenged and partook of, was essentially androcentric and masculinist, yet that it also demonstrated, more than any other sector of American society, a consistent concern for women's issues.

The painful and sometimes wry anecdotes of women writers like Josephine Herbst, Meridel LeSueur, and others amply testify to the sexual politics of life in the literary Left. For example, Herbst writes to Katherine Anne Porter about the "gentle stay-in-your-place, which may or may not be the home," she received from her husband, John Herrmann, when she wished to join him at a "talk fest" with Gold, Edmund Wilson, Malcolm Cowley, and others.

> I told Mister Herrmann that as long as the gents had bourgeois reactions to women they would probably never rise very high in their revolutionary conversations, but said remarks rolled off like water.[29]

Olsen herself remembers that at the American Writers Congress, James Farrell informed her that she and another attractive young woman present were "the two flowers there," compared with the other "old bags." Because she was not really a part of the literary circles of the Left, their sexual politics had less impact on Olsen than on writers who were more involved, like Herbst and LeSueur. If for Herbst it was her gender that prevented her from moving freely in the heady circles of the literary Left, for Olsen it was more the depth of her own class loyalties to the rank and file. The sexism she experienced in her daily life mostly reflected the structure of gender-role assignments in society as a whole, although she does recall some incidents peculiar to life on the Left, such as the pressure on YCL women to make themselves available at parties as dancing partners especially to black and Mexican-American men, whether the women wanted to dance or not. As a writer, though, Olsen was keenly aware of the male dominance of Left literature and criticism and the relative absence of women's subjects and concerns.

If one examines the composition of the editorial boards of Left magazines of culture and criticism, one finds that the mastheads are largely male; in 1935, one woman wrote to the *New Masses* complaining at the underrepresentation of women writers,[30] although a few women writers, like Herbst and LeSueur, were regular contributors. The numerical dominance of men in the literary Left paralleled the omnipresence of a worker-figure in literature and criticism who almost by definition was male; proletarian prose and criticism tended to flex their muscles with a particularly masculinist pride. Here, for example, is a passage from Gold's famous *New Masses* editorial, "Go Left, Young Writers," written in 1929:

> A new writer has been appearing; a wild youth of about twenty-two, the son of working-class parents, who himself works in the lumber camps, coal mines, and steel mills, harvest fields and mountain camps of America . . . . He writes in jets of exasperated feeling and has not time to polish his work . . . . He lacks self-confidence but writes because he must—and because he has a real talent.[31]

An even more pronounced masculinism prevails in Gold's "American Needs a Critic," published in *New Masses* in 1926:

> Send us a critic. Send a giant who can shame our writers back to their task of civilizing America. Send a soldier who has studied history. Send a strong poet who loves the masses, and their future . . . . Send one who is not a pompous liberal, but a man of the street . . . . Send us a man fit to stand up to skyscrapers . . . . Send no saint. Send an artist. Send a scientist. Send a Bolshevik. Send a man.[32]

Gold's worst insult to a writer was that he was a pansy, his art, effeminate.[33] Gold, of course, was an extreme example of working-class male chauvinism, but he was not atypical. Even as late as 1969, when Joseph North edited an anthology of *New Masses* pieces, masculinity predominates. North's Prologue praises the *New Masses* for capturing the essence of American life in its portrayals of the industrial proletariat, in its emphasis on the "day of a workingman," that of a miner, a locomotive engineer, a weaver. "Its men," he says, "its writers and artists understood this kind of a life existed."[34] In spite of his once-favorable notice of Tillie Lerner's work, he does not mention its women.

When women writers on the Left did write about explicitly female subjects from a woman's perspective, they were sometimes criticized outright, sometimes ignored. LeSueur has remembered that she was criticized for writing in a lyrical, emotive style about sexuality and the reproductive process.[35] I have already noted Chambers's attack on her for writing about the conditions of women on the breadlines without building in a revolutionary dialectic. Elinor Langer, having worked for several years on a biography of Herbst, believes that one of the reasons Herbst's impressive trilogy of novels failed to win her the recognition she deserved was that she was a woman and the central experience in two of the three novels is that of female characters.[36] Not that the scorn or neglect of male Left critics was reserved exclusively for women writers. The more dogmatic of them viewed any literature concerned primarily with domestic and psychological subjects as suspect. One novel focusing on the experience and perceptions of a child of the working classes, Henry Roth's *Call It Sleep* (1935), which Olsen read and admired during the later stages of her work on *Yonnondio*, was one of the more intricate, imaginative works in the proletarian genre. Yet the *New Masses* dismissed it in a paragraph, concluding, "It is a pity that so many young writers drawn from the proletariat can make no better use of their working class experience than as material for introspective and febrile novels."[37]

In writing *Yonnondio*, Olsen was consciously writing class literature from a woman's point of view, incorporating a dimension that she saw ignored and neglected in the works of most contemporary male leftists. All of Olsen's work, in fact, testifies to her concern for women, her vision of their double oppression if they are poor or women of color, her affirmation of their creative potential, her sense of the deepest, most intractable contradiction of all: the unparalleled satisfaction and fulfillment combined with the overwhelming all-consuming burden of motherhood. Indeed, her writings about mothering, about the complex, painful, and redemptive interactions between mother and child, have helped a new generation of women writers to treat that subject with a fullness and honesty never before possible in American literature.

In *Yonnondio*, Anna as mother wants for her children what she can no longer dream for herself: the freedom to live fully what is best in them; to the extent that the circumstances of their lives prevent this, her love is also her despair. Anna has a special kinship with her oldest daughter, Mazie, in whom her own intelligence and early hunger for knowledge are reincarnated. Mirroring each other's dreams and capacities, the two mirror also the anguish of women confronting daily the poverty of their class and the assigned burdens of their sex. At times they protect one another—Anna, Mazie's access to books, to literature; Mazie, Anna's physical well-being, she herself becoming temporarily mother when Anna lies unconscious after a miscarriage. Mazie's painful sensitivity—the sensitivity of the potential artist—makes her as a child deeply susceptible to both the beauty and ugliness around her; overcome at times by the ugliness, it is to her mother that she turns for renewal. For example, one of the gentlest, most healing of *Yonnondio's* passages is the interlude of peace when Anna and Mazie pause from gathering dandelion greens, and Anna is transported by the spring and river wind to a forgetful peace, different from her usual "mother look," the "mother alertness . . . . in her bounded body" (p. 120). Absently, she sings fragments of song and strokes Mazie's body:

> The fingers stroked, spun a web, cocooned Mazie into happiness
> and intactness and selfness. Soft wove the bliss round hurt and fear
> and want and shame—the old worn fragile bliss, a new frail
> selfness bliss, healing, transforming. Up from the grasses, from the
> earth, from the broad tree trunk at their back, latent life streamed
> and seeded. [P. 119]

The transformation here is not the political conversion that was to have taken place later, but one based on human love, on the capacity to respond to beauty, and on the premise of a regenerative life cycle of which mother and daughter are a part.

To be sure, Olsen wanted to weave this emphasis on "selfness," and this image of a regenerative life cycle that prefigures, but does not itself constitute, social and economic regeneration into a larger structure that would incorporate both personal and political transformation. Yet the hope *Yonnondio* offers most persuasively, through its characterizations, its images and events and its present conclusion, is less a vision of political and economic revolution than an assertion that the drive to love and achieve and create will survive somehow in spite of the social forces arraigned against it, because each new human being is born with it afresh.

It is with this "humanistic" rather than "Marxist" optimism that the novel now ends. In the midst of a stifling heat wave, Baby Bess suddenly realizes her own ability to have an effect on the world when she makes the connection between her manipulations of the lid of a jam jar and the noise it produces, so that her random motions become, for the first time, purposeful: "Bang, slam, whack. Release, grab, slam, bang, bang. Centuries of human drive work in her; human ecstasy of achievement; a satisfaction deep and fundamental as sex: *I can do, I use my Power; I! I!"*

(p. 153). And her mother and sister and brothers laugh, in spite of the awesome heat, the rising dust storms. Then for the first time the family listens to the radio on a borrowed set, and Mazie is awed at the magic, *"transparent meshes of sound, far sound, human and stellar, pulsing, pulsing"* (p. 153). This moment of empowerment and connection *is* linked to the revolutionary vision, and Anna's final, "The air's changin', Jim. I see for it [the heat wave] to end tomorrow, at least get tolerable" (p. 154), certainly hints at the possibility for greater change. Still, there is a great gulf between socialist revolution and the temporary individualized relief of this final passage. Yet the end seems right; indeed, today, the novel hardly seems unfinished, because it offers in its conclusion the affirmation most fully embedded in the texture of the novel as a whole: an affirmation of human will, familial love, and, at least in the child not yet deadened and brutalized by the struggle for sheer survival and the corrupt influence of social institutions, the drive toward achievement and creation.

To say this is not to diminish the power of *Yonnondio* as an indictment of society; Olsen makes it clear that the Holbrooks do not merely suffer—they are oppressed, in quite specific ways, as a working-class family in a capitalist system. The whole fabric of the book deals with how poverty, exploitation, and what today we would call sexism combine to extinguish gradually the very qualities Olsen values most. The loss of creative capacity is not, as Wordsworth would have it, the inevitable price of growing up, but rather the price of growing up in a society *like this one*.

In according that creative capacity especially to women and children, as in detailing the impact of social circumstance on the dailiness of family life, Olsen added a significant dimension to the largely masculine and public world of the proletarian novel. Women's work in preserving and nurturing that creative capacity in the young is shown in *Yonnondio* to be an essential precondition to social change.

Although in this regard, Olsen's work was deliberately oppositional to the androcentrism of the Left literary milieu, and although the tenets of proletarian criticism would not have validated this feminist and humanist dimension without the projected Marxian resolution, Olsen's affiliation with the Left undoubtedly encouraged and informed her writings about women in at least two ways.

First, there was the fact that in spite of the sexism of the Left milieu, the existence of serious analysis of women's status and roles meant that, in Olsen's circles at least, women's capacities were recognized and supported, however inconsistently, and women's grievances were recognized as real. It is certainly true, as Olsen recalls today, that on "those things that come particularly to the fore through consciousness-raising, having to do with sexuality, with rape, and most of all with what I call maintenance of life, the bearing and rearing of the young," the circles of the Left were little better than those of society as a whole—in spite of a body of theory on housework and the frequent bandying about of Lenin's observations on its degrading nature. And Olsen is in accord with Peggy Dennis, married for years to party leader Eugene Dennis, on the "explicit, deliberate and reprehensible sexism" of the party's leadership.[38] Yet Olsen also knew party women who brought their own husbands up for trial on charges of male chauvinism, one of them herself a party activist whose husband refused to help with childcare; he was removed from his leadership position when her charges were upheld. She remembers seeing women in the party, women like herself, grow in their capacities and rise to positions of leadership; she herself helped set up, after much debate about the pros and cons of autonomous women's formations, a separate Women's Division of the Warehouse Union to which Jack Olsen belonged, establishing thereby a whole secondary leadership of women. This process of women's coming to strength and voice was to have been central to *Yonnondio*, and if, paradoxically, her own activism in the Left helped prevent her from finishing the novel, her experience in that milieu nevertheless gave her, too, a sense of confidence and worth essential to both her political work and her writing.

She wanted, moreover, to pay tribute to, to memorialize, the women she knew on the Left: women like her YCL comrades and especially immigrant women like her own mother—strong women, political women, but sometimes also women defeated by their long existence in a patriarchal world. Sometime in 1938 she wrote in her journal:

> To write the history of that whole generation of exiled revolutionaries,
> the kurelians and croations, the bundists and the poles; and the
> women, the foreign women, the mothers of six and seven . . . . the
> housewives whose Zetkin and Curie and Bronte hearts went into
> kitchen and laundries and the patching of old socks; and those who
> did not speak the language of their children, who had no bridge . . . .
> to make themselves understood.

Tell Me a Riddle is dedicated to two such women, and its central character, Eva, is a vividly drawn composite of several; Eva, a passionate socialist organizer and orator in her youth, who is silenced by years of poverty and tending to others' needs, only to find her voice and vision again when she is dying. The publications of the Left in the thirties are full of tributes to women like Mother Bloor, Clara Zetkin, Krupskaya; in a way, *Yonnondio* and *Tell Me a Riddle* are both extensions and demystifications of such portrayals, renderings of the essentially heroic lives which circumstances did not allow to blossom into public deeds, art, and fame.

Second, the theoretical analysis of crucial aspects of women's experience was encouraged by articles, lectures, party publications devoted solely to women's issues, and study groups on the Woman Question. Olsen herself taught a class on the Woman Question at YCL headquarters on San Francisco's Haight Street. A self-styled feminist even then, she had read not only Marxist theory, but also works from the suffragist movement like the *History of Woman Suffrage* and the *Woman's Bible*, and she invited suffragists to her class to talk about their own experiences in the nineteenth-century woman's movement, establishing a sense of the history and continuity of women's struggles.

Theory about the Woman Question undoubtedly helped to shape her own thinking about women's issues. Communist Party theory on women, like its practice, certainly had weaknesses. Most arose from the fact that gender was not identified as a fundamental social category like class. Thus, working-class women could be viewed as suffering essentially the same oppression as their husbands, directly if they were workers, by extension if they were wives. Consequently, they would presumably benefit from the same measures. Analysis tended to focus on women in the paid labor force; and although housework did receive a substantial amount of critical attention, few analysts, except perhaps in special women's columns or special women's publications like the *Woman Worker*, suggested seriously that men should share equal responsibility for it, although many argued—not strongly enough, according to Olsen—for its collectivization.[39]

The socialist writers of the earlier years of the century tended to be fuller in their analyses of sexuality and "life styles" than the Communist party in the thirties, which generally avoided such discussions, failing to link political revolution and sexual freedom as Agnes Smedley had at the close of the twenties. *Yonnondio* is far more reticent than *Daughter of Earth* on this subject. Although it includes the painfully explicit rape of wife by husband, and although it is better than a history book at raising issues of women's health, *Yonnondio* is largely silent about women's sexuality per se—even though this is a topic which Olsen speaks of freely in her early poems and sometimes in her journals. That silence may well have something to do with the rather puritanical and conservative attitudes of the Communist party on sexuality throughout the 1930s.[40]

Still, in no other segment of American society at that time were there such extensive discussions about the sources of women's oppression and the means for alleviating it. A recent article by Robert Shaffer, "Women and the Communist Party, USA, 1930-1940," provides a useful summary of the nature of women's status and roles in the Communist party, its theory about the oppression of women, its publications and organizations designed to counteract such oppression, its involvement in mass work among women and around women's issues, and its views on the family and sexuality. He concludes that "despite its important weaknesses, the CP's work among women in the 1930s was sufficiently extensive, consistent, and theoretically valuable to be considered an important part of the struggle for women's liberation in the United States."[41]

Shaffer discusses two books by Communist women published in the 1930s that were important contributions to the analysis of women's issues. The first, by Grace Hutchins, focused on *Women Who Work*—that is, women in the paid work force; according to Shaffer, it underplays male chauvinism and sometimes blames women for their own oppression, but it also scrupulously documents the conditions of working women and formulates important demands to better them. The second book, written in 1939 by Mary Inman, takes a position reflecting the less sectarian consciousness of the Popular Front Years. Inman argues that all women are oppressed, not just working-class women, and that one of the symptoms of this oppression is their isolation in their homes; that working-class men sometimes oppress their wives; and that housework must be viewed as productive labor—positions rejected by the party's East Coast leadership, but supported in the West, where *People's World* was published and read. She also discusses how girls are conditioned to a "manufactured femininity" by childrearing practices and the mass media.[42] Inman eventually left the party over the controversy her book engendered, but clearly the ideas it expressed had some currency and support in Left circles at least on the West Coast.

In many ways, *Yonnondio* anticipates in fiction Inman's theoretical formulations. The conditioning of children to accept limiting sex roles is an important theme in *Yonnondio*. One thinks, for example, of the children's games that so cruelly inhibit the pre-adolescent Mazie, or of the favorite text—"the Movies, selected"—of twelve-year-old Jinella, who with Mazie as partner plays a vamp from *Sheik of Araby, Broken Blossoms, Slave of Love, She Stopped at Nothing.*[sic] *The Fast Life*, and *The Easiest Way* (pp. 127-28), her imaginative capacity absurdly channeled by her exposure to these films, her only escape from her real life as Gertrude Skolnick. Even Anna, full of her own repressed longings, imparts the lessons of sex roles to her children. "Boys get to do that," she tells Benjy wistfully, talking of travel by trains and boats, "not girls" (p. 113). And when Mazie asks her, "Why is it always me that has to help? How come

Will gets to play?" Anna can only answer, "Willie's a boy" (p. 142). Olsen, then, suggests throughout *Yonnondio* that both women and men are circumstanced to certain social roles, and that these roles, while placing impossible burdens of responsibility on working-class men, constrict the lives of women in particularly damaging ways.

Olsen understands and portrays the double oppression of working-class women in other ways as well. Anna's spirit is almost broken by her physical illness—"woman troubles"—connected with pregnancy and childbirth and compounded by inadequate medical care. Her apparent apathy and incompetence make her a target for her husband's rage; he strikes out at and violates her because he has no other accessible target for his frustrations and fears until her miscarriage forces him to a pained awareness and reawakened love. Few other American novels, perhaps none outside the radical tradition of which *Yonnondio* is a part, reveal so starkly the destructive interactions of class and sex under patriarchal capitalism.

In *Yonnondio*, as in Olsen's other work, the family itself has a contradictory function, at once a source of strength and love, and a battleground between women and men in a system exploiting both. This, of course, is a profoundly Marxian vision; it was Marx and Engels who wrote in the *Communist Manifesto:*

> The bourgeois clap-trap about the family and education, about the
> hallowed relation of parent and child, becomes all the more
> disgusting, the more, by the action of Modern Industry, all family
> ties among the proletarians are torn asunder . . . .[43]

The vision of the family in *Yonnondio* is formed both by Olsen's own experience and by her familiarity from childhood on with socialist ideas.

Another aspect of that vision is Olsen's treatment of the relationship between housework and paid labor in *Yonnondio*. One of the novel's crucial structural principles is the juxtaposition of men's (and women's) work in the paid labor force and women's work in the home—especially in the final chapter, which shifts back and forth between Anna's canning at home, as she tends to the demands of her older children and juggles Baby Bess on her hip, and the hellish speedup of the packing plant where Jim works. The overwhelming heat, prelude to the great droughts and dust storms of the thirties, becomes a common bond of suffering. There is nothing redeeming about the brutal and exploitative labor at the plant; Anna at least is engaged in production of goods the family will use and in caring for children whom she loves through her exhaustion. Olsen makes it clear that both forms of work are essential, and that the degrading conditions of both have the same systemic causes. If she is finally unable in *Yonnondio* to suggest a systemic solution, her instincts were perhaps more historically accurate than those of other Marxists writing in the same period.

Yonnondio, of course, is far more than ideology translated into fiction. Olsen wrote from what she had lived, what she had seen, at last incorporating "the common hysteria" of factory work, the bodily nausea and weariness, along with the incessant demands of work in the home. But her understanding of those events, the nature of her protest, although in many ways going beyond Communist party theory and practice of the early thirties, could only have been deepened by the very presence in her milieu of theory and controversy on the Woman Question.[44]

On the whole, in spite of the Left's demands on her time and energies, the prescriptiveness of its more dogmatic criticism, and the androcentrism or outright sexism of many of its spokesmen, there is no doubt but that Olsen's Marxian perspective and experience ultimately enriched her literature. In a talk in 1974 at Emerson College, in Boston, explaining some of the reasons why she is a "slow" writer, she discusses without using the terminology of the Left the differences between her own concerns and what a Marxist would identify as bourgeois ideology:

> My vision is very different from that of most writers . . . . I don't
> think in terms of quests for identity to explain human motivation and
> behavior. I feel that in a world where class, race, and sex are so
> determining, that that has little reality. What matters to me is the
> kind of soil *out* of which people have to grow, and the kind of climate
> around them; circumstances are the primary key and not the personal
> quest for identity . . . . I want to write what will help change that
> which is harmful for human beings in our time.[45]

In the fifties, partly out of a spirit of opposition to the McCarthy era, and blessed with increased time as the children grew up and there were temporary respites from financial need, Olsen began to do the work that gave us the serenely beautiful but still politically impassioned stories of the *Tell Me a Riddle* volume. Olsen's enduring insistence that literature must confront the material realities of people's lives as shaping circumstances, that the very categories of class and race and sex constitute the fabric of reality as we live it, and that literature has an obligation to deepen consciousness and facilitate social change are part of her—and our—inheritance from the radical tradition.

NOTES

1. To my knowledge, the connections between the contemporary women's movement and the Old Left have never been sufficiently explored, although its roots in the civil rights movement and the New Left are well-documented, as in Sara Evans's, *Personal Politics: The Roots of Women's Liberation in the Civil Rights Movement and the new Left* (New York: Random House, 1979). It would be interesting, for example, to look at the number of feminist leaders and spokeswomen with family or other personal ties to the Old Left.

2. The earlier version of this article was delivered at a session on Women Writers of the Left at the National Women's Studies Association convention in Bloomington, Indiana, June 1980. Olsen's comments on that version were made mostly during an eight-hour tape-recorded conversation in Fall 1980. I have quoted extensively from that discussion as well as from earlier interviews, without attempting to distinguish between them.

3. "Tillie Olsen, "A Note About This Book," *Yonnondio: From the Thirties* (New York: Dell, 1975), p. 158. All references are to this edition, and page numbers will be supplied in parentheses in the text.

4. Selma Burkom and Margaret Williams, "De-Riddling Tillie Olsen's Writings," *San Jose Studies* 2 (1976): 65-83. In spite of some inaccuracies, this important study is the best source of biographical and bibliographic information on Olsen outside of her own writings.

5. Ellen Moers, *Literary Women* (New York: Doubleday, 1976); and Elaine Showalter *A Literature of Their Own: British Women Novelists from Brontë to Lessing* (Princeton, N. J.: Princeton University Press, 1977).

6. Walter B. Rideout, *The Radical Novel in the United States, 1900-1954* (New York: Hill and Wang, 1956), p. 3; and Daniel Aaron, *Writers on the Left* (New York: Harcourt, Brace & World, 1961).

7. Aaron, *Writers on the Left*, pp. 336-37.

8. From an unmailed letter to Harriet Monroe, apparently intended as a cover letter for poems Olsen was planning to submit for publication in Monroe's influential *Poetry: A Magazine of Verse.*

9. From Elinor Langer's transcription of her introduction to a talk given by Olsen at a Reed College symposium in Portland, Oregon, in Fall, 1978.

10. In "Divided Against Herself: The Life Lived and the Life Suppressed," *Moving On* (April-May 1980): 15-20, 23, I explored the theme of the "buried life" in women's literature, as it appears in the work of leftist feminist writers like Olsen and Agnes Smedley. In "Tell Me a Riddle," the buried life in [sic] Eva's engaged, articulate, political self, whereas in Smedley's *Daughter of Earth*, it is the maternal, domestic self. Both works testify to the pain of denying part of one's being, and both condemn the society that does not allow women to be whole.

11. Burkom and Williams reprint these poems in their article "De-Riddling Tillie Olsen"; "I Want You Women up North to Know," pp. 67-69, and "There Is a Lesson," p. 70.

12. Tillie Lerner, "The Iron Throat," *Partisan Review* 1 (April-May 1934): 3-9.

13. Tillie Lerner, "Thousand-Dollar Vagrant," *New Republic* 80 (29 August 1934): 67-69; and "The Strike," *Partisan Review* 1 (September-October 1934): 3-9, reprinted in *Years of Protest: A Collection of American Writings of the 1930s,* ed. Jack Salzman (New York: Pegasus, 1967), pp. 138-44.

14. Salzman, ed., *Years of Protest,* p. 138.

15. Ibid., p. 144.

16. One of the best accounts of the importance of these clubs for young writers, in spite of his ultimate disillusionment with the Communist party, is Richard Wright's 1944 essay printed in *The God That Failed,* ed. Richard H. Crossman (New York: Harper, 1950).

17. This is Olsen's recollection; I did not locate the actual source.

18. Cited in Burkom and Williams, "De-Riddling Tillie Olsen," p. 71.

19. Among those who signed the call to the conference and/or attended were Nelson Algren, Kenneth Burke, Theodore Dreiser, Waldo Frank, Joseph Freeman, Granville Hicks, Langston Hughes, Edwin Seaver, and Nathaniel West.

20. Langer mentions this drawing in her talk at Reed College cited above. Olsen has a copy of the cartoon in her files, and Salzman includes it with twenty others in *Years of Protest,* p. 307.

21. The selections in Salzman's chapter on "The Social Muse," in *Years of Protest,* pp. 231-307, are well chosen to represent various positions in this debate.

22. Rideout's discussion of the efforts of the Left to define the "proletarian novel" is particularly helpful and more detailed than I can be here; see *Radical Novel in the United States,* especially pp. 165-70.

23. Printed in this issue of *Feminist Studies.*

24. Burkom and Williams, "De-Riddling Tillie Olsen," p. 69.

25. Rideout, *Radical Novel in the United States,* pp. 171-98. In only three of the many novels Rideout discusses do female characters play a major role: those by Josephine Herbst.

26. From an unpublished paper by Elaine Hedges, "Meridel LeSueur in the Thirties," first presented at the Modern Language Association Convention in San Francisco.

27. Mike Gold, "Proletarian Realism," reprinted in *Mike Gold: A Literary Anthology,* ed. Michael Folsom (New York: International Publishers, 1972), p. 207.

28. Rachel Blau DuPlessis, in an editorial comment on this paper.

29. Elinor Langer, "'The Ruins of Memory': Josephine Herbst in the 1930's," unpublished; also in Langer, "If In Fact I Have Found a Heroine . . . , "*Mother Jones,* 6 (May 1981), p. 43. Meridel LeSueur has mentioned similar episodes in talks at a conference on women writers at the Women's Building in Los Angeles in 1972 and at the National Women's Studies Association Conference in Lawrence, Kansas, 1979.

30. Robert Shaffer, "Women and the Communist Party, USA, 1930-1940," *Socialist Review,* no. 45 (May-June 1979): 93, note. I am indebted to Shaffer's article throughout the final section of this paper.

31. Folsom, ed., *Mike Gold,* p. 188.

32. Ibid., p. 139.

33. See, for example, Gold's "Wilder: Prophet of the Genteel Christ," in Salzman's *Years of Protest,* pp. 233-38.

34. Joseph North, *New Masses: An Anthology of the Rebel Thirties* (New York: International Publishers, 1969), p. 24.

35. Meridel LeSueur, in talks cited above and personal conversations with her on those occasions; also see Hedges, "Meridel LeSueur in the Thirties," p. 7.

36. Langer, "'The Ruins of Memory,'" p. 16.

37. In Rideout, *Radical Novel in the United States,* p. 189.

38. Peggy Dennis, *The Autobiography of an American Communist: A Personal View of a Political Life, 1925-1975* (Berkeley, Calif.: Creative Arts Books, 1977), p. 294.

39. Shaffer, "Women and the Communist Party," pp. 94-96.

40. Ibid., especially pp. 104-107.

41. Ibid., p. 10.

42. Ibid., pp. 83-87. I am also grateful to historian Sherna Gluck for discussing Inman's work and the controversy surrounding it with me.

43. This version is from Barbara Sinclair Deckard's *The Women's Movement: Political, Socioeconomic, and Psychological Issues,* 2d ed. (New York: Harper & Row, 1979), p. 234

44. Olsen's concern with the Woman Question continued into the forties. She authored for a few months in 1946 a women's column in *People's World,* writing articles like "Wartime Gains of Women in Industry," and "Politically Active Mothers—One View," which argued like Inman that motherhood should be considered political work. Also in the forties she participated actively in some of the organizations targeted by the Communist party for mass work on what the party considered to be women's issues—health and education—work related also, of course, to her own deepest concerns.

45. From a tape transcription in Olsen's files.

Voices: Bakhtin's Heteroglossia and Polyphony, and the Performance of Narrative Literature[*]

Linda M. Park-Fuller

Post-structuralism, particularly deconstructionist theory, has contributed much to interpretation studies focusing on the social contexts of performance.[1] By calling into question assumptions about the process of interpretation and the nature of texts, such theories have allowed expanded definitions of performance and text and considerations of the socio-political aspects of performed texts, performance conventions, and performance contexts.[2]

On the other hand, deconstructionist theory has very little to offer interpretation studies focusing on the aesthetic experience of performed literature and on the act of performing individual literary texts. Jill Taft-Kaufman cautions:

> We, who distinguish ourselves by our involvement with the oral performance of individual texts, must ask ourselves whether critical theory which vivisects the practices that underlie our emotional involvement with and appreciation of individual texts might not pose more problems for the survival of our discipline than it solves.[3]

Clearly, deconstructionist theory cannot answer all questions nor address the interests of everyone. Recognizing this, Mary S. Strine has encouraged a dialogue between studies about performance as socio-cultural fact and studies about performance as phenomenological, aesthetic act.[4] Just as importantly, I would assert, critics and performers should investigate post-structuralist theories that consider the socio-political aspects of interpretation without the deconstructionist's bias against individual texts.

The writings of Mikhail Bakhtin offer a useful framework for the study of individual texts and their potentials for performance while at the same time acknowledging the social, cultural, and political nature of all texts, and the primacy of context to textual meaning. Indeed, his dialogic theory, based on a perception of the inherent relationship between ideology and utterance, addresses the socio-political fact of literary performance and provides analytical tools relevant to the act of performing literature.

[*] Reprinted from *Literature and Performance* 7.1 (Nov. 1986): 1-12.

In this essay, I shall apply Bakhtin's dialogic theory in an examination of Tillie Olsen's novel, *Yonnondio: From the Thirties.*[5] Olsen's novel invites a dialogic reading on three levels. First, as a Marxist rejoinder in a 1930s political dialogue, *Yonnondio* demonstrates Bakhtin's perceptions of language and literature as dynamic, ideology-infused processes. Second, as an unfinished novel published nearly thirty years after its writing, the book has both engendered a dialogue between two decades and called into question formalist aesthetic theories.[6] Third, the texture of voices in Olsen's novel provides rich examples illustrative of Bakhtin's concepts of heteroglossia and polyphony. In the interests of illustrating most directly the value of Bakhtin's theory to performance of literature, this essay will focus on the third area. Specifically, I shall address the complexity of the novel's narrative voice and the layers of voices and languages embedded within that voice.

According to Bakhtin, all speech utterances are heteroglot and polyphonic in that they partake of "different-languages" and resonate with "many-voices." Heteroglossia (other-languagedness) and polyphony (many-voicedness) are the base conditions "governing the operation of meaning in any utterance."[7] By "other-languagedness," Bakhtin does not mean only national languages (though a national language determines, in part, the meaning of any utterance). More generally, heteroglossia refers to the ideologies inherent in the various languages to which we all lay claim as social beings and by which we are constituted as individuals: the language and the inherent ideologies of our profession, the language and inherent ideologies of our age group, of the decade, of our social class, geographical region, family, circle of friends, etc.[8]

Polyphony refers not literally to a number of voices, but to the collective quality of an individual utterance, that is, the capacity of my utterance to embody someone else's utterance even while it is mine, which thereby creates a dialogic relationship between two voices. For example, I quote or report someone's speech and thereby "dialogue" with his/her opinions; I appropriate the speech pattern of an admired person and associate myself with that person's linguistic-ideologic community; or I mock someone and dissociate myself from him or her. These are obvious examples, but Bakhtin further maintains that polyphony is inherent in all its words or forms: "Each word tastes of the context and contexts in which it has lived its socially charged life; all words and forms are populated by intentions."[9]

For Bakhtin, this layering of voices within one voice is nowhere more obvious than in the novel. The novel's epic mode permits the writer to embed voices within voices (e.g., character speech within narrator speech, narrator speech within authorial speech, etc.), and to orchestrate a dialogue among them. In *Yonnondio*, for example, the layering of character speech within narrative discourse allows Olsen to present a rich diversity of human voices and ideologies on one hand, and on the other, to collect those diverse, particularized voices and ideologies into a resounding social protest against an alien capitalist society.

The dialogic nature of the novel is not limited to the distinction between narrator speech and character speech, however. In *Yonnondio*, at least three levels of voices comprise the novel's internal discourse. These include: 1) the stratification of the narrator's voice into two distinct voices, 2) undramatized voices and linguistic-ideological communities embedded in the narrative voice, and 3) voices of characters, including undramatized voices and communities embedded in character discourse. In the remainder of this essay, I shall explain and illustrate these levels and indicate some performance implications for each.[10]

The narrator of *Yonnondio*, cast as a third-person observer, chronicles the lives of Jim and Anna Holbrook and their children as they battle the forces of economic depression. From the novel's opening in a Wyoming mining town, to the interlude of tenant farming in Dakota, to the conclusion in the slums of Omaha (where Jim finds work first in the sewers, and later in a packing plant), the narrator shows us a depression-era family whose love and tenderness for one another are constantly threatened by an uncaring capitalist society. The narrator does not limit herself to observation, however. In numerous passages she breaks out of the literary convention and engages in direct address to the reader or to a character. Such inconsistency of posture is not simply a shift in narrative point of view, but rather a stratification of one voice into two voices, specifically in this case, an oral voice embedded within the literary voice.

Throughout the novel, the narrative voice moves between two types of discourse—literary discourse and oral discourse *(skaz)*.[11] The primary distinction between these two orientations is precisely the degree of oral characteristics (oral syntax, oral intonation, etc.), embodied in the speech. In its literary orientation, the narrative voice tends toward an objective style of speech—relating the action as something happening to someone else, to the characters. As readers, we can detect a separation between the situation of the voice telling the tale and the situation of voices within the tale. The oral orientation collapses this separation. The narrator becomes not only the telling voice but also a voice coming from within the tale, a voice that exists on a level between the literary voice and character voices, which shares with the characters qualities of oral speech.

At times, the oral voice will emerge from within a literary passage, as it does in the sequence predicting the fate of the young miner, Andy Kvaternick:

> Andy Kvaternick stumbles through the night. The late September wind fills the night with lost and crying voices and drowns all but the largest stars. Chop, chop goes the black sea of his mind. How wild and stormy inside, how the ship-wrecked thoughts plunge and whirl. Andy lifts his face to the stars and breathes frantic, like an almost drowned man.
>
> But it is useless, Andy. The coal dust lies too far inside; it will be there forever, like a hand squeezing your heart, choking at your throat. The bowels of earth have claimed you.
>
> Breathe and breathe. (pp.6-7)

In this sequence, the use of present tense in the literary narrative of the first two sentences prefaces the emergence of the oral voice in the third sentence. Characterized first by oral syntax, and later by direct address to the character, this second voice belongs neither to Andy Kvaternick nor to a narrator who stands outside of the story. Instead, it seems to originate from within the story. In addition to the oral characteristics of syntax and direct address, the voice also contains oral intonations. The final sentence, "breathe and breathe," repeated frequently as the passage continues, has an ironically soothing, lulling quality that is distinctively oral in its reminiscence of the soothing sounds one makes to comfort a child. Thus, in its orientation toward oral *skaz*, the voice partakes of both narrative and character speech.

This vocal alterity serves two purposes. First, as Bakhtin explains, an oral narrator represents the common people: "a storyteller [oral narrator] . . . is not a literary person; he belongs in most cases to the lower social strata, to the common people (precisely this is important to the author)—and he brings with him oral speech."[12] Thus, through *skaz* or oral speech, the narrator achieves a common identity with the characters and can therefore serve as their representative—a spokesperson for their grievances. Conversely, it is through literary discourse—through a distanced perspective, metaphorical imagery, an elevated language style, etc.—that the narrator achieves the ideological clarity, structure, and verbal delineation necessary to articulate the characters' grievances. This layering of voices, this movement between literary and oral narration, accounts for the narrator's capacity as a dynamic unifying and diversifying force in the novel.

Secondly, this double-voiced narrative discourse functions to cast suspicion on our expectations of narrative discourse. By blurring the

distinctions between narrator and character situations, and between the
fictive world and the real world, the oral narrative subverts the notion of
a purely objective, detached aesthetic that would free the author and
reader from social responsibility. In the alternation between these
orientations, the one voice comments on the other.

In some instances, the oral narrative seems to encompass the literary
narrative rather than emerge from within it. For example, Chapter Four
opens with a series of oral exclamations and present participles that
situate the narrator at a point within the story, close to the characters
she describes: "The farm. Oh Jim's great voice rolling over the land. Oh
Anna, moving rigidly from house to barn so that the happiness with
which she brims will not jar and spill over. Oh Mazie, hurting herself
with beauty" (p. 41).

In other cases, the oral narrative voice interrupts the action to address
directly the listener/reader:

> Perhaps it frightens you as you walk by, the travail of the trees against the
> dark crouched house, the weak tipsy light in the window, the man sitting on
> the porch, menacing weariness riding his flesh like despair. And you hurry
> along, afraid of the black forsaken streets, the crooked streets, and look no
> more. (pp. 103-104)

In this example, the direct acknowledgement of the addressee's presence
as an active participant in the narrative discourse gives the narration an
oral quality that tends to decompose the boundaries between art and life,
between oratory and literary narration.

For the performer, director, or adaptor, the stratification of the
narrative voice provides rich implications for guiding performance
decisions. In group performance, for example, the adaptor or director
might choose to cast two performers in the role of the narrator, assigning
lines on the basis of literary or oral orientations, and thereby illustrating
the dialogic relationship between these two voices. On the other hand, a
solo performer cast in the role of the narrator might develop and present
a double-voiced character—one whose physical manner and vocal tone
shifts with the shifting orientation of the narration. In any case,
experimentation with performance techniques such as tone, focus, stance,
gesture, movement, and stage-positioning offers numerous ways to
illustrate the dialogical nature of the narrative voice.

In addition to the shifting orientation between literary discourse and
skaz, the narrative voice also contains embedded discourse of unobjecti-

fied or undramatized voices. As Bakhtin notes, speaking persons in a novel need not necessarily be incarnated in character.[13]

While undramatized voices populate the narrator's discourse throughout the novel, nowhere are they more multiple and varied than in the sequence describing the fate of Jim Tracy—the young individualist who quits his job in the sewers, believing that he can find a better job. The passage begins with quasi-direct discourse. Cast in Jim Holbrook's speech style, the speech reflects his resentment and envy in witnessing Tracy's act: "All right for Tracy to talk, all right, he didn't have a wife and kids hangin round his neck like an anchor" (pp. 88-89). Soon, however, the narrator casts off the embedded speech of Jim Holbrook, and continues in her own oral style:

> And Tracy was young, just twenty, still wet behind the ears, and the old blinders were on him so he couldn't really see what was around and he believed the bull about freedomofopportunity and a chancetorise and ifyoureallywanttoworkyoucanalwaysfindajob and ruggedindividualism and something about a pursuit of happiness. (p. 89)

Continuing to "carnivalize" through parody and distortion the platitudes of capitalist-individualism, the ensuing lines incorporate, without demarcation, a variety of voices, speech acts, and genres. For example, included in the passage are Jim Tracy's individualistic protests: "I'm a man, and I'm not takin crap offn anybody"; the voices of the unemployed, and of companies that are not hiring: "nojobnojob nothingdoingtoday"; period songs: "buddy . . . can you spare a dime"; the voices of railroad bulls: "keep movin keep movin"; distorted children's games: "sing a song of hunger the weather four below holes in your pockets and nowhere to go"; distorted biblical references to "God Job": "even among the pious who heed and prostrate themselves It's [*sic*] wrath is visited, for Many Are Called But Few Are Chosen"; and the voices of underprivileged children forced to recite platitudes after the teacher: "we-are-the-rich-est-country-in-the-worr-uld" (pp. 89-91).

The effect of this diversity of speech acts resembles a surrealistic carnival of distorted voices acting to deconstruct the monolithic capitalist-individualist voice against which the novel protests. Accordingly, the passage ends with a reconstruction of the narrator's collective socialist voice, promising redemption through organized protest:

> And there's nothing to say, Jim Tracy, I'm sorry, Jim Tracy, sorry as hell we weren't stronger and could get to you in time and show you that kind of individual revolt was no good, kid, no good at all, you had to bide your time

and take it till there were enough of you to fight it all together on the job, and bide your time, and take it, till the day millions of fists clamped in yours, and you could wipe out the whole thing, the whole goddamn thing, and a human could be a human for the first time on earth. (pp. 91-92)

Taken as a whole, the passage describing the fate of Jim Tracy is a study in miniature of the novel's entire utterance. It encompasses the diversifying and unifying strategies of the narrator's voice in one forceful stroke, garnering the myriad voices of a verbal-ideological world into a choral refutation of capitalist individualism.

Undramatized voices generate additional ideas for performing the narrative discourse. For example, the orchestration of voices in the above passage implies a choral quality that, in turn, suggests casting the narrator as a narrative chorus. A group of performers who speak individually at times, and in unison at other times, could demonstrate in performance both the individualized and collective qualities of the narrator's speech. Other possibilities for performing embedded voices include vocal recordings, music, and projections of photographs or film-footage from the depression-era which, if presented with the narrative speech, could enhance and extend its polyphonic quality.

Examples of heteroglossia and polyphony, so clearly evident in *Yonnondio's* narrator discourse, are no less abundant at the level of character discourse. While no character voice in *Yonnondio* attains the collective ideological structure of the narrator's voice, the individual voices are rich with embedded socio-linguistic communities, emerging ideologies, and the legacy of human speech diversity.

The novel's opening dialogue between Anna and Jim Holbrook establishes these characters' membership in several socio-linguistic communities:

"What'll ya have? Coffee and eggs? There aint no bacon."
"Dont bother with anything. Havent time. I gotta stop by Kvaternicks and get the kid. He's starting work today."
"What're they going to give him?"
"Little of everything at first, I guess, trap, throw switches. Maybe timberin."
"Well, he'll be starting one punch ahead of the old man. Chris began as a breaker boy." (pp.1-2)

The passage begins with an abbreviated form of communication identifying the characters as members of the same family unit who share knowledge and can conduct unspoken dialogue. For example, Anna does not need to explain why there is no bacon for breakfast, nor to remind Jim why there is no bacon. He knows there is no money with which to buy it; and if Anna is reproaching him in that regard, he both comprehends and evades the reproach.

At the same time, the opening sentences link the couple with a broader socio-linguistic community. Their inattention to standard grammatical rules and precise diction suggest that neither Anna nor Jim, nor the people with whom they associate, have time (literally or figuratively) for "correct" speech.[14] The ensuing sentences also contain indications of a job-related linguistic community in their references to specific occupational positions in mining work.

As the dialogue continues, other linguistic communities become evident, and speech acts and ideologies become further stratified. "Marie was tellin me, it would break Chris's heart if he only knew. He wanted the kid to be different, get an edjication." In this example of reported speech, embedded within character discourse, Anna reveals a sociolinguistic community of women—characterized by the sharing of confidences. Further embedded in Marie's reported speech are Chris's ideological aspirations for his children. This type of verbal-layering, weaving one speech act into another, and then another, illustrates heteroglossia and polyphony within a single utterance. Furthermore, Anna's decision to report Marie's speech without apparent contradiction of its inherent ideology, suggests that, at least tentatively, Anna shares that ideology. In response to Anna's report, Jim, who seemingly feels he cannot permit himself such lofty dreams for his children, counters with a comment designed to dissociate himself (and Anna) from the Kvaternicks socio-linguistic community: "Yeah? Them foreigners do have funny ideas."

As Anna continues to probe the subject of social conditions, she reveals Marxist ideology embedded in Marie Kvaternick's speech:

> She keeps talking about the old country, the field, and what they thought it would be like here—all buried in da bowels of earth, she finishes . . . . And she talks about the coal. Says it oughta be red, and let people see how they get it with blood.

Finally, in his fear of the implicit ideology in Anna's speech—which, if embraced, could cost him his job—and in his failure to dissociate himself and Anna from the Kvaternicks, Jim ends the dialogue by dissociating himself from Anna: "'Quit your woman's blabbin,' said Jim Holbrook, irritated suddenly. 'I'm going now'" (pp. 2-3). In this way, the characters' speeches embody diverse languages, ideologies, and voices within individual utterances.

Examples of polyphony occur throughout the novel, serving both to distinguish the characters as individuals and to illustrate their common humanity. In some cases, as in the example above, polyphony takes the form of reported speech in which diverse ideologies and ethnic groups are represented. At other times, voices seem to be resurrected from the past as fleeting memory—without delineation of their source. An example of such an anonymous voice occurs when Anna lies worrying about the possibility of a mine disaster: "In her a deep man's voice suddenly arose, moaning over and over, 'God, God, God'" (p. 3). Such intrusions from the past create the illusion that the novel is populated by more characters than one actually meets in the story.

The communal sharing of ideas and words also contributes to the learning process, as illustrated by Mazie Holbrook's attempts to understand her world. Early in the novel, six-year-old Mazie appropriates Marie Kvaternick's words and uses them to develop her own understanding of the coal mine: "A phrase trembled into her mind, 'Bowels of earth.' . . . It was mysterious and terrible to her. 'Bowels of earth. It means the mine. Bowels is the stummy. Earth is a stummy and mebbe she ets the men that come down'" (p. 5).

Throughout the book, such distinctive speech styles and socio-ideological languages provide a smattering of human diversity and unity. Among these are the foreign dialects of the Kvaternicks, the Kryczskis, and Mrs. Skolnick; Elsie Bedner's syrupy expressions ("dearie, honey"); Erina's biblical quotations ("suffer little children . . . "); and the inevitable anonymous comments on the weather: "Is it hot enough for you? In a dozen dialects, is it hot enough, hot enough, hot enough for you?" (p. 160).

The language of popular media and other folk genres are particularly worthy of note. For example, in the city, the Holbrook children discover and master the language of film. Will Holbrook internalizes the physical vocabulary of a popular movie star: "(. . . *Even outwardly: Will's eyes are narrowed now, his mouth drawn up at the corner, his walk—when he remembers—loose; for the rest of his life he will grin crooked:* Bill Hart)" (p. 156). The character who most completely internalizes the language of film, however, is Gertrude Skolnick—a young Polish immigrant who attempts to deny her old-world heritage by posing as a glamorous actress: "Say vamp me, vamp me. I'm Nazimova. Take me to the roadhouse. I want to make whoopee. Hotcha. Never never never. O my gigolo, my gigolo. A moment of ecstasy, a lifetime of regret" (p. 158).

Children's games, chants, and rhyme also abound in the novel, ranging in tone from the humorous and sad nonsense rhyme Mazie recites on the Dakota farm, "O Were I a Lum Ti Tum Tum/In the land of the alivoo fig/I'd play on the strum ti tum tum/To the tune of the thinguma jig" (p. 49); to the lighthearted game, "alley, alley 'ats in free' (p. 136); to the frightening chant, "Doctor, Doctor, will I die?/Yes. You will. And so shall I" (p. 159). The presence of these folk genres, like the influence of popular media, serves to reinforce the folk artistry of the People, and thus, additionally, to subvert the authority of individualistic bourgeois, aesthetic philosophies.

Among the folk genres included in the novel, none is more indicative of human bonding than is the sharing of songs. In three separate instances, the characters are able to transcend their isolation and individual circumstances through music.

The first instance occurs on the family's journey to the Dakota farm. Here, Anna and Jim's act of singing evokes pleasant memories and elicits happy plans for a new life. Presented through narrative discourse, the family experiences the binding power of the harmonious sounds: "Their voices were slow curving rhythms, slow curving sounds. Voices rising and twining, beauty curving on rainbows of quiet sound, filled their hearts heavy, welled happy tears to Mazie's eyes" (p. 39). At their visit to the Bedners, after they have moved to the city, the family again experiences the sweet-sadness of this unifying force: "They sang and sang, and a longing, a want undefined, for something lost, for something never known, troubled them all. The separate voices chorded into one great full one, their faces into beauty" (pp. 75-76).

The third example of the binding power of song occurs when Anna and Mazie are hunting "greens" for salad. Here, under the shade of a catalpa tree—for one brief moment free of household responsibilities—Anna sings to herself and to her daughter, stroking Mazie's hair; and the song and touch release them from their individual social roles and bind them to a broader human society:

"Fair, fair, with golden hair," her mother sang.
"Under the willow she's weeping." Mazie felt the strange happiness in her mother's body, happiness that had nought to do with them, with her, happiness and farness and selfness.
"Fair, Fair, with golden hair, under the willow she's sleeping."
The fingers stroked, spun a web, cocooned Mazie into happiness and intactness and selfness. Soft wove the bliss round hurt and fear and want and shame—the old worn fragile bliss, a new frail selfness bliss, healing, transforming. Up from the grasses, from the earth, from the broad tree trunk at their

back, latent life streamed and seeded. The air and self shone boundless. (p. 146)

In this instance, the introduction of the actual song lyrics develops the communal-voice quality on yet another level. The words of the narrator, the embedded voice of the character, and the further embedded voice of the song-writer blend into a chorus of three voices. Moreover, if the reader knows the song, its lyrics evoke its melody; and, in our imaginative constitution of the song, we lend our own vocal music to the passage, thus, contributing further to its polyphonic quality.

While by no means exhaustive, this discussion demonstrates some of the ways in which heteroglossia and polyphony contribute to *Yonnondio's* verbal-ideological texture. Through the use of literary and oral narrator voices; embedded discourse of dramatized characters and undramatized voices; parody and distortion of alien ideology; implication of diverse socio-linguistic communities; reported speech, appropriated words, dialects, speech styles, popular media, and folk genres; Olsen weaves a composition as rich and as delicate as a fugue. In orchestrating the diverse voices of the 1930s American Depression, she gives to these voices a sense of unity and harmony: "The separate voices [chord] into one great full one, their faces into beauty."

While an awareness of levels of character speech and undramatized voices embedded within them can result in a variety of staging possibilities, the most obvious contribution of Bakhtin's theory at this level (though applicable to all levels) lies in its potential for character analysis and development. For a performer, a director, or a teacher of performance, Bakhtin's concepts of heteroglossia and polyphony provide a new vocabulary for exploring *subtextual levels* of characterization. While the perimeters of this study do not permit a detailed exploration of that potential, it would seem obvious that performers could benefit from understanding the various speech acts and linguistic-ideological communities embedded in character speech as a means toward understanding the more traditional analytical elements of character attributes, motives, attitudes, and disposition.

Because of its emphasis on voices, Bakhtin's dialogic theory of literature presents particularly rich potential for performance studies of literary texts; and, conversely, performance offers an effective and engaging medium through which to dialogue with a text. One one hand, the adaptor, director, or performer of narrative literature can utilize Bakhtin's method of analyzing embedded voices to guide performance choices regarding line assignments, vocal orchestration, production concepts, and subtextual levels of characterization. On the other hand, established techniques for performing embedded voices—including bifurcation of narrators and characters, multiple casting, choral speech, and the use of electronic media—can not only demonstrate polyphony and heteroglossia, but can also serve as tools for uncovering new insights into the various levels of voices that populate a novel.[15]

Such a dialogic exchange between performance and text is only one kind of exchange that Bakhtin's theory affords,[16] but it is one that I believe Bakhtin would readily endorse. He states:

> The work and the world represented in it enter the real world and enrich it, and the real world enters the work and its world as part of the process of creation, as well as part of its subsequent life, in a constant renewing of the work through the creative perception of listeners and readers.[17]

NOTES

1. For a general overview of social context studies, see Kristin M. Langellier, "From Text to Social Context," *Literature in Performance*, 6 (April 1986), 60-70.

2. The relationship between post-structuralism and performance is explored in essays by Eric E. Peterson, John Hollwitz, Kay Ellen Capo, Jacqueline Taylor, Carol Simpson Stern, Kristin M. Langellier, Kristina Minister, Jill Taft-Kaufman, and Stanley Deetz in "Symposium: Post-Structuralism and Performance," ed. Mary S. Strine, *Literature in Performance*, 4 (November 1983), 21-64.

3. Taft-Kaufman, "Deconstructing the Text: Performance Implications," *Literature in Performance*, 4 (November 1983), 58. For a similar viewpoint, see Stern, "Deconstruction and the Phenomenological Alternative," *Literature in Performance*, 4 (November 1983), 41-44.

4. Strine, "Between Meaning and Representation: Dialogic Aspects of Interpretation Scholarship," *Renewal & Revision: The Future of Interpretation*, ed. Ted Colson (Denton, Texas: NB Omega Publication, 1986), 69-91. (See also Strine's Forum essay in this issue of *Literature in Performance*.)

5. Tillie Olsen, *Yonnondio: From the Thirties*, (New York: Delacorte Press/Seymour Lawrence, 1974). Subsequent references appear in text.

6. For various responses to Olsen's novel, see, for example, Bell Gale Chevigny, rev. of *Yonnondio*, *The Village Voice*, (May 23, 1974), 38-39; Sally Cunneen, "Tillie Olsen: Storyteller of Working America," *The Christian Century*, (May 21, 1980), 570-73; Erika Duncan, "Coming of Age in the Thirties: A Portrait of Tillie Olsen," *Book Forum*, 4,2 (1982), 207-22; Deborah Rosenfelt, "From the Thirties: Tillie Olsen and the Radical Tradition," *Feminist Studies*, 7 (Fall 1981), 371-406.

7. Michael Holquist, editor's glossary, in M. M. Bakhtin, *The Dialogic Imagination: Four Essays*, ed. Michael Holquist, trans. Caryl Emerson and Michael Holquist, (Austin: University of Texas Press, 1981), p. 428.

8. For Bakhtin, an individual's inner life, or consciousness is directly dependent on one's social self. As he notes, "ideological differentiation, the growth of consciousness, is in direct proportion to the firmness and reliability of the social orientation. The stronger, the more organized, the more differentiated the collective in which the individual orients himself, the more vivid and complex his inner world will be." See, [sic] V. N. Vološinov/Bakhtin, *Marxism and the Philosophy of Language*, trans. Ladislav Matejka and I. R. Titunik, (New York: Seminar Press, 1973), p. 88. As Vološinov's authorship is disputed, and there is growing evidence that Bakhtin wrote the book, I attribute the statement to Bakhtin.

9. Bakhtin, *The Dialogic Imagination*, p. 293.

10. These levels are not as mutually-exclusive as they might be in a formalist, dramatic, or another type of rhetorical analysis; they are used here primarily to orient the reader and to provide a general format for this discussion. While it is possible to situate an utterance in a linguistic-ideological framework or a "character zone," to insist on a strict demarcation among, say, authorial voice, narrator voice, and character voices risks ignoring the novel's dominant characteristic of the overlap or "dialogue" among these voices—a dialogue wherein "voices" are defined not only by speech styles but by the latent experiential-ideological perceptions that they express. Thus, for example, a speech by a narrator that expresses a character's inner experience belongs both to the category of narrator voice and the category of character voices. See Bakhtin, *The Dialogic Imagination*, pp. 301-331.

11. In his discussion of discourse in Dostoevsky's works, Bakhtin differentiates between narration by a narrator *(skaz)*, and first-person narration *(Ich-Erzählung)*. Olsen's oral narrator partakes of both types of discourse. Because it is the oral quality of speech *(skaz—*in the strictest sense of the term) that best distinguishes this narrative orientation, I shall refer to this orientation as "oral narration" or *"skaz."* See Bakhtin, *Problems in Dostoevsky's Poetics*, ed. and trans. Caryl Emerson, (Minneapolis: University of Minnesota Press, 1984), p. 190.

12. Bakhtin, *Problems in Dostoevsky's Poetics*, p. 192.

13. Bakhtin, *The Dialogic Imagination*, p. 335.

14. At an authorial level, Olsen's decision to omit the apostrophe in the contractions contained in the dialogue serves both to represent the dialect and to suggest that the sub-standard speech is politically motivated (i.e., that the omission indicates a conscious rejection of so-called "standards" of speech).

15. Numerous studies in interpretation suggest techniques for performing voices in narrative literature. See especially, Robert Breen, *Chamber Theatre*, (Evanston, Illinois: Wm. Caxton Ltd.), 1978, 1986; and Judith C. Espinola, "The Nature, Function, and Performance of Indirect Discourse in Prose Fiction," *Speech Monographs*, 41 (August 1974), 193-204. At another level of dialogue, a comparison of my 1983 production record essay with this essay reinforces the affinity between performance theories and Bakhtin's theory. While I was not aware of Bakhtin's work at the time that I adapted and directed the production of *Yonnondio* (nor when I wrote the production record essay), my decision to

assign the narration to a controlling narrator and a narrative chorus (based on an appreciation of the narrative point of view and studies of the Greek dramatic chorus), reflects a shared interest in embedded voices that Bakhtin's theory addresses in specific relation to the novel. Similarly, the kinds of insights into Olsen's narrative speech styles that arose in the process of choreographing that production would seem as appropriate to this type of dialogic analysis as to that dialogic activity. See Park-Fuller and Tillie Olsen, "Understanding What We Know: *Yonnondio: From the Thirties," Literature in Performance* 4 (November 1983), 65-74.

16. For examples of performance studies that apply Bakhtin's theory in various ways, see Strine (note #4 above); see also, Dwight Conquergood, "'A Sense of the Other': Interpretation and Ethnographic Research," *Proceedings of the Southwest Conference on Oral Traditions,* ed. Isabel Crouch (Las Cruces, New Mexico: New Mexico State Univ.), pp. 148-155; Conquergood, "Performance and Dialogical Understanding: In Quest of the Other," *Communication and Performance,* ed. Janet Larsen Palmer (Tempe, Arizona: Arizona State Univ., 1986), pp. 30-37; and Conquergood, "Between Experience and Meaning: Performance as a Paradigm for Meaningful Action," *Renewal and Revision: The Future of Interpretation,* pp. 26-59 (note #4 above). Additional studies incorporating a dialogic approach include two articles in *The Carolinas Speech Communication Annual,* 2 (1986): Beverly Whitaker Long, "Where is the (Other) Voice Coming From? Dialogic Prompting for Rehearsing the Performance of Lyric Poetry," 8-14; and John M. Allison, Jr., "The Rehearsal Process: A Brief Descriptive Analysis," 24-30.

17. Bakhtin, *The Dialogic Imagination,* p. 254.

Labor Activism and the Post-War Politics
of Motherhood: Tillie Olsen in the *People's World*

Michael E. Staub

In the spring and early summer of 1946, Tillie Olsen contributed a column to the *People's World* that has never before been discussed. The *People's World* was a daily labor and radical newspaper based in San Francisco and associated with (but hardly limited to) the West Coast branch of the Communist Party. With circulation in the tens of thousands during the 1940s, the *People's World* influenced a broad-based progressive audience that included California intellectuals, Hollywood stars, and liberal supporters, in addition to the rank-and-file of key West Coast labor organizations, like the International Longshoremen's and Warehousemen's Union.

Under the banner "Tillie Olsen Says," Olsen's first column on April 18, 1946, was greeted with unusual editorial fanfare. A generous editorial statement began by noting that their new columnist was "an old friend of many of our readers," thus acknowledging Olsen's role as staff writer during the early 1930s for the *Western Worker*, the *People's World's* predecessor. It also listed Olsen's more recent accomplishments, both personal and political: "Mrs. Olsen, mother of three, and veteran in the labor movement, has a rich background of experience and study in the problems of women workers. Former Northern California Director of CIO War Relief, past president of California CIO auxiliaries; active in the Parent-Teacher Association; one-time member of the San Francisco Board of Education's child care committee—these activities have given Mrs. Olsen an expert's insight in her field."[1]

Olsen quickly staked out her "field" of expertise as the interrelationship between working women and political activism. The columnist wasted no time before striking a dramatic chord, beginning her inaugural column this way:

> There won't be much space in this "woman's column" for best buys, household hints, and time-saving, money-saving recipes. We need such information. They're part of women's necessary tools for daily living. But jostling on them, crowding them out, are other women's problems; problems intertwined and interacting on the problems of trade unions and the whole progressive movement; problems so swollen and urgent they must be seen, and said, and acted upon, or this last great fight of humanity's for survival and a free life is endangered.

Stating that the great majority of women worked as homemakers and mothers, while many others labored at "all types of work, work which is the most monotonous, the dirtiest, the least organized—and of course, the lowest paid," Olsen emphasized the absolutely critical responsibility of the progressive movement to take seriously these individuals and their economic and social concerns.[2]

In the weeks that followed, Olsen's columns continued to stress the progressive movement's obligation to defend in peacetime the economic advances made by working women during the war. "The classification of jobs as 'men's work' and 'women's work' was proved as having no basis in fact," Olsen wrote in a column on "the struggle to maintain women's wartime gains."[3] She added: "Women demonstrated they could do 80 per cent of all jobs and industrial processes, by doing them . . . For the first time in history, the majority of women who worked on the same kinds of jobs as men, received the same kinds of wages."[4] Pressing her opinion even more forcefully in a later column, Olsen strove to eliminate the blind spots she believed union men had about working women. She posed questions she must have suspected would bring unencouraging replies:

> How's YOUR score on the women in your industry, brother steward and union officials? When management deliberately lays off women so they can be replaced by men, do you let them get by with it? . . . When a vet comes back for his job which a woman had been doing for the duration, do you just say "too bad, sister, goodbye," or do you find a place for her in the plant according to her seniority and skill? When a woman quits, do you try to see another woman has a chance to replace her? When a "good" job comes up, the kind a woman never had a crack at before the war, [but] did OK at during the war, do you see that a woman gets the same chance at that better job as a man?[5]

The column acknowledged that improving attitudes towards working women would not be easy for union men who "have been consciously taught to look at the woman in industry as a cut-throat competitor who does not do as well, and will work for less, and doesn't need to work in the first place, but is just there for pin-money or to give her husband a bad time." She continued: "Without thinking about it, men feel they have the right to the best jobs, the best wages, and seniority over women—and this is the one place union rules don't apply."[6] But as she stressed, that kind of attitude toward working women could only weaken the workers' cause as a whole "through creating bitterness, jealousy, resentment, and pitting worker against worker."[7]

Up to this point, or more than three weeks since her first column, there had been no responses to Olsen's column, either in letters to the editor or in other forums the newspaper provided for writers to express their opinions. Therefore, and while it is not possible to establish how Olsen's audience reacted to her demands for the equal rights of women to work, if the controversy which soon followed is any indication, there would have been *some* response had her proposals run strongly counter to the views of her readership.

Olsen's difficulties with the *People's World* began on May 9, 1946. On the same day (and the same page) that the just-mentioned Olsen column appeared, there also appeared a guest column by a Mrs. Joan Garson entitled "A progressive's problem: Can a housewife be politically active?" Garson and her husband both wished to remain fully active in Communist Party organizations, but the birth of their first child made dual political obligations increasingly difficult to pursue. Though a sitter could be found on infrequent occasions, most evenings when Mrs. Garson and her husband both had meetings, one of them had to remain home. A concluding editorial note requested readers' responses: "Mrs. Garson raises a very serious problem faced by many active women in the labor and progressive movement. We invite our readers to send in their experiences and comments that may help achieve a solution."[8]

On May 23, 1946, under the banner "What Do You Think?: 'Politically active' mothers—one view," Tillie Olsen wrote a response to Joan Garson. It may have been her undoing. "Do you remember the letter that appeared on this page several weeks ago from a new mother who wanted to know, how could she continue to be politically active?" the column opened. Olsen addressed herself to Garson:

> Dear Sister Garson, so tensely concerned with how you're going to manage to carry on the same kind of activity as you did before, and how many afternoons and evenings you can arrange to get out: RELAX. Relax and have fun with your baby. Be a good mother. That's your primary job and social function right now. That's your first political responsibility . . . Let go, Sister Garson, and mother your baby so that he'll be secure and happy. Feel that that's a social function. And if activity comes along that interferes with your doing that job well, wave it away.[9]

Olsen did, in addition to celebrating "the richness you will win as an individual participating in the miracle of human grow[th] . . . the fierce, jet-propelled impetus loving your baby will give you," suggest a number of concrete ways a stay-at-home mother could advance the progressive movement. She pointed out that the most important way "to change this world" is through "living agitation from person to person," "to be WITH people, to be a part of people, to know what is troubling and stirring people," and she indicated that the experience of motherhood would equip

Garson "as never before to work with women out of your closeness to their common experiences and needs." She also pointed out that now Garson would have the time to develop a social life with the families of her husband's coworkers and union comrades, and she argued that neighborhood work was as vital to the movement as shop-floor work. Highlighting the urgent need for door-to-door agitation, and yet acknowledging sadly that "we usually do [this work] awkwardly, unnaturally," Olsen insisted that as a trusted neighbor and confidante to other mothers and their children Garson would make an absolutely essential political contribution. And finally, Olsen concluded, the attitudes in party and union organizations simply would have to change to accommodate the special needs of "our mother-members":

> Seeing that you can function as a member of the organization to which you belong, must become a responsibility of that organizations [sic], not yours. Maybe they'll need to finance a baby sitter for you so you can come to meetings; maybe (heretical thought) they may need to see you get help on your housework so you can do other things.[10]

But despite Olsen's concluding efforts to urge changes in both labor movement attitudes and practices, and despite her recommendations to use the home as a base for innovative approaches to building and strengthening the working-class cause, the published reaction from working-class mothers was hostile, and riveted onto Olsen's initial glowing glorification of motherhood, and her suggestion that political responsibilities could be "waved away." One anonymous letter-writer from Berkeley bitterly told how she had had to work during the time her husband was in the service, despite her two children. With the war over, "I am [still] working now; my husband has been unemployed for two months since his discharge, and when he finds employment it will be at wages inadequate for a family of four, and with a continuous threat of unemployment." She responded to Olsen: "I feel that I am in a good position to say that Mrs. Olsen's advice does not answer the problems of working class women. The bourgeois cliches which she uses have no place in The People's World. Her position is an anti-working class one which can only be interpreted as the reactionary's position that the woman's place is in the home." Charging that "a normal mother does not need to be told to love her baby," she reminded her readers as well that

> housewives are forced to perform tasks which are dull and unstimulating, because capitalism does not find it profitable to organize household tasks in the same way that production of commodities for sale is organized, with

efficient and modern equipment. Let us talk about why these things are true, and how we can fight against them. Let us not talk about staying home and loving it.[11]

A second letter, signed "A Working Mother of two Pre-School Children," demanded to know: "If we are wiping revisionism out of our ranks, may I ask, what is Tillie Olsen's latest article doing in our press? . . . If The People's World can't find anything more enlightening than this on the woman question the editors would do well to go back to quoting from earlier works—and that's not a bad idea."[12]

June 6, 1946, the day *People's World* printed the second letter, was also when Olsen's final column for the *People's World* appeared. It did not respond directly to the criticism, but rather summarized and elaborated further on many of the same opinions about working women the column had begun with two months earlier. Reporting with outrage on the ways women pushed out of their wartime work were being forced into exploitative piecework jobs at pathetically low wages, Olsen urged a greater role for women in union leadership, calling on women to "convert the present meaningless unions into fighting organizations" and to campaign for equal pay, a higher minimum wage, and publicly-funded childcare.[13] While the controversy over the dilemmas faced by working and activist mothers continued for several more weeks, Olsen's column ended without editorial announcement or commentary.[14]

The cessation of Olsen's *People's World* column might have had most to do with what the author would describe so eloquently decades afterwards in *Silences:* "In the twenty years I bore and reared my children, usually had to work on a paid job as well, the simplest circumstances for creation did not exist."[15] Or it might have been the result of internal disputes in a political milieu quick to cast out those who had been charged with "revisionism." Or the author may have been discouraged by the criticisms leveled against her. In any event, it seems that Olsen did not publish for a Communist Party newspaper again. When she returned to writing in the mid-1950s, it would be the short fiction later collected in *Tell Me A Riddle.*

NOTES

1. Editorial commentary introducing Tillie Olsen, "Tillie Olsen Says: No time for 'household hints,'" *People's World* (April 18, 1946), 5.
2. For all quotes in this paragraph, see Tillie Olsen, "Tillie Olsen Says: No time for 'household hints,'" *People's World* (April 18, 1946), 5.

3. Tillie Olsen, "The struggle to maintain women's wartime gains," *People's World* (May 2, 1946), 5.

4. Ibid.

5. Tillie Olsen, "Wartime gains of women in industry," *People's World* (May 9, 1946), 5.

6. Ibid.

7. Ibid.

8. See Joan Garson, "A progressive problem: Can housewife be politically active?" along with the appended editorial commentary in *People's World* (May 9, 1946), 5.

9. Tillie Olsen, "What Do You Think?: 'Politically active' mothers—one view," *People's World* (May 23, 1946), 5.

10. For all quotes in this paragraph, see ibid.

11. For all quotes in this paragraph so far, see "An Answer to Tillie Olsen," *People's World* (June 3, 1946), 5.

12. "On Olsen," *People's World* (June 6, 1946), 6.

13. Tillie Olsen, "Tillie Olsen Says: Back to the slave shops?" *People's World* (June 6, 1946), 5.

14. See "A woman worker expresses her views on home, family and politics," *People's World* (June 11, 1946), 5; and Gerda Lerner and Virginia Warner, "This isn't a problem for mothers to solve alone . . . ," *People's World* (July 26, 1946), 5.

15. Tillie Olsen, *Silences* (New York: Delta/Seymour Lawrence, 1979), 19.

THE 1950s-1970s:
FICTIONS OF STRUGGLE
& SURVIVAL

Stories: New, Old, and Sometimes Good[*]

Irving Howe

Tillie Olson [*sic*][**] is a woman in her forties who has raised a family and then returned to her earlier ambition to write short stories. It is a common pattern these days in the life of the American middle class, though seldom do the results so thoroughly justify the risks. About Mrs. Olson one is not inclined to say, as might have been said about Bernard Malamud or Philip Roth on their first appearance, that here, no matter what comes of it, is a rich outpouring of talent. Mrs. Olson's stories depend heavily on her own experience, and that experience seems to be narrow. But, to judge from the stories, it is also one that she has felt very deeply and pondered and imaginatively absorbed. The one remarkable story in her book, "Tell Me a Riddle," is a *tour de force* which pits aging and dying immigrant Jews against their native-born children, prosperous, troubled and helpless. Mrs. Olson treats this familiar subject with balance, a cool humaneness, as if she were trying to see through the eyes of both generations and accept the self-pity of neither.

[*] Excerpt reprinted from *New Republic* 13 Nov. 1961: 22.
[**] Editor's note: The misspelling of Olsen's name continues throughout the review without further recognition.

The aging Jewish couple, now living in bored retirement and feeding on each other's resentments, are quasi-intellectuals of a kind familiar to anyone who has moved through the Jewish trade unions or communal organizations. They trundle from one child to another waiting for death, tormenting each other, until the wife is stricken with cancer and they must spend her few remaining months on a California seashore, lost in an America they neither made nor understand. The squalor of the setting is matched by the misery of their decline. And then comes the brilliant stroke of the story, a piece of imaginative daring absolutely true to the nature of such lives: the dying woman, her mind and tongue loosened, turns away from the petty family concerns of her old age and floats back into the past, into the days of her revolutionary ardor in Czarist Russia, and old phrases from speeches on socialism and Tolstoyan humanitarian-ism come streaming out of her, first to shock her husband and then to stir him into the pain of remembered love.

Mrs. Olson writes with steady hardness of tone, clinging to the one perception—the perception of loss and forgetting—which controls her story. In some passages she presses too hard, trying for verbal effects, intensities upon intensities, she cannot quite control, and not allowing her fable to move freely on its own. Nevertheless, the story is a remarkable piece of work, and one can only hope that Mrs. Olson, having been possessed by the powers of memory, may now move ahead to fiction in which everything depends on the powers of invention.

The Many Forms Which Loss Can Take*

Richard M. Elman

Four stories make up this first book by a gifted, mature artist with an uncanny sense of compassion. Rarely, at least in recent years, has the literature of alienation been engaged in such devout service of the imagination. In writing which is individualized but not eccentric, experimental but not obscure, Mrs. Olson [sic]** has created imagined experience which has the authenticity of autobiography or memoir. With a faultless accuracy, her stories treat the very young, the mature, the dying—poor people without the means to buy or invent lies about their situations—and yet her writing never succumbs to mere naturalism.

Some critics will persist in finding analogies to Mrs. Olson's work in the socially conscious literature of the thirties. They are there, if one wished to be blind to everything else, but the truth is that Mrs. Olson has been more daring. Sometimes she is able to compress within the space of a single sentence or a brief paragraph the peculiar density of a career, a lifetime, in the manner of lyric poetry. It follows that the poverty which she describes never strikes one as formulary or anachronistic, but as an image for contemporary experience. Although addicted to metaphorical language, she uses it flexibly and unself-consciously to record, to analyze and then to judge, fusing it with thought and feeling in such a way that the prose becomes the central intelligence of these dramas. "For forty-seven years they had been married," she begins the title story of her collection. "How deep the quarrel reached, no one could say—but only now when tending to the needs of others no longer shackled them together, the roots swelled up visible, split the earth between them, and the tearing shook even to the children, long since grown."

Some of these stories have their faults, but they are faults of enthusiasm. Occasionally the prose will get out of hand, or, in choosing to be on such intimate terms with her characters, Mrs. Olson will descend to a literal-mindedness which is her humanity unrestrained. Even so, there are stories in this collection which are perfectly realized works of art.

The foremost of these is a dramatic monologue entitled "I Sit [sic]*** Here Ironing," in which an unnamed and physically nondescript woman (a voice really), after a lifetime of deprivation, explains as she does the

*   Reprinted from *Commonweal* 8 Dec. 1961: 295-96.

**   Editor's note: Misspelling of name continues throughout the review.

***   Editor's note: Error in title of "I Stand Here Ironing" continues without further recognition. Other minor title errors will *not* be noted.

day's ironing the growth of her estrangement from her homely, first-born daughter. As she describes the early slights and disasters which brought such a relationship about, one has revealed the many human forms which loss can take. Mrs. Olson's woman is burdened with exhaustion, a victim of a world in which all the panaceas have been discredited. To say that she seems ordinary or without stature indicates only the costume she may be wearing, for her suffering is made extraordinarily vivid and historic.

At one point she reflects: "In this and other ways she leaves her seal, I say aloud. And startle at my saying it. What do I mean? What did I start to gather together, to try and make coherent. I was at the terrible growing years. War years. I do not remember them well. I was working, there were four smaller ones now. She had to help to be a mother, and housekeeper, and shopper. She had to set her seal. Mornings of crisis and near hysteria trying to get lunches packed, haircomb, coats and shoes found; everyone to school or child care on time, the baby ready for transportation. And always the paper scribbled on by a smaller one, the book looked at by Susan and mislaid, the homework not done. Running out to that huge school where she was one, she was lost, she was a drop; suffering over the unpreparedness, stammering and unsure in her classes. . . ."

"I Sit Here Ironing" is a catalogue of the failure of intimacy; yet it forces us to understand precisely because it is so intimate.

The other stories in this remarkable collection have equally remarkable titles. One is called "Hey Sailor What Ship"; another tersely, "O Yes." The title story is Mrs. Olson's longest and most ambitious work. Although she had explored the possibility of multiple consciousnesses functioning within the same dramatic situation in the earlier "Hey Sailor What Ship," one feels that in the final story she has actually fleshed two protagonists of equal vigor, enmeshing them in a marriage which seems as real and as permanent as any one will encounter in recent fiction. "Tell Me A Riddle" is a modern day "Ivan Illych [sic]." The death of Mrs. Olson's heroine is the death of social consciousness itself, gruesome, alienated, and without consolation. In the death-struggle of this old activist and her mate (with both continually pitting their dignities against the other), Mrs. Olson has envisaged a true tragedy of human mortality. In the last grim acts of a social protest which sprang from love, not cant, she puts it more eloquently than I can, in the words of the desolated old man who has been left behind, when he says: "Aaah, children . . . how we believed, how we belonged."

The Passion of Tillie Olsen[*]

Elizabeth Fisher

The title story is her masterpiece. My first reading of it was one of those shattering discoveries, an experience that, at first, reminded me of coming on Henry Roth's *Call It Sleep*, because that book, too, had been "buried," had a strong emotional impact, and dealt with poor immigrant Jews. However, Olsen's work has neither the particularity nor the special faults of Roth's; it has such compression and such scope that the analogy made by a friend of mine—her first reading of "The Death of Ivan Ilyitch"—seems to me a better one. With this difference: Tillie Olsen is not only a great writer, she is a feminist artist. Till the very end, we do not even know the name of the old woman whose long dying is the framework on which "Tell Me a Riddle" evolves. She is the mother, the wife, the grandmother. Only in the last 3 pages do we learn that she is Eva. But in the magic weaving of past and present which goes from Olshana in pre-revolutionary Russia to death in a strange impersonal Los Angeles, what comes out most strongly is the disadvantaging of woman, the denial of intellect and aspiration, the utter thanklessness of the mother's role. Seven children are brought up, through the vicissitudes of a working-class life during the past fifty years, and make the successful climb into the middle classes, but at what a cost, what a cost. The young girl steeped in 19th-century idealism gives way to the exigencies of 20th-century American materialism. Always "don't read, put your book away," and she dies shutting out her husband, babbling of the great world of books and culture, philosophy and music of which she has had only the most fleeting glimpses in her practical everyday life: "The children's needings; that grocer's face or this merchant's wife she had to beg credit from when credit was a disgrace; the scenery of the long blocks walked around when she could not pay; school coming, and the desperate going over the old to see what yet could be remade; the soups of meat bones begged 'for the dog' one winter . . . . " About Olsen's men it might be said, as of the husband in Beckett's "Happy Days," how can they help others when they can't even help themselves? Her women can, but it is never enough, never right, never whole.

"The love—the passion of tending—had risen with the need like a torrent; and like a torrent drowned and immolated all else . . . . Only the thin pulsing left that could not quiet suffering over lives one felt but could no longer hold nor help." People have drawn on her, feeding, demanding

---

[*] Excerpt reprinted from *Nation* 10 Apr. 1972: 427, 474.

more, more, so that, at last, drained without replenishment, she says, no enough.

"Never again to be forced to move to the rhythms of others. Being at last, able to live within, and not to move to the rhythms of others." This is the refrain of the tired old woman, battered by too much life, but free at last on her own limited terms. "If they would but leave her in the air now stilled of clamor, in the reconciled solitude to journey to her self." Hunched in the closet, she hides from the hurly-burly of family, from her daughter's "spilling memories," unable to touch the baby, "warm flesh like this that had claims and nuzzled away all else and with lovely mouths devoured . . . the drawing into needing and being needed." And later, "at the back of the great city" where her husband had brought her "to the dwelling places of the cast-off old," as she makes for "the far ruffle of the sea . . . though she leaned against him, it was she who led." What images and what economy, what a world is here compressed!

"I Stand Here Ironing" is the story told by a mother of how, wanting to do the best for her daughter, she was so often forced to do the worst, and it is one that every parent can recognize. In tight, economical prose she tears us with the parental experience, how we listen, wrongly, to other people, or are just imprisoned by events we could not fore-see—desertion, poverty, expanding families; it is also a hopeful story of how children survive, sometimes even making strength, or talent, out of the deprivations they've endured. Tillie Olsen's is an unsparing but tender vision in which love is need that is rarely answered, a vision of communication on strange, imperfect levels, and, above all, of resilience, a belief that human beings are not passive, that there is more in them "than this dress on the ironing board, helpless before the iron."

The two other stories in this volume, strong and well worked, would be accounted great if someone else had written them; they fade only beside the raw strength of the first-named ones. "Hey Sailor, What Ship?" tells of an alcoholic seaman who cannot survive ashore and who yet seeks the warmth of a family; it tells also of the limitations and cruelties and affections of the family trying to hold on to an earlier time's hope and community.

In "O Yes" there is a marvelous evocation of the black religious experience: "The crucified Christ embroidered on the starched white curtain leaps in the wind of the sudden singing"; "You not used to hearing what people keeps inside, Carol!"; and a depiction of the snob and class pressures that drive apart two 12-year-old girls, one black, one white. The white girl doesn't want to be oppressed by life; "Why is it like this and why do I have to care?" Her mother knows, but is helpless with her own unassuaged needs, as she answers, inside to herself, "Caring asks doing. It is a long baptism into the seas of humanity."

Olsen's women alternatively reject and demand the full intensity of life. They are conscious, terrifyingly frighteningly conscious, and it is this that makes their pain and ours. Mortality presses on them with an awful weight, the finiteness of the human animal as opposed to the infinitude of the human spirit, or even to the possibilities of the human being. *"Humankind one has to believe."* And we feel with Lennie, Eva's son, *"for that in her which never lived (for that which in him might never live) . . . good–bye Mother who taught me to mother myself."*

What is wonderful is that, engaged, feminist, Olsen's work is also utterly transcendent—a contradiction of the art-for-art's sake purists. Though the subject matter may be autobiographical, the author is everywhere and nowhere; this is indeed writing that consumes all impediments; incandescent, it glows and it burns. Read the stories; they will not be forgotten.

Limning: or Why Tillie Writes[*]

Ellen Cronan Rose

Tillie Olsen was born in Nebraska 65 years ago. In 1960, when she was 50 years old, she published her first book, a slim volume of short stories called *Tell Me A Riddle*. In 1974 she finally published a novel—*Yonnondio*—she had begun in 1932 and abandoned in 1937. To women in "the movement" she is a major literary figure, not so much despite as because of the paucity of her publications.

Since 1971, when Delta reissued *Tell Me A Riddle* in paperback, Olsen has been stumping the country, speaking about women who have been prevented by their sex from utilizing their creative talents. These are her words:

> In the twenty years I bore and reared my children, usually had to work on the job as well, the simplest circumstances for creation did not exist. When the youngest of our four was in school, the beginnings struggled toward endings . . . . Bliss of movement. A full extended family life; the world of my job; and the writing, which I was somehow able to carry around with me through work, through home. Time on the bus, even when I had to stand, was enough; the stolen moments at work, enough; the deep night hours for as long as I could stay awake, after the kids were in bed, after the household tasks were done, sometimes during. It is no accident that the first work I considered publishable began: "I stand here ironing." In such snatches of time I wrote what I did in those years but there came a time when this triple life was no longer possible. The fifteen hours of daily realities became too much distraction for the writing.
>
> As for myself, who did not publish a book until I was 50, who raised children without household help or the help of the technological sublime' . . . who worked outside the house on everyday jobs as well . . . . The years when I should have been writing, my hands and being were at other (inescapable) tasks . . . . The habits of a lifetime when everything else had to come before writing are not easily broken, even when circumstances now often make it possible for the writing to be first: habits of years: response to others, distractibility, responsibility for daily matters, stay with you, mark you, become you. I speak of myself to bring here the sense of those others to whom this is in the process of happening (unnecessarily happening, for it need not, must not continue to be) and to remind us of those (I so nearly was one) who never come to writing at all. We cannot speak of women writers in our century without speaking also of the invisible: the also capable: the born

[*] Reprinted from *The Hollins Critic* Apr. 1976: 1-13.

to the wrong circumstances, the diminished, the excluded, the lost, the silenced. We who write are survivors, 'onlys.' One—out of twelve.

I heard Olsen speak these words to a class at Dartmouth College last year, and I observed their galvanic effect on the students—mostly women—who heard them. My first exposure to Tillie Olsen was to Olsen the feminist. It was with this preparation that I first read *Tell Me A Riddle* and *Yonnondio*. I was thus unprepared for their impact on me.

II

For in her books, Olsen is no politician, but an artist. Her fictions evoke, move, haunt. They did not seem, when I read them, to belong to any movement, to support any cause.

And so I returned to Olsen's words about the situation of the woman writer to see if there was something I had missed, something the women's movement had missed.

In "Silences: When Writers Don't Write," originally delivered as a talk to the Radcliffe Institute for Independent Study in 1963, Olsen asks, "What are creation's needs for full functioning?" The answer *women* have heard is an echo of Virginia Woolf's "£500 a year and a room of one's own"—independence, freedom, escape from the restriction of traditional feminine roles. This is the answer Olsen herself gives on the lecture circuit. But in this early Radcliffe speech, her question seems not so much political as aesthetic.

Wondering what keeps writers from writing, Olsen turns to what writers—*men* writers—have themselves said about their unnatural silences, not periods of gestation and renewal, but of drought, "unnatural thwarting of what struggles to come into being, but cannot." She points to Hardy's sense of lost "vision," to Hopkins, [*sic*] "poet's eye," curbed by a priestly vow to refrain from writing, to Rimbaud who, after long silence, finally on his deathbed "spoke again like a poet-visionary." She then turns to writers who wrote continuously, in an effort to understand what preserved them from the unnatural silences that fore-shortened the creativity of Hardy, Hopkins, Rimbaud, Melville, and Kafka. She cites James's assertion that creation demands "a depth and continuity of attention," and notes that Rilke cut himself off from his family to live in attentive isolation so that there would be "no limit to vision." Over and over in these opening paragraphs of "Silences," Olsen identifies the act of creation with an act of the eye.

In order to create, the artist must see. Margaret Howth, in Rebecca Harding Davis's novel of that name, is the type of the artist for Olsen, "her eyes quicker to see than ours." And one of the special handicaps of the woman writer, confined traditionally to her proper sphere in the drawing room or the kitchen, is that she is restricted to what Olsen calls "trespass vision" of the world beyond that sphere. But although she echoes Charlotte Bronte's lament that women are denied "facilities for observation . . . a knowledge of the world," Olsen does not equate the reportorial with the creative eye. Vision is not photography. Olsen quotes, approvingly, Sarah Orne Jewett's advice to the young Willa Cather: "If you don't keep and mature your force . . . . what might be insight is only observation. You will write about life, but never life itself."

In Rebecca Harding Davis's *Life in the Iron Mills*, to which Olsen has added an appreciative biographical afterword, the distinction between vision and mere seeing is dramatized in the reactions of two views to the statue Hugh Wolfe has sculpted out of slag. The mill owner's son has brought a party of gentlemen to see the mill. On their way back to the carriage, they stumble on Hugh's statue, the crouching figure of a nude woman, with outstretched arms. Moved by its crude power, the gentlemen ask Hugh, "But what did you mean by it?" "She be hungry," he answers. The Doctor condescendingly instructs the unschooled sculptor: "Oh-h! But what a mistake you have made, my fine fellow! You have given no sign of starvation to the body. It is strong,—terribly strong." To the realist, a portrait of starvation must count every rib. But Mitchell, who is portrayed as the dilettante and aesthete, a stranger to the mill town and of a different cut than the doctor, foreman, and newspaperman who round out the party, "flash[es] a look of disgust" at the doctor: 'May,' [sic] he broke out impatiently, 'are you blind? Look at that woman's face! It asks questions of God, and says, "I have a right to know." Good God, how hungry it is!'"

So Olsen's vision is, in a sense, trespass vision. It is "insight, not observation," the eye's invasion of outward detail to the meaning and shape within. It is this creative trespassing that Rebecca Davis commends in Margaret Howth, whose eyes are "quicker to see than ours, delicate or grand lines in the homeliest things." And it is precisely that quality in Rebecca Davis herself that makes her so significant to Tillie Olsen, who says of her that "the noting of reality was transformed into comprehension, Vision."

Tillie Olsen's edition of *Life in the Iron Mills*, published by the Feminist Press, is central to an understanding of what she means by the creative act. It may or may not be one of the lost masterpieces of American fiction. Olsen herself admits that it is "botched." But it fascinates her because it is a parable of creation, a portrait of the artist. And significantly, that artist is a sculptor.

One of the unsilent writers Olsen quotes in "Silences" is the articulate Thomas Mann, who spoke of the act of creation as "the will, the self-control to shape a sentence or follow out a hard train of thought. From the first rhythmical urge of the inward creative force towards the material, towards casting in shape and form, from that to the thought, the image, the word, the line." Vision is perceptive seeing, which sees beneath and within the outward details the essential shape of the meaning of the thing perceived. Doctor May saw only the anatomy of Hugh's statue; Mitchell saw through to the woman's soul.

Sculpting is cutting away the exterior surface to come to the shape within the block of marble. Hugh spends months "hewing and hacking with his blunt knife," compelled by "a fierce thirst for beauty,—to know it, to create it." His struggle is first to see the beauty within and then to give it form. Mann's urge towards the material and then casting it in shape and form.

Olsen writes of Davis's art in similarly sculptural words: "It may have taken her years to embody her vision. 'Hewing and hacking'" like Hugh. The first pages of *Life in the Iron Mills* are the narrator's injunction to the reader to "look deeper" into the sordid lives of the mill workers, to ask whether there is "nothing beneath" the squalor. This preamble concludes with the artless confession that "I can paint nothing of this" inner reality, "only give you the outside lines." But the strength of the tale is in Davis's ability to sculpt that inner reality, to dissolve the outside outlines and uncover the moral shape of her simple tale. For Olsen it is "a stunning insight . . . as transcendent as any written in her century."

Vision is not photography. Sculpting is not cameo carving. Rebecca Harding Davis excoriated the Brahmins she met on her trip north from her native Wheeling, West Virginia. Emerson and Bronson Alcott, she wrote in her journal, "thought they were guiding the real world, [but] they stood quite outside of it, and never would see it as it was . . . .their views gave you the same sense of unreality, of having been taken, as Hawthorne said, at too long a range." In other words, they imposed their vision of the world on the world of fact, pasted their carvings on the surface of things. Davis criticized them for ignoring the "back-bone of fact." To see the inner shape, you have at least to acknowledge the contour of the surface.

In her own tale of the down-trodden, *Yonnondio*, Olsen addresses the Brahmins of our day:

And could you not make a cameo of this and pin it onto your aesthetic hearts? So sharp it is, so clear, so classic. The shattered dusk, the mountain of culm, the tipple; clean lines, bare beauty—and carved against them dwarfed by the vastness of night and the towering tipple, these black figures with bowed heads, waiting, waiting.

The aesthetic eye sees "at too long a range." It abstracts from surface detail a pleasing pattern. But the creative eye, the visionary eye, apprehends the surface in order to comprehend the inner shape which gives it meaning.

Thus by accreted detail, Olsen's definition of the creative act comes into focus. The artist stands, always, in relation to a world of fact. He can record it or he can transform it. In the one case, the standard by which he measures his achievement is fidelity to fact. In the other, his standards are formal. Between these extremes, Tillie Olsen places the creative act. Fidelity to fact, but essential fact. Form and pattern, but exposed, not imposed.

It is not surprising that, of all the literary people she met on her northern trip, Rebecca Davis should have been drawn to Hawthorne. This aesthetic stance in relation to reality that I have discerned in Olsen and Davis is also, as I understand it, the method of Hawthorne's romances. Coming to Hawthorne's tales in her early life, Davis was "verified" in her feeling that "the commonplace folk and things which I saw every day had mystery and charm . . . belong to the magic world [of books] as much as knights and pilgrims." *Ethan Brand,* that tale of another furnace tender, sees under the surface of fact a fable of the unpardonable sin; *Life in the Iron Mills,* as Olsen points out, is about "another kind of unpardonable sin," but its method of uncovering that sin is akin to Hawthorne's. It is not an abstraction from reality—that is the method of the cameo cutter, the formalist—but a reduction of facticity to its primary form.

III

When I began this study of Tillie Olsen, I was motivated by my sense that beneath the polemic about the predicament of the woman writer lay something like this more comprehensive aesthetic. What gave me this sense, or suspicion, was Olsen's fiction, which transcends her oratory. But before I turn to an appreciation of that fiction, I want to examine briefly the source of the disparity between Olsen's real aesthetic and her current feminist articulation of it.

Throughout her non-fiction writing, as we have seen, Olsen uses the metaphor of sculpture to define the creative act. To be a writer, one must "be able to come to, cleave to, find the form for one's own life comprehensions." But in an article published in *College English* in 1972, "Women Who Are Writers in Our Century: One Out of Twelve," Olsen uses this sculptural imagery to describe, not the artist, but the situation of women who are "estranged from their own experience and unable to perceive its shape and authenticity," prevented by social and sexual circumscription from the essential act of self-definition and affirmation. The paradox of female reality, as Olsen understands it, is that immersion in life means loss of perspective, or vision.

The artist-visionary can supply that perspective, can "find the form" which constitutes the "shape of authenticity" of what Olsen calls "common female realities."

Thus in "One Out of Twelve" and on the lecture circuit, Tillie Olsen exhorts women artists to take women's lives as their subject matter, finding a therapeutic link between the situation of women in our society and the peculiar kind of discovery implicit in the aesthetic creation. Accordingly she feels "it is no accident that the first work I considered publishable began: 'I stand here ironing'."

It is possible to read the first of the four stories that comprise *Tell Me A Riddle* as an exemplum of Olsen's feminist aesthetic. The mother-narrator of "I Stand Here Ironing" looks back over a life where there has been no "time to remember, to sift, to weigh, to estimate, to total." Caught in the mesh of paid work, unpaid work, typing, darning, ironing, she has suffered, but never had time and leisure to perceive and shape, to understand, the passionate arc of motherhood. Helplessly she looks back over her memories of her daughter's childhood and concludes, "I will never total it all."

What Olsen does, in "I Stand Here Ironing," is to perceive and give form to the meaning of her narrator's motherhood, that "total" which the mother has no time to sum. As every female reader I have spoken to attests, this story movingly succeeds in articulating what Olsen calls "common female realities."

It is also possible to fit the title story of the collection into the Procrustean feminist aesthetic Olsen propounds in "One Out of Twelve." "Tell me a riddle, Grammy. I know no riddles, child." But the grandfather "knew how to tickle, chuck, lift, toss, do tricks, tell secrets, make jokes, match riddle for riddle." Why? Clearly because during all the years when she "had had to manage," to contend with poverty, to raise five children, to preserve domestic order, he "never scraped a carrot or knew a dish towel sops." The man is free, the woman bound. Women cannot "riddle" or form the experience they are utterly immersed in.

But "Tell Me A Riddle" is far more than a feminist document. In it, Olsen riddles the inscrutable by perceiving the meaning beneath and within the old woman's life and death. But this service is not rendered solely to the grandmother, but to all the characters in the story, and to the reader as well. Lennie, her son, suffered "not alone for her who was dying, but for that in her which never lived (for that which in him might never live)." And keeping his vigil by the dying woman's bedside, the grandfather achieves an epiphany, which the reader shares:

> The cards fell from his fingers. Without warning, the bereavement and betrayal he had sheltered—compounded through the years—hidden even from himself—revealed itself,
> uncoiled,
> released,
> *sprung*
> and with it the monstrous shapes of what had actually happened in the century.

"Tell Me A Riddle" is a story about "common female realities," but it is also a story about "common *human* realities." We are all bound slaves, all immured in immanence, pawns of economic and political forces we cannot comprehend. Stepping from moment to moment, we do not see that we are pacing out the steps of a "dance, while the flutes so joyous and vibrant tremble in the air."

Olsen has made the mistake, in her recent oratory, of confusing the general human situation and the particular plight of women in our society. What she empathically knows because she is an artist she thinks she knows because she is a woman, that our greatest need is to "be able to come to, cleave to, find the form for [our] own life comprehensions." In her fiction, if not in her rhetoric, Olsen does not reserve that need to the female half of the race.

Like the mother in "I Stand Here Ironing," the protagonist of "Hey Sailor, What Ship?", the second of the *Tell Me A Riddle* stories, has spent his life day by day, immersed in "the watery shifting" from one port to another, the animal rhythm of work/ pay check/ binge/ hangover. Yet Olsen rescues this inchoate history into meaning, by showing how Whitey fits in to a larger pattern, of which he himself is unaware. To his old friends in San Francisco, to whom he continually returns no matter how wide the arc of his dereliction, he is "a chunk of our lives." When Jeannie, the ruthless teenager, says, "he's just a Howard Street wino, that's all," her mother insists, "You've got to understand."

Understand. Once they had been young together. To Lennie he remained a tie to adventure and a world in which men had not eaten each other; and the pleasure, when the mind was clear, of chewing over with that tough mind the happenings of the times or the queernesses of people, or laughing over the mimicry. To Helen he was the compound of much help given, much support: the ear to hear, the hand that understands how much a scrubbed floor, or a washed dish, or a child taken care of for a while, can mean.

With understanding, Whitey's sordid life is illuminated and valued. For us, who view it by way of Olsen's trespass vision, his life has meaning.

IV

If Olsen, like Rebecca Harding Davis, owes her aesthetic to Hawthorne, it is with another American writer that she shares her sympathies. In a revealing remark to a class of Dartmouth students, Tillie Olsen said that when she began writing her tale "From the Thirties" in 1932, she knew she would call it *Yonnondio*. Furthermore she has another unfinished novel she also calls *Yonnondio*. Like Walt Whitman's, from whom she borrowed the name, her fiction is one continuous poem, dedicated to the common man.

Yonnondio, as the subtitle reminds us, is a tale "From the Thirties." It records several years in the life of the Holbrook family, as they move from a mining town in Wyoming to a tenant farm in South Dakota to the slaughter-houses of Denver. But although the settings and their squalor have equivalents in other writing "from the thirties," Olsen is neither Upton Sinclair nor John Steinbeck. *Yonnondio* is not a protest, but a perception.

Olsen told the Dartmouth students she was "fortunate" to have been brought up "working class, socialist." She thus credited her strength as an artist, not to her sex, but to her roots, her heritage, her sense of belonging to a living culture. It is her sympathetic love for the common people she identifies with that leads her to perceive in their lives the luminous beauty she limns, to articulate the inarticulate, to give voice to what might otherwise be a note as fleeting as JimJim's song in *Yonnondio:*

a fifth voice, pure, ethereal, veiled over the rest. Mazie saw it was Jimmie, crouched at the pedals of the piano. "Ma," she said after the song was done, "it's Jimmie, JimJim was singin too." Incredulous, they made him sing it over with them and over and over. His words were a blur, a shadow of the real words, but the melody came true and clear.

Olsen's ears are quick to catch that ethereal melody, and her pen is incomparable at notating it.

Olsen's fiction is full of privileged moments, instants prised from the flux of time and illumined by a vision of their essential meaning. For the character, the moments are fleeting. At the end of a day of gathering greens and weaving dandelion chains, a day wrested from the stink and squalor of Slaughterhouse City, Mazie sees her mother's face transfigured, senses in her "remote" eyes "happiness and farness and selfness." Anna's peace suffuses the place where she sits with the children, so that "up from the grasses, from the earth, from the broad tree trunk at their back, latent life streamed and seeded. The air and self shone boundless." But the sun sinks. Ben gets hungry for supper, and "the mother look" returns to Anna's face. "Never again, but once, did Mazie see that look—the other look—on her mother's face."

For Mazie, the privileged moments are so evanescent that she sometimes wonders if they ever occurred: "Where was the belted man Caldwell had told her of, lifting his shield against a horn of stars? Where was the bright one she had run after into the sunset? A strange face, the sky grieved above her, gone suddenly strange like her mother's." Snatched from the grinding, degrading poverty of her life's daily texture, such moments of beauty as Mazie had with the old man Caldwell, who directed her naïve eyes to Orion and his luminous companions, are so rare that they might never have existed, might be dreams, or promises, like the books the dying Caldwell wills her and her father sells "for half a dollar."

More often, the privileged moments do not "come to writing" for Olsen characters. "Come to writing," a favorite phrase of Tillie Olsen's, expresses her vitalistic conception of the creative process. It means the inarticulate finding words, the dumbly sensed becoming sensible, the incipient meaning finding form. For the writer, it is breaking silence. For the actor in an Olsen fiction, it is a moment of perceiving, of knowing that there is shape and direction in the ceaseless flow of what must be. Mazie comes to writing occasionally; so does her mother, Anna, who "stagger[s]" in the sunlight and moves beyond the helpless "My head is balloony, balloony" to sing her love for her eldest child and her joy in motherhood: "O Shenandoah, I love thy daughter,/ I'll bring her safe through stormy water."

But more often when Mazie is immersed in a potentially luminous moment, she perceives it as "stammering light" and when "she turns her hand to hold" it, "she grasps shadows." Anna moves through the daily drudgery "not knowing an every-hued radiance floats on her hair." As for Jim, her husband, "the things in his mind so vast and formless, so terrible and bitter, cannot be spoken, will never be spoken—till the day that hands will find a way to speak this: hands."

The hands are Olsen's hands, grasping her pen to copy a fragment of Walt Whitman's poem as the epigraph to her novel "From the Thirties":

No picture, poem, statement, passing them to the future:
Yonnondio! Yonnondio!—unlimn'd they disappear;
To-day gives place, and fades—the cities, farms, factories fade;
A muffled sonorous sound, a wailing word is borne through the air for
   a moment,
Then blank and gone and still, and utter lost.

Yonnondio! That evocative word is the emblem of Tillie Olsen's aesthetic. It is her plea, and her pledge: that the unobserved should be perceived, that the fleeting should be fixed, that the inarticulate should come to writing.

"I Stand Here Ironing":
Motherhood as Experience and Metaphor[*]

Joanne S. Frye

Motherhood as literary metaphor has long been a cliché for the creative process; the artist gives birth to a work of art which takes on a life of its own. Motherhood as literary experience has only rarely existed at all, except as perceived by a resentful or adoring son who is working through his own identity in separation from the power of a nurturant and/or threatening past. The uniqueness of Tillie Olsen's "I Stand Here Ironing" lies in its fusion of motherhood as both metaphor and experience: it shows us motherhood bared, stripped of romantic distortion, and reinfused with the power of genuine metaphorical insight into the problems of selfhood in the modern world.

The story seems at first to be a simple meditation of a mother reconstructing her daughter's past in an attempt to explain present behavior. In its pretense of silent dialogue with the school's guidance counselor—a mental occupation to accompany the physical occupation of ironing—it creates the impression of literal transcription of a mother's thought processes in the isolation of performing household tasks: "I stand here ironing, and what you asked me moves tormented back and forth with the iron."[1] Indeed, this surface level provides the narrative thread for our insights into both Emily and her mother. The mother's first person narrative moves chronologically through a personal past which is gauged and anchored by occasional intrusions of the present: "I put the iron down" (p. 12); "Ronnie is calling. He is wet and I change him" (p. 17); "She is coming. She runs up the stairs two at a time with her light graceful step, and I know she is happy tonight. Whatever it was that occasioned your call did not happen today" (p. 19).

As we read the story, then, we are drawn through a knowledge of the present reality and into participation in the narrative process of reconstructing and visualizing the past. With the narrator, we construct an image of the mother's own development: her difficulties as a young mother alone with her daughter and barely surviving during the early years of the depression; her painful months of enforced separation from her daughter; her gradual and partial relaxation in response to a new

[*] Reprinted from *Studies in Short Fiction* (Summer 1981): 287-92.

[1] Tillie Olsen, "I Stand Here Ironing," in *Tell Me a Riddle* (New York: Dell, 1976), p. 9. Subsequent references will be indicated within the text.

husband and a new family as more children follow; her increasingly complex anxieties about her first child; and finally her sense of family equilibrium which surrounds but does not quite encompass the early memories of herself and Emily in the grips of survival needs. We construct, too, an image of the stressful growth of the daughter from infancy through a troubled, lonely childhood, an alienating relationship to schools and friends, and an unsettled adolescence—and finally into the present nineteen-year-old, who "needs help," as the counselor insists, but who has also found a strong inner resource in her talent for mime and in her own sense of self.

The story is very fundamentally structured through the mother's present selfhood. It is her reality with which we are centrally concerned, her perception of the process of individuation to which the story gives us access. Her concerns with sorting through Emily's past are her concerns with defining the patterns of her own motherhood and of the limitations on her capacity to care for and support the growth of another human being. As she rethinks the past, she frames her perceptions through such interjections as "I did not know then what I know now" (p. 11) and "What in me demanded that goodness in her?" (p. 12)—gauges taken from the present self to try to assess her own past behavior. But throughout, she is assessing the larger pattern of interaction between her own needs and constraints and her daughter's needs and constraints. When she defines the hostilities between Emily and her sister Susan—"that terrible balancing of hurts and needs" (p. 16)—she asserts her own recognition not only of an extreme sibling rivalry but also of the inevitable conflict in the separate self-definitions of parent and child. Gauging the hurts and needs of one human being against the hurts and needs of another: this is the pattern of parenthood. But more, it is the pattern of a responsible self living in relationship.

The story's immediate reality continually opens onto such larger patterns of human awareness. Ostensibly an answer to the school counselor, the mother's interior monologue becomes a meditation on human existence, on the interplay among external contingencies, individual needs, and individual responsibilities. The narrative structure creates a powerful sense of immediacy and an unfamiliar literary experience. But it also generates a unique capacity for metaphorical insight into the knowledge that each individual—like both the mother and the daughter—can act only from the context of immediate personal limitations but must nonetheless act through a sense of individual responsibility.

The narrator sets the context for this general concern by first defining the separateness of mother and daughter: "You think because I am her mother I have a key, or that in some way you could use me as a key? She has lived for nineteen years. There is all that life that has happened outside of me, beyond me" (p. 9). Almost defensively, she cites too the difficulties of finding time and being always—as mothers are—susceptible to interruption. But in identifying an even greater difficulty in the focus of her parental responsibility, she highlights the thematic concern with guilt and responsibility: "Or I will become engulfed with all I did or did not do, with what should have been and what cannot be helped" (p. 9). She is, in other words, setting out to assess her own responsibility, her own failure, and finally her need to reaffirm her own autonomy as a separate human being who cannot be defined solely through her parental role.

When she identifies the patterns of isolation and alienation between herself and her daughter, she is further probing the awareness of her own separateness and the implicit separation between any two selfhoods. The convalescent home to which she sent Emily as a child is premised on establishing an "invisible wall" between visiting parents and their children on the balconies above (p. 14). But, in fact, that wall is only an extreme instance of an inevitable separateness, of all the life that is lived "outside of me, beyond me" (p. 9). Even in her memory of deeply caring conversations with her daughter, the mother can only claim to provide an occasional external eye, a person who can begin to narrate for the daughter the continuity of the daughter's own past and emergent selfhood but who must stand outside that selfhood separated by her own experiences and her own needs.

In Emily's concern with her physical appearance we can see, distilled, the limitations of a parent's capacity to foster a child's growth in selfhood and finally of the possibilities of any full bridging of human separateness. Emily insists on being told "over and over how beautiful she had been—and would be, I would tell her—and was now, to the seeing eye. But the seeing eyes were few or non-existent. Including mine" (p. 10). The particular poignancy in Emily's own circumstances and needs does not lessen the power of the general insight: a human being cannot rely on the perpetual presence of external seeing eyes to validate her own authenticity as a separate self. Emily, feeling her isolation, and Emily's mother, feeling helpless to overcome her daughter's painful alienation, together give us a powerful lens on the vulnerability to external perceptions of selfhood: "the unsureness, the having to be conscious of words before you speak, the constant caring—what are they thinking of me? . . . " (p. 17). Consequently, Emily's achievement of external validation as a gifted performer of pantomime cannot be expected to overcome her isolation: "Now suddenly she was Somebody, and as imprisoned in her difference as she had been in anonymity" (p. 19). And in watching her daughter's moving performance, the mother herself had confronted a new consciousness of separateness as she lost her sense of recognition for her own daughter: "Was this Emily?" (p. 19).

One of the central defining premises for the working out of separate personal identity for both mother and daughter is the power of cultural circumstances. The narrative is laced with references to the depression, the war, the survival needs which dictate unsatisfactory child care arrangements and equally unsatisfactory work circumstances. Even the dictates of pediatric treatises on breast-feeding by the decree of the clock (p. 10) become a part of the general cultural pressure which operates to define and limit the power of individual choice. Over and over, we are told of the limitations on choice—"it was the only way" (p. 11); "They persuaded me" (p. 13)—and verbs of necessity recur for descriptions of both the mother's and Emily's behavior. In the attempt at summing up, the mother concludes: "She kept too much in herself, her life was such she had to keep too much in herself. My wisdom came too late. She has much to her and probably little will come of it. She is a child of her age, of depression, of war, of fear" (p. 20).

In such statements as "my wisdom came too late," the story verges on becoming an analysis of parental guilt. But though the mother expresses frequent regret for her own past limitations and failings, she is not at all insisting on guilty self-laceration. Rather she is searching for an honest assessment of past behavior and its consequences and for an accurate understanding of the role of cultural necessity which nonetheless allows for individual responsibility. She recognizes that there are some questions "for which there is no answer" (p. 16) and some causal relationships which cannot be deciphered: "Why do I put that first? I do not even know if it matters, or if it explains anything" (p. 10). At the same time, she insists upon the power and significance of her own actions within those limiting circumstances: that, of course, is the premise for the whole narrative reconstruction of the past through the self-awareness founded in present knowledge.

This claim to her own self-validation remains primarily a general premise of the story rather than a specific claim at points within the narrative. Her actual absolution—to the extent that she is seeking absolution from parental guilt—does not come in the particular recognition of past success or failure. Rather it comes in the growing emphasis upon Emily's separateness and Emily's right to make her own imprint upon the world in which she lives. The narrative's first interruption by immediate maternal necessity—the crying of the younger brother with wet diapers—marks the beginning of a clearer resistance to the forces of external necessities through this acceptance of Emily's separate selfhood. As Ronnie says "Shoogily," the family word for comfort which originated with Emily, the mother recognizes the impact of Emily's presence and personhood: "In this and other ways she leaves her seal" (p. 18). The narrative then moves quickly into the identification of Emily's own special talent in pantomime and the balancing of external necessity, parental responsibility, and the assumption of Emily's own ultimate self-responsibility: "You ought to do something about her with a gift like that—but without money or knowing how, what does one do? We have left it all to her, and the gift has as often eddied inside, clogged and clotted, as [sic] been used and growing" (p. 19). Consequently, the second interruption—in Emily's own return from school—reaches toward the story's tenuous resolution in relinquishing the claim to controlling her daughter's destiny; the mother returns to her private monologue/dialogue, thinking: "She is so lovely. Why did you want me to come in at all? Why were you so concerned? She will find her way." (p. 20).

The tension in Emily's personality—which has continually been defined as light and glimmering yet rigid and withheld—comes to a final focus in the self-mocking humor of her allusion to the most powerful cultural constraint on human behavior: nothing individual matters because "in a couple years we'll all be atom-dead" (p. 20). But Emily does not, in fact, succumb to that despairing view; rather she is asserting her own right to choice as she lightly claims her wish to sleep late in the morning. Though the mother feels more heavily the horror of this judgment, she feels its weight most clearly in relation to the complexity of individual personhood and responsibility: "because I have been dredging the past, and all that compounds a human being is so heavy and meaningful in me, I cannot endure it tonight" (p. 20). And when she goes on from her despairing inability to "total it all" to the story's conclusion, she recenters her thoughts on the tenuous balance between the powerful cultural constraints and the need to affirm the autonomy of the self in the face of those constraints: "Let her be. So all that is in her will not bloom—but in how many does it? There is still enough left to live by. Only help her to know—help make it so there is cause for her to know—that she is more than this dress on the ironing board, helpless before the iron" (p. 21).

Her efforts, then, "to gather together, to try and make coherent" (p. 18) are both inevitably doomed to failure and finally successful. There cannot be—either for parent or for story-teller—a final coherence, a final access to defined personality, or a full sense of individual control. There is only the enriched understanding of the separateness of all people—even parents from children—and the necessity to perceive and foster the value of each person's autonomous selfhood. Though that selfhood is always limited by the forces of external constraints, it is nonetheless defined and activated by the recognition of the "seal" each person sets on surrounding people and the acceptance of responsibility for one's own actions and capacities. At best, we can share in the efforts to resist the fatalism of life lived helplessly "before the iron"—never denying the power of the iron but never yielding to the iron in final helplessness either. We must trust the power of each to "find her way" even in the face of powerful external constraints on individual control.

The metaphor of the iron and the rhythm of the ironing establish a tightly coherent framework for the narrative probing of a mother-daughter relationship. But the fuller metaphorical structure of the story lies in the expansion of the metaphorical power of that relationship itself. Without ever relinquishing the immediate reality of motherhood and the probing of parental responsibility, Tillie Olsen has taken that reality and developed its peculiar complexity into a powerful and complex statement on the experience of responsible selfhood in the modern world. In doing so she has neither trivialized nor romanticized the experience of motherhood; she has indicated the wealth of experience yet to be explored in the narrative possibilities of experiences, like motherhood, which have rarely been granted serious literary consideration.

Olsen's "O Yes": Alva's Vision as Childbirth Account*

Naomi M. Jacobs

A passage in Tillie Olsen's "O Yes" contains imagery which had long puzzled me. Alva, a black working woman with three children, is remembering the dream-vision she had when, an abandoned fifteen-year-old, she was pregnant with her first child:

> . . . waiting there in the clinic and maybe sleeping, a voice called: Alva, Alva. So mournful and so sweet: Alva. Fear Not, I have loved you from the foundation of the universe. And a little small child tugged on my dress. He was carrying a parade stick, on the end of it a star that outshined the sun. Follow me, he said. And the real sun went down and he hidden his stick. How dark it was, how dark. I could feel the darkness with my hands. And when I could see, I screamed. Dump trucks run, dumping bodies in hell, and a convey line run, never ceasing with souls, weary ones having to stamp and shove them along, and the air like fire. Oh I never want to hear such screaming. Then the little child jumped on a motorbike making a path no bigger than my little finger. But first he greased my feet with the hands of my momma when I was a knee baby. They shined like the sun was on them. Eyes he placed all around my head, and as I journeyed upward after him, it seemed I heard a mourning: "Mama Mama you must help carry the world." The rise and fall of nations I saw. And the voice called again Alva, Alva, and I flew into a world of light, multitudes singing, Free, free, I am so glad.[1]

Of course, in the context of a story which includes a lengthy description of a Black church service, the "little small child" must be read at one level as the infant Jesus, though hardly the Jesus of conventional religious iconography, and the passage can be seen simply as a Christian vision of hell and salvation. But many specific details—particularly the recurrent emphasis on mothers and children—are inadequately accounted for by this reading.

The passage was recently clarified for me by several women students who have had children. Independently of each other, they had read the passage as a description of the physical and psychological experience of childbirth. The "screaming" is that of Alva and the other women in labor in this charity clinic; the "weary ones" are doctors and nurses too exhausted to do more than "shove them along." The "Eyes all around" Alva's head are the hot, bright lights of the delivery room, making her feet shine "like the sun was upon them." Alva's descent into hell is a first-

* Reprinted from *Notes on Contemporary Literature* 16.1 (Jan. 1986): 7-8.

time mother's experience of abandonment, disorientation and fear from which she is delivered by a "little child" who makes a path "no bigger than my little finger," the almost impossibly narrow path that is made and traveled by a child being born.

Based on their own experiences, my students saw the rather confusing tonal and perspectival shifts in the passage to be evidence of Alva's confusion of her own identity with that of her child and that of her mother. It is Alva herself, the abandoned teenager, who sees the clinic as a hellish "convey line" that never ceases to produce children damned to poverty and prejudice from the moment of their births in this human dumping ground. But Alva simultaneously is the child trying to be born, trapped in the claustrophobic darkness of the womb, a darkness that can be felt with the hands; sped on her way by the hands of her own mother, the mother of her infancy, she reverts to that infancy in this ordeal and journeys, as a child, with her child into a world of light, freedom, and gladness. At the same time, Alva becomes her mother, who survived childbirth, who tended and loved Alva, and who now brings to Alva the strength she will need to do the same. When that anonymous and intimate call, "Mama Mama," comes, it is at once a call from Alva the frightened girl-mother seeking help from her mother; a call from Alva's birthing baby to Alva; and a call from all sorrowing children in the world to their mothers, all mothers. As she is delivered of her child, the voice calls her by name, and she returns to her own separate identity; yet she brings with her a new knowledge of the responsibilities she must bear, not only to her children but to the whole world.

The story is many things, including an eloquent account of the effects of racial bias and the functions of religious ecstasy, but it is also, like much of Olsen's work, an inquiry into what she has elsewhere called "comprehensions possible out of motherhood"[2]:comprehensions of the ways in which our connections to other people are as painful, inexorable, and rewarding as the biological processes which compel a woman to complete the terrifying and ecstatic experience of giving birth.

NOTES

1. Tillie Olsen, "O Yes," in *Tell Me a Riddle* (1961; rpt. New York: Dell, 1981), p. 61.

2. Tillie Olsen, *Silences* (New York: Delacorte Press/Seymour Lawrence, 1978), p. 202.

Polar Stars, Pyramids, and "Tell Me A Riddle"*

Edward L. Niehus and Teresa Jackson

Much of the obscurity of Tillie Olsen's "Tell Me A Riddle" arises from the difficulty in understanding the motives and attitudes of Eva, the dying woman. This difficulty results not only from her general incommunicativeness but increasingly from her delirium as she nears death. As she shifts in and out of consciousness and rationality, her train of thought often seems random and discontinuous. Fragmented memories from her past spring up as she searches for a way of understanding and expressing the riddles of life and death as she has experienced them. Memories of her revolutionary youth in Russia filter back into consciousness and details of her year of exile in Siberia are revealed. One traumatic incident appears to be of particular importance in understanding Eva and her ideas.

Speaking to her son and his wife, Eva explains that their daughter is reminiscent of her childhood friend and mentor:

> In a half-whisper: "Like Lisa she is, your Jeannie. Have I told you of Lisa, she who taught me to read? Of the highborn she was, but noble in herself. I was sixteen; they beat me; my father beat me so I would not go to her. It was forbidden, she was a Tolstoyan. At night, past dogs that howled, terrible dogs, my son, in the snows of winter to the road, I to ride in her carriage like a lady, to books. To her, life was holy, knowledge was holy, and she taught me to read. They hung her. Everything that happens one must try to understand why. She killed one who betrayed many. Because of betrayal, betrayed all she lived and believed. In one minute she killed, before my eyes (there is so much blood in a human being, my son), in prison with me. All that happens, one must try to understand."[1]

At this point in what seems to be a crucial statement, Eva's mind takes an apparently random, irrational leap, and she begins to babble about Egyptian tombs and astronomy:

> "The name?" Her lips would work. "The name that was their pole star; the doors of the death houses fixed to open on it; I read of it my year of penal servitude. Thuban!" very excited, "Thuban, in ancient Egypt the pole star. Can you see, look out to see it, Jeannie, if it swings around *our* pole star that seems to *us* not to move."

* Reprinted from *ANQ* 24 (Jan./Feb. 1986): 77-83.

This may seem to be the cryptic and irrelevant meandering of a disoriented mind, but some basic astronomy and late nineteenth century pyramidology can clarify the passage and may help to reveal its significance to the preceding paragraph and the story as a whole.

II

Thuban, also known as Alpha Draconis, is one of the brightest stars in the constellation Draco (the Dragon) which winds its way between the Big and Little Dippers in the northern sky of the northern hemisphere. It is one of the circumpolar stars, so-called because as seen from the northern temperate zone they rotate around the north celestial pole without ever sinking beneath the horizon. The celestial poles are those points where a line drawn through the north-south axis of the earth would seem to intersect the heavens. At present the north celestial pole is most nearly marked by Polaris, The North Star, which therefore seems to be a fixed, unchanging marker around which the rest of the heavens revolve. In fact, Polaris is about one degree from the true pole, and five thousand years ago it was Thuban which appeared motionless while the rest of the stars, including Polaris, revolved around it.

The cause of this remarkable alteration in the apparently eternal guiding light of the heavens is a phenomenon known as the precession of the equinoxes. Three earthly cycles alter our visions of the skies. Two, the daily rotation on the earth's axis and the annual rotation around the sun, are brief enough to be recognizable and familiar in their effects. But precession, the third movement in the "celestial ballet," is "so slow that it is scarcely perceptible during a human lifetime."[2] The precessional cycle is completed over 25,700 years, a period known as the "Platonic" or "great" year.

Precession is caused by a slight shifting in the earth's axis as the earth rotates around it. This shifting of the axis might be compared to the motion of an unsupported gyroscope or to the wobble of an imperfectly balanced top. In the earth's case the wobble is the result of a slight bulge around the equator. Like the tip of the gyroscope or the top, the pole of the earth's axis moves in a very slow circle even as the earth itself continues to rotate with relative speed.[3]

By imagining the earth's axis extending upward we can visualize the north celestial pole moving ever so slowly through the northern sky, approaching and passing a series of stars, each of which in turn would seem to be a fixed center and point of reference for generations of earthdwellers in the northern hemisphere. Astronomers can track the progress of the pole, naming past and future pole stars and predicting the recurrence of each star's tour of duty as guiding light every 25,700 years (Figure 1).[4]

During the third millenium B. C. when the pyramids were being built, Thuban would have been perceived as the pole star. One astronomer even suggests that "Thuban was much closer to the true pole of the heavens than Polaris is at the present time, and for that reason must have seemed an absolutely fixed centre round which all other stars revolved."[5] Although the full extent and sophistication of ancient astronomy is still hotly debated, it has long been recognized that some ancient civilizations observed very closely the related movements of the sun, moon, and stars, the dependability of their cycles providing the bases for essential measurements of time and space.

Rumors have descended from the Greeks and medieval Arabs that the Egyptian pyramids had been used as observatories.[6] But it was only during the nineteenth century that professional and amateur investigators begin to link the orientation and inner construction of the pyramids, espe-

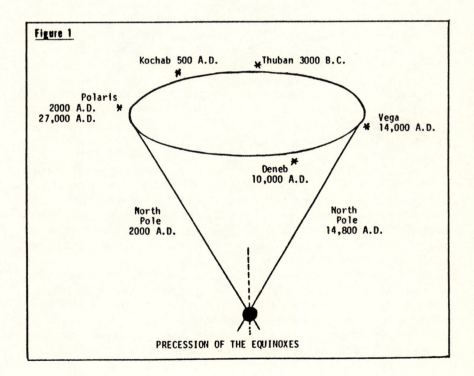

Figure 1

Kochab 500 A.D.

Thuban 3000 B.C.

Polaris
2000 A.D.
27,000 A.D.

Vega
14,000 A.D.

Deneb
10,000 A.D.

North
Pole
2000 A.D.

North
Pole
14,800 A.D.

PRECESSION OF THE EQUINOXES

cially the Great Pyramid, with the configuration of the heavens as they appeared to those who built the enormous tombs. In 1798 the French savants accompanying Napoleon's troops into Egypt determined that the Great Pyramid was accurately oriented to the cardinal points of the compass. One of these scholars even speculated that from the bottom of the long passage descending from the entrance on the north face, 'the [sic] ancients might have been able to see the transit across the meridian of some circumpolar star, and thus have previously established true north and correctly oriented the building."[7] Becoming intrigued by this possibility during his explorations of the pyramid in 1837-38, the British colonel Richard Howard-Vyse made inquiries of the astronomer Sir John Herschel. Herschel informed him that the angle of the passage would have allowed a small patch of sky just below the celestial pole to be seen, but Thuban and not Polaris would have been visible in that location at around 3400 B. C. and again around 2200 B. C. (Figure 2).

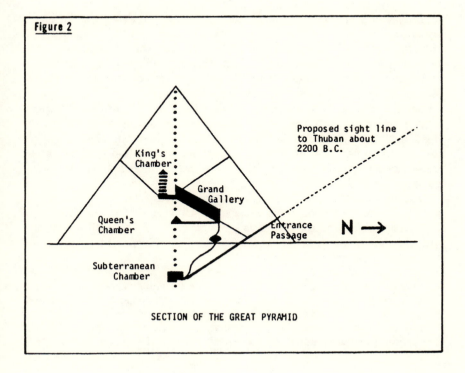

Figure 2

Proposed sight line to Thuban about 2200 B.C.

King's Chamber

Grand Gallery

Queen's Chamber

Entrance Passage

N →

Subterranean Chamber

SECTION OF THE GREAT PYRAMID

Building on this suggestion and some mathematically based religious theories of John Taylor *(The Great Pyramid: Why Was It Built & Who Built It* [London, 1959]), Charles Piazzi Smyth, Astronomer Royal for Scotland, developed fantastically elaborate theories about the scientifically sophisticated and divinely inspired nature of the Great Pyramid. When they were published in London in 1864 as *Our Inheritance in the Great Pyramid,* Smyth's ideas stirred so much interest and controversy that four expanding editions were called for by 1880. The next few decades were to see such a rush of speculative pyramidology that by the turn of the century, when the imprisoned Eva read about Thuban and the death houses,

> a veritable army of eccentrics, romantics, visionaries and frauds were swarming over [the Great Pyramid's] stone tiers with tape measures and copybooks, checking, measuring, and discovering everything from the chronology of the Old Testament to prophecies of a new world order.[8]

Among the outpouring of material on Egyptian astronomy at this time, there were two books worth mentioning as possible influences on the ideas Eva was picking up in her reading. Richard A. Proctor's *The Great Pyramid: Observatory, Tomb, and Temple* (London, 1883) suggests that the structure of the pyramid was such that when the entrance door was open Thuban would have shown down the descending passage and been reflected in a pool of water where it could have been observed by someone sitting in the King's chamber at the end of the ascending passage. A somewhat more substantial and less sensational linking of the Egyptians' astronomy with their religious and funereal practices appeared in Sir Joseph N. Lockyer's *The Dawn of Astronomy* (London, 1894). Lockyer attempted to demonstrate that not only the pyramids but many of the other Egyptian tombs and temples were situated and constructed to serve as astronomical observatories or almanacs.

Although many of these nineteenth century theories about the pyramids are now considered little more than the curious offspring of mysticism and pseudoscience, Eva's basic idea that the death houses are linked to one of the circumpolar stars is still generally accepted. According to the Egyptologist A. J. Spencer,

> One of the earliest beliefs contained in the Pyramid Texts states that the king would become on [sic] of the circumpolar stars, regarded as a symbol of performance because they are never seen to set when viewed from Egypt. The stellar concept of the afterlife probably accounts for the location of the earliest pyramid temples on the north side of the Third Dynasty step

pyramids, and . . . certainly determined the orientation of the entrances toward the north in all pyramids of the Old Kingdom.[9]

III

Eva's transition from her memory of Lisa to her recollection of the pyramids and pole stars turns out to be a natural process of association. Both memories are linked in time and place of origin and both deal with the mystery of death which inevitably preoccupies a dying woman. In her last days, as Eva tries to understand her own life and death, her mind drifts through the past examining the riddles of other deaths: her son and millions like him who have died because of humankind's cruelty and stupidity, her mother and grandmother who at Jeannie's age had already buried children, the idealists and revolutionaries whose visions have never been realized, and on back through the centuries to the Egyptians who confidently built for eternity but whose tombs were soon plundered and whose civilization is long dead. Betrayal, suffering, failure seem to suffuse the history of the race, and yet the dance of life goes on with ever renewed faith, endurance, and creativity: Eva clings to her belief that life is holy, that it "may be hated or wearied of, but never despised." All humanity—past, present, and future—share in the struggle to endure and prevail. For the Egyptians, for Lisa, for Eva, and for Jeannie the riddles and paradoxes of the human experience are essentially the same, and we must go on trying to understand our place and responsibility in the history and the future of the human community.

This need to understand, emphasized in the passage about Lisa and a persistent theme in all of Olsen's works, is linked to the concept of the pole stars. For the naive and idealistic Eva, Lisa had probably appeared to be what Thuban had seemed to the Egyptians, a fixed and dependable guide through the voyages of life and death, an unquestioned and absolute truth among the riddles of existence. When Lisa "betrayed all she lived and believed," the shock of disillusionment for the youthful Eva must have seemed comparable to the discovery that something as apparently fixed and eternal as the pole star could be subject to change. The older Eva expressed the necessity of trying to understand the circumstances, pressures, and weaknesses which make it so difficult for any human beings to develop their full potential or to be true to their highest ideals. All of us betray and are betrayed; we must try to understand and keep faith.

The center or pole of an individual's or a society's life may seem fixed and clear, but life is never so simple for Olsen. Circumstances change, necessity intrudes, the demands of self, family, and society conflict. As Eva has painfully learned, one goal or potential must be neglected in order to pursue another, one need denied in order to satisfy another. Every gain entails some loss. Olsen presents a vision of human life which is filled with complex riddles, with the paradoxes of suffering and joy, of frustration and fulfillment, and then she demands of her characters and readers: "All that happens, one must try to understand."

When Eva asks Jeannie to see if Thuban "swings around *our* pole star that seems to *us* not to move," her emphasis points to an important aspect of the need to understand. Throughout "Tell Me A Riddle," as in her other writings, Olsen is concerned with narrow or egocentric visions which result in distorted or limited perceptions of truth and reality. It is all too easy for individuals, groups, and generations to see the world only in terms of their own experience and self-interest. Conditioned perceptions or transient situations are too readily assumed to reflect universal and permanent truths. For Olsen, it is essential that we escape the insular and relativistic attitudes which blind us to the significance of the past and the reality of other people. Only by coming to know and understand the past can we possess its heritage, preserving its virtues and avoiding its errors. Only by trying to understand other people, past and present, in terms of their own experience and reality can we see them as more than the roles defined by our own needs and expectations.

By realizing the limitations, prejudices, and relativism of our own perspectives, we may be able to understand that which seems alien, different, repugnant. We may be able to see beyond appearance to reality, and perhaps even beyond what is to what might be. History and circumstances create barriers of time, culture, and opportunity, of class, sex, and race. These barriers can only be transcended when we see beyond the superficial differences and conflicts of humanity to its shared needs, goals, and fate. In order to do this we must escape the egocentric, ethnocentric, and anthropocentric blinders which prevent us from questioning those transient circumstances and misunderstood realities which we, like the Egyptians, too readily presume are fixed and eternal truths.

NOTES

1. Tillie Olsen, "Tell Me A Riddle" in *Tell Me A Riddle* (New York: Dell, [1971]), pp. 103-04. All quotations from the story come from these two pages.

2. Harry L. Shipman, *The Restless Universe* (Boston: Houghton Mifflin, 1978), p. 50.

3. Stephen Ionides and Margaret Ionides, *Stars and Men* (New York: Bobbs-Merrill, 1939), p. 238.

4. Shipman, p. 50.

5. Mary Proctor, *Evenings with the Stars* (London: Cassell, 1924), pp. 22-23.

6. See Colin Wilson, *Starseekers* (Garden City, NY: Doubleday, 1980), p. 47, and Peter Lancaster Brown, *Megaliths and Masterminds* (New York: Scribner, 1979), p. 175.

7. Peter Tompkins, *Secrets of the Great Pyramid* (New York: Harper & Row, 1971), pp. 46-47.

8. James Cornell, *The First Stargazers* (New York: Scribner, 1981), pp. 106-07.

9. A. J. Spencer, *Death in Ancient Egypt* (Harmondsworth, England: Penguin, 1982), p. 140.

Tillie Olsen: The Writer as a Jewish Woman[*]

Bonnie Lyons

That Tillie Olsen's work is radically perfectibilistic in spirit and vision is obvious to most of her readers. Less obvious is that the two principal sources of that vision derive directly from her experience as a Jew and as a woman.

What is most deeply Jewish in Olsen is the secular messianic utopianism she inherited from her immigrant parents. That is, her political and social ideology directly reflects the radical Jewish background in which she grew up. But while her Jewish background provides a foundation for Olsen's basic political vision, it would be a mistake to view Jewishness itself as the living core, either in theme or imagery, of her work. Her experience as a woman is much more central, and is especially noticeable in her patterns of imagery. From the weak propagandistic early poetry to the great "Tell Me a Riddle," Olsen repeatedly emphasizes the human body and the mother/child relationship, aspects of human experience strongly identified with the female.

This is not to suggest that Olsen's explicit "femaleness" makes her work restricted in scope or marginal. Her habitual focus on the body does not suggest, for example, that the human is *merely* a body. On the contrary she grounds the spiritual *in* the body in very concrete and physical terms, emphatically insisting on the wholeness of the human. For Olsen the physical body makes the spiritual condition manifest: disfigurement, mutilation, and especially starvation are body images or ideas employed repeatedly to reflect both self-estrangement and estrangement from the world. Generally, hunger, eating, and feeding (nurturing) are the pivotal experiences that directly link the mother/child relationship on the one hand to the Jewish radical political vision on the other.

Olsen's vision lies between the Realist emphasis on victimization and the puniness of the individual, and the over-optimistic emphasis on the sheer human potentiality of some of the Romantics. In Olsen, human beings experience ravening hungers of all kinds: physical, emotional, intellectual, spiritual. But when these hungers are fed, the individuals develop their potential and give to others and to the world at large: fulfilled people are productive and nurturing in turn. In Olsen's view the deepest human hunger is to be fruitful, so human beings satisfy their own needs best by giving. The negative conclusions of the Rousseauvian view are likewise drawn: those who are prevented by circumstances from

[*] Reprinted from *Studies in Jewish American Literature* 5 (1986): 89-102.

developing their productive and nurturing natures will be inclined in turn to become victimizers and stultifiers of others.

The Rousseauvian dimension of Olsen's work is most obviously demonstrated by the fact that in each of her fictions there is a child at or near the center of the story. The child poetically embodies mankind's two dominant characteristics: potential and hunger. Moreover, since she sees each individual human life and all human life in general as parallel journeys toward greater consciousness, what happens to the child is emblematic of the condition and fate of humankind.

Since for Olsen the deepest human hunger is to be fruitful, mothering, in its ideal form, is an example of intense fulfillment. It is also a source of knowledge. Through the experience, the mother discovers human potential and all the forces that operate to limit it; she comes to see human beings as born with enormous possibilities for joy, growth, and productivity which are unnaturally thwarted through class, age, sex and race prejudice.

What is implicit about nurturing and motherhood in her fiction is made explicit in *Silences*, where she insists on the "comprehensions possible out of motherhood" and specifies that these comprehensions include *"the very nature, needs, illimitable potentiality of the human being—and the everyday means by which these are distorted, discouraged, limited, extinguished."*[1] Moreover, Olsen asserts that because motherhood is a neglected theme in literature (neglected because mothers are not usually able to become writers), these comprehensions have not yet "come to powerful, undeniable, useful expression." Thus there are "aspects and understandings of human life as yet largely absent in literature." Olsen's own fiction is itself an attempt to redeem that "loss in literature."

The next section of this essay will explore what is Jewish in Olsen's work, the following two will focus on what is female: first, her treatment of the body and second, the mother/child relationship both as fact and metaphor. Tillie Olsen has said "What is Yiddish in me. . . is inextricable from what is woman in me, from woman who is mother."[2] The concluding section will suggest the accuracy of that self-analysis.

II
"Still Eva Believed and Still I Believe"

Olsen's Jewishness is a thorny subject. Because her mother was a non-Jew, for Orthodox Jews Olsen is not, in fact, Jewish. Moreover, Olsen considers herself an atheist and proudly describes her father as "incorruptibly atheist to the last day of his life." Nonetheless, Olsen considers herself a Jewish atheist, and "Tell Me a Riddle," her greatest fiction, is also one of the finest works of American Jewish literature.

Olsen hardly affirms all things Jewish. She looks at traditional Judaism as having served a useful purpose in the past by providing a sense of solidarity and strength, a refuge in a terrible world of oppression. But for all its positive effects, traditional Judaism for Olsen is inextricably linked with much that is negative or limiting: superstition, patriarchy, parochialialsm [sic], and an enclosed, static life which reinforced life-stifling traditions as the price of security and continuity.

In an interview, Olsen recently remarked, "I still remain with the kind of *Yiddishkeit* I grew up with."[3] By this she refers to her Jewish socialist background. According to her, that background fostered two essential insights. First, "knowledge and experience of injustice, of discrimination, of oppression, of genocide and of the need to act against them forever and whenever they appear." And second, an "absolute belief in the potentiality of human beings."[4]

Olsen's vision of the world parallels Eva's in "Tell Me a Riddle," and Eva is on the one hand a spiritual portrait of the artist as an old woman and, on the other a wonderfully moving evocation of a segment of the Jewish community. That is, even Eva's insistence "Race, human; religion, none," is a not atypical Jewish response.[5]

Olsen has said that she began "Tell Me a Riddle" in order to "celebrate a generation of revolutionaries," and her portrait of Eva and David is indeed a celebration of fervent Jewish revolutionaries during the early years of the century and of a time of boundless hopes and richly humanist fervor. These Jewish socialists, whom Irving Howe also celebrates in *World of Our Fathers,* were dedicated to building a new society, a world-wide international community in which all human beings "would live without want in freedom and fulfillment."[6] Theirs was a socialism that was more than political and economic; it was founded on a profound idealism, an idea of human liberation and secular utopia. Opposed to traditional Judaism, socialist Jews transferred messianism, one of the traditional elements of Jewish experience, to secular dreams.

"Tell Me a Riddle" then is a deeply Jewish story. The Yiddish-inflected speech and "old country curses" are obviously of Jewish origin. David's ideal, to retire in dignity and community to his workers' haven evokes memories of Jewish Workmen's Circles. Even the bait with which David unsuccessfully tempts Eva to the home is particularly Jewish; he tells her there is a reading circle which studies Chekhov and Peretz, a Russian and a Jewish author united by their understanding and love of the ordinary person, of basic, unimproved humanity.

Through Eva, Olsen makes her clearest fictional statement about traditional Judaism. When one of her children tells Eva that the hospital puts patients on lists so that "men of God may visit those of their religion" and that she is on the Jewish list, Eva responds: "Not for rabbis" (p. 80). It is not that Eva denies being Jewish but that she refuses the religious views and consolation of the rabbis.

When asked by her daughter Hannah to light the Sabbath candles, Eva refuses and accuses Hannah of doing it for ignoble reasons: "Not for pleasure she does it. For emptiness. Because his [her husband's] family does. Because all around her do" (p. 86). She calls Hannah's heritage and tradition "superstition! From the savages afraid of the dark, of themselves: mumbo words and magic lights to scare away ghosts" (p. 81). Eva's dismissive attitude toward ritual parallels that of her "real life" contemporaries: in the early years of the century young Jewish radicals held costume balls on Yom Kippur to flaunt their separation from a "benighted" past. What infuriates Eva most is Hannah's nostalgia for the past. For the forward-looking Eva the past means "dark centuries" when religion stifled women and encouraged the poor to buy candles instead of bread. It was when the poor chosen Jew was "ground under, despised, trembling in cellars" and later a Holocaust victim—"and cremated. And cremated" (p. 81). When her husband David asks whether the terrible victimization of the Jews is the fault of religion, Eva does not answer. But clearly she sees Judaism as a backward religion and has no faith in a God who permits his chosen people to suffer so excruciatingly. Instead of traditional religion she believes Hannah should teach universal humanism: "to smash all ghettos that divide us—not to go back, not to go back" (p. 81).

Eva's undying faith in their youthful messianic hopes, "Their holiest dreams" is the story's vision of a secular utopia. Both the vision and the faith in human possibility mirror Jewish socialism of the early years of the century and Olsen's own abiding *Yiddishkeit*: "*that joyous certainty, that sense of mattering, of moving and being moved, of being one and indivisible with the great of the past, with all that freed, ennobled man*" (p. 113). Although Eva's sacred text is not the Bible but the Book of Martyrs, and Socrates not Moses is her hero, her vision embodies both the messianic hope and universalist worldview of a particular kind of secular Jew.

The complete familiarity with Jewish immigrant culture revealed in "Tell Me a Riddle" is particularly striking because Jewishness barely touches Olsen's other work. In *Yonnondio* it appears and disappears suddenly and briefly. Enroute to a farm after finally escaping from a brutalizing coal mining town, Anna Holbrook momentarily blossoms with memories and plans: "School for the kids, Jim working near her, on the earth, lovely things to keep, brass lamps, bright tablecloths, vines over the doors, and roses twining."[7] Suddenly a memory flashes: "her grand- mother bending in such a twilight over lit candles chanting in an unknown tongue, white bread on the table over a shining white tablecloth and red wine" (pp. 38-39). Elenore Lester has suggested that "the way Anna's Jewishness is injected and then withdrawn without casting some subtle coloration over her, suggests that the author was cauterizing a rich vein of associations which might have worked for her."[8] Since the novel was never completed there is no way of knowing for sure if or how Olsen would have developed this Jewish thread. As is, the very slightness of the Jewish memory functions to keep the Holbrooks a representative American proletarian family and supports the universalizing aspects of the novel. To explore or develop Anna's Jewishness may well have seemed to the young Olsen to risk parochialism and to undermine the one world vision. The word Jewish itself is mentioned as one of many nationalities, neither first nor last: "Na-tion-al-it-ies American Armenian Chinese Croatian. . . Irish French Italian Jewish Lith. . ." (p. 63).

The candle lighting ceremony links *Yonnondia* [sic] with "Tell Me a Riddle." That candle lighting is clearly positive in the early novel and denounced by Eva in the later story superficially suggests a change in Olsen, a deepening disaffection and disavowal of her Jewish roots. But the contexts and function of the scenes differ crucially in the two texts. In *Yonnondio* candle lighting is positive to Anna because her recent past has been so physically and spiritually crippling. Candle lighting in her mind is linked with order and beauty, with home and sweet domesticity. In "Tell Me a Riddle" the candle lighting occurs in the home of Eva's son- in-law, a Jewish doctor. That is, in an affluent, educated home where there is no real need to look back, no need for religion whose purposes have been, in Eva's and Olsen's eyes, outgrown.

"O Yes," the only other Olsen story mentioning Jewishness even obliquely supports this analysis of Olsen's religious attitudes. That story celebrated the Negro church as a place where oppressed Negroes release pent up emotion and "the preaching finding lodgment in their hearts" (p. 51). When her daughter Carol becomes hysterical because of all the intense feeling in the church, Helen thinks of explaining that emotion is *"a characteristic of the religion of all oppressed peoples, yes your very own great-grandparents"* (p. 60). Traditional religion as a resource, a rock for oppressed people is affirmed, but only as a stage along the way. This is Olsen's overt message. Interestingly, however, at the end of "O Yes" Helen is unable to explain the cruelty and suffering of the world to Carol and feels her own emptiness: "her own need leapt and plunged for the place of strength that was not" (p. 62). What Helen is missing is the warmth and comfort of the church "where one could scream or sorrow while all knew and accepted, and gloved and loving hands waited to support and understand." The Negro church and the religion of their grandparents seem equally impossible solutions.

III
"We are the injured body"

A section of *Silences* ends with the words, *"We are the injured body. Let us not desert one another"* (p. 176). Throughout her work Olsen expresses the ways people are psychologically as well as physically thwarted and diminished through bodily images. In her earliest, rather obvious polemical poetry, she denounces capitalist exploitation by envisioning the effects on the workers' bodies. Here the body, standing for the whole self, is destroyed in various ways; in particular, the poor workers' bodies are *consumed* by the rich.

In "I Want You Women Up North to Know," the seamstresses' bodies are stitched into the garments bought by the wealthy.[9] The dainty dresses that the poor women sew are "dyed in blood," stitched in wasting flesh; "bodies shrivel" in "parching heat." Skeletons and starved children abound. Parallel examples of exploitation and bodily disfigurement and consumption are portrayed: women reduced to prostitution and venereal disease, and an injured male worker "remembering a leg, and twenty-five years cut off from his life by the railroad." Didactic and simplistic, the early poems divide the world into innocent victims whose bodies are eaten, and wicked victimizers with fat, bloated bodies.

The novel *Yonnondio*, also begun in the thirties, evokes a similar vision of the world and employs similar body imagery. In the first chapter the nameless narrator mourns the waste of a young boy's life as he enters the coal mines and contrasts the "skeletons of starved children" with the "fat bellies" of the capitalists (p. 14). Later in the novel when the Holbrook family loses their farm despite their unceasing work, the politicians are seen as vultures, and the father, Jim Holbrook, says that the banks "batten on us like hogs" (p. 51).

Olsen also uses two body images to integrate major sections of the novel and to establish parallels and contrasts between the two sections. The opening section (part of which was first published under the title "The Iron Throat") is dominated by an image of the mine as the "earth's intestines," as a place where the earth "sucks you in" (pp. 13-14).[10] The climax of the terror comes when an insane miner (a victim turned into a crazed victimizer) attempts to throw a child, Mazie Holbrook, into the mine: the miner imagines the mine as a ravenous woman "hungry for a child" to devour (p. 20). The very fact that the miner sees woman as devourer rather than nurturer demonstrates the extremity of his condition, a result of the economic and social conditions in general.

The third major section of *Yonnondio,* like the opening one, is dominated by a nightmare body image: the packing house is a monstrous heart, which, rather than pumping healthy blood, pumps "the men and women who are the streets' lifeblood, nourishing the taverns and brothels and rheumy-eyes stores, bulging out the soiled and exhausted houses, and multiplying into these children playing so mirthlessly in their street yards where flower only lampposts" (p. 60).

In the stories the human condition is not seen in such dichotomous terms—victims and victimizers—but the same body and eating imagery abounds, developed in subtler, more complex ways. In these stories Olsen often uses eating as symbolic of a character's sense of self and world, as the link between the individual and the universe. Eating is a clear indication of a character's psychic state, and healthy eating indicates a sense of total wellbeing, an at-homeness in the universe.

Eating is significant because to eat is to assert and fulfill the claims of the self. Eating also means taking a part of the world, making it part of the self, absorbing part of the world. In Olsen's work the eating process reflects the ultimate mystery of life and death and an awareness that humans kill other living organisms in order to survive. For Olsen the proper response to the plant or animal sacrifice necessary to human life is a kind of reverence or natural piety. Her characters express this natural piety by eating, not to become bloated, but in order to grow and produce and, in turn, nourish others: they eat so that they can feed others.

In "I Stand Here Ironing" the daughter Emily's thinness, her early inability to eat, and her subsequent ravenous appetite all suggests her lack of nourishment on every level. Although the narrator/mother remembers the "sleek" young society women who raise money for an institution where children like Emily wear "gigantic red bows and ravaged looks" (pp. 80-81), it is not just the fat bellies who cause Emily's thinness. Sent to an institution to gain weight by a well-meaning mother and social worker, Emily returns thin and stays thin. As her mother tells it, "'Food sickened her, and I think much of life too'" (p. 7).

Here the problems are not all solvable by eliminating the vultures of the earth. Emily's hunger and subsequent legendary appetite have many causes, including her mother's youth and anxiety, her father's cowardice and withdrawal, her own slowness and darkness in a world that prizes quickness and blondness. Her hunger also has one surprisingly positive effect: out of her despair, expressed by both her early thinness and later insatiable appetite, she develops a gift, the art of comic mimicry. And while the memory of a heartless teacher who belittled Emily for her fear has "curdled" in the mother's memory, the mother refuses to see Emily as doomed or as passive victim—a dress "helpless before the iron" (p. 12).

"Hey Sailor, What Ship?" also interweaves body and eating imagery into its texture in important ways. Some of the imagery reflects the so-cial/political concerns of the earlier work. For Lennie, Whitey is a tie to *"a world in which men had not eaten each other"* (p. 36). One of the memories Whitey tries to drown in liquor is the time of brotherhood when *"whoever came off the ship fat shared"* (p. 25). Now part of Whitey's problem with authority on the ship stems from his complaint about "rotten feed"—symbolic of the exploitation of the workers.

Whitey's present failing condition is also given digestive terms: he hardly eats, and he drinks not to nourish himself, but to poison himself. The key to his woes also seems bodily: he cannot have sex unless he is drunk. And now he also drinks because there are *"memories to forget, dreams to be stifled, hopes to be murdered"* (p. 34). His body expresses his estrangement from himself and the world; now he has a *"decaying body, the body that was betraying him"* (p. 37). His desperate attempt to connect with Lennie and Helen and their children, who represent not only family but also his memories, his earlier self, and a hopeful future, is symbolized by his attempt to provide and share a meal with them, a communion through shared food.

In "Tell Me a Riddle," the deepest hungers are embodied, hungers of every kind. In Russia, Eva and David experienced physical hunger as well as hunger for learning, for holy knowledge. In America they had hungry children and hungry souls—hungry for beauty, meaning, sense of purpose, and progress. As the story progresses, Eva wastes away, consumed by cancer until the final day when the "agony was perpetual" (p. 115). Still she refuses to give up the dream of fulfilled human life which is embodied in the old Russian revolutionary song she continues to sing. At the climax of the song, which is interrupted by a "long strangling cough," her husband suddenly awakens from his years-long sleep and self-blindness: "Without warning, the bereavement and betrayal he had sheltered . . . revealed itself,/uncoiled,/releases,/*sprung*/ and with it the monstrous shapes of what he had actually happened in the century" (p. 111). His reaction is immediate and "Olsenian": "ravening hunger or thirst seized him" (p. 111).

Despite the bitterness, recriminations, rage, and disappointment, Eva and David and their love finally triumph. On her last night and in

Jeannie's picture they are holding hands: "their hands, his and hers, clasped, feeding each other" (p. 115). The image of love as mutual nourishment, as two people *feeding* each other, is the antithesis of and the "answer" to the earlier vision of a world of eaters and eaten. And this image of mutual nourishment is linked to another: David looks at Jeannie's art, her drawing of Eva and himself "and as if he had been instructed he went to his bed, lay down, holding the sketch (as if it would shield against the monstrous shapes of loss, of betrayal, of death) and with his free hand took hers [Eva's] back into his." Their life, their love, their humanity nourish Jeannie's art, which in turn, nourishes and instructs their life: life and art feed each other.

Silences is about artists' failure to produce because of inadequate nourishment: here Olsen analyzes the multiple causes that produce silence—all the nagging hungers that thwart productivity. The hunger/feeding metaphor is pursued insistently at every level. In the very acknowledgements of the book Olsen mentions earth, air, and others as "sustenance" for her own efforts. The major theme of her long afterword to Rebecca Harding Davis's *Life in the Iron Mills* is Davis's hunger to make use of herself and her powers, her hunger to give and produce. Olsen explores the many kinds of hunger in Davis's life and the lives of her characters, whose miserable circumstances meant soul starvation. As Davis identifies with her characters, so Olsen identifies with Davis, especially her "hunger to know" (p. 53).

Repeatedly Olsen blames unsatisfied hunger for non-productivity. Analyzing Katherine Anne Porter's long delay in finishing *Ship of Fools*, Olsen observes that "subterranean forces" need feeding: "before they will feed the creator back they must be fed, passionately fed" (p. 13). Similarly, Olsen describes the destruction of her own powers as a failure in the necessary mutual feeding of art and life: "'So long they feed each other—my life, the writing —;—the writing or hope of it, my life —; but now they begin to destroy;" (p. 20).

IV
"Mama Mama you must help carry the world"

Mothers and children are at the heart of almost every Olsen work. The child embodies man's potential greatness and his needy vulnerability. The degree to which adults can mother and nurture children is frequently a sign of their own psychic condition. Because the link between the individual family and the family of man everywhere penetrates Olsen's work, her focus on the nuclear family does not seem narrow or claustrophobic.

In *Yonnondio* Olsen repeatedly uses the word "baby" to suggest beauty and tenderness. Mazie feels a breeze as "soft, like the baby laughin'" (p. 12). Gorgeous colors of fire seem to her "like babies' tongues reaching out to you." The healing beauty of the baby-tongued fire melts "the hard swollen lump of tears" into a "swell of wonder and awe" (p. 19). And when the Holbrooks escape from the coalmines, "the sun laid warm hands on their bodies" and "the air was pure and soft like a baby's skin" (p. 34).

Erina, the epileptic, crippled child from an impoverished, brutalized, and brutalizing family, symbolizes the most humiliated, abused humanity: the child or human as innocent sufferer. The horror of Erina's life is most movingly evoked through her linguistic errors. In the author's brilliant use of children's linguistic errors and connections, *Yonnondio* resembles another Thirties novel, Henry Roth's *Call It Sleep*.[11] But while the confusion of Roth's David Schearl about the ordinary coal and the coal which purified Isaiah's lips is central to a redemptive vision, Olsen's two most memorable uses of this technique are unequivocally pathetic. Olsen first uses the technique early in the novel when Mazie confuses the word "operator" with the idea of a surgical operation and cannot understand how the privileged coal operator "cut up a mine" (p. 18). In the reader's mind the error is suggestive, for the coal operator does indeed cut up the land and the miners themselves. The later use of the device is much more chilling. The monstrous distortions of her life have taught Erina, a most Dostoevskian character, to interpret the Biblical line, "suffer the children," as "the children suffer." Erina's twisting of the meaning of the word *suffer* from "allow" into "bear painfully" perfectly embodies Olsen's outraged sense of the world's derangement. It is worth noting that even Erina is not totally reduced to inhumanity. On her way home, "where she will be beaten," she sees a bird "bathing itself, fluttering its wings in delight" (p. 147). Erina feels in herself "the shining, the fluttering happiness" and for a few minutes walks "in the fluttering shining and the peace."

Erina is the novel's deepest and most frightening image of human suffering; Bess, the Holbrook baby, represents human possibility and power. In the midst of an oppressive heat wave, Bess, while playing with a fruit-jar lid, discovers her powers: "Lightning in her brain" (p. 153). the [sic] novel celebrates her coming to consciousness: "Centuries of human drive work in her; human ecstasy of achievement; satisfaction deep and fundamental as sex: *I can do, I use my powers; I! I!*"(p. 153). With her "eternal dream look" (p. 67) Bess is the promise, the possibility.

In "I Stand Here Ironing," the mother speaks of Emily as a tender young plant, bemoans the fact that Emily never had "the soil of easy growth," and concludes that "all that is in her will not bloom" (p. 12). She also remembers Emily's miraculous capacity for learning and delight when she was a baby and trusts that "there is enough left to live by." Similarly, the uncollected story "Requa" suggests that early damage can be overcome, that a hurt, withdrawn child can be reclaimed, that later care can revive a wilting plant.[12]

In "Hey Sailor" Whitey's sense of loss, of his lost past and empty future, is most acute when he touches his friends' children: "It is destroying, dissolving him utterly, this helpless warmth against him, this feel of a child—lost country to him and unattainable" (p. 20). Even more terrible to him is the general horror: "The begging children and the lost, the thieving children and the children who were sold" (p. 21). The relative financial and emotional security of Lennie and Helen's home coupled with their sympathy and moral sense will help to bring their children to fruition, but the reality of other children's lost and wasted lives is not forgotten, never forgiven.

In several of her stories Olsen focuses more on the mother and nurturing process than on the child. In particular, "O Yes" is a story of mothering, especially the moral and emotional aspect. Two women "mother" Carol. Parry's mother Alva tries to teach Carol about the meaning of their release and ecstasy in church, and Helen tries to ease Carol through the *"long baptism into the seas of humankind"* (p. 61). Alva's classic death and rebirth dream-memory embodies several mother/child relationships. A small boy leads Alva on her journey; in order to ascend, Alva needs her own mother's hands, and the final injunction to Alva as mother completes the journey. The child leads the mother whose journey is helped by her own mother and who is enjoined as mother to " 'help carry the world' " (p. 52). Nurturing is thus the road and the rule.

In *Silences* Olsen describes motherhood as both the *"core* of woman's oppression" and her "transport as woman" (p. 202). This dual description of motherhood is most vividly embodied in "Tell Me a Riddle," which brilliantly evokes the complexity and depth of the mother/child relationship, as well as the wisdom and richness that motherhood has brought to this aging mother and grandmother.

Eva looks back at her youthful mothering and remembers the poverty and want, the "old humiliations and terror," and the "endless defeating battles" of housekeeping (pp. 67 and 68). Part of her bitterness is about the poverty, and part is directed at her husband who never thought of her needs, never helped at home, never stayed with the children so that she could have some life outside the home.

But her memory is not just of the chafing limitations but also "the love—the passion of tending" that had "risen with the need like a torrent." Eva has now lived through that period: "the need was done." Unlike more limited, traditional women suffering from the empty nest syndrome, she is sure there is more: "Somewhere an older power that beat for life" (pp. 83 and 84).

Eva is characterized as more than just a biological mother of a large family; she is also a woman concerned since her youth about developing human potential. When she first sees the Pacific Ocean, she looks "toward the shore that nurtured life as it first crawled toward consciousness the millions of years ago" (p. 94). As biological and symbolic mother, Eva looks back at her own family history and at human history, especially the history of life in this century. She sees the revolutionary dreams and the monstrous facts, including millions with "'no graves—save air,'" the holocaust victims (p. 104). As the seashore reminds Eva of the developing human infant, the aged, including her pathetic friend Mrs. Mays, suggest the terrible waste, the incompletion. The unfulfilled aged suggest that the overall direction may not be higher consciousness but rather destruction and self-destruction: "Everywhere unused the life . . . . Century after century still all in us not to grow" (p. 99).

V
"A song, a poem of itself—the word itself a dirge"

Directly, as in the early poetry, and indirectly, as in Eva's dream in "Tell Me a Riddle," Olsen celebrates human potential, mourns what has been lost, and anticipates a time when the world will be changed so that human capacities will not be wasted.

"A song, a poem of itself—the word itself a dirge," these three phrases of Whitman's introductory explanatory note to his poem "Yonnodio [sic]" are emblematic of Olsen's vision and her borrowing of this title for her one and only novel is noteworthy. In Olsen's art, the song and dirge are the poles of human life: the fruit and the blight.

The dirge is not primarily a response to any natural calamity or death. This is clearest in "Tell Me a Riddle." There Eva's excruciating physical decline into death is not the deepest source of pain. In fact, her decision tp [sic] experience her own death—refusing the sterile, painless, numb hospital death—is a personal triumph: she has chosen a death of her own. She stays with her family and experiences everything, including her own terrible physical pain. For her and for the reader, the deepest agony is, on the contrary, the realization of what has died prematurely in her, what through unnatural causes never flowered. For her the dirge laments what has been thwarted by circumstances—primarily poverty but also rigid sex role prescriptions. Even more than the limitations of her own life, Eva and the author mourn Eva's (and mankind's) dream of peace, freedom, education, humaneness: the fulfillment of the individual and a harmonious society. The deepest dread is the either/or that mankind faces—growth and progress or annihilation. Wasted lives, unused potential, and the threat of nuclear holocaust—this is the dirge in Olsen's work.

The song, the other pole, celebrates what mankind can experience and express. It is the possibility, the undying hope, that never totally relinquished dream. It is the part of Olsen that, in *Silences*, after listing the lost and ruined writers and analyzing the multiple causes of the blight, insists, "**AND YET THE TREE DID—DOES BEAR FRUIT**" (p. 258). It is embodied in Eva (with whom Olsen explicitly identifies in *Silences*) who continues to dream, whose continued hope keeps the dream alive and verifies its essential value and possibility: the "stained words" of her youthful dream song, stained by what the century did to kill the dream, "on her working lips came stainless" (p. 112).

Olsen's exploration of the dirge and song of human life reflects her experience as a Jew and as a woman. Her ideology recapitulates the radical Jewish socialist background in which she grew up; her analysis in terms of the body and the mother/child relationship reflect her deeply felt experiences as a woman. Song and dirge alike emerge from the one radical (in the sense of root, fundamental) condition: the single individual in all his vulnerability, hunger, and yearning potentialities. The uncanny bitter-sweet harmonies Olsen has created by interweaving dirge and song, by vividly depicting the sheltering of or preying upon vulnerabilities, the nurturing or starving of hungers, the fulfillment or blighting of potentials—these give her own music its intense emotional resonance, as the song and dirge merge into a luminous, all encompassing chord: "'the poem of itself.'"

NOTES

1. *Silences* (New York: Delacorte Press/Seymour Lawrence, 1978). p. 202.
2. Unpublished Olsen interview with Naomi Rubin conducted in May 1983.
3. Unpublished Rubin interview.
4. Unpublished Rubin interview.
5. "Tell Me a Riddle," in *Tell Me a Riddle* (New York: Delta/Dell, 1961), p. 80. All subsequent references to this story and to the other three stories of the collection ("I Stand Here Ironing," "Hey Sailor, What Ship?" and "O Yes") are to this Delta/Seymour Lawrence paperback edition and are noted parenthetically in the text.

6. Irving Howe, *World of Our Fathers* (New York: Harcourt Brace Jovanovich, 1976), p. 323.

7. *Yonnondio: From the Thirties* (New York: Dell, 1975), p. 38. Subsequent references are to this edition and are noted parenthetically in the text.

8. Elenore Lester, "The Riddle of Tillie Olsen," *Midstream,* (January 1975), p. 77.

9. The poem, signed I. [sic] Lerner, appeared in *The Partisan,* (March 1934), 4. Selma Burkom and Margaret Williams reprint and analyze the poem in "De-Riddling Tillie Olsen's Writings," *San Jose Studies,* 2 (1976), 65-83. The bibliography of Olsen's works appended to Burkom and Williams' essay includes Olsen's early poetry, essays, and various of her fiction.

10. "The Iron Throat," *Partisan Review,* 1 (April-May 1934), 3-9.

11. See the accessible paperback edition of *Call It Sleep* (New York: Avon, 1964). *Yonnondio* and *Call It Sleep* are strikingly similar in their exploration of the terrors of slum life, interest in the child' [sic] developing mind, and use of experimental typography and Whitmanesque lists.

12. "Requa," *Iowa Review,* 1 (Summer 1970), 54-74, rpt. as "Requa I," *Best American Short Stories 1971,* ed. Martha Foley and David Burnett (Boston: Houghton Mifflin, 1971), pp. 237-265.

Death Labors[*]

Joanne Trautmann Banks

They look so different on the page, these two seemingly similar stories.[1] Tolstoy's paragraphs are long, his sentences complete and declarative, his words richly abundant. His page is filled in. In contrast, Olsen works with empty space as if it were as important an element as language. Many of her sentences are fragments, italicized, parenthetical. These are not only styles of writing for Tolstoy and Olsen; they are also, as I hope to show, styles of living for their main characters. It is the deepest irony that in order to die well, the characters must reconstitute—even repudiate—the very styles that the authors have used so brilliantly.

It is all, finally, a matter of identity. Can these two people, Olsen's old woman[2] and Tolstoy's Ivan Ilych (or can any of us, for that matter), die as they (or we) have lived? Can they carry into the last scene of their lives' dramas the same roles, the same selves, that they have built with such energy in the preceding acts? Tolstoy and Olsen say "no." The people who go to meet death in these stories are not the people who existed before their illnesses intervened. Cancer has challenged every dimension of their lives.

Before her cancer, the old woman in "Riddle" had largely based her identity on her service to others, rather than on her own primary needs. The field theory psychologists, who believe that one's personhood can be explained as the focus of one's relationships, would probably find her a clear instance of their concepts.[3] As Olsen develops her, however, the elements of her identity are loosely connected. There are significant spaces between them. There is a literal one, for instance, in her geographical identity. The early part of her life was spent in revolutionary Russia; all the rest, in America. Metaphorically, the experience in America is separated by a vast space from her intellectual, political life in Russia. Even apparently intimate spaces are wide. To her daughter's statement that the mother lived all her life *for* people, she replies, "'Not *with*'" (p. 76, italics mine). The spaces are not precisely voids, any more than the spaces between Olsen's paragraphs mark major hiatuses. Some sort of meaning inheres in them. But, like Rosencrantz and Guildenstern in Tom Stoppard's play of that name about Hamlet, the old woman has perhaps not been the main character in her own drama. She has had to work out

[*] Reprinted from *Literature and Medicine* 9 (1990): 162-71.

her identity in the parentheses, as it were, between other people's utterances. She has found her self in life's interstices.

The same phenomenon can be described in terms of space's correlative, time. There was never time in the old woman's life to finish a project in the way she would have preferred, seldom time even to finish reading a story by her favorite, Chekhov, let alone live a life of the mind. She believes that all her life she has been *"forced to move to the rhythms of others"* (p. 68),[4] and thus there are major discontinuities in her experience of her self.

"Discontinuity"—that's Olsen's term. In her study of the barriers to creativity, she suggests that discontinuity is a pattern imposed on women's lives.[5] In context, it's clear that she means women whose lives are defined for many of their adult years by maternal exigencies and the Sisyphean tasks of daily housekeeping. She cites the old woman in "Riddle" as an instance. In her case, the discontinuities and spaces are the inevitable consequences of having so many children to raise in a condition of constant poverty, and with a passionate husband (she grants that his desires are the "most beguiling" interruption of them all [p. 67]). She is an "outsider" not only because of her gender and her class, but also because of her Jewishness.[6] Even within that tradition, she is an outsider, an atheist who spits on religion's conventions as oppressive. Outsiders prowl the circle of society, taking on such identities as they have in opposition and at great cost to creativity.

Then comes the cancer. When the disease is doing its initial damage, the old woman does not, of course, know about it—at least in the usual sense of "knowing." She knows in terms of D. H. Lawrence's fleshly knowing.[7] Her body has a consciousness of sorts, and it immediately begins to communicate with her mind: in concert they prepare to die. For instance, there is good reason to blame the agitation she feels on outside causes, namely, her husband's insistence that they sell the house where she feels comfortable and move to a retirement community. But she wonders "if the tumult was outside, or in her" (p.70). She "knows" she has cancer. It "knocks" on "the great ear pressed inside" (p. 90). Because of its insistence, she begins to explore her life and to rebuild the identity she will need in the near and urgent future.

But "explore" implies cognitive acuity, and the old woman's disease eventually attacks that function. Early on, as is common in age, her recent memories fade in favor of those from long ago, and finally she expresses herself only in isolated snippets. It would seem that in a grotesque extension of her lifelong habits, her identity in the final days lies scattered around her, as if—in a phrase of Yeats from another context entirely—"the centre cannot hold" ("The Second Coming"). And yet she *is* exploring. "'No pills, let me feel what I feel'"(p. 105). Even in neurological disarray, the old woman has the power she needs.

Significantly, her given name is not revealed until now, when the story is nearly over. She has always been "Ma" or one of a series of insulting epithets hurled by her husband in their mutual game of bitterness—"Mrs. Unpleasant," "Mrs. Excited Over Nothing," "Mrs. Word Miser." Her name is Eva.

Eva's job, her last one, is to recollect herself. She accepts this position without question. It is what she must do before she can die meaningfully. Her method will be to undo, to reverse in some ways, and to balance the style by which she has lived thus far. That is, she will fill in some of the gaps in space and time that have prevented her from having a solid self. She will attempt to connect the prose of her life as a beleaguered mother and wife with the poetry that somehow still fuels her.[8]

At her core there is solitude. But it is not, she discovers, the same thing as emptiness. In fact, at this stage of her life, she relishes it, refusing to give it up by moving to a communal life, even creating it artificially, if necessary, by turning off her hearing aid. She senses that from the silence will come the identity she needs: "in the reconciled solitude, to journey to herself" (p. 84). Eva moves, instinctively Olsen seems to suggest, to the ocean's edge, there to look "toward the shore that nurtured life as it first crawled toward consciousness the millions of years ago" (p. 94). Eva is herself engaged in seeking her beginnings.

Soon the necessary data come. Though they come in scraps, they also come in torrents—words from beloved books and speeches, music from her idealistic youth. Her husband is shocked; she has not spoken of these things for decades. Hiding in the body of this frail, embittered, and normally silent woman is the young girl with noble dreams for humankind. She has survived all this time in the memory cells. At this point, Olsen introduces a poetic image for a scientific truth: it seems to Eva's husband that "for seventy years she had hidden a tape recorder, infinitely microscopic, within her, . . . it had coiled infinite mile on mile, trapping every song, every melody, every word read, heard, and spoken" (p. 109). The memories are so intense that they are almost real presences for Eva in her deteriorating but (or therefore?) receptive state. She is reunited in this sense with her girlhood friend and mentor, the aristocratic rebel Lisa, for whom, because she is a follower of Tolstoy, knowledge is holy and to be shared among all classes.

If times and spaces have thereby been reconnected for Eva, the achievement has been bought at a terrible price. This woman, whose hands were always busy with a child, now can scarcely bear to touch one. In Sylvia Plath's memorable image from "Three Women," a baby's cries are "hooks that catch and grate like cats." Eva's grandchildren are vessels of vitality, from which she knows she must detach herself. The full context of a phrase quoted above is: "Somewhere coherence, transport, meaning. If they would but leave her in the air now stilled of clamor, in the reconciled solitude, to journey to herself" (p. 84). One grandchild entreats her to tell him a riddle, but she is not playful. She has not time for life's inherent ambiguities. Her task requires that she leave even her husband. As he listens to the "tape recorder" of her past, he hears nothing of their springtime love or their joyful hours as a family. For him, it is the moment of bitterest grief. By her last day, Eva has left present time entirely. She is now ready to enter the final turnstile, as she must, alone.

It would be wrong to conclude that Ivan Ilych has the simpler task just because for most of his life he has a more secure sense of self. I am inclined to think, as a matter of fact, that constructing an identity from scraps is easier than dismantling a rigid one. But the latter is precisely what Ivan Ilych must do if he is to die in peace.

His problem has its origins, as Eva's did, in the literary choices made by the author. It is almost as if a certain style of dying is irrevocably linked with certain aesthetic conventions. Olsen's organization and rhythms are basically lyrical;[9] her point of view, essentially a post-Jamesian center of consciousness, wherein the world is only as real as an individual's perception of it. The poetic subjectivity extends to her title, which begs for multiple interpretations. Tolstoy works within a very different mode. He has the advantages, and the limitations, of a linear, realistic style. From the bluntly explicit title on, he and his readers assume some truthful correspondence between what he describes and the world as we agree to see it. His voice is the one long known in narrative theory as *omniscient*. Because Tolstoy's talent and insight persuade readers that he deserves to declare such a perspective on human events, the narrator speaks with great authority. This powerful presence has philosophical consequences for Ivan Ilych. Consider, for instance, the finality that sounds in this famous sentence: "Ivan Ilych's life had been most simple and most ordinary and therefore most terrible" (p. 104). Like realists before and after him, Tolstoy takes the nature of society as his arena. He also practices satire as an extension of both his social interests and his omniscient stance. That is, the satire results from his looking closely at institutions such as the family, law, and medicine, and judging them wittily on the basis of firmly held values. A story that will end as powerfully as any in literature, begins hilariously as a satirical look at the behavior of self-centered "mourners," who see Ivan Ilych's death solely in terms of interruption of their own affairs.

Ivan Ilych's life style partakes of Tolstoy's literary stances, and, with one necessary exception,[10] might even be seen as a parody of them. True, Ivan Ilych is not a purveyor of satire among his friends (at least so far as we know), but he has the satirist's smug certainty that his or her values are the proper ones from which others depart at their peril. He thus tells himself the story of his own life omnisciently without every questioning his assumptions. Furthermore, he is firmly anchored in society's abundant details, and this too is a parallel with Tolstoy's style. If Eva is an outsider, Ivan Ilych is clearly an insider, living in the public world of power. "Think: If Tolstoy had been born a woman," muses Olsen in *Silences.*[11] Socially created realities are for Ivan Ilych the only realities. He derives his identity from the opinions of others of his rank and time.

Ivan Ilych has not so much lived his life as built a résumé. His professional credentials are impeccable. He has accepted the ladder as a metaphor for success, and he has moved up it at regular intervals, ending pleasantly above the midpoint of the judicial bureaucracy. He is, in Willy Loman's pitiful phrase from *Death of a Salesman,* not only liked, but well liked, chiefly because he conducts his relationships with propriety and decorum (two terms that are very important to him). When he furnishes a house, he chooses those items that will make him appear to be rich; it has nothing whatever of the personal about it. But neither has his personal life. In his youth, his sexual relationships were conducted "with clean hands, in clean linen, with French phrases" (p. 106). When it is time to marry, he chooses a woman whose background will look good, as it were, on his résumé under the biographical details section. That the marriage turns hostile distresses him chiefly because of his wife's "coarse" demands for attention (p. 109). He has had a few setbacks, but in his opinion everything has gone on the whole very satisfactorily indeed, and the evidence indicates that the second half of his life should be even better.

He has allowed no space for major contingencies. His illness nearly breaks him in two, so rigid has he become. In contrast, Eva bends like a bamboo tree in the wind. She accepts her coming death far more easily and sets to work on what must be done. For Ivan Ilych, disease is a gross impropriety against which he rages ineffectually for much of the story.

At the same time, his anger serves as a powerful corrosive that begins little by little to weaken the false girders of his life. I need not repeat the phases of his torment and terror. They have in fact been given a kind of renewed fame among medical educators by virtue of their being a nearly perfect example of Kübler-Ross's stages of dying.[12] But it is important to my argument to note that the process involves the tearing down of almost all his previously held tenets. That moving *up* and *on,* for instance, is the only criterion for success. Is he now a failure, and his life meaningless, because he is horizontal? That cleanliness in bodily functions somehow mysteriously insures the social order. Now that he must be helped with his excretions, has all turned to shameful chaos? That professional people ought always to affect indifference to their clients. Since the doctors he consults do not listen to him, what does that say about his years in the law? That a certain aloofness in human relationships, even in marriage, maintains decorum. Why will not his friends and his family comfort him? That a gentleman does not ask too many questions about life. Do gentlemen, then, live in basic and mutually supportive deceit, especially as regards the absolute fact of one's death? Perhaps most insidious of all: that he is a man, when inside he is a little boy crying out to be pitied. Ivan Ilych has "to live thus all alone on the brink of an abyss" (p. 127).

Of course, there is pain. The pain is ghastly and ought not to be paraphrased, even if that were possible. But just as *Ivan Ilych* prefigured Kübler-Ross, so does the story demonstrate what many clinically experienced philosophers and theologians have said about the distinction between physical agony (pain) and mental agony (suffering). Suffering is the worse torture. If suffering can be reduced, pain can be endured. If life has been meaningful, death can be likewise.

As part of his attempt to understand, Ivan Ilych takes a journey that is at one point similar to Eva's. Both return to their youth for sub-stance—Eva to connect with what she already feels to be good and true, Ivan Ilych to understand his child self for the first time. To be sure, his early venture into childhood memories elicits one of the most poignant passages in the story. Thinking of the well-known syllogism that ends "therefore Caius is mortal" (p. 131), Ivan Ilych refuses to accept that *he* is mortal. Caius is abstract logic. But he, Ivan Ilych, had once been a little boy called Vanya with a mamma and a papa and a beloved striped ball. Little Vanya cannot die!

Near the end, he returns more often to his childhood, savoring what we would now call Proustian sensations. Life, he concludes, was better and more vital then. In fact, the closer he comes to his beginnings, and the farther he gets from death, the more real he feels. That may be fear speaking, but it leads to another conclusion that carries more conviction: his entire life has been lived in false rectitude except for those "scarcely perceptible attempts to struggle against what was considered good by the most highly placed people" (p. 152). They alone had been real. This awareness is hardly freeing. In fact, with this insight, he has reached the bottom of his despair. Immediately, his pain multiplies tenfold. Ivan Ilych has come as far as he can alone.

But why is he so isolated? Where, in particular, are the doctors and the nurses? Part of the answer is that in both *Ivan Ilych* and "Tell Me a Riddle," doctors are portrayed as scarcely necessary to the dying people. Olsen is not negative about them;[13] they simply do their jobs at the periphery of the central drama. Tolstoy goes farther. His physicians make themselves irrelevant by virtue of their self-importance. They deceive their patient and themselves. After putting on an inappropriately cheerful, "there now" face in the mornings, they cannot take it off (p. 141). Ivan Ilych eventually consults several doctors, each of whom disagrees pompously with the others. If their characterizations were not set into the midst of an otherwise tragic tale, their essential natures—which are straight out of a Molière comedy—would be clearer.

The nurses are another matter altogether. The servant Gerasim performs nursing functions for Ivan Ilych, and, in "Riddle" Eva's granddaughter Jeannie, who is in fact a professional nurse, does the nursing alongside Eva's husband. Neither Gerasim nor Jeannie accomplishes very much in terms of a conventional plot. Gerasim has very few sentences to himself, and Jeannie does nothing overtly dramatic. Oddly, that is good news for everyone who attends a dying person. It seems to demonstrate that in these two situations, at least, a great deal can be accomplished with the simple means available to most of us. On the plot level that I have been developing, the nurses are really midwives who assist in the paradox of the eleventh-hour birthing.[14]

Gerasim exemplifies Tolstoy's well-known view of the peasant as a kind and simple type. Innocent of the supercilious posturing of Ivan Ilych's family, friends, and doctors, Gerasim alone acknowledges directly that Ivan Ilych is going to die: "Only Gerasim recognized it and pitied him" (p. 138). The young servant finds caring for Ivan Ilych's body neither distasteful nor burdensome, but a natural, democratic act that he hopes will one day be done for him. He thereby helps Ivan Ilych in his central task of breaking down his rigid ideas about propriety. With Gerasim, Ivan Ilych is able to practice intimacy, never a valued part of his identity until now. Jeannie is more sophisticated than Gerasim, but her reactions to dying are, like his, direct, kind, and nonjudgmental. With perfect tact, she brings Eva a Mexican cookie, the "Bread of the Dead," made by a mother in the likeness of the little girl she has just lost. The cookie becomes the occasion for a conversation about grief in which Eva participates comfortably. She says that Jeannie is like the Russian Lisa, that mentor-midwife from long ago.

Eva is an atheist. I am not sure whether or not she is to be taken for a good person. But there is something deeply spiritual about how, in the face of physical agony, she yet makes a last-minute search for meaning among the shards of humankind's attempts to connect. Jeannie senses this. She is nearly incoherent in expressing it—but when has transcendent experience ever been easy to verbalize? To explain her "radiant" face of love to her grandfather, she replies "'my darling escape' . . . 'my darling Granny'" (p. 107). Olsen expands the thought: "(Shameful the joy, the pure overwhelming joy from being with her grandmother; the peace, the serenity that breathed.)" Thus is the midwife paid.[15]

As for Eva herself, has she reached her goal by the time she dies? We have only Jeannie's report: "On the last day, she said she would go back to when she first heard music, a little girl on the road of the village where she was born. She promised me. It is a wedding and they dance, while the flutes so joyous and vibrant tremble in the air" (pp. 115-16). Vibrant flutes—this is not the way Eva remembered the scene earlier: *a bare-footed sore-covered little girl . . . danced her ecstasy of grimace to flutes that scratched at a cross-roads village wedding* (p. 97). Therefore, if Jeannie has repeated her grandmother's words accurately, it may be that Eva has indeed seen through to the truth. We can follow Eva no farther towards her wished-for reunion.

Tolstoy lets us experience the fulfillment. When Ivan Ilych realizes that his life has been false, his task is almost completed, though he does not yet know it. He has not only broken down the past, he appears to have emptied himself of any identity at all. He is like an empty vessel, waiting to be filled. And he is filled, with light and with joy. His rebirth occurs just as his pathetic little son comes into the room, takes up his hand, and, weeping, kisses it.

People have offered theological, psychological, and something like scientific interpretations of such a phenomenon. For Tolstoy, the theological, as understood in the Western world, is paramount. Ivan Ilych is rewarded with peace at that moment when he asks for forgiveness from God. Suddenly, "there was no fear because there was no death" (p. 155). This cannot mean that there is no dying, for Ivan Ilych goes on immediately to die, but that because of faith, death has no sting, the grave no victory.[16] His pain too is still real, but now just a given, and no longer a reminder of his absurdity: "'Let the pain be'" (p. 155). Therefore, he is infused with light and joy. Psychologically, Ivan Ilych changes at the moment when he sees others as real. He feels his son's pain, and later his wife's, and he is relieved of the burden of himself. The result is light and joy. Using the methods of the social sciences, the authors of two recent books have concluded that, whether for physiological reasons or others, many dying people do in fact report seeing light, feeling joy, and going gladly.[17]

Much mystery remains. Fortunately, I am obliged to pick up only one small part of it. I have tried to establish that Olsen's and Tolstoy's literary styles parallel the lifestyles of their main characters—loose, personal, and fragmented in the first case; tight, social, and linear in the second—and that, to die happily, the characters must at least partially revise the authors. If I am right, why does this revolt of character against creator happen? It is possible, though unlikely in these cases, that the authors intend it. So the unconscious gapes. I cannot believe that the revolt is due to the authors' unconscious self-hatred, wherein they are punished by their very own creatures. In fact, something healthy may be going on. Here is how my thinking runs: These authors are enormously successful. But success tends to reinforce past methods, and the method that succeeds sooner or later becomes the method that limits. Maybe the unconscious minds of these two deeply creative writers have allowed their characters to break down old forms, not in revolt but in exploration of new possibilities for Tolstoy and Olsen. If so, the pattern is recognizable. It is that type of death labor we call evolution.

NOTES

1. I have used the Louise and Alymer Maude translation of Leo Tolstoy's 1886 novella *The Death of Ivan Ilych and other Stories* (New York: New American Library/Signet 1960), 95-156. Tillie Olsen's story "Tell Me a Riddle" was first collected in *Tell Me a Riddle* (New York: Dell, 1961), 63-116. Copyright 1961 by Tillie Olsen. Reprinted by permission of Tillie Olsen and Dell Publishing. All subsequent quotations are from these editions and are cited parenthetically in the essay.

2. She is only sixty-nine, an age our society no longer considers old, but that is how Olsen conceives of her. In Tillie Olsen's *Silences* (New York: Dell, 1983), 58, she makes a reference to the character as "old mother, grandmother."

3. E.g., Harry Stack Sullivan and Kurt Lewin.

4. Like several others in the story, this phrase is italicized as if to underscore meaning seized on the run.

5. Olsen, *Silences*, 58.

6. "Outsider" is Virginia Woolf's term in *Three Guineas* (1938), a feminist volume that Olsen frequently cites in public lectures and private conversations.

7. D. H. Lawrence developed this concept throughout his work. See, e.g., his letter to Ernest Collings (17 January 1913) in *The Portable D. H. Lawrence* (New York: Viking, 1947), 563: "My great religion is a belief in the blood, the flesh, as being wiser than the intellect."

8. "Only connect the prose and the passion, and both will be exalted": a phrase from E. M. Forster's novel, *Howards End* (1910), and used, in part, as its epigraph.

9. In the sense defined by Ralph Freedman in his influential study, *The Lyrical Novel: Studies in Hermann Hesse, Andre Gide, and Virginia Woolf* (Princeton, N.J.: Princeton University Press, 1963); that is, a fiction that emphasized personal experience as revealed through poetic methods more than strictly narrative forms.

10. The clarity that derives from Tolstoy's fervent Christianity.

11. Olsen, *Silences*, 268.

12. Elisabeth Kübler-Ross, *On Death and Dying* (New York: Macmillan, 1970).

13. Eva's first physician misses the diagnosis, but this serves an aesthetic rather than moral goal in that it allows Olsen to observe what I have termed Eva's "Laurentian" behavior while the cancer is still unknown to her intellect.

14. It may be helpful to see their methods as Rogerian. Carl R. Rogers, who believed that the good therapeutic relationship was paradigmatic of any good interpersonal activity—and that the object of both was to help others become persons—outlined three conditions for the helper. He or she was to be "congruent" (i.e., genuine), to have "unconditional positive regard" for the client, and to evince "accurate empathy." See "The Necessary and Sufficient Conditions of Therapeutic Personality Change," *Journal of Consulting Psychology* 21 (1957): 95-103.

15. Cf. Mary de Santis, the private duty nurse in Patrick White's novel, *The Eye of the Storm* (New York: Viking, 1974), for whom the care of an elderly, disintegrating woman is a religious experience.

16. 1 Corinthians 15:55 (KJV).

17. Karlis Osis and Erlendur Haraldsson, *At the Hour of Death*, rev. ed. (New York: Hastings House, 1986); and Raymond A. Moody, Jr., *Life After Life* (New

York: Bantam Books, 1976). Cancer, or any lingering terminal illness, provides time for this kind of death labor, but Moody accumulates evidence that the same process, much condensed, also occurs in some traumatic near-death experiences.

"No One's Private Ground": A Bakhtinian Reading of Tillie Olsen's *Tell Me a Riddle*[*]

Constance Coiner

"Commitment" is more than just a matter of presenting correct political opinions in one's art; it reveals itself in how far the artist reconstructs the artistic forms at his [/her] disposal, turning authors, readers and spectators into collaborators.

> — Terry Eagleton, referring in his *Marxism and Literary Criticism* to Walter Benjamin's "The Author as Producer"

In the stories collected in *Tell Me a Riddle* Tillie Olsen examines the marginalization and potential empowering of various groups of oppressed people, particularly women, by experimenting with potentially democratizing modes of discourse. Deborah Rosenfelt has rightly placed Olsen in

> . . . a line of women writers, associated with the American Left, who unite a class consciousness and a feminist consciousness in their lives and creative work, who are concerned with the material circumstances of people's lives, who articulate the experiences and grievances of women and of other oppressed groups—workers, national minorities, the colonized and the exploited—and who speak out of a defining commitment to social change. ("Thirties" 374)

Although *Tell Me a Riddle* shows a range of marginalized lives, Olsen is far from content with merely portraying this multiplicity in American society. As Rosenfelt observes, Olsen writes out of a "commitment to social change," and I will discuss some of Olsen's narrative/political strategies that exemplify that commitment.

The modes of discourse with which Olsen experiments in developing her narrative strategies are those she has derived and recreated from long and careful listening to the voices of marginalized people. The cacophony of their voices, Olsen recognizes, comprises a potentially democratizing force. Noting some of Olsen's uses of empowering discursive forms in *Silences*, Elizabeth A. Meese writes that "by means of a polyvocal chorus she [Olsen] questions silence and allows others to participate in the same process . . . . She then calls upon the reader to write the text—no longer

[*] Reprinted (with revisions) from *Feminist Studies* 18.2 (Summer 1992): 257-81.

her text, but occasioned by it and by the voices speaking through it" (110). The experiments noted by Meese as well as several other experiments pervade *Tell Me a Riddle*.

Some of Olsen's specific uses of discursive modes and the political/social changes they work to bring about are prefigured in Mikhail Bakhtin's general concept of "heteroglossia." For Bakhtin there are two competing forces in language use: "Every concrete utterance of a speaking subject serves as a point where centrifugal as well as centripetal forces are brought to bear" (*Dialogic* 272). The "centripetal" or "monologic" force presses toward unity, singularity of meaning; it attempts to assert its dominance by silencing uses of language that deviate from it. On the other hand, the "centrifugal" or "heteroglossic" force resists the dominance of monologism by fragmenting and disrupting it. The myriad heteroglossic voices of the marginalized comprise a social and political force against the tyranny of dominant discursive modes in any language community. Those such as Olsen who observe, record, and honor the multiple heteroglossic voices engage in the democratizing enterprise of amplifying dominated and marginalized voices.

Bakhtin's metaphor of "carnival" displays the nexus of heteroglossia and political/social power. Carnival, with its various simultaneous activities, is a site in which many of the usual societal impositions of class and order are suspended while the populace participates in multiple ways of parodying or mimicking the dominant culture's behavior. Terry Eagleton has described Bakhtin's notion of carnival in these terms: "The 'gay relativity' of popular carnival, 'opposed to all that [is] ready-made and completed, to all pretence at immutability,' is the political materialization of Bakhtin's poetics, as the blasphemous, 'familiarizing' language of plebeian laughter destroys monologic authoritarianism with its satirical estrangements" (*Against* 117). In *Tell Me a Riddle*, in several instances of carnival-like atmosphere, heteroglossia is unleashed to engage in a powerful, playful satirizing of the dominant culture.

The nurturing and recording of heteroglossia has democratizing potential, but heteroglossia itself and the recording of it also contain hazards both for the multiplicity of speakers and for those who listen to their voices. The collection of stories in *Tell Me a Riddle* presents a wide range of individual, marginalized voices competing for our attention. Unless readers/listeners make connections among a variety of voices, many of which are foreign to their own, the potential for genuine democracy latent within the cacophony of heteroglossia is lost. If they remain unconnected from each other, the competing voices lapse into a white-noise excess of sound that becomes unintelligible. Rejecting many traditional modes of authorial control, Olsen refuses opportunities to make connections for us and presses us to make connections among those voices ourselves. The social/political act of connecting otherwise isolated and marginalized voices realizes the democratizing potential of hetero-glossia, and Olsen demands that we participate in such action.

To participate properly, we must be permeable to multiple voices, and in some characters in *Tell Me a Riddle*, Olsen shows us both the benefits and risks of receptivity to heteroglossia. Multiple voices often compete within a single character, displaying that character's complex web of ties to others and to the past. Heteroglossia on this level often operates in *Tell Me a Riddle* and other works by Olsen to undermine and offer alterna-tives to bourgeois individualism. But Olsen does not idealize the individual permeable to heteroglossia; she shows us hazards that exist in individual manifestations of heteroglossia (e.g., Whitey's isolation in "Hey Sailor, What Ship?" and the multiple voices that threaten to overwhelm the narrator of "I Stand Here Ironing"). *Tell Me a Riddle* asks us to be cognizant of the dangers we face as we assume the role Olsen insists we assume—that of active readers alert to the connections among a multiplic-ity of marginalized voices.

Throughout the stories in *Tell Me a Riddle* Olsen pits heteroglossic modes of discourse she associates with the oppressed against oppressors' monolingual/monological modes of discourse. In the title story, Jeannie's sketch of Eva "coiled, convoluted like an ear" suggests Olsen's narra-tive/political strategies. Olsen's writing, like an ear "intense in listening," is permeable to the heteroglossic differences constitutive of a complex social field. The stories collected in *Tell Me a Riddle* strain away from the prevailing narrative and social order by "hearing" and incorporating the suppressed voices of mothers, those of the working class, and the dialects of immigrants and African-Americans; by deconstructing the opposition between personal and political; and, in the title story, by honoring the communal polyphony of a dying visionary.

A second and related narrative/political strategy is a reworking of traditional relationships among writer, text, and reader. The stories collected in *Tell Me a Riddle* subvert the concept of textual ownership, affirming the reader not as an object but, reciprocally, as another subject. Many dominant discursive practices still take for granted that the act of reading will be a subjection to a fixed meaning, a passive receiving of what Bakhtin terms "monologue." In Bakhtin's view of monological discourse, the writer directly addresses the readers, attempting to anticipate their responses and deflect their objections; meanings are seen as delivered, unchanged, from source to recipient. In Bakhtin's terms, monologue is "deaf to the other's response; it does not await it and does not grant it any *decisive* force" (cited in Todorov 107).

Heteroglossic discourse, on the other hand, acknowledges "that there exists outside of it another consciousness, with the same rights, and capable of responding on an equal footing, another and equal *I*" (107). *Tell Me a Riddle's* heteroglossia acknowledges the other consciousnesses that exist outside the text. As Meese indicates about similar strategies in *Silences*, *Tell Me a Riddle* activates its reader-subjects while subverting authorial domination; in the tradition of Bertolt Brecht's theater and Jean-Luc Godard's cinematic montage, it turns writer and readers into collaborators.

The two categories of Olsen's narrative/political strategy I have identified—her recording of heteroglossia and her reworking of relationships among writer, text, and reader—constitute this essay's two major divisions.

In *Tell Me a Riddle's* first story, "I Stand Here Ironing, "Olsen begins her recording of heteroglossia by exploring problems that fragment lives and discourse and by experimenting with narrative forms that display that fragmentation. Emily, the daughter of the unnamed narrator, had been born into "the pre-relief, pre-WPA world of the depression," and her father, no longer able to "endure . . . sharing want" with the 19-year-old mother and child, had left them when Emily was eight-months old (10). The infant "was a miracle to me," the narrator recalls, but when she had to work, she had no choice but to leave Emily with "the woman downstairs to whom she was no miracle at all" (10). This arrangement grieved both mother and child: "I would start running as soon as I got off the streetcar, running up the stairs," the narrator remembers, and "when she saw me she would break into a clogged weeping that could not be comforted, a weeping I can hear yet" (10-11). Then came months of complete separation, while the child lived with relatives. The price for reunion was Emily's spending days at "the kinds of nurseries that [were] only parking places for children . . . . It was the only place there was. It was the only way we could be together, the only way I could hold a job" (11). Their situation improved with the presence of "a new daddy" (12). Although the narrator still worked at wage-earning jobs, she was more relaxed with her younger children than she had been with Emily: "it was the face of joy, and not of care or tightness or worry I turned to them." But, the narrator adds, by then it was "too late for Emily" (12).

The narrative is laced with references to the pressure of circumstance, the limits on choice: "when is there time?"; "what cannot be helped" (9); "it was the only way" (11); "We were poor and could not afford for her the soil of easy growth" (20); "She is the child of her age, of depression, of war, of fear" (20). Both mother and daughter have been damaged: While Emily expresses fear and despair casually ("we'll all be atom-dead"), her mother suffers because "all that is in her [Emily] will not bloom" (20). All the narrator asks for Emily is "enough left to live by" and the consciousness that "she is more than this dress on the ironing board, helpless before the iron" (21).

The story includes two major discursive forms. The form that appears through most of the story is indirect, circling, uncertain; it is heteroglossic. The other form, which Olsen points out and discards in one paragraph near the story's end, is direct, clipped, and assertive.[1] It is a version of the reductive dominant discourse contributing to the pressure of the circumstances in which Emily and her mother struggle to survive. With these two forms of discourse Olsen introduces issues that concern her in all the stories in *Tell Me a Riddle*: language as power; dominant versus subversive modes of discourse; heteroglossia.

The second major discursive form, the direct, is introduced by the narrator of "I Stand Here Ironing" in this way: "I will never total it all. I will never come in to say: She was a child seldom smiled at. Her father left me before she was a year old. I had to work her first six years when there was work, or I sent her home and to his relatives. There were years she had care she hated" (20). What the narrator offers here is what she will not say and what she will not do. She will not "total"—sum up—Emily's life in a direct, linear, cause-and-effect way.

The other major discursive form—with its many modes of indirectness, false starts, and uncertainties—is signalled in the form of address at the beginning of the story. The narrator says, "I stand here ironing, and what you asked me moves tormented back and forth with the iron" (9). This "you" (never clearly identified, but likely one of Emily's high school teachers, a guidance counselor, or a social worker) is the ostensible audience to whom the narrator's discourse is directed. However, in this most indirect form of address, the entire story takes place in the mind of the narrator, who is speaking to herself as though rehearsing her discourse for the "you." We do not know whether this discourse ever passes from the silence of the mother's mind to the hearing of the audience (the teacher or counselor) for whom it is being rehearsed.

The narrator's discourse is persistently marked by indirectness, false starts, and uncertainties—the forms on which the narrator must rely as she looks back over her life with Emily: "Why do I put that first? I do not even know if it matters, or if it explains anything" (10); "In this and other ways she leaves her seal, I say aloud. And startle at my saying it. What do I mean? What did I start to gather together, to try and make coherent?" (18). These fitful "digressions" typify the movement of the story's first major discursive form. The user of that form, far from reducing her subjects to linear, cause-and-effect patterns, displays in multifaceted discourse her own complicated and ultimately irreducible forms of interdependence with her subjects. The form is heteroglossic; it is a "voice" made of many voices: Caught in the memory of conflicts between Emily and her sister, Susan, "each one human, needing, demanding, hurting, taking," the mother says, "Susan telling jokes and riddles to company for applause while Emily sat silent (to say to me later; that was *my* riddle, Mother, I told it to Susan)" (16-17). As employed in this and other stories in the collection, heteroglossia is not solely a matter of multiple voices within or among cultures or subcultures; it is often the multiple and conflicting voices that make up one person. Olsen's displays of individual heteroglossia, the fragmenting of voices constituting a self and that self's interdependence with others, become one means by which her work offers alternatives to bourgeois individualism.

At the beginning of the story, the words of the unidentified teacher or counselor and the mother's reaction to those words create a complex intermingling of voices. The mother has been asked to assist in helping Emily: "'I wish you would manage the time to come in and talk with me about your daughter. I'm sure you can help me understand her. She's a youngster who needs help and whom I'm deeply interested in helping.'" The next line of the story is "'Who needs help.'. . ." (9; ellipsis Olsen's). Who indeed? This entangling of the helpers and the helped, including the suggestion that the mother is being asked for the very aid she herself may need in order to assist Emily, is indicative of the ways in which the narrator's thinking and discourse proceed. She cannot, in language, fully demarcate herself from Emily or from those whose lives became entangled with Emily's in the past, such as an unsympathetic nursery school teacher: "And even without knowing, I knew. I knew the teacher that was evil because all these years it has curdled into my memory, the little boy hunched in the corner, her rasp, 'why aren't you outside, because Alvin hits you? that's no reason, go out, scaredy'" (11). Facing the incessant pressure of time and circumstance—"And when is there time to remember, to sift, to weigh, to estimate, to total?"—the narrator recognizes that multiple voices and memories constantly threaten to engulf her (9).

The nonlinear mode of discourse is so often replete with complexity of meaning that it risks falling into meaninglessness and the equivalent of silence. In this story that risk is most acute at moments when the mother cannot find the language to respond to Emily. While looking back over her life with Emily, the mother returns to times when she could respond to her daughter with nothing more than silence.

> There was a boy she loved painfully through two school semesters. Months later she told me how she had taken pennies from my purse to buy him candy. "Licorice was his favorite and I bought him some every day, but he still liked Jennifer better'n me. Why, Mommy?" The kind of question for which there is no answer. (15-16)

On the night in which this story takes place the mother is remembering such details of Emily's life and instances of failed communication between mother and daughter. The cumulative details from the various stages of Emily's life and the crowding of voices force the narrator to say near the story's end: "because I have been dredging the past, and all that compounds a human being is so heavy and meaningful in me, I cannot bear it tonight" (20). A richness of meaning approximating meaninglessness and the equivalent of silence weighs on the mother when she says of Emily, "This is one of her communicative nights and she tells me everything and nothing as she fixes herself a plate of food" (19). Yet for the narrator a reliance on nonlinear discourse with its attendant hazards is not only a matter of what her circumstances have forced upon her. It is also a matter of choice.

The narrator must use nonlinear heteroglossic modes if her goal in telling Emily's story is, as she says it is, to "Let her [Emily] be." The complicated, conflicting stuff of which human beings are made can be discussed only nonreductively in nonlinear discourse, in a manner that has some chance of "letting them be." To adopt the dominant, linear, reductive mode of discourse is to usurp and control Emily, and it is to abandon the hope with which the story ends: the narrator's hope that Emily will know "that she is more than this dress on the ironing board, helpless before the iron" (20).

The two major discursive forms in "I Stand Here Ironing"—the indirect, uncertain, circling form, and the direct, clipped, assertive form—appear again in "Tell Me a Riddle," and, again, Olsen uses them to explore language as power; dominant versus subversive modes of discourse; and heteroglossia. The story begins with a battle between Eva and David, who have been married for 47 years, most of them spent in poverty. In the dialect of Russian-Jewish immigrants, they bitterly dispute whether to sell their home and move to a retirement cooperative operated by David's union. He craves company while Eva, after raising seven children, will not "exchange her solitude for anything. *Never again to be forced to move to the rhythms of others*" (76). David and Eva use a not-always-direct, but relentlessly assertive, and minimal form of discourse in their perpetual quarreling. We find that mode of discourse in their opening fray:

"What do we need all this for?" he would ask loudly, for her hearing aid
was turned down and the vacuum was shrilling. "Five rooms" (pushing the
sofa so she could get into the corner) "furniture" (smoothing down the rug)
"floors and surfaces to make work. Tell me why do we need it?" And he was
glad he could ask in a scream.

"Because I'm use't."

"Because you're use't. This is a reason, Mrs. Word Miser? Used to can get
unused!" (73)

They poke at each other with as few words as possible, using words not
as instruments of communication but as weapons of combat and control.
Further, each uses any available means to suppress the other's minimal
discourse. She turns down her hearing aid and turns on the vacuum
cleaner. He turns on the television "loud so he need not hear" (75).

The text only gradually reveals Eva's long-ago status as a revolutionary
orator; only through fragments of dialogue and interior monologue do we
learn that this obdurate, rancorous woman, who now wields power only
by turning down her hearing aid, was once an orator in the 1905 Russian
revolution. Models for Eva's revolutionary commitment included that of
Olsen's own mother, Ida Lerner. Another was Seevya Dinkin, who shares
"Riddle"'s dedication with Genya Gorelick.[2]

"Tell Me a Riddle" illuminates, as no polemic could, the terrible cost of
a sexual division of labor. David, who has worked outside the home, has
sustained a vitality and sociability. But he has lost the "holiest dreams" he
and Eva shared in their radical youth, seems to accept American
"progress," and would rather consume TV's version of "This Is Your Life"
than reflect on his own (119; 83). Insulated at home, Eva has felt less
pressure to assimilate, to compromise her values, and has preserved those
dreams. But the many years of 18-hour days, of performing domestic
tasks "with the desperate ingenuity of poverty" (years in which David
"never scraped a carrot") have transformed her youthful capacity for
engagement into a terrible need for solitude (Rosenfelt, "Divided" 19;
TMR 74).

As Eva is dying she slips into the indirect discursive mode. After years
of bitter silence, she begins to speak, sing, and recite incessantly.
Fragments of memories and voices, suppressed during her years of
marriage and motherhood, emerge as the old woman nears death. Eva,
like the mother in "I Stand Here Ironing," becomes an individual
embodiment of heteroglossia. Eva had announced her desire for solitude,
but ironically she returns in her reverie to the time when she was
engaged with others in a revolutionary movement. She sings revolutionary songs from her youth and in a "gossamer" voice whispers fragments

of speeches she had delivered in "a girl's voice of eloquence" half a century before (119). Her babble is a communal one; she becomes a vehicle for many voices.

Eva's experiences while dying may have been partly modelled on those of Ida Lerner. "In the winter of 1955," Olsen reports in *Mother to Daughter, Daughter to Mother*, "in her last weeks of life, my mother—so much of whose waking life had been a nightmare, that common everyday nightmare of hardship, limitation, longing; of baffling struggle to raise six children in a world hostile to human unfolding—my mother, dying of cancer, had beautiful dream-visions—in color." She dreamed/envisioned three wise men, "magnificent in jewelled robes" of crimson, gold, and royal blue. The wise men ask to talk to her "of whys, of wisdom," but as they began to talk, "*she saw that they were not men, but women: That they were not dressed in jewelled robes, but in the coarse everyday shifts and shawls of the old country women of her childhood, their feet wrapped round and round with rags for lack of boots. . . . And now it was many women, a babble*" (261, 262). Together, the women sing a lullaby.

Like Ida Lerner, on her deathbed Eva becomes the human equivalent of a heteroglossic carnival site.

> One by one they [the thousand various faces of age] streamed by and imprinted on her—and though the savage zest of their singing came voicelessly soft and distant, the faces still roared—the faces densened the air—chorded into

children-chants, mother-croons, singing of the chained love serenades, Beethoven storms, mad Lucia's scream, drunken joy-songs, keens for the dead, working-singing. . . . (106)

Olsen blurs the distinction between high and popular culture in the diversity of cultural forms that sustain Eva: her beloved Chekhov, Balzac, Victor Hugo; Russian love songs; revolutionary songs; a "community sing" for elderly immigrants; and *Pan del Muerto*, a folk-art cookie for a dead child.

The barrage of voices and references that constitute Eva at her death return us to the danger I referred to in discussing "I Stand Here Ironing"— that multivocal, heteroglossic discourse may result in the equivalent of silence. Despite the danger, heteroglossia's cacophony is preferable to the dominant discourse's reductive forms. As for Emily in "I Stand Here Ironing," what will "let Eva be" is heteroglossia. After years of living in silence and near silence, Eva emerges in heteroglossia. Yet in both stories the richness of meaning released in Emily's and Eva's heteroglossic utterances threaten to result in the equivalent of silence.

In *Tell Me a Riddle* mimicry provides examples of subversive, indirect modes of discourse jousting with dominant monolithic modes; however, in mimicry Olsen finds the occasion to examine hazards in marginalized discourse's competing with the dominant discourse. Like other forms of parody, mimicry comprises a powerful form of heteroglossia. Aimed against an official or monologic language, mimicry divides that system against itself. However, mimicry's ability to oppress the oppressor may be a snare for the mimic. To make her mother laugh, or out of the despair she felt about her isolation in the world, Emily, in "I Stand Here Ironing," imitates people and incidents from her school day. Eventually her gift for mimicry, pantomime, and comedy lead to first prize in her high school amateur show and requests to perform at other schools, colleges, and city- and state-wide competitions. However, her talent and achievement do not remedy her isolation: "Now suddenly she was Somebody, and as imprisoned in her difference as she had been in anonymity" (19). By exercising her parodic talent, Emily unwittingly exchanges one form of marginalization for another.

Like Emily, Whitey in "Hey Sailor, What Ship?" has a knack for mimicry, which he exhibits, for example, when telling Lennie about the union official who fined him: "(His [Whitey's] old fine talent for mimicry jutting through the blurred-together words.)" (44). Whitey, a seaman being destroyed by alcoholism, is no less isolated than Emily in "I Stand Here Ironing." Lennie and Helen, who have been Whitey's friends and political comrades for years (Whitey saved Lennie's life during the 1934 Maritime Strike), and their three daughters are his only friends—indeed, the only people he can "be around . . . without having to pay" (43).[3]

Mimicry deals Whitey a fate similar to Emily's. However, an irony of "Hey Sailor, What Ship?" is that it is mimicry of the mimic, Whitey, that contributes to Whitey's fate. The family engages in an affectionate mimicking of the salty language that sets Whitey apart from their other acquaintances:

> Watch the language, Whitey, there's a gentleman present, says Helen. Finish your plate, Allie.
> [Whitey:] Thass right. Know who the gen'lmun is? I'm the gen'lmun. The world, says Marx, is divided into two classes. . . . [ellipsis Olsen's]
> Seafaring gen'lmun and shoreside bastards, choruses Lennie with him.
> Why, Daddy! says Jeannie.
> You're a mean ole bassard father, says Allie.

> Thass right, tell him off, urges Whitey. Hell with waitin' for glasses. Down the ol' hatch.
>
> *My* class is divided by marks, says Carol, giggling helplessly at her own joke, and anyway what about ladies? Where's *my* drink? Down the hatch. (35)

Thus mimicry functions in "Hey Sailor, What Ship?" as one form that entices Whitey out of isolation and into the family, while simultaneously diminishing the importance of Whitey as "other." The behavior of the family in relation to Whitey, despite what seems to be their shared political beliefs and practice, becomes a microcosm for the dominant culture's behavior in relation to much marginalized discourse. Charmed by difference (the history of music in U.S. popular culture exemplifies the point), the mainstream culture co-opts the marginalized discourse, stripping it of its power as "difference," and diminishes its force in a process of homogenization. Olsen's references to mimicry in these stories comprise part of her running commentary on the power of dominant and subversive modes of discourse and the complications of identity that marginalized people and their discourses face.

In addition to mimicry, "Hey Sailor, What Ship?", like other stories collected in *Tell Me a Riddle,* manifests heteroglossia by incorporating genres that "further intensify its speech diversity in fresh ways" (Bakhtin, *Dialogic* 321). Although this strategy is not uncommon among fiction writers, Olsen employs it more than many. In "Hey Sailor, What Ship?" Olsen has inserted a valediction (because the story is a farewell to Whitey, this insertion becomes a valediction within a valediction). Whitey learned it as a boy from his first shipmate, and one of the children asks him to recite it. Originally delivered in 1896 by the Phillipine hero Jose Rizal before he was executed, it concludes:

> Little will matter, my country,
> That thou shouldst forget me.
> I shall be speech in thy ears, fragrance and color,
> Light and shout and loved song. . . .
>
> Where I go are no tyrants. . . . (42)

Jose Rizal would have been an insurgent against both Spanish and American domination of the Philippines, and the recitation implicitly condemns American imperialism and the Cold War, at its height when Olsen wrote "Hey Sailor, What Ship?"

Whitey's recitation also eulogizes his (and Olsen's) youthful hopes for a socialist America, which have been snuffed out by Cold War strategists:

Land I adore, farewell. . . .
Our forfeited garden of Eden. . . .

Vision I followed from afar,
Desire that spurred on and consumed me,
Beautiful it is to fall,
That the vision may rise to fulfillment. (41)

Moreover, the valediction associates Whitey, who has been destroyed as much by *"the death of the brotherhood"* as by alcoholism, with political martyrdom. Whitey, who has attempted to keep '30s militancy alive in a period of political reaction, feels estranged from the complacent younger seamen. "These kids," he complains to Lennie, "don't realize how we got what we got. Beginnin' to lose it, too." One "kid," who had overtime coming to him, "didn't even wanta beef about it" (44). As the ship's delegate, Whitey nevertheless took the grievance to the union, which had become a conservative, alien bureaucracy, and was fined for "not taking it [the grievance] up through proper channels" (44). The younger seamen also lack the sense of solidarity Whitey and Lennie experienced during the '30s: "'Think anybody backed me up, Len?' . . . *Once, once an injury to one is an injury to all. Once, once they had to live for each other. And whoever came off the ship fat shared, because that was the only way of survival for all of them . . . . Now it was a dwindling few . . .* " (45). And, finally, because Whitey's efforts to stay sober have consistently failed and his health is rapidly deteriorating, Jose Rizal's valediction also functions as his own farewell address.

Yet there is a dimension to Whitey that cannot be explained in political or economic terms. Even in his youth, when both he and the Left were robust, Whitey was tormented by an emotional disorder that manifested itself in an inability to have sexual relations except when *"high with drink."* Many years later, at "the drunken end of his eight-months-sober try," Lennie and Helen hear a "torn-out-of-him confession" that the psychosexual problem persists, and likely, it will remain a riddle (44, 46). The story ends with its plaintive refrain— "Hey Sailor, what ship?"—which mourns the tragic waste of Whitey's life as well as suggests the disorientation, diminished options, and uncertainty of radicals in a period of right-wing ascendancy.

Both Whitey and Emily exemplify dangers in heteroglossic, subversive modes of discourse. Emily's and Whitey's individual talent allows each of them to joust with the dominant discourse. However, those individual talents, unlinked to other heteroglossic voices also intent upon jabbing at the dominant discourse, leave both Emily and Whitey without the supporting network of similar subversive voices. Without that support, they experience the dominant discourse's subsuming power and are returned to marginalized positions and forms of silence.

Mimicry and the two major forms of discourse—the direct and the indirect, and the risk that the cacophony of multivocal discourse may result in the equivalent of silence—play major roles in "O Yes." Helen, Lennie, and their daughters appear again in this story about the difficulty of sustaining a friendship across racial lines. Lennie and Helen's 12-year-old, Carol, is white; Parialee, her neighbor and closest friend from their earliest years, is African-American. "O Yes," which begins with Helen and Carol's attending Parialee's baptismal service, is permeable to the speech of "others"—songs by three church choirs; parishioners' shouts; Parialee's newly-learned jivetalk; and Alva's African-American dialect. Carol, who has never before experienced the intense emotionalism that erupts during the service (chanting, shrieking, fainting), is a stranger in the world of an all-African-American congregation. Trapped in heteroglossia's cacophony, Carol falls into the silence of a near faint, and once again, an abundance of meaning approaches silence.

Yet, in the first of the story's two parts, a far more reductive and controlling mode of discourse—an assertion/affirmation form of "dialogue"—presents itself as a counter to heteroglossia. In the dialogue's highly structured environment, the preacher takes the lead by making assertions that the congregation affirms. The dialogue includes the preacher's words, such as "And God is Powerful," and the congregation's response, "O Yes" and "I am so glad" (52, 54). The reductive and controlling mode of discourse in which the assertions are assigned to the figure of power, the preacher, and the affirmations to his followers, the congregation, replicates the structure of society outside the church. Exercising their role in the dialogue, the parishoners seem to be playing out the subservient parts African-Americans have so often been assigned within the society. Yet, within the church, heteroglossia persistently strains against the constraining mode of discourse. In "O Yes," as throughout *Tell Me a Riddle*, two major discursive forms—heteroglossia and, in this case, the countering assertion/affirmation dialogue—vie for power.

A complicated version of mimicry is prominent in "O Yes." What I identified earlier as a conventional assertion/affirmation structure placed in the midst of a swirling heteroglossia contains complex elements of a form of mimicry in which the preacher and congregation wittingly or unwittingly dramatize the roles of dominant and marginalized people, oppressor and oppressed. As the drama of the dialogue intensifies, it threatens to overpower heteroglossia by reducing it to the near monological assertion/affirmation exchanges between a leader and followers. Much of that drama takes place in the sermon delivered at Parialee's baptismal service. The narrator tells us that the subject of the sermon is "the Nature of God. How God is long-suffering. Oh, how long he has suffered" (51). The narrator has shown us a version of the classic Christian mystery of incarnation: God as the maker of human beings who suffer and God as the human victim of suffering. This dual role of perpetrator and victim becomes central to the sermon-response's dialogic structure. Early in the sermon the preacher chants, "And God is Powerful," to which the congregation responds "*O Yes*" (52). Here, again, we find an assertion/affirmation structure in which the preacher assumes the lead in the dialogue by making assertions that the congregation, in its role as follower, responds to by affirming.

Other dimensions of the dialogue quickly emerge. The preacher, working the theme of the great judgment day, blows an imaginary trumpet and announces: "And the horn wakes up Adam, and Adam runs to wake up Eve, and Eve moans; Just one more minute, let me sleep, and Adam yells, Great Day, woman, don't you know it's the Great Day?" (53). The basic assertion/affirmation structure is still operating, but within that structure the preacher in godlike fashion now creates characters who in turn engage in their own dialogues. The scene becomes increasingly heteroglossic. Immediately after the created Adam's rousing call to a sleeping Eve ("Great Day, woman, don't you know it's the Great Day?"), one of the choirs responds, "*Great Day, Great Day*" (53). Is the choir responding to the voice of the created Adam or to the preacher? The answer is of little consequence. What is important here is that the structure of the assertion/affirmation dialogue has dictated conditions that the congregation follows. Whichever "leader," real or imaginary, they respond to in the course of the sermon, they persistently replicate their role as affirmers of the leader's assertion. Thus what emerges from this heteroglossic scene is a powerful counter to heteroglossia, a discursive structure that imposes unity and control by locking participants into predetermined traditional roles.

The force for unity within heteroglossia intensifies as the imaginary dimension of the dialogue escalates. The preacher moves from assertions about God and the creation of characters such as Adam and Eve to assuming the role of God, and with that move the form of his discourse shifts from assertion/affirmation to promise/affirmation. Having just asserted the multiple roles of God in relation to human beings (friend, father, way maker, door opener), the preacher proclaims: "I will put my Word in you and it is power. I will put my Truth in you and it is power." The response is "*O Yes*" (55). Soon after, the narrator says, "Powerful throbbing voices. Calling and answering to each other" (56). The narrator captures the vibrant force of the unity within heteroglossia when she says, "A single exultant lunge of shriek" (56).

What are we to make of this univocalizing of heteroglossia? The sexual implications that have been accumulating in this scene and that culminate in the orgasmic "single exultant lunge of shriek" invite an instructive digression into Mae Gwendolyn Henderson's discussion of an orgasmic "howl" in Toni Morrison's *Sula*. Henderson, who skillfully employs Bakhtinian analysis, observes of Sula's orgasmic cry: "The howl, signifying a prediscursive mode, thus becomes an act of self-reconstitution as well as an act of subversion or resistance to the 'network of significa-tion' represented by the symbolic order. The 'high silence of orgasm' and the howl allow temporary retreats from or breaks in the dominant discourse" (33). The "single exultant lunge of shriek" has very similar functions in the church scene in "O Yes." The parishioners have repeated-ly experienced the intense repetition of the constraining asser-tion/affirmation and promise/affirmation structures that mimic the dominant discourse of power to which the congregation members are subjected outside the church. The shriek becomes an act of "self-reconsti-tution" and, at the same time, a "subversion or resistance to the 'network of signification'" that constrains the parishioners.

Henderson argues persuasively that Sula's orgasmic howl occurs at the moment at which she is located "outside of the dominant discursive order" but also when she is poised to re-enter and disrupt the discursive order. For Henderson, Sula's howl becomes a primary metaphor for African-American women writers whose objective is not "to move from margin to center, but to remain on the borders of discourse, speaking from the vantage point of the insider/outsider" (33, 36). This point of difficult balance is, I suggest, where Olsen places the African-American congrega-tion at the moment of the "single exultant lunge of shriek."

But what more is there in the story to justify such a reading of this univocalizing of heteroglossia? Alva, Parialee's mother, will give us some indications. After Carol's near-faint, Alva blames herself for not having been more attentive to Carol's being brought into a situation she had no basis for understanding. Attempting to explain the situation to Carol after the fact, Alva says, "You not used to people letting go that way. . . . You not used to hearing what people keeps inside, Carol. You know how music can make you feel things? Glad or sad or like you can't sit still? That was religion music, Carol.'" Speaking of the congregation Alva says, "'And they're home Carol, church is home. Maybe the only place they can feel how they feel and maybe let it come out. So they can go on. And it's all right'" (59-60). So we seem to have our answer. The univocalizing of heteroglossia is a shared singular escape of people who are trapped in multiple ways. They seem to choose to surrender the heteroglossia of their suffering to the univocal escape of the church/home. But is it "all right"?

The story's first section ends with an italicized rendering of what Alva did not say to Carol. This reverie—which remains silent, unspoken to Carol—stands as a response (like the earlier italicized responses of the congregation and the choirs) to an earlier series of the preacher's assertions. Earlier in the sermon the preacher proclaims: "He was your mother's rock. Your father's mighty tower. And he gave us a little baby. A little baby to love." The congregation responds: "*I am so glad*" (54). Alva's silent reverie begins:

> *When I was carrying Parry and her father left me, and I fifteen years old, one thousand miles away from home, sin-sick and never really believing, as still I don't believe all, scorning, for what have it done to help, waiting there in the clinic and maybe sleeping, a voice called: Alva, Alva. So mournful and so sweet: Alva. Fear not, I have loved you from the foundation of the universe.* (61)

Alva follows the voice "*into a world of light, multitudes singing,*" and the reverie ends: "*Free, free, I am so glad*" (61). The reverie's mixture of dream and reality parallels the mixture of the imaginary and the real in the sermon situation and seems to stand as Alva's singular response (not an affirmation) to the preacher's assertions in the sermon. But this is not a completely singular response, and it is not totally devoid of affirmation. When Alva acknowledges, "still I don't believe all," she locates herself, like Henderson's African-American female writer, both within and outside the church, inside yet resisting the univocality, outside yet resisting the conflation of the imaginary and the real. But we must remember that this is what Alva does *not* say to Carol, or to Helen, or as far as we know to anyone other than us. What is the force that creates this silence? Is it the circumstances of Alva's daily life? Is it the church?

We cannot begin to answer these questions without looking at the structure of the second part of the story. Just as Alva's reverie functions as a response to the sermon, the second part of the story stands as a response to the first part. In the second part, which takes place in the world of Helen and Len (or Lennie) and their daughters, Carol and Jeannie, a univocalizing force parallels that of the church in part one. In the second part the force against heteroglossia is the junior high school, which officially and unofficially attempts to separate Carol and Parialee, univocalizing Carol and other white students while shutting out Parialee and other African-American students. Because she is African-American, Parialee will not be tracked into Carol's accelerated classes; and even if she were initially admitted to them, the necessity to care for younger siblings while her mother works the four-to-twelve-thirty night shift would quickly put her behind in her studies. Carol is "college prep," whereas Parialee will likely not finish junior high, predicts Jeannie, a 17-year-old veteran of the public school system. According to Jeannie, "you have to watch everything, what you wear and how you wear it and who you eat lunch with and how much homework you do and how you act to the teacher and what you laugh at. . . .[ellipsis Olsen's] And run with your crowd" (63). Peer pressure is tremendous, and Carol and Parialee would be ostracized for attempting to be friends. Jeannie contrasts their "for real" working-class school with one in a nearby affluent neighborhood where it is fashionable for whites and African-Americans to be "buddies": " . . . three coloured kids and their father's a doctor or judge or something big wheel and one always gets elected President or head song girl or something to prove oh how we're democratic" (65).

The junior high school has its parallel to the preacher—the teacher, Miss Campbell (nicknamed "Rockface")—and in this parallel Olsen further suggests dangers in the monologic impulses within the church's hetero-glossia. Godlike in the junior high school kingdom, the bigoted teacher has the power to decide whether Parialee can be trusted to take Carol's homework assignments to her when Carol has the mumps: "Does your mother work for Carol's mother?" Rockface asks Parialee. "Oh, you're neighbors! Very well, I'll send along a monitor to open Carol's locker but you're only to take these things I'm writing down, nothing else" (67). Like the preacher, Rockface has the power to make Parialee respond. In drill master fashion, Rockface insists: "Now say after me: Miss Campbell is trusting me to be a good responsible girl. And go right to Carol's house . . . . Not stop anywhere on the way. Not lose anything. And only take. What's written on the list" (67). However, we know of this not because Parialee told Carol. The account of Rockface appears in a passage that parallels Alva's reverie—what she did not say to Carol. The passage in which Parialee accounts for Rockface appears in a section in which she has been talking to Carol, but the Rockface passage begins: "*But did not tell.*" The knowledge we have of Rockface from Parialee is, like the knowledge we have of Alva's inner world, one more silence in Carol's world.

What are we to make of this chilling structural parallel between the worlds of the dominant and the marginalized, the oppressor and the oppressed? Certainly we must hear Olsen's warning that the marginalized imperil their identities by replicating, even through mimicry, structures of the dominant discourse. The African-American congregation risks imposing on itself the dominant culture's reductive and oppressive structures. But has the congregation yet succumbed? Perhaps not. Perhaps they as a collective, unlike the individuals Emily and Whitey, keep their identities apart from what they mimic (or in Whitey's case, what mimics him). Perhaps insofar as the assertion/affirmation structure (so dangerously reminiscent of the dominant discourse's reductive structures) remains embedded in a cacophonous atmosphere of heteroglossia, it remains a viable form of mimicry and the African-American church maintains a delicate ecology of inside/outside with alternative structures and voices constantly checking and offsetting the structures of an oppressive discourse. Certainly the scene within the church approximates what Bakhtin identifies as heteroglossia in its fullest play—carnival—in which people's multiple voices play in, around, and against the dominant culture's hierarchical structures. Perhaps insofar as the African-American church remains a world about which Alva can say, "still I don't believe all," a world where she can be simultaneously inside and outside, it remains a dynamic social unit capable of resisting its own oppressive impulses.

Those readers who are strangers to the powerful culture of the African-American church cannot be sure how to assess that world and, like Carol, experience an abundance of meaning that approaches silence. In fact, Carol is a very useful point of reference for Olsen's readers. The story is a tangled web of explanations Carol never hears about historical circumstances that have enmeshed her. Carol hears neither Alva's reverie, which partly explains the phenomenon in the church, nor Parialee's account of Rockface. Further, as the story nears its end, Carol in desperation asks Helen a basic question, openly pleading for a response: "'Mother, why did they sing and scream like that? At Parry's church?'" But in place of a response we find:

> *Emotion,* Helen thought of explaining, *a characteristic of the religion of all oppressed peoples, yes your very own great-grandparents*—thought of saying. And discarded.
> *Aren't you now, haven't you had feelings in yourself so strong they had to come out some way?* ("what howls restrained by decorum")—thought of saying. And discarded.
> Repeat Alva: *hope . . . every word out of their own life. A place to let go. And church is home.* And discarded.
> *The special history of the Negro people—history?—just you try living what must be lived every day*—thought of saying. And discarded.
> And said nothing. (70)

Once more, Carol is met with silence.

We as readers may, like Carol, expect answers to our many questions about the disjunctures and potential connections among the lives and worlds of the story's characters. But Olsen, no more than Helen, supplies definitive answers. We are privileged to hear more than Carol hears, but Olsen does not answer our questions about how the lives and worlds might be connected. Is Helen's silence at the end of "O Yes" a failure in relation to her daughter? Is Olsen's silence in relation to us a failure of authorial responsibility?

To address these questions I turn to my discussion's second major division, Olsen's reworking of relationships among writer, text, and reader. Helen's silence provides insight into Olsen's designs on us as readers and our relationships to issues of dominant and marginalized people and their discourses. To return to Meese's previously-cited observation, Olsen repeatedly "calls upon the reader to write the text—no longer her text, but occasioned by it and by the voices speaking through it" (110). Helen thinks but does not say: *"Better immersion than to live untouched"* (71). Structured immersion is what Olsen plans for us. Olsen demands that we not be passive receptors, but that we, in Bakhtinian terms, join in the heteroglossia. Olsen has skillfully structured textual gaps and developed strategies for readers' identifying with characters—structures and strategies that require readers to contribute to the emergence of heteroglossic meaning. In those gaps and moments of identification we are not given free rein as readers, but we are asked to act responsibly as members of a complex human community.

To observe Olsen's craft in teasing out our active participation, I return first to "Tell Me a Riddle." Eva craves solitude: *"Never again to be forced to move to the rhythms of others"* (76). And she is tired of the talk: "'All my life around babblers. Enough!'" (82). Eva exercises her greatest control and feels triumphant when she manages to gain and maintain periods of silence. Olsen has given us a difficult kind of central character, one whose fierce desire for the silence she believes she has earned resists the telling of her story. We as audience are caught in the uncomfortable position of hearing the story of someone who wants her story left in silence. We are interlopers. We, like David, violate Eva's solitude and silence, and the narrator, seemingly torn between telling the story and honoring Eva's longing for silence, contributes to our discomfort.

The story's title and the presence of the phrase "tell me a riddle" in the story itself indicate sources of our uneasiness. In the story, the phrase "tell me a riddle" appears in the context of the "command performance." On the visit to daughter Vivi's, a visit Eva felt forced to make when she really wanted to go home, the narrator tells us very nearly from Eva's own perspective: "Attentive with the older children; sat through their performances (command performance; we command you to be the audience) . . . ." (94). Here the traditional notion of "command performance" is reversed. It is not the performer who enacts her role by command; it is the audience who performs its role by command. Eva is trapped. She is once again at the mercy of others' needs and desires.

In her role as command audience, Eva "watched the children whoop after their grandfather who knew how to tickle, chuck, lift, toss, do tricks, tell secrets, make jokes, match riddle for riddle" (94). She watched David interact with the grandchildren in the expected ways, in all the ways in which she would not: "(Tell me a riddle, Grammy. I know no riddles, child)" (94). Eva, the command audience, plays her attentive role up to a point, but she does not fully meet expectations. To the command "Tell me a riddle" she responds with a form of her prized silence, thwarting conventional expectations about grandparent-grandchild interactions.

Conventional expectations about interactions between us as audience and Eva and her story are also thwarted. We cannot be merely passive listeners to Eva's story. Whereas monologic discourse is, again, as Bakhtin asserts, "deaf to the other's response," even the title "Tell Me a Riddle" signals the necessity of our response. From the moment we read the title, we are told to act: "Tell Me a Riddle." We expect to hear a story, but we are told to tell a riddle. We, like Eva, are a command audience, and we, like Eva, find ourselves responding with our own versions of silence. We, the command audience, have been identified with Eva, the command audience, and with her desire for silence. Again, we are put in the uncomfortable situation of wanting to be silent listeners to the story of someone who wants her story left in silence.

Why should we be submitted to this discomfort? On one level we are put in this position because of the narrator's sympathy with Eva's desires. Eva's is a story that needs to be told, yet the narrator sympathizes with Eva's hunger for silence. The compromise for the narrator is to disrupt our complacency as audience. We will hear the story, but not on our terms: We will hear the story as a command audience. What better way to force us to realize the complexity of Eva's situation than to force us into a position resembling Eva's experience as command audience? But there is another reason for our discomfort. As in *Yonnondio* and *Silences*, Olsen disrupts our passivity, demanding that we as readers share responsibility for completing Eva's story.

But how do we exercise our responsibility? We have some clues in David's response to Eva. To David it seemed that for 70 years she had hidden an "infinitely microscopic" tape recorder within her, "trapping every song, every melody, every word read, heard, and spoken" (118). She had caught and was now releasing all the discourse around her: "'you who called others babbler and cunningly saved your words'" (119). But the harsh realization for David was that "she was playing back only what said nothing of him, of the children, of their intimate life together" (118). For David, the air is now filled with sound; yet that sound is the equivalent of silence. To him the danger referred to in my discussion of "I Stand Here Ironing"—that multivocal, heteroglossic discourse may result in the equivalent of silence—has become reality.

However, here we have a new perspective on the danger. The danger lies not in the discourse but in the audience. Because David hears nothing of Eva's life with him, the sounds become meaningless. His is an individualistic, self-centered response. But, crucially, what are these sounds to us as command audience? We have experienced the discomfort of being listeners to the story of one who does not want her story told, but now, at the end of her life, she speaks. If we identify with David's individualistic perspective, we will not understand Eva; her sounds will be the equivalent of silence. However, if we value Eva's identification with all humankind, we are an audience for whom Eva's last words have meaning.

Olsen aids us in valuing Eva's links to all humankind. One of those aids is a resuscitated David with whom we are invited to identify once he has remembered what he had long forgotten. Finally, David comes to a partial understanding of Eva's last words. When she brokenly repeats part of a favorite quotation from Victor Hugo, David remembers it, too, reciting scornfully: "'in the twentieth century ignorance will be dead, dogma will be dead, war will be dead, and for all humankind one country—of fulfillment'? Hah!" (120). But Eva's feverish cantata finally awakens in the old man memories of his own youthful visions:

> Without warning, the bereavement and betrayal he had sheltered—compounded through the years—hidden even from himself—revealed itself,
> > uncoiled,
> > released,
> > *sprung*
> and with it the monstrous shapes of what had actually happened in the century. (120)

David realizes with sudden clarity the full price of his assimilation into America's "apolitical" mainstream: "'Lost, how much I lost'" (121). He and Eva "had believed so beautifully, so . . . falsely?" (122; ellipsis Olsen's):

"Aaah, children," he said out loud, "how we believed, how we belonged."
And he yearned to package for each of the children, the grandchildren, for
everyone, *that joyous certainty, that sense of mattering, of moving and being
moved, of being one and indivisible with the great of the past, with all that
freed, ennobled.* Package it, stand on corners, in front of stadiums and on
crowded beaches, knock on doors, give it as a fabled gift. (122)

David also realizes that Eva's revolutionary faith did not die with his:
"*Still she believed?* 'Eva!' he whispered. 'Still you believed? You lived by
it? These Things Shall Be?'" (123). This story's epigraph, "These Things
Shall Be," is the title of an old socialist hymn expressing hope for a future
just society. Another riddle, then, is the puzzle of revolutionary consciousness: Under what circumstances does it develop, dissipate? How does it
sustain itself when confronted by "monstrous shapes"—the rise of fascism,
two world wars, the extermination of nine million Jews, the threat of
global extinction?

The second aid Olsen provides us in valuing Eva's ties to all humankind is Eva's granddaughter, Jeannie (the same Jeannie of "Hey Sailor,
What Ship?" and "O Yes," now in her twenties) to whom the legacy of
resistance is passed on. Jeannie, who works as a visiting nurse and has
a special political and artistic sensibility, cares for Eva in the last weeks
of her life. "'Like Lisa she is, your Jeannie,'" Eva whispers to Lennie and
Helen, referring to the revolutionary who taught Eva to read more than
50 years before. It is at the end of the passage in which Eva compares
Jeannie to Lisa that Eva says, "'All that happens, one must try to
understand'" (112, 113).

Those words comprise Eva's hope for Jeannie and Olsen's most basic
demand on us as active readers. Recognizing the persistent threat of
being so flooded with meaning that we may be faced with meaninglessness and the equivalent of silence, we must persist in the attempt to
understand. In that attempt we must recognize the dangers of the
bourgeois individualism into which we, like David, are constantly tempted
to retreat. Olsen provides structures, such as the command audience
structure I have discussed, to force us out of our passive individualistic
roles as readers and to invite us into a web of interconnected, heteroglossic roles.[4] If we accept the invitation, we must do more than value
Eva's identification with all humankind: We must remember if we have
forgotten (the model of David) or learn if we have never known (the
model of Jeannie) the complicated histories of worlds like those in which
Eva lived and struggled. At the least, we are required to do our part in
keeping alive the historical circumstances of oppressive czarist Russia and
the connections among all oppressed groups. Eva and Olsen require us to

learn the very histories to which America's "apolitical" mainstream would have us remain oblivious. With Jeannie, we are challenged to carry on Eva's legacy of resistance.

Olsen provides one further aid in valuing Eva's links to all humankind, an aid not limited to the collection's final story. The subject of motherhood so prominent in "I Stand Here Ironing," "O Yes," and "Tell Me a Riddle" provides a crucial reference point for our accepting a heteroglossia linking all humankind. Olsen has rightly referred to motherhood "as an almost taboo area; the last refuge of sexism . . . the least understood" and "last explored, tormentingly complex *core* of women's oppression." At the same time, Olsen believes that motherhood is, potentially, a source of "transport" for women, moving them beyond some of the constraints of individualism.[5] Responsible for what Olsen terms "the maintenance of life," mothers are often exposed to forms of heteroglossia, with their attendant benefits and hazards (*Silences* 34). In exploring the complexity of motherhood, Olsen renders versions of it that are "coiled, convoluted like an ear"—versions that may serve as models for the necessary hearing of heteroglossia.

I return to Helen's silence at the end of "O Yes." We can read Helen's silence as one of several textual comments on the limits of authority; indeed, it may have been through the experience of parenting that Olsen learned the limits of authorial control, which her texts so willingly concede. As an involved parent, one is forced to live intensely "in relation to," as the boundary between self and other is constantly negotiated. Such negotiating provides a model in which the ability to listen to constantly changing, heteroglossic voices is prized. When Carol asks, "why do I have to care?", the narrator tells us the following about Helen:

> Caressing, quieting.
> Thinking: *caring asks doing. It is a long baptism into the seas of humankind, my daughter. Better immersion than to live untouched* . . . . [ellipsis Olsen's] *Yet how will you sustain?*
> *Why is it like it is?*
> Sheltering her daughter close, mourning the illusion of the embrace.
> *And why do I have to care?*
> While in her, her own need leapt and plunged for the place of strength that was not—where one could scream or sorrow while all knew and accepted, and gloved and loving hands waited to support and understand. (71)

Although we risk being flooded by a multiplicity of meaning that approaches meaninglessness and the equivalent of silence, we as readers must submit to the "immersion," the "long baptism" that allows us to be the proper "ear" for the complexity of heteroglossia.

We have similar models at the end of "I Stand Here Ironing" and "Tell Me a Riddle." The mother listens to Emily on "one of her communicative nights . . . [when] she tells me everything and nothing" (19). The mother does not respond to Emily, but says to herself, to the teacher or counselor, and to us, "Let her be. So all that is in her will not bloom—but in how many does it? There is still enough left to live by" (20-21). In "Tell Me a Riddle" Jeannie, who has listened carefully to Eva's dying heteroglossia, is not actually a mother; but, like a mother, she is a caretaker, a nurturer, a listener.

However, Olsen asks more of us than listening. As Helen says to herself, "*caring asks doing.*" In none of these models in *Tell Me a Riddle* is the mother figure a passive listener; rather, she is a listener responsive to heteroglossia. Even when multiple voices so overwhelm her that she is caught in silence (Emily's mother, Helen, Eva), she can sometimes caress or embrace, knowing the communicative power of such actions. As active readers, then, we are provided models of careful listening, leading to action. Olsen does not proscribe the field of political/social action that we as active readers might enter. However, she does demand that we work to understand the many voices of the oppressed. In "I Stand Here Ironing," the mother says of Emily, "Only help her to know," a command the dying Eva echoes: "All that happens, one must try to understand." These words comprise imperatives for us. And these mother figures, who live compassionately and interdependently in a multicultural and heteroglossic dynamic, become models for us as readers.

Olsen demands another, related form of action from her readers. In the collection, *Tell Me a Riddle*, we have been exposed to many moments in which characters sensitive to heteroglossia have been so inundated with complexity of meaning they have lapsed into silence. We have heard what the unnamed mother in "I Stand Here Ironing," Alva, Helen, and Eva have *not* been able to say to those most immediately connected to them. If the silence is perpetuated, these characters risk, as do Emily and Whitey, being subsumed by the dominant discourse. Olsen requires us, as readers of the complete collection, to hear the various oppressed voices and to make and articulate connections among them, connections the separate characters may not be able to see, or may only partially see. With such actions we become collaborators with Olsen in the democratizing enterprise of amplifying dominated and marginalized voices. We join her in a commitment to social change.

The "riddle" which Olsen's work challenges us to engage requires that we consider political activity not as something confined to a single class, party, gender, ethnic group, or cause but as something undertaken within a kaleidoscopic social field and, simultaneously, within "the fibres of the self and in the hard practical substance of effective and continuing relationships" (Williams 212). Olsen's genuinely democratic content articulates itself in multivocal texts that prefigure postindividual cultural forms. In a sense, Olsen's sociopolitical vision has enabled her to write what cannot be written. *Tell Me a Riddle's* form represents a *"pre-emergence,* active and pressing but not yet fully articulated, rather than the evident emergence which could be more confidently named" (Williams 126). With Virginia Woolf in "The Leaning Tower," Olsen's texts proclaim: "Literature is no one's private ground; literature is common ground" (125).

NOTES

1. For discussions of history of reading strategies and earlier defenses of indirect and figurational structures against schemes for linguistic reductionism, see Bartine.

2. In the edition of *Tell Me a Riddle* I have used for this essay, the title story is "for two of that generation, Seevya and Genya." In the 1989 edition, Olsen also dedicates the story to her parents. Genya Gorelick had been a factory organizer in Morzyr, a famous orator, and the leading woman of the Jewish Workers' Alliance, the Bund of pre-revolutionary Russia. Her son, Al Richmond, has written about the role Gorelick played in the 1905 revolution, when she was just nineteen:

> ... the 1905 revolution burst forth like the splendid realization of a dream, shaking the Czarist regime enough to loosen its most repressive restrictions, so that revolutionaries at last could address the public, not any more through the whispered word and the surreptitious leaflet but openly and directly in large assemblies. She discovered her gifts as a public orator. She was good, and in her best moments she was truly great. (8; cited in Rosenfelt, "Divided" 19)

3. Olsen told me in an interview (11 July 1986, San Francisco) that she modelled Whitey partly on Filipino men she knew "in the movement" who hungered for contact with families at a time when U.S. immigration law kept Filipino women and children from entering the U.S.

4. Patrocinio P. Schweickart outlines a promising model for reading based on a joining of reader-response theory and feminist theory. Her model contains some of the characteristics Olsen's writing demands of readers. Schweickart finds that feminist theory can move "beyond the individualistic models of [Wolfgang] Iser and of most reader-response critics" toward a "collective" model of reading. Describing the goal of that model, Schweickart observes that "the feminist reader hopes that other women will recognize themselves in her story, and join her in her struggle to transform the culture" (50, 51). It must be added that Olsen, like Schweickart, would have women and men "join her in her struggle to transform the culture."

5. *Silences* 202. For an enlightening discussion of *Tell Me a Riddle* in relation to other works dealing with motherhood, see Gardiner. Gardiner also suggests Jeannie's function as a model for readers when she notes that "at the end of the story, Jeannie has absorbed her grandmother's consciousness," allowing Eva to be "the agent of a revolutionary and transcendent ideal that can be passed from woman to woman, of a commitment to fully human values" (163).

WORKS CITED

Bakhtin, M.M. *The Dialogic Imagination.* Ed. Michael Holquist. Trans. Caryl Emerson and Michael Holquist. Austin: U of Texas P, 1981.

Bartine, David. *Early English Reading Theory: Origins of Current Debates.* Columbia: U of South Carolina P, 1989.

———. *Reading, Culture, and Criticism: 1820-1950.* Columbia: U of South Carolina P, 1992.

Eagleton, Terry. *Against the Grain, Essays 1975-1985.* London: Verso, 1986.

———. *Marxism and Literary Criticism.* Berkeley and Los Angeles: U of California P, 1976.

Gardiner, Judith Kegan. "A Wake for Mother: The Maternal Deathbed in Women's Fiction." *Feminist Studies* 4 (June 1978): 146-165.

Henderson, Mae Gwendolyn. "Speaking in Tongues: Dialogics, Dialectics, and the Black Woman Writer's Literary Tradition." *Changing Our Own Words: Essays on Criticism, Theory, and Writing by Black Women.* Ed. Cheryl A. Wall. New Brunswick: Rutgers UP, 1989.

Meese, Elizabeth A. *Crossing the Double-Cross: The Practice of Feminist Criticism.* Chapel Hill: U of North Carolina P, 1986.

Olsen, Tillie. *Mother to Daughter, Daughter to Mother.* Old Westbury: Feminist Press, 1984.

———. *Silences.* New York: Dell, 1978.

———. *Tell Me a Riddle.* 1961. New York: Dell, 1979.

Richmond, Al. *A Long View from the Left: Memoirs of an American Revolutionary.* New York: Dell, 1972.

Rosenfelt, Deborah. "Divided against Herself." *Moving On* April/May 1980: 15-23.

———. "From the Thirties: Tillie Olsen and the Radical Tradition." *Feminist Studies* 7 (Fall 1981): 371-406. Rept. in Judith Newton and Deborah Rosenfelt, eds., *Feminist Criticism and Social Change: Sex, Class, and Race in Literature and Culture* (New York: Methuen, 1985), 216-48.

Schweickart, Patrocinio P. "Reading Ourselves: Toward a Feminist Theory of Reading." *Gender and Reading: Essays on Readers, Texts, and Contexts,* eds. Elizabeth A. Flynn and Patrocinio P. Schweickart. Baltimore: Johns Hopkins UP, 1986.

Todorov, Tzvetan. *Mikhail Bakhtin: The Dialogical Principle*. Translated by Wlad Godzich. Minneapolis: U of Minnesota P, 1984.

Williams, Raymond. *Marxism and Literature*. Oxford: Oxford UP, 1977.

Woolf, Virginia. "The Leaning Tower." *The Moment and Other Essays*. London: Hogarth, 1952.

Re-reading Tillie Olsen's "O Yes"

Nancy Huse

Tillie Olsen's multivocal narrative style evoked the complexities of race/ethnicity, class, and gender well before this set of terms had become critical tools in the academy. And, unlike writers who object to readers' departure from their own sense of intentionality, Olsen acknowledges the range of meanings possible for each text, when readers "fill it in with their own lives."[1] Her dense, poetic prose, carrying rich traces of her political commitments as well as gaps drawn from silences about her personal life, invites and rewards numerous readings.[2]

Olsen's work seems kaleidoscopic; while composed of "genuinely democratic content" it nonetheless can be seen differently with each change of critical perspective.[3] The narrative style and complex historical vision, drawn from an aesthetic at once socialist and feminist, modernist and postmodernist, make her a writer particularly subject to "misreadings," or critical acts involving as much of readers' own concerns as textual evidence. Olsen's writing challenges me as a teacher, because the meanings I draw from her work often differ radically from the responses of my students, at least upon their first reading. Olsen herself urges respect for readers, and she is certain that students engage ably with her writing. But she also sets an example of claiming authority over the interpretive process. For example, at an MLA panel on working class women writers, she reiterated her conviction that the Communist Party of her youth took an active stance against sexism.[4]

Like Olsen, I want my own understandings incorporated into discussion of the stories in *Tell Me a Riddle,* but—equally committed to feminist pedagogy—do not want to stifle the insights brought by students. Just as Olsen offered her comments after critics had given their papers, hoping that future interpretive work would attend to the evidence she offered, I want students to engage with Olsen's texts using the personal resources they demonstrate in other discussions. Yet, I am restive with this process. What seem to me narrow or mistaken emphases occur; for example, in my twenty years of teaching Olsen's work, many students have anguished over the disintegrating marriage of Eva and David in "Tell Me a Riddle," seldom foregrounding Jeannie in their interpretation of the story, much less pondering, as I hope they will, Eva's social and aesthetic beliefs. To avoid transmission pedagogy, I need ways to ground my students better in the contexts from which Olsen writes, and I do make efforts to sequence material accordingly. But I have just so much time to teach a given course, and must account for many needs—those of students just beginning their literary educations, those of students preparing for

graduate school, and those of students hoping for a course relevant to
their life experience. One cannot (or I, at least, cannot) always adhere to
sequencing of materials in ways suited to each student's perceived needs.
Like the narrator of "I Stand Here Ironing," I know that "I will never total
it all" or bring out the critical potential of my students to the fullest.[5]

Usually white and middle class women in their early twenties, my
students assume themselves competent in literary analysis. Many are
embarrassed when they recognize what they have "missed" on a first
reading. I have thus begun emphasizing how often Olsen does evoke
misreadings from skilled critics, and how useful these can be as part of
a fluid interpretive process. Mickey Pearlman, for example, points with
exasperation to Janet Silverman Van Buren's statement that Eva and
Jeannie, of "Tell Me a Riddle," both had abortions.[6] While I agree with
Pearlman that no textual evidence supports Van Buren, I am intrigued
by the way this misreading heightens the female independence of both
characters. Moreover, Pearlman describes what I consider a misreading
of her own, though of a different kind, when she relates how she asked
Olsen about the "disorder" in her stories. Olsen shifts Pearlman away
from this interpretation, to my satisfaction.[7] But Pearlman's emphasis
in reading Olsen strikes a resonant chord with my own response, even
though before encountering Pearlman I had not recognized in my own
reading strategies the affinity for fragmentation I bring to modernist
texts.

Because Pearlman and I both respond to Olsen by immersion in the
nonsequential, occluding processes of her stories, our different descriptions of them (hers as an unexpected "disorder," mine as a "fragmentation"
to be looked for) suggest a limited, not an infinite, range of meanings
available in a literary experience, a point important to classroom contexts
where various readers bring different assumptions and experience into
play. In Chris Weedon's terms, a finite number of competing discourses
circulate in a given culture; the "conflict between these discourses . . .
creates the possibility of new ways of thinking and new forms of
subjectivity."[8] Combining an emphasis on misreading as a potentially
helpful stage with an understanding that teacher and students can give
one another permission to propose connections and disjunctions not all
share can help with the sensitive issues Olsen deals with: reproduction,
memory, class oppression, and in "O Yes," the effect of racism on two
young girls, their families and communities, and—crucially—on writers and
readers.

The need for readers to grow and change, accepting that mistakes or
misreadings can further growth and that the range of responses is defined
by cultural practice, is essential if certain works, including "O Yes," are to

become part of our cultural knowledge. Few critics have written about this text, and most readings of it occur in essays or books dealing with Olsen's entire canon.[9] Toni Morrison points out that critics have been relatively silent about the use made by white writers of the presence of African American people in their narratives.[10] In part, silence about how white authors deal with what Morrison calls "Africanism"—"the denotative and connotative blackness that African peoples have come to signify"—results from the fact that one can hardly speak about racism without employing racist understandings, a problem similar to that feminists have dealt with in claiming language for women.[11] In order to claim language for building a non-racist society, Morrison challenges critics to begin looking at writers' struggle to depict our racialized society.

As an attempt to deal with the difficult issue of how race-inflected discourses function in the construction of meanings, I offer the following analysis of a class discussion that moved from students' race-inflected discourse to my race-inflected discourse, with reflection on the implications of acknowledging misreadings even while valuing our own responses to the text. Indicative of Olsen's complexity as a writer, each move brings out the impossibility of being finished with commentary, of knowing exactly what Olsen's story means, or even ought to mean. But because my students and I engaged in misreadings relevant at once to Olsen's structural treatment of reproduction (including child-*rearing* as well as child-*bearing*) and our different notions of how to deal with racism, we provided each other, as white middle class women of varied ages, with ideas for our next readings of "O Yes." And in my case, taking my students' comments seriously meant a deeper understanding of what it is to be predetermined by cultural and social constraints even as writers and critics struggle against those constraints. In the shifts between age-related perceptions of Parry's oppression and Helen's duty to live morally in an unjust world, my students and I can be found engaging in a quest for change central to Olsen's work, and not entirely ruled out by the nature of the language.

A misreading of Alva's dream vision occurred in my classroom when a student introduced the idea that Alva had been waiting for an abortion before Parialee's birth. Though she admitted she had little to go on textually, the word "clinic" in the italicized passage had sent her on a responsive journey marvelling at the way Alva's religious imagination had both led her to choose motherhood at fifteen and sustained her later as head of a family gathered for Parialee's baptism. Bringing children into the world against the odds, responding to the little child in her vision as he mourned, "'Mama Mama you must help carry the world'" (52), Alva became an ideal for this student, and for the rest of us, as she argued persuasively that Alva's carrying of Parialee grounded the beauty of the story as a narrative of reproductive choice undermined by racism. Another student commented that Alva's daughter was, in the eyes of the white middle-class school environment, really a "Pariah-lie," both a little pariah, and a false or not-pariah, a brave defiance of repressive systems which crush difference.

The class did not, as I recall, go on to link Carol's dream sequences with that of Alva, or to ask why Alva dreams of a great love and a little child, while Carol dreams of swimming through Alva's workplace, Hostess Foods, with her, and is awakened by both Alva and Helen. In a later instance, Carol sleeps after a painful visit by Parry ending their friendship; again, she is awakened by Helen, this time because Helen's radio sends black gospel singing into Carol's consciousness. Rather than drawing from these allied dream sequences the initiation issues common to Alva and to Carol as they mature into female adulthood in late capitalist, racist environments, my students pursued the fate of Alva's daughter, Parry, born when Alva was fifteen and, at the time of the story, priding herself on "what newly swelled above and swelled below" her wide cinch belt (58). Though Alva seemed a figure of wise strength, my students worried about her daughter.

For my students, the implied question was, "How does Alva's mothering fail Parry, and why?" For me, it was "Who is mothered and unmothered in this story, and why?" Students at that moment did not move from their insights about Parry's birth and naming to a consideration of how Carol's name—"Carry"—is a key word in Alva's vision of mature womanhood, and the occasion of Parry's baptism is also that of Carry's, into a class, race and gender system she will not be comfortable in, seductive though it is, like the dream of unconditional love in Alva's dream and Helen's final yearning for "the place of strength that was not—where one could scream or sorrow while all knew and accepted, and gloved and loving hands waited to support and understand" (62).

My students, that day at least, poured out their responses as a way of valuing Parry, whom they perceived as a victim of race and class bias that turned bittersweet Alva's birthing of her. I remember feeling both elated and saddened at the discussion, recognizing Alva as a pivotal character but wondering how to "get at" what I considered essential Olsen—her social vision and hope. My students wanted to mourn; only now do I accept that the "O Yes" of the congregation, like Alva's acceptance of motherhood and Carry's recognition of her flawed humanity, has a dark side, of a piece with Parry's resistant language and Helen's leaping and plunging need. My students had their own vision of the story, one which makes more sense to me now than it did when they proposed it. Naomi

M. Jacobs has described how her own students, in this case women who had had children, arrived independently of each other at a reading of Alva's dream-vision as a literal account of the "physical and psychological experience of childbirth."[12] Like my abortion-minded student, they traced the bright lights and impersonal care offered to Alva in textual clues related to the word "clinic." They noted the child on his motorbike "making a path no bigger than my little finger" as a reference to the birth canal and the maturation of Alva through the birth experience. The terror and ecstasy of giving birth became a ready (and convincing) interpretive theory for these students. My own, younger students, on the threshold of their reproductive lives, validated the truth of the caste system they recognized in high school and in college. Alluding to Parry's language, they found both deprivation and strength in comparison to Carol's somewhat "prissy" idiom. To follow up on their interest in Olsen's use of varied discourses, I pursued my own misreading with their help.

My own misreading of "O Yes," schematizing the friendships of the mothers and the daughters into a tightly woven network of affirmation, involves imagining Helen as a guide for Parry, in the way Alva is a guide for Carol. Nothing supports this desire in the text, to my knowledge. In fact, Helen's yearning for the loving community of the black church and for the unconditional acceptance she believes Alva can find there, suggests how vulnerable she is within her own rational, dialectical family. Parry, too, is vulnerable, but not only within her own culture; she is coming into her own as a young black woman able to dress, dance, and engage in word play—and perhaps, as my students feared, to be a teen-aged mother. She is vulnerable within the world of rational and conventional white middle class behavior and language, somewhat (though the comparison is tenuous) the way Helen, the white mother hoping to preserve friendship and yet support her daughter's acceptance within the dominant culture, suffers from the inexorable grip of that culture, exemplified by her husband Lennie and her older daughter Jeannie as they analyze class bias. Though Lennie believes in social change—"Don't you think kids like Carol and Parry can show it doesn't *have* to be that way" (54)—he cuts off Jeannie's protest when he fears it is becoming irrational, that like Carol she will lose conscious control of her faculties. In contrast, Helen asks Jeannie to repeat her outburst so that she can focus on the daughter rather than on herself. The white family's distance from the intuitive and expressive modes of the black community endangers Carol's friendship with Parry and (by implication) endangers all.

My concern for Helen as she mourns a racist and classist gulf while rocking and soothing the newly conscious Carol competed with my students' grief for Parry. As they moved to a discussion of junior high pressures they remembered well, I wondered how Helen endured. Like Jeannie, they observed Parry's acceptance by her own group, but unlike her they expressed no concern for Carol, whose fainting at church they seemed to disapprove. Since Olsen must always be "misread" because of the layers of meaning evoked by the use of dialogue and silences, with narrative reportage of characters' inner thoughts, I felt free to ask students' patience with my need to turn the discussion toward the interaction of the two mothers and the two daughters. For part of my job as a teacher, like Helen's as a mother, is to show them a vision other than their own. One such vision is a recognition of Olsen's treatment of a complex issue, the friendship of white women and black women. For the framework I cannot fit into the story, my dream that Helen shows, directly, a care for Parry parallel to Alva's for Carol, is not unrelated to my students' sense that Parry was harmed by a racism infused with class and gender inequities. If I heard my students "othering" Parry and Alva, I heard myself "sameing" the mothers and daughters in the story, wanting to close the gap of direct guidance to Parry, regardless of what I know about how people learn things through experience and constructing their own discourses. In short, just as my students' anxiety around reproduction was behind their misreading, so mine around teaching evoked another misreading. Using our own small certainties, my students and I positioned ourselves within the narrative. As white women recognizing some of the ways Olsen alludes to racism in "O Yes," we had begun what proved to be a painful process, especially for me, as I continue to think about re-reading "O Yes."

From a study of novels by American women, Nancy Porter concludes that "white women writers develop the dark-skinned friend as mirror or mentor of the white character whose identity and growth are the novel's central concern."[13] Overall, "white writers do not appear sanguine about the durability of black-white friendship in a racist world." Nonetheless, Porter sees a variety of female interracial friendships available in novels, offering an opportunity for readers' growth by recognizing how white guilt and black distrust provide a connection between the private realm of friendship and the need to transform the public realm of power. Citing Sherley Anne Williams and Toni Morrison as black novelists who have altered the pattern of failed friendship/white guilt/black distrust, Porter causes me to wonder how Olsen's earlier short story fares when I shift attention to the wider context of American fiction. Helen and Alva continue their friendship, but "Parry never drops by with Alva for Saturday snack to or from grocery shopping" (57). Parry is spending more of her time caring for her sister, brother, and cousins while Alva works the four to twelve-thirty shift; Carol is "off to club or skating or library or someone's house" after school (56). It is Carol who, overall, is the focus of the story—she will grow into a white woman with a double, divided consciousness, thanks to the mentoring of Parry's church and family as well as to the care of her own family. Seen in this way, with Carol's guilt and Parry's distrust the basis of the story, my students' outpouring of care for Parry seems no less mature than my own example of white guilt. My concern—that Alva mothers Carol overtly, but Helen's care for Parry is not conveyed to her directly—seems dangerously stereotypical: black women can mother the world, white women are limited by class and race privilege to an ineffectual silence. Is Helen's yearning for Alva's religious community, as the story closes, a sign of her unmothered life? Olsen presents Alva's partial resistance to religious community in the dream-vision passage; Alva is both intuitive and rational at once. For Helen, rationality is no defense; Carol's grief evokes her caress, but not an explanation. She does speak from betrayal and shame about the possibility of friendship: "Brought herself to say aloud: 'But may be friends again. As Alva and I are'"(61). These are the last of Helen's spoken words except for her "Yes, lambie" in the midst of Carol's recognition that she resembles a black girl whose spiritual gifts make her an outcast in the world. The story ends with Helen's yearning for "the place of strength that was not" (62).

Friendship between the two mothers survives although the discourse systems of their communities fail them. It is implied that Carol will be a socially conscious white woman, that Parry will be a socially conscious black woman—but guilt and distrust seem embedded in that social consciousness. Olsen's story, though well within the pattern of endangered friendships between black and white women found in other literature by white women, rests in the emphasis she places on the domestic. Alva and Helen have the habit of seeing each other on Saturdays, in a break from household chores; and they share a concern about child-rearing. Each berates herself for not attending well enough to one of Helen's girls. Alva is confident that her children understand the church ritual, but wishes she had prepared Carol for it. We are not told what Alva thinks about Parry's resentment of her mother as the girl plans to go to a party on Saturday night "if Momma'll stay home. IF" (58). That the story attends to Carol, not Parry, has a certain truth to it; and my students' movement into the narrative is to take on the voice of Helen explaining things to Parry as Alva explains them to Carol—possibly futile, but caring gestures. This reflection, then, constructs my students' response as a meeting of my own need to have Helen mother Parry. "Caring asks doing," she practices as she silently holds Carol (61). My own act of authority, showing the intersection of student and teacher concerns, is understandable, yet subject to a verdict of insufficiency.

The competing discourses of students and teacher, like the competing discourses of mothers and daughters within the story, can move readers toward a recognition of the many conflicts—youth and age, male and female, black and white, working class and middle class, rational and irrational, silence and speech, protest and action—Olsen recognizes and dramatizes for our attention and care. No one discourse can deal adequately with these; care for Parry, concern for Helen, are only two of the possible and necessary responses and arguments. My students and I each drew from our consciousness of white privilege, but differently. They "mothered" Parry. I "sistered" Helen. In the terms sketched by Cheryl Wall, an African American critic, we had engaged in an appropriate process, because "white women need to reflect on how they have been marked by race and *positioned* in a system of racial privilege."[14] When Toni Morrison breaks silence about Cather's *Sapphira and the Slave Girl*, her analysis emphasizes how Cather must leave her fiction and move into memoir in order to explore the "meaning of female betrayal as it faces the void of racism" (28). Unlike many critics of this work, Morrison acknowledges the effort to "undertake a dangerous journey" it represents. Likewise, Olsen embarks into a forbidden and dangerous world when she allows Parry's baptism to serve as Carry's. My students' sorrow for Parry conveyed also the easily recognizable concept of the victim as "other." In wanting the white woman to be more like Alva, to speak kindly and firmly to the black woman's daughter, I was asking Helen (and myself) to be more "human." I wanted the white mother to engage in the "self-contradictory features of the self," Morrison's summation of how blackness is depicted in writing by whites, and break out of the mute-ness/implacability of whites' "correct" use of speech. (59) For a terrifying moment, I see that Olsen offers Helen's silence and yearning as a model of mothering and a model of teaching more efficacious and culturally acceptable than Alva's futile directness; then I remember Helen's soft-sounding repetitions that Parry and Carol can continue to be friends, repetitions her own family set aside. She, too, engages in futile directness, albeit not (within the narrative) to Parry. The focus of the narrative is on Carol and Helen, not Parry and Alva. They are the mentors/mirrors of the white women, in the story and outside of it. Parry's baptism provides Carol's. Her rebellion necessitates Carol's growth (Carol enters Parry's version of reality, standing on her head at one point to act out the way Parry depicts her by turning their graduation picture upside down). It is Carol and Helen whose epiphanies are dramatized—Carol entering the "waters of life" through immersion into painful realities of race, class, and self-doubt, Helen momentarily drowning in that stream as she yearns for rescue by a believing and caring community.

Morrison's admonition to critics, and by implication to readers like my students and me, is "to avert the critical gaze from the racial object to the racial subject; from the described and imagined to the describers and imaginers; from the serving to the served" (90). Using Alva as our mentor, mirror and—to use the term other women of color have revealed as a central metaphor for their experience—as our *bridge,* to the story, to each other, my students and I must recognize our double consciousness, the separation between what we desire and what we are.[15] To recognize Olsen as "playing in the dark" just as we are, despite her brilliant and complex vision, is to make our next reading of "O Yes" more dangerous, more painful, more admiring. To turn our gaze toward ourselves as describers and imaginers, as dreamers, is to "carry the world"—not Alva's job alone, nor Olsen's either.

NOTES

1. Tillie Olsen, quoted in Marilon Yalom, "Tillie Olsen," *Women Writers of the West Coast: Speaking of their Lives and Careers,* ed. Marilon Yalom (Santa Barbara: Capra, 1983).

2. Linda Ray Pratt, "The Circumstances of Silence: Literary Representations and Tillie Olsen's Omaha Past," forthcoming in *The Critical Response to Tillie Olsen,* ed. Kay Hoyle Nelson and Nancy Huse (Westport: Greenwood, 1993).

3. Constance Coiner, "'No One's Private Ground': A Bakhtinian Reading of Tillie Olsen's *Tell Me a Riddle*" in *Feminist Studies* 18 (Summer 1992), 280.

4. Personal tape of Tillie Olsen responding to panelists at MLA, 1988.

5. Tillie Olsen, "I Stand Here Ironing," in *Tell Me a Riddle* (New York: Dell, 1960), 12. Further references to stories in *Tell Me a Riddle* are to this edition.

6. Mickey Pearlman and Abby Werlock, *Tillie Olsen,* (Boston: G.K. Hall, 1991), xi. See also Janet Silverman Van Buren, *The Modernist Madonna: Semiotics of the Maternal Metaphor* (Bloomington, IN: University of Indiana Press, 1989), 166.

7. Pearlman, 6.

8. Chris Weedon, *Feminist Practice and Poststructuralist Theory,* Oxford: Basil Blackwell, 1987, 135.

9. See Pearlman and Werlock, and Coiner, for two examples.

10. Toni Morrison, *Playing in the Dark: Whiteness and the Literary Imagination* (Cambridge: Harvard University Press, 1992).

11. Morrison, 14.

12. Naomi M. Jacobs, "Olsen's 'O Yes': Alva's Vision as Childbirth Account," *Notes on Contemporary Literature* 16 (January 1986), 7-8.

13. Nancy Porter, "Women's Interracial Friendships and Visions of Community in *Meridian, The Salt Eaters, Civil Wars,* and *Dessa Rose"* in *Tradition and the Talents of Women,* ed. Florence Howe (Urbana: University of Illinois Press, 1991), 252.

14. Cheryl A. Wall, *Changing our Own Words: Essays on Criticism, Theory, and Writing by Black Women,* Cheryl A. Wall, ed. (New Brunswick: Rutgers University Press, 1989), 5.

15. Cherie Moraga and Gloria Anzaldua, *This Bridge Called My Back: Writings by Radical Women of Color* (New York: Kitchen Table Women of Color Press, 1981).

After Long Silence: Tillie Olsen's "Requa"[*]

Blanche H. Gelfant

No one has written so eloquently about silences as Tillie Olsen,[1] or shown as poignantly that a writer can recover her voice.[2] In her most recent fiction, a long story called "Requa," she reclaims once more a power of speech that has proved at times extremely difficult to exercise. Silence followed the publication, almost fifty years ago, of sections from her early and still unfinished novel *Yonnondio*.[3] Then came *Tell Me a Riddle*,[4] bringing Olsen fame but not the sustained power to write she needed, and for another long period her voice was stilled. In 1970 "Requa" appeared, an impressive work which received immediate recognition and was reprinted as one of the year's best stories.[5] For apparently fortuitous reasons, it is now little known, though as Olsen's most innovative and complex work of fiction, it deserves critical attention it has yet to receive. Complete but unfinished, "Requa" is a still-to-be-continued story that develops the theme of human continuity in ways which seem almost subversive. Its form is discontinuous, as though to challenge its theme, and the text is broken visibly into fragments separated from each other by conspicuous blank spaces, gaps the eye must jump over and the mind fill with meaning. However, the story repudiates the meanings that might be inferred from its disintegrated form and from its imagery and setting, both influenced by literary traditions of the past that Olsen continues only to subvert. She draws obviously upon poetry of the twenties for her waste land motifs, and upon novels of the thirties for her realistic portrayal of America's great Depression. Waste and depression are Olsen's subjects in "Requa," but Olsen's voice, resonant after long silence, is attuned to her vision of recovery.

In his poem "After Long Silence," Yeats had defined the "supreme theme" of recovered speech as "Art and Song." Patently, these are not the themes of Olsen's story. "Requa" is about uneducated, unsung working people struggling against depression, both the economic collapse of the thirties and the emotional depression of its protagonist, fourteen-year-old Stevie. The story begins with Stevie traumatized by his mother's death and the loss of everything familiar. Alone and estranged from the work, he is being taken by his Uncle Wes from his home in San Francisco to a small California town set by the Klamath River. Here men fish for salmon, hunt deer, and lead a life alien to a city boy. Stevie arrives at this town, named by the Urac tribe Rek-woi, or Requa, broken in body and

[*] Reprinted from *Studies in American Fiction* 12.1 (Spring 1984): 61-69.

spirit. A wreck of a child, still dizzy from the long bumpy truck ride, heaving until he "can't have 'ary a shred left to bring up," he seems utterly defeated, unable "to hold up." From the beginning, his obsessive deathwish leads to Stevie's withdrawal: "All he wanted was to lie down" (p. 54). He refuses to speak; he sees human faces dimly or not at all; he huddles in bed, hiding under his quilt and rocking. A "ghostboy" with dazed eyes and clammy green skin, he seems ready to lie down forever. But the story turns aside from death to describe a miraculous recovery, nothing less than Stevie's resurrection, for at the end the silent boy springs spectacularly to life. In the "newly tall, awkward body" he has grown into, he runs, "rassles," "frisks" about like a puppy; and when at last Stevie does lie down, he falls into a sweet sleep from which, it seems, he will awaken rested and restored.

Given the time and place, that recovery should become the pervasive action of the story seems as miraculous as a boy's resurrection. The time is 1932, and the setting a junkyard, the natural stopping-place for dispossessed people on the move during America's great Depression. "Half the grown men in the county's not working," Wes tells the boy, no jobs anywhere. Wes himself works in the junkyard, a realistic place described in encyclopedic detail and a symbolic setting suitable to the theme of loss and recovery.[6] At the junkyard mounds of discarded and disjunct things represent tangibly a vision of disorder, disintegration, and waste. "U NAME IT—WE GOT IT," the yard sign boasts: tools, tees, machine parts, mugs, quilts, wing nuts, ropes, reamers, sewing machines, basket hats, "Indian things," baby buggies, beds, pipe fittings, five-and-dime souvenirs, stoves, victrolas. These wildly proliferating abandoned things form "Heaps piles glut accumulation" (p. 64), but the growing lists of material objects Olsen interjects into the story—or rather, makes its substance—undermine a common assumption that accumulation means wealth. On the contrary, things can reveal the poverty of a person's life. All the souvenirs that Stevie's mother had accumulated, now passed on to her son, are "junk." The more souvenirs the story mentions, the more it shows how little the mother had, though obviously she wished to possess something pretty even if it was only "a kewpie doll [or a] green glass vase, cracked" or a "coiled brass snake Plush candy box: sewing stuff: patches, buttons in jars, stork scissors, pin-cushion doll, taffeta bell skirt glistening with glass pinheads" (p. 60).

But things that at first seem worthless take on a strange incandescence in the story, initially perhaps because of the narrator's tone, a musing, mysterious, reverent tone that imbues isolated objects with emotional meaning. And the lives that seem wasted in the story also begin to glow. The dead mother's felt presence becomes stronger and brighter, shining through characters who help her son and through Stevie himself as he begins to recover. Even the junkyard changes. Piled with seemingly useless things, it gives promise of renewal, for the "human mastery, [the] human skill" which went into making machines, now broken and disassembled, can be applied again and the strewn parts made to function. Olsen's waste land inspires "wonder" at the technological genius that can rehabilitate as well as invent, though it has rampantly destroyed. Olsen expresses no nostalgia for a bygone pastoral past which many American writers wish recovered. She visualizes instead a reclamation in the modern world of the waste its technology has produced. In her story everything can be recycled, and anything broken and discarded put to new use. Nothing is beyond the human imagination that can create even out of waste, the "found" objects in a junkyard, a poetic text. Placed side by side, the names of these objects begin to form a concrete poem the story will interrupt, continue, and complete as it moves along. The first stanza, a listing of ingenious devices, implicitly extols human inventiveness and skill: "Hasps switches screws plugs faucets drills Valves pistons shears planes punchers sheaves Clamps sprockets coils bits braces dies" (p. 65). If these disconnected nouns form also a litany of waste, it is one that introduces the hope of redemption, for Olsen describes "disorder twining with order," a combination which qualifies chaos and may signify its arrest. Moreover, Olsen's final inchoate sentence traces a search through the "discarded, the broken, the torn from the whole; [the] weathereaten weatherbeaten: mouldering" for whatever can still be used or needed, for anything that can be redeemed (p. 65).

At the junkyard, Stevie sees people as depleted as himself still hoping for redemption. The faceless, nameless migrant workers who stop to pick up a used transmission or discarded tire reflect widespread social disintegration, but like the migrant workers in John Steinbeck's *The Grapes of Wrath*, they persist in trying, struggling, moving. Battered as they are, they refuse the temptation to lie down, and they trade their last possession, a mattress or gun, for whatever will keep them going. "We got a used everything," Evans the yard-owner says, seeing to it that trashed and broken things are fixed and made usable again for people on the move. Evans is tough and wants the "do-re-mi," but whatever his motives, he is crucially involved in the process of recovery. His yard attracts people whose lives have been shattered, the dispossessed migratory workers and, in time, Stevie. The junkyard also sustains Wes, who keeps his self intact as he makes broken parts useful, working capably and even happily, "singing . . . to match the motor hum as he machines a new edge, rethreads a pipe" (p. 65). Meanwhile Wes is trying to make a new life for his nephew: "I'll help you to catch hold, Stevie," he says, "I promise I'll help" (p. 61). Other characters, barely identified, also help, and the story sketches in the outlines of people variously involved in the boy's recovery. Besides Evans, who gives Stevie a chance to work, the Chinese cook at the boardinghouse keeps him company, and the sympathetic landlady takes him on an outing that will complete his recovery.

As "Requa" describes the "concern" underprivileged or struggling characters show for each other, it raises Olsen's thematic questions about human responsibility and about the relationship between love and survival. Implicitly it asks why Wes, a lone workingman, should give his skill and energy to make trash useful to others and an alienated boy valuable to himself, and why anyone should care, as everyone does, whether a "ghostboy" recovers. The story thus restates Olsen's recurrent riddle, which is, essentially, the mystery of human survival as evidenced by people who continue to live and to care even though their lives seem broken and futile, and life itself full of pain. If human existence has meaning, as Olsen's fiction asserts, then suffering, bereavement, poverty, despair, all inseparable from day-to-day survival in a waste land, must be explained. So must the secret of recovery, which prevails against depression.

This is a complicated achievement already described in Olsen's earlier stories. In "I Stand Here Ironing," a pock-marked girl becomes beautiful, her talent realized, her unhappy deprived childhood, never forgotten, transcended; and a mother, recalling this childhood, straightens out confused emotions and gains a sense of her own identity.[7] Before the Grandmother dies in "Tell Me a Riddle," she too searches through the past to see what of value she can retrieve; and as she becomes reconciled to her own painful life, now coming to an end, she finds meaning and continuity in all human existence. Olsen can describe such recoveries because she has a strong sense of history as both a personal past that gives one a continuous identity and a social legacy that links generations. This legacy, however, is neither whole nor complete, for history is a dump-heap strewn with broken promises and wrecked hopes, among which lie examples of human achievement. Someone must sort through the junk of history, redeem its waste, and salvage whatever can be useful for the next generation. This is the task of reclamation Olsen has assumed as a writer and assigns to her characters, often unnoted, unlikely, inarticulate people for whom she speaks. Indeed, this is why she must recover her own speech, no matter how long her silence, so that Wes, and Stevie, and the dying Grandmother can have a voice.[8]

In "Requa" Stevie continues the quest of the Grandmother in "Tell Me a Riddle." Different as they are, the resurrected boy and the dying woman are both searching for a transmittable human past that will give significance to their present struggle. Both need a history as reusable as Wes's re-threaded pipes. The Grandmother finds hers in the record of humanity's continuous progress toward self-realization. She appropriates this history as a shared "Heritage": "How have we come from the savages, how no longer to be savages—this to teach. To look back and learn what humanizes man—this to teach" (p. 81). Young as he is, Stevie also looks back to learn from his past the secret of recovery, of how he might claim his rightful place as a human being. As the story begins he seems dehumanized, so broken and apathetic that he is unable to relate to anyone else or to himself, unable to see the people in the boarding-house or the beauty of the countryside that will in time shake him with "ecstasy." Described as a "ghostboy," he appears doomed to inanition, but the story struggles against this fate and insists in hushed portentous tones that something will save him: "The known is reaching to him, stealthily, secretly, reclaiming" (p. 65). Both mysterious and obvious, the *known* is Stevie's personal past, experiences from which he will in time draw the strength to live. This strength comes mainly from the remembered love of his mother, the person in his past who has provided him with a "recognizable human bond" which must sustain him and matter more than the losses that life makes inevitable. Even in his withdrawal, a quest for "safety" from the shocks he has suffered, Stevie recognizes that the bond is holding, that Wes is taking the place of his mother by showing "concern." Wes is in Stevie's "corner," willing to share whatever he knows. "I got so much to learn you" (p. 64), he says, looking to the future; and looking back at the past, he vows not to let Stevie "[go] through what me and Sis did" (p. 56). Though he is an orphan, Stevie belongs to a family bound together by ties Olsen insists can remain irrefragable, even in a landscape of waste. When Wes becomes helpless, falling on his bed in a drunken stupor, Stevie tends to his uncle as once he had been cared for by his mother. He takes off Wes's muddy shoes and covers his body with blankets: *"There now you'll be warm,* he said aloud, *sleep sweet, sweet dreams* (though he did not know he had said it, nor in whose inflections)" (p. 70). Then he stares at the sleeping face in a crucial moment of recognition: "Face of his mother. *His* face. Family face" (p. 71).

Once Stevie can see clearly the *"human bond"* created by the human family, he begins to see objects and people that had been vague: The windows in the dining room which had been "black mirrors where apparitions swam"; the Indian decorations on the wall; the bizarre family resemblance between a bearded face and the face of his landlady. The forces of reclamation are finally reaching Stevie, forces shaped by the care and concern that have linked generations together in an endless chain of human relationships. Thus, though "Requa" describes the fragmentation of a life disrupted by death, it creates in the end a vision of relatedness that gives the displaced person somewhere to belong. Wes's loyalty to his sister's child makes possible Stevie's recovery of the life he lost when his mother died; and Stevie's consciousness of recovery begins when he recognizes the face of his mother in any human being who cares for another, his uncle, his landlady, himself. In an unexpected way, Olsen speaks of the power of mother love as a basis for the continuity of one's self and of one's relationships with others. History keeps a record of these relationships, preserving and fostering the ties of one generation to another; and literature extends these ties as it creates a bond of sympathy between the reader and such unlikely characters as Stevie, whose experience of depression and death is universal.

As the story continues, work reinforces a recovery made possible by extended acts of love, and Stevie's apprenticeship period at the junkyard proves therapeutic. Understanding perhaps that he can learn from things as broken as he is, Stevie has begged to work with Wes rather than attend school. As he undertakes the task of sorting out the accumulated junk in the yard, the story begins to sort out its contents, separating order from disorder; and Stevie sorts out his life. He bungles and fails at his job in the junkyard, but he keeps trying because *"the tasks"* are there, *"coaxing."* Describing these tasks, ordinary daily labor, Olsen dignifies the menial worker and his work. Stevie sees Wes showing "concern" for a trashed car as "he machines a new edge, rethreads a pipe." A man's labor expresses his love; and a boy's tasks pull him "to attention, consciousness"; they teach him "trustworthiness, pliancy"; they force him "to hold up" (p. 65). The salvaging effect of work, even the work of salvaging, dramatizes the theme of "Requa" and shows Olsen's experience of the 1930s still shaping her social vision. During the Depression she had seen jobless men lose their self-respect, and she learned a simple tautological truth: economic recovery, as well as the recovery of a broken individual, comes with work. Even the most menial task, as she would show in "Requa," can be redemptive. Instinctively, Stevie knows this and wants a job, "a learn job, Wes. By you" (p. 63). Work will bond him to another and teach him the secret of survival. At the junkyard Stevie slowly acquires skill and patience, which give him a sense of self-respect. He can put things together, including himself. As he sorts through heaps of waste, he finds a rhythm to his life: The incremental repetition of tasks produces a sense of pattern and continuity, of meaning. He is becoming someone who keeps working, making order, and making himself into an integrated person, like Wes. Slowly, "coaxed" by his tasks, he too is showing "concern."

The climactic moment of Stevie's return to life occurs, oddly enough, as he commemorates the dead. On Memorial Day, Mrs. Edler, the landlady, takes Stevie to church for a requiem celebration and then to several cemeteries. At church, encountering other "families, other young" who remember their dead, he realizes that loss, like love, constitutes a human bond. Moreover, as long as the dead are remembered they are never entirely lost, for the human community includes both mourners and the mourned. At the cemetery, Stevie embraces a stone lamb that may represent the ultimate inexplicability of death, the mystery of its arbitrariness as it claims an infant's life. The quaint consoling verse on the lamb tells that the baby is safely sleeping, and it seems to lull Stevie to rest: "The lamb was sun warm . . . . He put his arm around its stone neck and rested" (p. 74). Calmly embracing a figure of death, Stevie at last finds peace at the Requiescat in Pace cemetery. His story, however, is not over, for the act of recovery is never entirely consummated. "Requa" concludes with the word "reclaiming," after which there is neither the end parenthesis the text requires nor a final period—as though the process of reclamation still goes on and will continue with no sign of ending.[9]

In the last scene, Stevie's "newly tall" body suggests that time has effected recovery simply by letting the boy grow; but the natural gathering of strength that comes with the body's maturation needs the reinforcement of human relationship and love. A faceless woman, merely a name in the story, Mrs. Edler or Mrs. Ed, has taken Stevie in hand and acted as catalyst for his recovery.[10] She does this, apparently, because she feels sorry for an orphan boy, though Olsen's characterization of Stevie raises questions of why she should mother him. Stevie is a silent, withdrawn, and ghostlike boy, if not sleeping then vomiting, and awake or asleep, dripping with snot. However, the characters in "Requa" have a clairvoyance that comes from caring, and they see beyond appearances, just as they communicate without words, or with curses and insults that express love. Throughout the story, Wes calls Stevie "dummy" and "loony" and swears the boy will end in the crazy house; but Wes's insults in no way affect his action nor show disaffection. Rather they express frustration as he waits for Stevie's recovery. Wes's happiest moment comes at the end of the story when he looks at the blissfully sleeping boy and says, "blowing out the biggest bubble of snot you ever saw. Just try and figger that loony kid" (p. 74).

Olsen's style in "Requa" is conspicuously varied. Lyrical passages are juxtaposed to crude dialectic speech, and stream of consciousness passages to objectively seen realistic details. Numerous lists of things represent a world of objects proliferating outside the self; but a mind encompasses these objects and tries to find in their disorder a way of ordering an inner tumult expressed by the roiling fragments of the story. Like the junkyard, the story is the repository of bits and pieces: sentences broken into phrases separated into words, words isolated by blank spaces. Single words on a line or simply sounds—"aaagh/ aaagh"—mark the end of narrative sections, some introduced by titles such as *Rifts* and *Terrible Pumps.* Even the typography is discontinuous, so that the text seems a mosaic of oddly assorted fragments. In creating a visibly discontinuous text, in effect turning "Requa" into a design upon the page, Olsen attracts attention to her form, which always refers the reader to a social world that "Requa" presents as real, recognizable, and outside the fiction. Still "Requa" exists as an object: its varied typography creates truncated patterns of print that catch the eye; words placed together as lists or as fragmentary refrains form distinct visual units; blocks of nouns separated from the text produce concrete poems; intervening spaces turn into aesthetic entities. Mimetic of her theme, Olsen's form is enacting the story's crucial phrase: *"Broken existences that yet continue"* (p. 65). As a text, "Requa" is broken and yet continuous, its action extending beyond its open-ended ending. The story transforms a paradox into a promise as it turns the polarities of fragmentation and continuity into obverse aspects of each other. Merged together, the broken pieces of "Requa" create an integrated self as well as an aesthetic entity. The story enacts a process of composition to show broken existences continuing, order emerging from disorder, art from images of waste, and speech from the void of silence.

Among the many reasons for silence that Tillie Olsen has enumerated, another may be added. Perhaps what the writer has to say is too painful to express: mothers die, children sorrow, working families are evicted from homes and left with nothing to trade for a gallon of gasoline. Olsen speaks of knowledge ordinarily repressed, and while she dignifies her characters and their work, her story denies the cherished illusion that childhood in America is a happy time of life. But "Requa" preaches no social doctrine; unlike the novel *Yonnondio,* which also describes a child caught in a period of depression, it preaches nothing at all, although a preacher's fragmentary phrases of consolation help restore the boy.[11] Rather, the story contains a secret that must be pieced together from disconnected fragments, inferred from blank spaces on the page, melded out of poetic prose and vomit, snot, and violence. This secret, that broken existences can continue, is stated explicitly. Left unsaid is another truth that both affirms and subverts the view of the poet. Yeats had described speech after long silence as an extended discourse upon Art and Song, "we descant and yet again descant." In "Requa," Olsen has said nothing about art. Her speech, resumed after ten years of silence, simply *is* art. This is the secret inherent in Tillie Olsen's story of recovery, in which a child's renewed will to live becomes inseparable from an artist's recovered power to write.

NOTES

1. This reading of "Requa" is based upon a talk honoring Tillie Olsen. The occasion was a conference on women writers held by the New England College English Association at Wheaton College in October 1982. Tillie Olsen was the guest speaker. My purpose was to bring to the attention of Olsen's readers a story which is comparatively recent and important to her career but still little known. It was also to pay tribute to her talent.

2. Tillie Olsen, *Silences* (New York: Delacorte Press, 1978).

3. *The Partisan Review* published sections of *Yonnondio* in 1934. See "The Iron Throat" *Partisan Review*, 1, No. 2 (1934), 3-9; and "The Strike," *Partisan Review*, 1, No. 4 (1934), 3-9. The novel appeared forty years later as a still unfinished work. See Tillie Olsen, *Yonnondio: From the Thirties* (New York: Delacorte Press, 1974).

4. Tillie Olsen, *Tell Me a Riddle* (New York: Dell Publishing Co., 1961). The stories in this collection had been published earlier, the first in 1956.

5. Tillie Olsen, "Requa," *The Iowa Review*, 1, No. 3 (1970), 54-74. Reprinted as "Requa I" in *Best American Short Stories*, ed. Martha Foley and David Burnett (Boston: Houghton Mifflin, 1971). "Requa" is part of a larger work-in-progress Olsen plans to complete. A long review-essay on Olsen refers to "Requa" briefly. See Selma Burkom and Margaret Williams, "De-Riddling Tillie Olsen's Writings," *San Jose Studies*, 2 (February, 1976), 79-80, 81-82.

6. Olsen's knowledge about the varieties of junk comes from her experience as an office worker in a junkyard.

7. For a discussion of this story, see Annette Bennington McElhiney, "Alternate Responses to Life in Tillie Olsen's Work," *Frontiers*, 11, No 1 (1977), 76-91. See also Joanne S. Frye, "'I Stand Here Ironing': Motherhood as Experience and Metaphor," *SSF*, 18 (1981), 287-92.

8. In reaffirming the radical aesthetics of the thirties which identified the writer's voice with the voice of "the people," Olsen recovers also a nearly lost legacy from the past that she values.

9. In effect, Olsen has recovered the site of Requa as she knew and loved it, for many aspects of her setting no longer exist. The graveyard was vandalized; the salmon are few; and the town of Klamath has become a shopping-center with that name. I am indebted to Tillie Olsen for this information as well as her plans concerning the continuation of her story.

10. Tillie Olsen intends the landlady, Mrs. Edler, to play a larger part in Stevie's life in the version of "Requa" she hopes to complete. Wes, apparently, will die, and Mrs. Edler will carry on his role as "mother."

11. On *Yonnondio* as "class literature from a woman's point of view," see Deborah Rosenfelt, "From the Thirties: Tillie Olsen and the Radical Tradition," *Feminist Studies*, 7, No. 3 (1984), 371-406. Note particularly pp. 397-405.

Rethinking the Father:
Maternal Recursion in Tillie Olsen's "Requa"

Elaine Orr

Sometime between 1932 and 1937—when she was in her early twenties and the mother of a daughter—Tillie Lerner wrote a scene in which a mother almost dies. The passage is included in her partial novel *Yonnondio: From the Thirties*. Pregnant with a fifth child and nearing physical collapse, Anna resists her husband's sexual advances. But Jim, unaware of the pregnancy, depressed by his own working conditions, and half drunk, demands his conjugal rights. The eldest child, Mazie, hears Anna's protest and later views her mother's unconscious body:

> Oh, Ma, Ma. The blood on the kitchen floor, the two lifeless braids of hair framing her face like a corpse . . . "Poppa, come in the kitchen, Mamma went dead again." (92)

The young Lerner revives Anna in the narrative, ending the novel with her voice; speaking ostensibly about the scorching summer heat, she looks for things to get "at least . . . tolerable" (154). Anna's survival is perhaps more historical accident than authorial choice. According to Tillie Olsen, her youthful plan for the novel's conclusion included the mother's death (Rosenfelt 390). But the young mother stopped work on the novel in 1937, never completing it.[1]

However accidental or fortuitous, Anna's physical survival prefigures the maternal index of Olsen's canon. An early unpublished story, "Not You I Weep For," puts into relief the fostering of the mother in Olsen's published work. In that story, a young woman (Nena Asarch) becomes pregnant, chooses an abortion, and ends up dying of pneumonia. But because Nena's name is an anagram of Anne, making her a precursor to Anna of *Yonnondio*, we might say that Olsen recuperates the mother at the beginning and in the middle of her novel.[2] When Olsen returned to writing in the fifties, she sustained the maternal center of her fiction. Collected in the order of their writing, the stories of *Tell Me a Riddle* build from the tentative and circular voice of the unnamed mother in "I Stand Here Ironing" to the affirming and multiple mothers' visions that structure "O Yes" and "Hey Sailor, What Ship?"[3] to the tumultuous life of Eva that dominates the title story, a life sustained, finally, in her granddaughter's.

Only in her last short story, one as yet uncollected and little read,[4] does Olsen begin with the death of a young mother, the death threatened in her first fiction. "Requa"[5] is set in 1932, the time that shaped *Yonnondio* and Olsen as a writer. As a story about an uncle who becomes a surrogate father, it is Olsen's only text to focus on the father/son dyad.[6]

Feminist critics have theorized the narrative death of the mother in a variety of ways. Riane Eisler reads the mother's death as symbolizing the overthrow of matriarchal by patriarchal culture, a reading representative of radical feminist theories: "In the *Orestia* every Athenian could see how even the ancient Furies . . . finally gave in. The male dominant order had been established" (80). Margaret Homans's *Bearing the Word* is one of several Lacanian based analyses that theorize the mother's death as the textualization of sons' (or male-identified daughters') entry into the Symbolic. Because language works by replacing the literal with the figurative and because the mother is the child's first and premier object, language as the locus of human value requires "not merely . . . the regrettable loss of the mother, but rather . . . her active and overt murder" (11). As Homans explains, "To kill and replace the mother is the same as language's search for substitutes for the object" (10).

In a recent consideration of the plots of women's writing, Marianne Hirsch reads the consistent death of the mother in nineteenth-century women's fiction as the psycho/social struggle of the writing daughter to escape her mother's history (*The Mother-Daughter Plot*). But the plotting of mothers' deaths by women writers well into the twentieth century causes Hirsch to ask whether the daughter can move beyond the mother without a mother's story.

What these theories share is a representation of the mother as contained threat (whether in history, language, or narrative). But what about Tillie Olsen's canon, which begins with and sustains a maternal center until her last fiction? Do we read her canonical "ending" as yet another instance of maternal containment?[7]

I will argue that in writing "Requa," Olsen seeks to expand her maternal subject, transmuting female presence into narration and remaking the father. As a performance of the mother's voice, the story explores the possibility of a father/son cathexis that remains connected to female subjectivity and gives rise to a caring practice among and between male subjects. In contrast to a scenario that displaces the mother in order to stage male sexual differentiation, then, Olsen's text dramatizes the male subject's turn to maternity.

"Requa"

As a writer influenced by personal observation of physical injury to mothers, by oral transmission of mothers' stories, and by written stories of mothering,[8] Olsen renders maternal pain for the purpose of exploring a maternally viable future. The death of the unnamed mother in "Requa" is neither a confirmation of patriarchal rule nor a transcendence of the feminine Literal to the masculine Symbolic. Instead, the story encodes maternal practices (holding, soothing, coaxing—imperfectly enacted by the mother) and patterns the narrative on these ways of being. Whether or not the text achieves a maternal "language," it hopes to negotiate with the thematic father and the interpreting reader to keep an abandoned boy alive. In this sense and in Olsen's fashioning of a visibly fragmented text, the story announces its "writerly" character.[9] The absence of a biological father makes the narrative task all the more imperative.

Olsen's novella is the limited omniscient narration of a boy's journey with his uncle to "Requa   March, 1932   13 years old" (239).[10] Stevie moves from city to town, from a fragile maternal sheltering to a fragile but "good enough"[11] paternal sheltering. The mother's death by exhaustion—("*Are you tired, Ma?   Tired to death, love*" [243, original emphasis])—underscores her working class status and exposes the limits of personal mothering. But some maternal imprint survives culture's attacks. Formerly separate and unknown to one another, Wes and Stevie (uncle and nephew) appear in the fissures created by the mother character's absence and yet in relation to a voice that speaks her former practices and so holds open a maternal space and identity.

The story begins in the middle of the journey, with "everything slid[ing], mov[ing]" (236). The narrator's repeated description of Stevie's trying to hold his head up ("having to hold it up forever" [237]) forces recognition of a missing piece (maternal holding) before readers know the death that prefaces the plot. The completion of the physical move initiates the emotional shift that the narrative tells. In Requa, Stevie's primary task commences: making connections with a new family, with Wes and the ethnically mixed collection of people he houses with (Mrs. Edler and men with names like Bo, Yee, and Hi). At the level of characterization, the task is signified through Stevie's shift from a maternal to a paternal attachment. Given the boy's age, we might read the story, then, as the traditional one of male maturation, of separation from the mother and "distant" identification with the father.[12] But the story's narration echoes a maternal voice. This sublimated presence returns the boy to the transitional stage of birth and hands him to a coextensive father. The story then unfolds through a series of sociopoetic lessons in which the mother is more than memory and other than a safely distanced maternal power. Olsen's maternal voice is the performing voice of the text: choreographing father and son in their co-nurturance and physical proximity, and revising the masculine bildungsroman—the journey out—as the journey home.

Other critics have described a maternal narrator in women's writing.[13] Blythe Forcey, for one, describes a narrator in Harriet Beecher Stowe's novels who makes her readers "at home" and then educates them through a series of textual lessons before sending them back into the world.[14] Like Stowe, Olsen situates readers in relation to maternal realities. But the working-class origins of Olsen's vision result in a narration more tenuous and more radical than Stowe's. The physical extremity that threatens the mother's life, for example, results in literal homelessness for Olsen's mother's child. Readers must accept a similar disorientation as they begin. At the same time, Olsen's text represents the limits of maternal voice through the narrative use of sentence fragments and breaks on the page. Alternately "holding" the boy and letting him go, the narrator of "Requa" must make a present father.

The hazardous, fragmentary character of Olsen's maternal voice is telescoped in the junkyard worked by Wes and Stevie as well as in the mother's things, sorted through and discarded:

Red plush valentine box: nestled in the compartments:
brown baby hair, ribbon tied   perfume bottle   empty
china deer miniature, the fawn headless   heart locket, stone
missing . . . (245-6).

These "broken existences" (252), however, are used to advantage by the writer. Metaphorically, they return Stevie to the liminal stage of gestation—each fragment recalling the mother—and restage his birth in the presence of his uncle; these pieces must be released in order for Stevie to emerge in new relationships. Not only does this work among fragments assist the text's "trying out" of gender inversions (of father as nurturer), but it tests biological borders, introducing the surrogate father as "close enough" to care for Stevie.[15]

On the way to Requa, Stevie sleeps on the ground beside the truck, "curling [up] . . . in a ball" under Wes's mackinaw (238); once in Wes's room, he builds a cave of boxes, another image reflective of gestation. A polyhyphenated word describing Wes's sense of being with Stevie—the "incomprehensible moil of with-that-boy"—serves to *show* the umbilicus, but now connecting boy and man. This word/phrase evokes the text's structuring ethos, remaking the father as physically present and actively caring. In turn, the reader is invited to internalize the lessons of the text, to identify the father in corporeal relation with *this* child. "Trying out" maternal subjectivity, male and female readers share the narrator's knowledge: her intimate assessments of the child's body, her concern for sheltering spaces, and her belief—based on her observation—that Stevie is growing in his sleep.

Father and reader are linked when Wes thinks he should get Mrs. Ed (the landlady) "to look in the doctor book" to find a diagnosis for Stevie's "laying around" and "actin nuts" (248). Wes's thought signifies a cultural desire to find another mother for the boy (Mrs. Ed) and also his assumption that women are better readers of children. Olsen, however, does not allow another mother in the story. Instead, "Requa" hands the boy to Wes, a textualization of maternal handling that affirms boundary transgression and argues for a male turn to the cultural work of bodily care. A series of vignettes illustrates this pattern:

> It seemed he had had to hold up his head forever. All he wanted was to lie down. Maybe his uncle would let him, there in that strip of pale sun by the redwoods, where he might get warm. (237)

> Everything slid, moved, as if he were still in the truck. He had been holding up his head forever. . . . Staying up to take care of his mother, afraid to lie down even when she was quiet, 'cause he might . . . not hear her if she needed him. (237)

> Sometimes he could sleep, sagged against his uncle who didn't move away. (238)

The first passage—opening the story—is written in an attitude of affinity with the boy. Aware of Stevie's need for sleep and warmth, the narrative voice makes clear the distance between the mother's and the "father's" knowledge. The second continues to represent the world from a position close to the boy, evoking the crisis that sets the story in action: the mother's illness and the ensuing requirement that *he* be mother to *her*. The last passage suggests the narrative project of remaking the father, as his body begins—like a mother's—to accommodate the boy.

The story progresses by closing the distance between the narrator's descriptions and the uncle's understanding, a shift reflected in the abridgement of their bodies. As a working class man, Wes is allowed little reprieve from material occupations and markings ("the work of the day [of the week, of years] slumped onto Wes" [243]). And yet he is far from grasping the meanings latent in *Stevie's* posture, in his exhausted sleep and stunned silence. The mother who once "tickl[ed Stevie], keeping him laughing while she dried his face" (258), is the knower whose perspective, transmuted into narration, coaxes "this man [Stevie] hardly knew" (243) into caring *for him.*

In an early passage, an actual wall separates boy and man, a clear rendering of those cultural structures that distance men from (their male) children:

> He stands with his back clamped hard against the door Wes has left open, and he has jumped up from the cot to close.
> Hey. Leave it open. My can's still draggin. A block behind.
> *No smile. Skinny little shrimp. Clutching at the door knob, knuckles white, nostrils flaring. Funny animal noises in his throat.)*
> Sleeping—all day? Cmon, you had to at least take a leak and put something into that belly . . . Mrs. Ed or Yee didn't stick their nose in? . . . *(Pale. Ol Ghostboy. Silent Cal.) (Natural—it's plenty raw yet.)* (239)

The compassionate exposure of these male bodies ("can . . . draggin," "knuckles white") challenges the divide, however, creating instead a narrative enfolding. Thus, the intervening and sympathetic voice ("little shrimp," "Silent Cal") serves to entangle what culture seeks to separate (body and narrative; animal and human; female and male). Reference to physical excess ("nostrils flaring," "animal noises," "plenty raw,") seems an authorial insistence on *"recognizable human bond[s]"* that are not entirely flattened or absorbed in language (252).

Echoing the boy's movement as he rocks himself, the text moves to the reader's interior the motion of the narrative:

> And the round and round slipping sliding jolting moved to inside him, so he has to begin to rock his body; rock the cot gently, down and back. (240)

The rest of this passage is punctuated by the rocking: "Down and back" repeated at regular intervals in the writing. "Down and back. . . " "Down and back . . . " (240-241). Between the rocking, the narrator shares Stevie's thoughts: "He couldn't remember, was it Bo had taken the [mother's] lamp?" "What had happened with the bloody quilt?" (241). Trying to hold together his mother's things as a way of holding onto her, the boy is sustained in the text by the sound and structure of the rocking and the close proximity of the narrator, something the uncle at first misunderstands. He thinks "the little bastard [is] jacking off," but realizes his error when he opens the door and sees "the boy—as usual—lying on the cot, arm over his face—yes, and rolled into *his* blanket" (244).

Rereading Stevie's body, Wes begins to understand that the boy is trying to get close to him: "into *his* blanket," a realization the reader has internalized through the text's rocking cadences. While the alliterative, pulsing sounds ("round and round slipping sliding") of the narrator's voice enfold readers textually, the father's vision envelops Stevie thematically. Rather than sexual initiation (and a break from the mother), the boy's rocking disrupts oppositional plotting and consolidates familial bonds. In effect, the text urges a continuation of maternal thinking[16] as a mechanism for the boy's maturation.

Uncle and boy journey toward one another just as Olsen's text invites readerly movement toward a maternal subjectivity. Not long after his arrival late one afternoon, Stevie looks one night at Wes and thinks he is his mother. The confusion moves the boy towards his uncle, wondering: "Was that his mother or his uncle sagged there in the weight of weariness" (243). When the boy—distraught by painful memories—urges Wes to put his feet up and "rub where [they] hurt," the uncle resists: "What are you twitchin your muscles like a flybit horse for? . . . And stop swallowin snot" (243). But the scene ends "with a shove that is half embrace" (244), so that the co-mingled images of mother and uncle distill into a loving paternal body.

The absent mother is transmuted in this passage as the maternal narrator who brings the boy together with his new father and the reader with both. Her body is appropriated but not in the inevitable plot of psychoanalytic and object relations theory (theories that require her jettisoning for a "healthy" male maturity).[17] Employed by a maternal narrator, the mother's body is more than the object of masculine exchange. Instead, the narrative use of her figure expands a gendered knowledge of care and foregrounds bodily connection. In Stevie's memory, we see her "sagged with weariness *like Wes* her stockings rolled down rubbing rubbing where the blue veins swoll [244, emphasis mine]."

Stevie's refusal of "learnin'" that separates him from Wes, even a beating will not convince him to go to school, signifies a male, if not masculine, rejection of meanings that require parental absence. He wants, instead, to go with his uncle to work: "A learn job, Wes. By you" (249). Convincing his uncle, Stevie is assigned the junk heap: sorting discarded objects, determining their *use* value, creating patterns through familiarity with the form and feel of things. Close to Wes, Stevie is able to read the most painful scripts. Seeing, for example, a discarded breadbox ("wheat wreathes enamelled"), he remembers a "pattern" and a "forgotten hunger" and, again, his mother's face (253). Pounding the box in rage, the boy redoubles the textual insistence on his mother's absence. His destruction of the associative image features his demand for *someone's accompanying body*. Olsen's plot provides for his need, but not in female form (neither mother nor wife is given).

Because Wes does not yet know how to appropriate his own text for Stevie—"*NEW   USED/ U NAME IT—WE GOT IT/ U ASK IT—WE FIX*

IT"—the narrator appropriates his trade words to turn the interpretive "I"
(the reading subject) toward the boy:

> Hasps switches screws plugs tubings drills
> Valves pistons shears planes punchers sheaves
> Clamps sprockets coils bits braces dies

Providing the text, the narrator glosses it:

> How many shapes and sizes; how various, how cunning in application. (252)

The father's metaphors—retooling, remaking—borrowed by the narrator
and offered to the reader, argue the connection between Wes's language
and the boy's body[18] while the onomatopoeic sounds of the poem
relocate the father's genius in his hands.

Just after the poem, the narrator represents Wes's internalized
learning, his pivoting between two "calls," the boy's and the job's:

> Wes: junking a towed-in car, one hundred pieces out of what had been
> one. Singing—unconscious, forceful—to match the motor hum as he machines
> a new edge, rethreads a pipe. Capable, fumbling; exasperated, patient;
> demanding, easy; uncomprehending, quick; harsh, gentle; *concerned* with
> him [Stevie]. (252)

This passage features no textual distance between the uncle's care in his
work and his care for the boy; instead the reduplicative narration moves
without a break from describing one to describing the other. The work of
the text is mirrored in this thematic and circular movement, as the
narrator closes the distance between her voice, the father's understanding, and the boy's need for care. The whispered assurance—*"But the
known is reaching to him, stealthily, secretly, reclaiming"* (252)—signifies
this necessary "closing" and the blurring of individual boundaries.

A transposition of the earlier scene of "viewing" further circulates the
narrative vision of the text. While the uncle's occasional drinking
threatens Stevie's new and hard won safety, one evening of carousing
occasions the boy's maturing—but not through his own initiation into
drinking and alcohol-induced sleep. Instead, the boy remains alert and
care-ful. Looking on the father's body with genuine empathy (it is neither
pity nor fear based), he rises from his cot to cover it. The action is
fulfilled through a percussive sounding of the mother's voice:

> The blanket ends wouldn't lap to cover. He had to pile on his coat, Wes's
> mackinaw, and two towels, patting them carefully around the sleeping form.

There now you'll be warm, he said aloud, *sleep sweet, sweet dreams* (though
he did not know he had said it, nor in whose inflections.) (259)

The chiasmic inflection—"*sleep sweet, sweet dreams*"—is, of course, his
mother's, the words also hers, but now transmuted as the narrator's and
repeated by Stevie. The mother's body as emblem for translation and
rereading is figured a second time and more extensively: "he leaned down
to . . . look . . . full on the sleeping face. Face of his mother. *His* face.
Family face" (259). If the child's humanity is mirrored initially in the eyes
of its mother, the textual slippage—"his mother . . . *His* . . . Family"—enacts a continuance of and return to that "view." Psychically and
narratively, *her* place is kept open. Thus, Stevie learns who his "father"
is through his own tonal representation of the mother. His gaze at
Wes—"His fly was open. How rosy and budlike and quiet it sheathed
there" (259)—recovers the father's body in child-like repose, a narrative
move deposing the social fiction of the Father's law and its psycho/social
threat: castration.

In the story's opening scene, Wes takes off his mackinaw and throws it
over the sleeping boy. At the level of plot, Stevie's covering of Wes in this
later scene keeps the action alive. The narrative consequence—embedded
in the boy's speech act: "[t]here now you'll be warm"—is the identification
of father and son in relation to a recursive maternal, the subject who dies
and tells this story. The enfolding character of these male acts of covering
recommends the double identity of pregnancy, not the attenuated identity
of phallic threat. As opposed to the heterosexual male fantasy of simple
return to the mother (to oneness and primal unity), the oscillation (in
viewing, caring) between Wes and Stevie exposes men's need for care and
dramatizes a male responsibility for and to maternity.

By the end of the story, Wes's understanding approximates the
narrator's. He knows the value of warmth to Stevie—("Don't this sun feel
good? Just smell") (262)—and though he continues to be exasperated with
the boy's awkwardnesses, he keeps inviting Stevie's participation beside
him. From the middle of the story until its end, an intervening narrative
voice gives way to more extended representations of father and child
interaction. Their entangled voices—sometimes lilting, sometimes
distraught—make the body of the text, as when Stevie tells Wes that his
singing is "for my head" and hears back: "Outa your head, you mean"
(262), or when Wes haltingly encourages: "I shouldn't have got so mad;
you're doin almost o.k. lately, sometimes as much help as trouble" (262).

The text's final lessons come through Stevie's readings. In its present
form, the story ends with Stevie accompanying Mrs. Ed to several
cemeteries on Memorial Day, a move Wes thinks will surely send him

back to his reclusive depression (264). At the first cemetery, Stevie
stumbles over a canning jar full of flowers. Bending, he reads the
tombstone: "Leo Jordan, 1859-1911, He is Not Dead but Sleeping" (264).
The modulated sentence—not dead but sleeping—reverberates in "Requa,"
a story Stevie has slept through. On another headstone, one commemo-
rating an infant, he reads: "Budded on earth/Blooming in Heaven" (264).
As in the beginning, the boy makes a bed, sitting down among the weeds,
reclining to embrace a stone lamb and to watch ants weaving in and out
of the grass. Sketched in the thin space of economic depression, "Requa"
whispers a human connection that brings people back from the dead: the
last words "*stealthily   secretly reclaiming.*"

The narrative choice to include Mrs. Ed in the final scene suggests
extra-familial extensions of a maternal voice and knowledge. Stevie's
reading of an artistic arrangement on her wall unfolds what began as
narrative adumbration: "he sees that it is not shadows that hang on the
wall around the bow, but Indian things: a feathered headdress, basket
hats, shell necklace. Two faces dream in shell frames. One, for all the
beard, Mrs. Ed's . . ./ *family face*" (261). The move from "[t]wo faces" to
"[o]ne . . Mrs. Ed's" to "*family face*" continues the text's circle of reason:
the child grows through ancestral recursion. The brief allusion to Native
American arts evokes as well this story's belief in spirits. Beyond the
ending of "Requa" (there is no concluding punctuation), Olsen conjures
her most abiding vision: reclamation of the women and men who bore us.

NOTES

1. The author's political activity with the Communist Party, the demands of
work, and an expanded maternity suspended the writing. The author began living
with Jack Olsen in 1936 and bore her second daughter in 1938. Two more
daughters were born in the forties. Jack rediscovered the fragments of the
manuscript. As Olsen says, she made choices among the narrative fragments in
order to publish it in 1974, but she did not actually revise the writing.

2. Pearlman and Werlock make this observation (11). Two versions of the
story are housed in the Berg Collection, New York Public Library. The second
version was apparently begun when Tillie Lerner was eighteen; see Pearlman and
Werlock 136.

3. Whitey is the protagonist of "Hey Sailor, What Ship?" but together, "O Yes"
and "Hey Sailor" tell the story of families, with Helen and Alva as sustaining
centers.

4. To date, only one critical article and two book chapters have been dedicated
to this story. See Gelfant, Orr, and Pearlman and Werlock.

5. "Requa" was reprinted as "Requa I" in *The Best American Short Stories 1971*. Both titles refer to the same story or to the first part of a novella, which remains, to date, incomplete. Internal notes refer to *Best American Short Stories*.

6. Precursors to the father figure in "Requa" include Jim, in *Yonnondio*, who holds his daughter occasionally but is not shown as physically close to his sons and who is only briefly identified as primary parent—when Anna is passed out or seriously ill. Lennie in "O Yes" and "Hey Sailor, What Ship?" is also shown holding a female child but not a son.

7. I do not mean to minimize the issue of Olsen's "slim canon." I would argue, for example, that it is small *because* of Olsen's own maternity. But I also don't want the witness of what is written to be silenced. That Olsen did sustain—in whatever abbreviated form—the mother as narrative center makes a difference in how we theorize her work and this last story in particular.

8. I draw these conclusions from interviews with Tillie Olsen, 1983-87. Traces of each claim can be found in her stories. In "Tell Me a Riddle," for example, she shows a mother begging for scraps to make soup (apparently a reflection from her own girlhood); in "O Yes," she has Alva tell a dream in which she appears as a mother; in "Tell Me a Riddle," she depicts Eva, as a young mother, struggling to hold two babies and read Chekhov.

See Orr (26-29), Rosenfelt (376), and Pearlman and Werlock (17) for discussions of Olsen's early reading, of her parents' lives, and of her early life.

9. Roland Barthes's term. The writerly text refers more properly to the occasion for rewriting and the process of remaking the text than it does to any material text. To refer to Olsen's text as "writerly" is to argue that its many gaps, openings, and beginnings provide an occasion for readerly intervention and that its indirect address to the reader helps to create conditions conducive to more writing.

10. The spacing here and elsewhere attempts to reflect Olsen's spacing in the story. See Gelfant's essay for further reproduction of the story's physical aspect.

11. "Good enough" mothering is D.W. Winnicott's phrase and a familiar concept in object relations theory.

12. I write "'distant' identification" because the son is thought to need identification with a father but the nature of that identity is separateness, difference. The notion that the boy must separate from the mother in order to establish his masculinity is basic to both Freudian and object relations theories. The difference is that Freudian theory figures the mother's primary power as threatening while object relations theorists tend to see her power as beneficent. But in both, the boy must establish identity through a literal move away from her.

13. I do not assume that only women can create maternal narrators; rather, it seems likely that some women writers who are mothers have made narrative use of a learned and practiced voice.

14. See her unpublished dissertation, "Harriet Beecher Stowe and the Emergence of the Maternal Narrator."

15. If we remember that Olsen was a single mother, abandoned by her child's father in 1932—the year in which she sets "Requa"—this provision for collaboration among male and female readers is particularly compelling. Her narrator is precariously situated on that divide between anger at the father's absence and the absolute need for his presence, an anger and need expressed in the story through the literal absence of Stevie's biological father (he is never mentioned) and the recreation of the father in Wes. The writer's lifetime partnership with Jack Olsen, who became surrogate father to her first daughter, is certainly suggested.

16. "Maternal thinking" is a phrase coined by Sara Ruddick (and the title to her book). I use it as she does to speak about knowledge unfolding from maternal practice.

17. According to Madelon Sprengnether (*The Spectral Mother*), the mother of sons, whether in Freudian or object relations theory, is figured primarily as object rather than as subject. Her body, in both theories, is a threat to masculinity and must be jettisoned for healthy maturation.

18. Olsen appropriates this "masculine" metaphor out of her own experience. In her youth and young adulthood, she worked in a junk shop (Orr 132).

BIBLIOGRAPHY

Barthes, Roland. *S/Z: An Essay*, trans. David Miller. New York: Hill & Wang, 1974.

Eisler, Riane. *The Chalice and the Blade.* San Francisco: Harper & Row, 1988.

Forcey, Blythe. "Harriet Beecher Stowe and the Emergence of the Maternal Narrator: Domestic Ideology, Object-Relations Psychology, and Narrative Strategy in *Uncle Tom's Cabin, Dred,* and *The Minister's Wooing.*" (Unpublished Dissertation. University of Colorado, 1992.)

Gelfant, Blanche. "After Long Silence: Tillie Olsen's 'Requa.'" *Studies in American Fiction* 12 (Spring 1984): 61-69.

Hirsch, Marianne. *The Mother/Daughter Plot: Narrrative, Psychoanalysis, Feminism.* Bloomington: Indiana UP, 1989.

Homans, Margaret. *Bearing the Word.* Chicago: U of Chicago P, 1986.

Olsen, Tillie. "Requa." In *The Best American Short Stories*, 1971. Eds. Martha Foley and David Burnett, 237-65. Boston: Houghton Mifflin, 1971. (This volume was dedicated to Tillie Olsen.)

——— . *Tell Me a Riddle.* New York: Dell, 1976.

——— . *Yonnondio: From the Thirties.* New York: Dell, 1981.

Orr, Elaine. *Tillie Olsen and a Feminist Spiritual Vision.* Jackson: UP of Mississippi, 1987.

Pearlman, Mickey, and Abby H.P. Werlock. *Tillie Olsen.* Boston: Twayne, 1991.

Ruddick, Sara. *Maternal Thinking.* Boston: Beacon Press, 1989.

Sprengnether, Madelon. *The Spectral Mother: Freud, Feminism, and Psychoanalysis*. Ithaca: Cornell UP, 1990.
Winnicott, D. W. *Playing and Reality*. New York: Basic, 1971.

The Circumstances of Silence: Literary Representation and Tillie Olsen's Omaha Past

Linda Ray Pratt

> I came to explore the wreck.
> The words are purposes.
> The words are maps.
> I came to see the damage that was done
> and the treasures that prevail.
>   Adrienne Rich, "Diving into the Wreck"

Tillie Olsen's *Silences* addresses "the relationship of circum-stances—including class, color, sex; the times, climate into which one is born—to the creation of literature"(xi). Olsen's primary concern is with those conditions that stop women from writing, but implicit in her pursuit of "unnatural silences" is the question of how situations affect *what* one writes. Like Virginia Woolf, Olsen is aware of how difficult it is for a woman to achieve a "totality of self" that can escape such circum-stances as "anxieties, shamings," "the leeching of belief," indeed, all the "punitive difference in circumstances, in history" that damage and inhibit the capacity to write (*Silences* 263, 27). Olsen candidly discusses those things that affected her opportunity to write, but *Silences* does not explore the relationship between her circumstances and what she did write. Many readers presume a connection exists between her fiction and her life, and Olsen has acknowledged that her stories may be in some sense "profoundly autobiographical" and that as a writer she dwells in the past. Most of the story of Olsen's past in the radical Jewish community of Omaha, Nebraska, has not been published before.[1] In a series of interviews about her Omaha years, Olsen recalled her early life and the use she has made of it in the fiction.[2] These accounts illuminate the autobiographical representation in the work, but also significant is what she does not use. Many of the ideological and ethnic circumstances which influenced the young Tillie Lerner are themselves silenced in the literary form.

Olsen's long residency in San Francisco and the general absence of a defined place in much of her work obscure the particulars of her heritage. Readers who know her through "I Stand Here Ironing" are often unaware of the author's Jewish background, and she rejects being categorized as a Jewish writer. Only the couple in "Tell Me a Riddle" are Jewish, and she has said many times that they represent a type and not her particular parents. Few readers associate her with Nebraska and fewer still with the Russian Jewish and Socialist community in Omaha. Tillie Lerner grew up in the immigrant working class that settled in north Omaha, a neighborhood once populated by many Jewish businesses and now the center of the city's Black community. The stories in *Tell Me a Riddle* (1961) and her novel of Depression life, *Yonnondio* (1974), draw heavily on her family's life in Omaha but usually without the specifics of a setting or ethnic culture. The Holbrooks in *Yonnondio* are abstractions of the Depression's working class poor, and the Jewish couple in "Tell Me a Riddle" live in an unnamed city. Yet Olsen grew up in a distinct kind of midwestern Jewish community where "the times, climate into which one is born" composed the often harsh "circumstances" of poverty, bias, and marginalization.

Olsen's belief that the valorizing of the individual self is patriarchal and central to the ethics of capitalism influences her rejection of a self-oriented autobiographical form. Her political belief in one international community of human beings limits the emphasis she is willing to put on ethnic and regional identities. In addition to the conscious role ideologies of politics, gender, and selfhood play in determining form, her responses to the painful nature of her past may also create the need for fictional abstractions and silences. In my interviews with Olsen she frequently returned to two themes: the richness of her radical past in a family of active Socialists, and the pain and embarrassment that went with being poor and different, even within one's own ethnic group. The Lerner family story is, in retrospect, representative of a certain kind of Jewish leftwing life among immigrants to the United States. Olsen recognizes her family as a significant type of their generation, but when she was living that life, she often felt a sense of rebellion and alienation. Yet, the intensity of these years make it her most important subject.

Discussing the autobiographical content of Olsen's work is difficult for her because not writing autobiographically is "what I'm all about" as an author who believes in "one human race without religion" (interview). "Should a writer write autobiography is a modern question," she says, noting that earlier authors were not scrutinized for the elements of their life in every piece of fiction they wrote. Yet, she characterized her story "I Stand Here Ironing" as "close to autobiography," "O Yes" as "profound autobiography," and "Tell Me a Riddle" as "very, very autobiographical" (interviews). "Autobiography takes many forms," Olsen comments, and explains that often the autobiographical elements in her stories are "probably deeper things" than the details of experiences and places. Her novel *Yonnondio* has some close parallels with her family's history, but she "was not writing an autobiographical novel" when she composed it. "I was not writing an immigrant saga," Olsen commented in response to questions about the lack of ethnic or religious identity attributed to the novel's fictional Holbrook family (interview). The novel was not "entirely different," however, and "a large part of it was what was in the neighborhood" (interview). Two questions I hope to examine are 1) what is the autobiographical experience out of which the author builds this fictional world? and 2) what does it mean for the literature that much of that experience is silenced in the fictional representation?[3]

I

Midwestern urban Jewish communities such as the one in Omaha were smaller than their East Coast counterparts and increasingly remote from involvement with radical politics and the labor movement. The Socialist beliefs which many Eastern European Jews such as Olsen's parents brought to the Great Plains were perhaps more susceptible to the pressure of acculturation and assimilation in an environment such as Omaha where a tradition of conservative politics, agrarian economics, and a largely homogeneous white Western European population dominated. Though many other Omaha Jews share the same Russian Socialist background, the Omaha Jewish community developed westward out of the urban center of the city and into the suburban middle class. This migration out of the urban neighborhoods and up the economic ladder was already underway in the late 1920's when Tillie Lerner was a student at Omaha's Central High.

Working class Socialists such as the Lerners were separated by ideology from the mainstream of the local Jewish community. Socialist Jews often had different economic attitudes and did not participate in the religious life around the synagogues. Radical Jews often rejected religion, and Olsen has described her father as "incorruptibly atheist to the last day of his life" (Rubin 3). Within a Jewish community already smaller and more isolated than those in large urban centers, Olsen's place was further marginalized when she broke with her family's Socialism to become a Communist. Olsen tried not to embarrass her family with her Communism, and she sometimes used aliases in her political work. In school she was aware of painful class differences compounded by being Jewish, working class, immigrant, poor, and female. Tillie Lerner's Omaha background of estrangement and alienation was a painful contradiction to her family's dream of an international society in which the comradeship of humanity transcended the divisions of race, ethnicity, and religion.

Olsen's parents came to the United States at a time when efforts were underway to relocate Jewish immigrants outside the urban areas of the East Coast. Samuel and Ida Lerner had met in Russia but did not begin their family until they settled on a farm near Mead, Nebraska. Samuel was from Odessa; Ida from Minsk. The family memory is that they had first met in Minsk where Samuel had gone to work for the Bund, the Jewish socialist movement organized in Russia in 1897 and devoted to secular Yiddish culture and internationalism.[4] After the failure of the 1905 Revolution in which they had participated, they fled Russian prisons and met again in New York. After working at least through 1907 with the Socialist Party in New York, Samuel made his way to Omaha where other Socialist Jews from Minsk and Odessa had already settled.[5]

The family history before 1918 is unclear. For a time the Lerners were tenant farmers in the Mead, Nebraska, area, but Olsen reports that at least one year was spent in Colorado where her father worked in the mines.[6] Olsen remembers that in Mead the children were harassed on their way to school because her father opposed the war and wouldn't buy bonds. *Yonnondio* draws on memories of the farm and mining years. The novel begins in a mining community in Wyoming, but the family moves on to South Dakota where they fail at farming and from there to a packing house city like Omaha. Unlike Anna in the novel, Olsen's mother spoke little English and was isolated in the rural community. The farm years were "terrible for my mother," Olsen said. Her father "loved being on the land," but her mother "had a hunger for a larger life" and desired to leave it (interview). After the move to Omaha Ida Lerner studied English in one of the many night classes that schools such as Kellom Elementary ran for immigrants. Some passages from an exercise her mother wrote in 1924 as part of her English class assignment suggest Ida's own sense of social values, maternal responsibility, and literary bent. The essay, dated December 10, 1924, and addressed to "Dear Teacher" reads in part:

> I am glad to study with ardor but the children wont let me, they go to bed late so it makes me tired, and I cant do my lessons. It is after ten o'clock my head dont work it likes to have rest. But I am in a sad mood I am sitting in the warm house and feel painfull that winter claps in to my heart. I see the old destroyed houses of the people from the old country. I hear the wind blow through them with the disgusting cry why the poor creatures ignore him, dont protest against him, that souless wind dont no, that they are helples have no material to repair the houses and no clothes to cover up their bodies, and so the sharp wind echo cry falls on the window, and the windows original sing with silver-ball tears seeing all the poor shivering creatures dressed in rags with frozen fingers and feverish hungry eyes.
>
> (personal correspondence)

Ida Lerner closes this essay with sentiments that begin, "So as a human being who carries responsibility for action I think as a duty to the community we shall try to understand each other." The character of Eva in "Tell Me a Riddle" echoes many of these sentiments, and she also shares the same sense of opportunities curtailed by the burdens of childcare. Olsen used a phrase from her mother's essay in "Tell Me a Riddle" where Eva's fragmented ruminations include the words, *"As a human being responsibility"* (114).

The family probably moved to Omaha no later than 1917. Olsen believes that they initially settled in South Omaha, the meat packing area of the city, but the first record of their Omaha residence is at 2512 Caldwell, the family's permanent home in North Omaha (Omaha *City Directory*, 1918). North Omaha was the section where Omaha's Jews clustered in the first two decades of the century. South Omaha, the center of the meat packing industry, was directly connected by 24th Street to the North Omaha area where the Lerners lived. Both areas were populated by ethnic and minority groups that migrated to the city to work in packing. Though not themselves in meat packing, the Lerners lived among packing house workers in a period of intense labor unrest in the industry.

In 1918 Samuel Lerner's occupation was listed in the City Directory as peddler. In 1920-23 Olsen's father worked at the Silver Star Confectionery at 1604 North 24th Street, one of many small Jewish businesses in the area at that time. Olsen's memory of shelling almonds for the candies her father made appears in some discarded pages of the *Yonnondio* manuscript where it became Mazie's experience. An unpublished fragment of the manuscript reads as follows:

> And then Mazie had a "job" for two weeks. Annamae told her about it, for just shelling almonds two blocks away she could get a quarter a day. Bitterly Anna ordered Mazie not to think about it, but then thought of Monday and the insurance man, and the 60¢ made her say yes. It wont hurt the kid, Jim had insisted. So Mazie sat at a high table in a top room filled with steam from the boiling nuts and the oil, her hands in hot water, peeling the almonds. Snap, snap, her fingers seemed independent of her body, red little animals snapping at brown skin.
>
> (correspondence)

After the confectionery failed, Sam Lerner worked as a painter and paper hanger.[7]

As Socialist Jews, the Lerners built their lives around political circles instead of the synagogue. Sam was active in his union, and both Sam and Ida were active in Workmen's Circles, a national Jewish Socialist organization with several chapters in Omaha. The Lerners were founding members of the Omaha Workmen's Circle, Branch 626, in 1920, and also helped found branches in Sioux City, Lincoln, and Des Moines. The Workmen's Circles served as political, social, and cultural centers for Jews whose socialist views and lack of traditional religious beliefs placed them outside the religious community. The Circles provided such traditional services of fraternal organizations as insurance policies, burial benefits, and retirement homes.

As part of the Workmen's Circles the Lerners helped to build Omaha's first Labor Lyceum at 22nd and Clark Streets. After the original labor lyceum was sold for public housing in the 1930's, Olsen's parents helped to build a new Labor Lyceum in 1940 at 31st and Cuming Street. No longer encompassed by small children, Ida Lerner was apparently active in this period, and some Omaha Jews recall her participation in Workmen's Circle activities. Both Sam and Ida spoke at the dedication ceremonies of the new Labor Lyceum which became the center for the district conferences of the Workmen's Circle. Sam Lerner was a president of the Midwest District Committee.

The family's Socialist activities were often in support of the labor struggles in the packing houses. Olsen recalls the impact of the packing house strike of 1921-22 on her family, especially her father.[8] By the 1920's the Socialist Party in the midwest had lost most of the members it had before World War I, but Olsen's father continued to be active.[9] He was secretary of the Nebraska Socialist Party and in 1928 was the party's candidate for Lt. Governor of the state. Family life was centered around party activities. On Sundays the children attended the Socialist Sunday School and sang of the worker's struggles from the *Socialist Sunday School Song Book*. Their house was a stopping point for prominent Socialists, Wobblies, and others on the Left who were traveling through Omaha.

Olsen's memories of her high school years are a mixture of the pleasures of discovering literature and the pain of recognizing her own marginalization. She had both teachers whom she credits with "saving" her and teachers that taught her painful lessons in class differences. Despite her Socialist home, Olsen has said that she "didn't really learn about class until I 'crossed the tracks' to Central High School."[10]   At Central, the best high school in the state, the curriculum was "college prep" and some of the students were from prominent and wealthy families in Omaha. As children of working class Jewish immigrants, the Lerners were, she says, "aliens in that school." Olsen remembers the striking contrasts in dress and ways, and that most students carried clean pocket handkerchiefs while the Lerner children had to make do with clean rags. "There were those things that were class differences that I had never encountered first hand," she recalls (interview).

Olsen singled out two teachers who had a strong influence on her—Sara Vore Taylor who taught English and Autumn Davies who taught Civics. Taylor introduced her to Coleridge, De Quincey, and Sir Thomas Browne. "I still have her old stylebook," Olsen says (interview). Taylor was also interested in recent poetry and urged students to go hear Carl Sandburg when he was in Omaha. Davies was "interested in my mind" and wanted Olsen to go to college. Despite occasional trouble with a few teachers because she would not silence her unorthodox and questioning mind, Tillie was praised for the humor column "Central Squeaks" which she wrote in the high school paper under the name "Tillie the Toiler." After the 1934 publication of "The Iron Throat" in *Partisan Review*, the Central High *Register* published an article on her literary success just six years after graduation. The paper notes that the column "Squeaks" "as run by Tillie was entirely natural and unhampered by rule." The article also noted her recent arrest "at the home of Communist friends" in California and that she was awaiting trial (clipping of *Register* article provided by Olsen).

Although some of her teachers encouraged her mind, Olsen also recalls the anti-semitism of others. The difficulty of her position as a Jew was perhaps compounded by also being part of a known radical family and by her own occasionally disruptive classroom behavior. A letter to her in 1934 from her brother Gene gives us an insight into the anti-semitic climate she found at school. The occasion of the letter from Gene was her arrest in California. At the time of the incident she was receiving her first serious attention as a writer after her story, "The Iron Throat," had appeared in *Partisan Review*. Gene's letter expresses his concern that her arrest might make the Omaha papers and give the "anti-semites" a "chance to say 'see what happens to the revolutionary Jew?'" (correspondence). He urges her to think what it would mean to succeed as a writer and imagines a moment of vindication:

> it would be the greatest happiness of my life to go to [name of teacher] and throw the book on her desk and say "look what the revolutionary Jew has done now"

(personal correspondence)

These sentiments strongly suggest the discrimination the Lerner children felt in school and the desire to prove themselves worthy of their heritage.[11] It also suggests the pressure to vindicate her family through her success as a writer, a need that may enter into Olsen's hesitation in publishing and her silencing of details that would reveal her family to be a major subject.

Olsen's "Tell Me a Riddle" mirrors the Russian Jewish political and intellectual values that Olsen learned at home. "There has been a real eclipsing of the beliefs of Jews of this generation," she observes, but they were people who saw their lives as committed to the liberation of an international human community (interview). Some members of the Omaha Jewish community characterized the Russian Socialist Jews as "a kind of intelligentsia," but as the community changed, those Jews who remained socialist and communists were less influential and less visible to the broader community.

Olsen broke with the family's Socialism when she joined the Young Communist League in 1931, a decision her parents could not approve. Although her parents were not happy with her decision, she says her decision to join the YCL "was not a rebellion against my home. My decision to join the YCL was rooted absolutely out of the beliefs in our house" (interview). Her break with her parents' views paralleled in many ways the splits taking place in the Socialist Party during the early days of the American Communist Party.[12] The decline of the Socialist Party after World War I may have contributed to the younger generation's interest in communism. From the early 1920's Communist and Communist Laborites had groups in Omaha, and some former Socialists had aligned themselves with them (W. Pratt, "Socialism on the Northern Plains" 27-9). Tillie's case was not unlike that of others whose parents had been Socialists in the 1900-1919 period but the children grew up to be Communists in the 1924-1939 period. Despite the unhappiness of her family at her decision, Olsen recalls her father saying to her mother, "Well, she didn't join the capitalist class." "My mother would have said, 'Never join the floggers against the flogged.' She always taught us that" (interview).

Because her family, well known as Socialists in the community, disapproved of her Communist affiliation, Olsen sometimes used aliases in her political work. The front page story of the Feb. 6, 1932 *Omaha Bee-News* features photographs of a "peaceful and small" crowd of about 100 members of the Omaha Council of the Unemployed marching to present their demands to Acting Mayor Arthur Westergard. Tillie Olsen identified herself as the woman speaker in one of the pictures under the name of "Theta Larimore, 2023 Burt Street," who is quoted as "shouting" "'What becomes of the women who lose their jobs? Save their respectability." In 1934 when she was arrested in California she apparently used the name "Teresa Landale" (correspondence). After joining the YCL she worked in packing houses and factories in Kansas City and St. Joseph, Missouri. In

Kansas City she was arrested for leafleting and jailed for five months. After she was released she returned to Omaha to recover her health, but by late 1932 Tillie Lerner left Omaha, first to Faribault, Minnesota, where she began writing *Yonnondio*, and then to California where she lives today.

The Lerner family history in Omaha ends in the late 1940's except for one sister who lived in Omaha until the 1980's. In the housing shortage after World War II Sam and Ida Lerner sold their home on Caldwell Street and moved to the Washington, D.C., area where Tillie's brother Harry lives. Tillie's mother died in January, 1956, and her father died in a Workmen's Circle retirement home in Media, Pennsylvania, in February, 1974.

II

The details of Olsen's family life and the identifying of incidents and characters that appear in her fiction give us an insight to how the work is autobiographical. Two points stand out: the extensive degree to which the work draws on family experience, and the centrality of the early period of her life to her fictional imagination. *Yonnondio*, written in the 1930's soon after Olsen left Omaha, sets a pattern that reappears throughout much of her work. Here the plot recasts experiences of her own family, the mother and child characters reflecting memories of her mother and herself, but the family as a whole is generalized to represent a type. Olsen commented that she identified with Mazie but that Mazie was "not a reader" and Tillie was. Mazie was also not "freaky in the same sense that I was freaky" Olsen observed (interviews). Mazie's response to the evening star and her school were the kinds of "deeper things" about the character that were autobiographical. Olsen's comment suggests that specific traits of Mazie were different but that Mazie's emotional responses are the "deeper" autobiographical part. Yet specific personal experiences and persons from her youth also appear in the novel. Mr. Caldwell, the farmer in the novel who wants to give the child some books, was, according to Olsen, mainly based on Dr. Alfred Jefferson, one of several Socialists the family knew. Jefferson was a physician who "loved talking to my mother and was good to me. He was interested that we read" (interview). The character of Jeff, "the little Negro boy" who hears a humming in his head "that would blend into music" (*Yonnondio* 91), was based on Jeff Crawford, the son of Suris and Mattie Crawford, the Black family who were neighbors to the Lerners on Caldwell Street, and whose daughter, Joe Eva, was Tillie's close girlhood friend. According to the *City Directory*, Suris Crawford worked as a butcher at Armours. The story "O Yes" in *Tell Me a Riddle* also reflects the friendship between the two families.

Olsen's memory of the city in *Yonnondio* is that she merged details from Omaha, Kansas City, and St. Joseph, all places where she worked briefly in meat packing. The details of the city, unnamed in the novel except that the father says the family may "go to Omaha—get on at the slaughterhouse," closely parallel the geography of South Omaha. Like the unnamed city in the novel, Omaha lies just west of the Missouri River on a series a bluffs with the packing plants in a shallow valley. The viaduct in the novel which the workers cross going to the packinghouse is like the Q Street viaduct which connects the ethnic neighborhoods on the bluffs to the packing houses and stock yards in the valley. The Armours plant is described in the novel as "way down, like a hog, a great hulk of a building wallowed. A—R—M—O—U—R—S gray letters shrieked" (85). Photographs of the Omaha area from the 1930's and 1940's show a massive packing house in the center of the district with "Armours" spelled in large letters across the wall. In *Yonnondio* "the children can lie on their bellies near the edge of the cliff and watch the trains and freights, the glittering railroad tracks, the broken bottles dumped below, the rubbish moving on the littered belly of the river" (61-62). The bluffs on the eastern edge of Omaha overlook the river, and a railroad track runs beside the river. Though the old meat packing district in Kansas City also was near the river, the placement of bluffs, factories, and streets in the novel all fit the topography of Omaha. Olsen's fictional intent seems to be that the Holbrooks and the city where they live function generically, but the mass of detail in the family history and the setting suggests that the fictional representation is also specific. The fictionalizing obliterates the ethnic, regional, and political details that would locate the story in a more defined historical context.

The story "O Yes" also draws on Olsen's childhood friendship with the Black child next door, but here she combines it with similar incidents in the lives of her own children. The story tells of two twelve-year-old girls, one white and one Black, whose friendship dissolves when they reach the age at which race and class consciousness begin to divide school children. Olsen says that "the story is fiction, but it is rooted in the real" (interview). The names of popular musicians date the story from her children's youth, but the memories of the Black church come from Olsen's own girlhood. In the story the white child is shocked at the intensity of the emotion in the Black church. "That sound and the church" in Olsen's mind were Calvary Baptist Church, located in Omaha at 25th and Hamilton Streets between 1901-1923, where she sometimes went to hear the music on summer nights. She used this material as the recitation in

Alva's mind in the story. The Black church, she remembers, was "a certain kind of community where you could let things out" (interview).

Olsen has repeatedly stated that Eva and David in "Tell Me a Riddle" are not specifically her parents, but the history of Sam and Ida Lerner, Socialists from Russia in 1905, parents of six children, active in the union, selling their house and retiring to a Workmen's Circle home, suggests how deeply rooted this story is in the lives of her parents. Many other Russian Jews of their generation came to the United States after the 1905 Revolution, but numerous details specific to her family fit the fictional characters. David and Eva have been married forty-seven years, and in 1956 when Olsen's mother died, her parents, who apparently had been united in Nebraska sometime between 1908 and 1910, had been together approximately forty-seven years. David and Eva have six living children, as did the Lerners. Like Sam Lerner, David was "an official" who had helped organize and run the Workmen's Circles. At one point when David is trying to convince Eva to sell the house, he tells her about the reading circles in the retirement home, and she says, "And forty years ago when the children were morsels and there was a Circle, did you stay home with them once so I could go?," an apparent reference to the Workman's Circle (75). Some of Eva's words are Olsen's mother's, as we have seen in the essay written by Ida. Olsen told me that the episode in *Yonnondio* in which Anna takes time from her laundry to teach her children how to blow bubbles with a green onion is based on a memory of her mother. This memory reappears in "Tell Me a Riddle" when Vivi recalls how Eva, also while washing clothes, taught her how to blow bubbles:

> Washing sweaters: Ma, I'll never forget, one of those days so nice you washed clothes outside; one of the first spring days it must have been. The bubbles just danced while you scrubbed, and we chased after, and you stopped to show us how to blow our own bubbles with green onion stalks . . . . (*Tell Me a Riddle* 97)

Looking at the text from the background of Olsen's Omaha life suggests that family and personal experiences are the crucial ground of her fiction. Yet much of the ethnic and radical past that she remembers so vividly and emotionally in interview is distanced or dropped in the fiction. In *Yonnondio* the "unlimn'd" who "disappear" and fade from "the cities, farms, factories" fade within the novel whose epigram promises to recall them. As abstractions of the Depression poor, the Holbrooks lack history, community, and beliefs, all of which were integral to the way of life among packing town families. "Tell Me a Riddle" reflects the Russian past before David and Eva's immigration but does not reflect the fifty years of ongoing political commitment in her parents' lives. Like the Holbrooks, David and Eva stand for a type within a generation but just what "type" can never be clear when characters lose so much context. These characters dramatize the pathos of lives constrained by poverty, of women whose energies are depleted by child care and housework, but the rich texture of a place, a heritage, and active beliefs that have historically given substance to immigrant culture, including the Lerner family of Omaha, are largely absent.

III

Olsen's decision to create characters who represent in the abstract the experiences of many fulfills her ideological and artistic principles, but her writing is most powerful when it escapes the generic and becomes culturally specific. The brilliant clarity given David and Eva's Jewish language and the poignancy of the lost youth in Russia contrast sharply with the featureless pathos of the Holbrooks. The closer Olsen writes to autobiography, the finer her work, as the weaknesses in "Requa" may also illustrate. The autobiographical background also suggests that family life is her essential subject. Paradoxically, however, her art often silences much of the richness in her imaginative sources. If the early years appear to be a major touchstone for her imagination, her often painful recollections in the interviews suggest that Omaha is where the silencing began. In those early years Olsen learned the lessons of discrimination on the basis of class, ethnicity, and gender. Olsen remembers both the strength she found in a socialist home and the marginalization she felt as a poor Jew who was also radical, female, and literary. Her tentative place in the wider community was underscored when her decision to join the Communist Party created anger and embarrassment at home. Those "circumstances" described in *Silences* that "blight" and damage the young woman writer match those she felt "in the vulnerable girl years" growing up in Omaha. *Silences* gives us "the barest of indications as to vulnerabilities, balks, blights; reasons for lessenings and silencings" that affect the young woman who hopes to write (263):

> Anxieties, shamings. "Hidden injuries of class." Prevailing attitudes toward our people as "lower class," "losers," (they just didn't have it); contempt for their lives and the work they do . . . . the blood struggle for means: . . . . class—economic circumstance; problems of being in the first generation of one's family to come to writing . . . "(263-64).

If these are the circumstances that silence creativity, it may also follow that the artist may wish to silence the silencers, may, indeed, have to silence them in order to write at all. When I asked about the power the past holds for her, Olsen said, "I certainly still dwell in that world in my writing" (interview).

Like Adrienne Rich's speaker, Olsen's stories "circle silently/about the wreck" amid "the evidence of damage," "back to this scene . . ."(Rich 24). The self that speaks, the artist in the woman, must counter that which silences. The particular eloquence of Olsen's work is in her portraits of women who survive with enough intact to be themselves in a world that does not open for them. In "I Stand Here Ironing" the mother explains what she did and could not do to protect her vulnerable daughter, Emily, a sensitive and artistic child "of depression, of war, of fear" (20). Though the past "will never total," the mother believes that in Emily "there is still enough left to live by" (*Riddle* 20-1). Perhaps this story can be seen as a metaphor for Olsen's own mothering of her artistic self, one without the "totality of self" that may exist where the past was full of love and wisdom, but one with "enough left" to build on what was strong and spoke of survival.

And like the young Omaha woman who used aliases when she did her Communist work, Olsen's fiction functions like an alias, too. Names are changed and events reformed, sometimes to universalize the specific; sometimes to protect herself and her family from the scrutiny that accompanies overt autobiography; and sometimes, perhaps, to distance the anguish of being marginalized by the surrounding world. The pain of being viewed as a radical in one's own ethnic community, as a troublesome Jew at school, and as a disappointment in one's own family may well leave one haunted by the past but unable to embrace it, remembering all the places and faces, and yet unwilling to speak their names.

NOTES

1. Deborah Rosenfelt's "From the Thirties: Tillie Olsen and Radical Tradition" examines her radical past after Olsen had moved to California.

2. Personal interview Dec. 30, 1990. This essay is based largely on a set of interviews and correspondence that began in the fall of 1987 and continued through 1991. In addition to telephone interviews, the two longest of which occurred on February 13, 1988, and Dec. 30, 1990, Olsen provided a number of newspaper clippings, family letters, manuscript fragments, and miscellaneous documents from her past. These materials will be cited in text either as

"interview" or "personal correspondence." I wish to express my gratitude to Olsen for her generosity in sharing her memories and allowing me to use these materials. An earlier sketch of the Lerner family was published locally as "Tillie Olsen's Omaha Heritage: A History Becomes Literature" in *Memories of the Jewish Midwest: Journal of the Nebraska Jewish Historical Society* (Fall 1989), 1-16.

3. Most of the criticism on autobiographical novels defines the genre from male-centered works such as *David Copperfield*. More useful to me were works on women's autobiography, especially Sidonie Smith's *A Poetics of Women's Autobiography*, and the essays in Shari Benstock's *The Private Self* and Estelle C. Jelinek's *Women's Autobiography*.

4. Olsen has discussed her understanding of the Bund and "what I feel is *my* Yiddishkeit, my Jewish heritage" in the interview article by Rubin. See also Howe, *World of Our Fathers*, 17.

5. Carol Gendler's M. A. thesis, "The Jews of Omaha," University of Nebraska-Omaha (1986), is the most extensive local history. See also *Our Story: Recollections of Omaha's Early Jewish Community 1885-1925,* Eds. Jonathan Rosenbaum and Patricia O'Conner-Seger, with Carol Gendler, for personal accounts, including several of immigrants from Minsk and Odessa.

6. All six of the Lerner children were born in Nebraska and attended Omaha's Central High. The first four (Tillie was the second in order) were apparently born on the farm, the last two in Omaha, though Tillie remains uncertain exactly where and when she was born. Previously published accounts that give a specific date, usually January 14, 1913, are inaccurate, according to Olsen, who unsuccessfully researched her birth date a few years ago when she applied for a passport.

7. The City Directory lists his occupation as "painter" beginning in 1925.

8. The strike was part of a nationwide effort that ended in the breakup of the union in South Omaha. For details, see William C. Pratt, "'Union Maids' in Omaha Labor History, 1887-1945."

9. See William C. Pratt, "Socialism on the Northern Plains, 1900-1924," for a detailed account of the Party at this time.

10. Zelenka, n.p. In *Silences* Olsen calls Central High her "first College-of-Contrast"(vii).

11. Another brother, Harry, was active in the Workmen's Circle. In 1940 he was Secretary of the Omaha Workmen's Circle, Branch 690E, and wrote an editorial for the *Labor Lyceum Journal* honoring the dedication of the new Labor Lyceum. The editorial is entitled, "Shall Youth Be Away?" and urges his generation to join the Workmen's Circles and learn to appreciate what it had meant to the parents. I wish to thank Mrs. Morris Fellman of Omaha for making this booklet available to me.

12. Minnesota author Meridel LeSueur is another case of children of well known Socialist parents who joined the Communist Party in the 1920's. Both LeSueur and "Tillie Lerner" signed the "Call for an American Writers' Congress"

in 1935. See Linda Ray Pratt, "Woman Writer in the CP," for details of LeSueur's CP involvement.

WORKS CITED

Benstock, Shari, ed. *The Private Self: Theory and Practice of Women's Autobiographical Writings.* Chapel Hill: U of North Carolina P, 1988.
Gendler, Carol. "The Jews of Omaha." University of Nebraska-Omaha, 1968.
Howe, Irving. *World of Our Fathers.* New York: Harcourt Brace, 1976.
Jelinek, Estelle C., ed. *Women's Autobiography.* Bloomington: Indiana UP, 1980.
Olsen, Tillie. *Silences.* New York. Delacorte Press, 1978.
———. *Tell Me a Riddle.* New York: Dell, 1961.
———. *Yonnondio: From the Thirties.* New York: Dell, 1974.
Pratt, Linda Ray. "Tillie Olsen's Omaha Heritage: A History Becomes Literature." *Memories of the Jewish Midwest: A Journal of the Nebraska Jewish Historical Society* (Fall 1989): 1-16.
———. "Woman Writer in the CP: The Case of Meridel LeSueur." *Women's Studies.* 14 (1988): 247-64.
Pratt, William C. "Socialism on the Northern Plains, 1900-1924." *South Dakota History.* 18 (Summer 1988): 1-35.
———. "'Union Maids' in Omaha Labor History, 1887-1945." in *Perspectives: Women in Nebraska History.* Lincoln: Nebraska Department of Education and Nebraska State Council for the Social Studies, 1984, 202-03.
Rich, Adrienne. *Diving into the Wreck.* New York: Norton, 1973.
Rosenbaum, Jonathan, and Patricia O'Conner-Seger, eds., with Carol Gendler. *Our Story: Recollections of Omaha's Early Jewish Community 1885-1925,* Omaha Section of the National Council of Jewish Women, 1981.
Rosenfelt, Deborah. "From the Thirties: Tillie Olsen and Radical Tradition." *Feminist Studies.* 7 (Fall 1981): 371-406.
Rubin, Naomi. "A Riddle of History for the Future." *Sojourner.* June 1983: 3-4, 18.
Smith, Sidonie. *A Poetics of Women's Autobiography: Marginality and the Fictions of Self Representation.* Bloomington: Indiana UP, 1987.
Zelenka, Julia. "Old Neighborhood Stays With Her." Omaha *World Herald.* August 5, 1980.

THE 1970s-1990s: MENTORINGS THROUGH WORD & DEED

Silences by Tillie Olsen [*]

Joyce Carol Oates

The highest art appears to contain an entire world in miniature: entering it, one experiences the illusion of entering into the very center of the human cosmos, penetrating immediately the depths of the human imagination. If the most perfect forms of art have the quality of being "static"—in Joyce's sense of the term—it is because they are beyond and above time. Of course they exclude a great deal, and yet they give the impression of excluding nothing. They are complete; they point to nothing outside themselves; one grasps them as esthetic wholes, moved by their authority.

There is no more powerfully moving a piece of fiction in recent years than Tillie Olsen's long story "Tell Me a Riddle," which was first published in *New World Writing* in 1960, and reprinted as the title story in Tillie Olsen's first book, in 1969. Forty-seven years of marriage, hard work and impoverishment and the dizzying passage of time, an old woman's death by cancer, a frightened old man's realization of love: bitter, relentless, supremely beautiful in its nuances, its voices and small perfect details: and certainly unforgettable. All of the stories of *Tell Me a Riddle* are superb but the title story is the one that remains most

[*] Reprinted from *New Republic* 29 July 1978: 32-34.

vividly in the mind. It will withstand repeated readings—and the sort of close, scrupulous attention ordinarily reserved for poetry.

Tillie Olsen tells us in her new book, *Silences,* that her fiction came very close to never having been written. The mother of four children, she was forced for many years to work at low-paying jobs in addition to her ceaseless labor as a wife and mother "without the help of the technological sublime." Since women are traditionally trained to meet others' needs before their own, and even to feel (in Olsen's words) these needs as their own, she was not able to write for 20 years, and did not publish her first book until she was 50. During this time she was haunted by the work that demanded to be written, which "seethed, bubbled, clamored, peopled me."

Some stories died. Deprived of the time and energy to imagine them into being—for writing requires not simply passion and self-confidence but periods of solitude that will allow for the slow maturing of work—Tillie Olsen lost them forever. The present book, *Silences,* is partly autobiographical, and partly a wide-ranging discussion of the phenomenon of "unnatural" silences in literary history. Its main focus is a feminist concern, and anger, with the enforced silences of women, but it also deals—in an informal, conversation, and frequently scattered way—with the "silences" of such disparate writers as Hopkins, Melville, Rimbaud, Hardy, and Baudelaire. Virginia Woolf is ubiquitous: in fact her voice seems to compete with Tillie Olsen's own. And there is a consideration of the meaning of certain statistics (as gauged by appearances in 20th-century literature courses, required reading lists, anthologies, textbooks, etc., there is only one woman writer for every 12 men) in terms of our patriarchal society.

A miscellany of Olsen's speeches, essays, and notes, written over a period of approximately 15 years, *Silences* is necessarily uneven, and it is certainly not an academic or scholarly study. It was written, as Olsen states in her preface, out of passion: love for her incomparable medium, literature, and hatred for all that, societally rooted, lessens and denies it. Most of its content consists of excerpts and quotations from other writers who have experienced the agony of being, for one reason or another, unable to write; and there is a complete section on the relatively unknown American writer Rebecca Harding Davis, whose "classic" *Life in the Iron Mills* was published in 1861 (and more or less forgotten until its reissue in 1972). Olsen's sympathy with her numerous subjects is evident, though one might wish that she had concentrated more on her own experiences, which would have been of great interest, and less on a recounting of familiar situations (Melville's fate of being "damned by dollars" and his subsequent silence, for instance). Admirers of Tillie

Olsen's fiction will be rather disappointed to discover in *Silences* dozens of extremely familiar passages from Virginia Woolf, a lengthy excerpt from *The Life of Thomas Hardy* (ostensibly by Florence Emily Hardy), parts of numerous poems by Emily Dickinson, and scattered quotations by artists as unlike as Van Gogh, Conrad, Katherine Anne Porter, Isaac Babel, Charlotte Bronte, and Henry James . . . and nothing but the most cursory and summary of remarks about Olsen's own life. (Yet the book is being advertised as "astonishingly autobiographical.")

The book's strengths lie, however, in its polemical passages. Olsen asks why so many more women are silenced than men; she asks why there is only one woman writer "of achievement" for every 12 men writers; why our culture continues to reflect a masculine point of view almost exclusively. She quotes disapprovingly Elizabeth Hardwick's remark (about Sylvia Plath's suicide), "Every artist is either a man or a woman, and the struggle is pretty much the same for both," and Cynthia Ozick's "The term 'woman writer' . . . has no meaning, not intellectually, not morally, not historically. A writer is a writer."

She notes the distressingly low earnings of "established" writers, men and women both, and the current unhealthy publishing situation, in which more and more publishing houses are owned by large conglomerates. She speaks critically of the literary atmosphere that sets writers against one another, breeding an absurd spirit of competition. One of her chapters lists the proportion of women writers to men writers in 20th-century literature courses (six percent women, 94 percent men), in critical studies (seven percent women, 93 percent men), in interviews (10 percent women, 90 percent men), in anthologies and textbooks (nine percent women, 91 percent men), in terms of various prizes and awards (the National Book Awards, for instance, in the years 1950-73, were given to 52 people, only six of them women). The figures are often rounded off, the estimates rough, but the message is certainly clear.

Norman Mailer is quoted and allowed to make a fool of himself once again ("I have a terrible confession to make—I have nothing to say about any of the talented women who write today . . . . I do not seem able to read them."); the English critic A. Alvarez speaks condescendingly toward Sylvia Plath (" . . . No longer a housewifely appendage to a powerful husband, she seemed made solid and complete. Perhaps the birth of a son had something to do with this new confident air."); Auden is quoted in one of his sillier passages ("The poet is the father who begets the poem which the language bears . . . . Poets, like husbands, are good, bad, and indifferent."). Books like *Silences* are enormously strengthening in that they polarize attitudes, freezing people into one camp or another, suggesting unlikely sisterhoods (Virginia Woolf, who wrote so many novels, and that marvelous Diary, and those essays and reviews—and those letters!—a sister to a woman writer who, thwarted by family responsibilities and lack of freedom, has never managed to publish a single word?) and bizarre bedfellows (Hopkins, Rimbaud, Scott Fitzgerald—who "sacrificed" his talent by writing *too much,* in order to live out his sophomoric notion of the Good Life).

One feels the author's passion, and cannot help but sympathize with it. Certainly women have been more generally "silenced" than men, in all the arts. But the book is marred by numerous inconsistencies and questionable statements offered as facts. Why, for instance, are Elizabeth Hardwick and Cynthia Ozick wrong? Their views differ from mainline feminist views but are not, surely, contemptible for that reason. Why are men in general the enemy, but some men—perhaps weaker men—welcomed as fellow victims, and their "unnatural silences" accorded as much dignity as that of women? Does Baudelaire's "silence" as a consequence of syphilitic paralysis have anything at all to do with Tillie Olsen's 20 years of "silence"? I see no connection, yet the book ends with excerpts from *My Heart Laid Bare,* as if they somehow summarized Olsen's position. And why are men who exploit women criticized on the one hand, and Rilke, who kept himself aloof from responsibilities to his family, admired, on the other hand, for being shrewd enough to guard his creative energies against emotional entanglements . . . ? We are told that women are not to be trapped into the role of being *women writers;* yet it turns out to be quixotic, and halfway traitorous, to "proclaim that one's sex has nothing to do with one's writing." Feminist homiletics are always troublesome not only because they are often self-contradictory but because they never seem to apply to anyone of originality or stature.

An angry book must stir anger. Hence there is little or no mention of successful women writers of our time—among them Doris Lessing, Flannery O'Connor, Eudora Welty, Isak Dinesen, Iris Murdoch, Elizabeth Bishop, Marianne Moore, Jean Stafford, Lillian Hellman, Mary McCarthy, Muriel Rukeyser, Penelope Mortimer, Joan Didion, Edna O'Brien, Margaret Drabble, Anne Tyler, May Swenson, and innumerable others. Tillie Olsen must have felt justified in subordinating—or silencing—her own considerable artistic instincts during the composition of *Silences,* and I would not quarrel with her decision. It was a generous one: she wanted to reach out to others, to the living and the dead, who have, evidently, shared her own agony. One must respect such an impulse. But the thinking that underlies *Silences* is simply glib and superficial if set in contrast to the imagination that created *Tell Me a Riddle* and *Yonnondio,* Olsen's novel. Unexamined, unverified, and indeed unverifiable statements are offered as facts again and again. For instance, someone at a national conference on creativity in 1959 said, "Creativity was in each one of us as a small child. In children it is universal. Among adults it is non-existent" [*sic*]*—not only a doubtful proposition, but sheer malarkey—and Olsen quotes it with approval.

She never confronts the most troublesome question of all: What has "creativity" as such to do with "art"? Are all silences equally tragic? On what basis can a writer resent his society's indifference to his art, so long as society is free to choose its values? I was reminded of that cruel but witty passage in the chapter "Economy" in *Walden,* in which Thoreau speaks of an Indian who has woven straw baskets no one wants to buy, and who is amazed and resentful at the world's indifference. He had not discovered, Thoreau says, that it was necessary for him to make it worth the other's while to buy them, or at least make him think that it was so. And there is Flannery O'Connor's sardonic response to a question put to her at a reading, about whether universities stifled writers. O'Connor replied: "They don't stifle enough of them." (Which is one of the reasons, I suspect, that O'Connor cannot be taken up by feminist critics with much comfort.)

A final comment on the book's editing, or lack thereof. Since the various chapters were published at different times there are many, many repetitions of key phrases and quotations. And nearly every page is marred by small, inconsequential footnotes that qualify or update statements made in the text. In practically every case these footnotes should have been incorporated into the text or eliminated: their busy, gnat-like presence is injurious to the reading experience, and in most instances their nature undercuts the seriousness of the book. For instance, in the chapter "One Out of Twelve: Writers Who Are Women," Olsen quotes Hortense Calisher with disapproval, and then admits in a footnote that her remarks are unfair, because the copy of Calisher's essay she read had an important (and unnoticed) page missing. "My abashed apologies," Olsen says. Yet surely it would not have been too much trouble to type over a single page and eliminate the negative reference to Calisher . . . ? These are signs of haste, and of an editor's indifference. In a book that sets itself up as a literary manifesto of the women's move-ment, one which has been eagerly anticipated by a considerable number of readers, offenses such as these are saddening, and inexplicable.

---

* Editor's Footnote: Olsen has noted that the sentence from *Silences* (261) reads "Among adults it is *almost* nonexistent [italics added to highlight omission]."

Obstacle Course[*]

Margaret Atwood

Tillie Olsen's is a unique voice. Few writers have gained such wide respect based on such a small body of published work: one book of short stories, "Tell Me a Riddle," and the unfinished novel, "Yonnondio: From the Thirties." Among women writers in the United States, "respect" is too pale a word: "reverence" is more like it. This is presumably because women writers, even more than their male counterparts, recognize what a heroic feat it is to have held down a job, raised four children and still somehow managed to become and to remain a writer. The exactions of this multiple identity cost Tillie Olsen 20 years of her writing life. The applause that greets her is not only for the quality of her artistic performance but, as at a grueling obstacle race, for the near miracle of her survival.

Tillie Olsen's third book, "Silences," is about this obstacle course, this ordeal, not only as she herself experienced it but as many writers have experienced it, in many forms. It begins with an account, first drafted in 1962, of her own long, circumstantially enforced silence. She did not write for a very simple reason: A day has 24 hours. For 20 years she had no time, no energy and none of the money that would have bought both. It may be comforting to believe that garrets are good for geniuses, that artists are made in Heaven and God will take care of them; but if you believe, as Tillie Olsen does, that writers are nurtured on Earth and nobody necessarily takes care of them, society cannot be absolved from the responsibility for what it produces or fails to produce in the way of literature.

Though Tillie Olsen begins with her own experience, she rapidly proceeds to that of others. The second part of the book is a grab bag of excerpts from the diaries, journals, letters and concealed autobiographical work of a wide range of writers, past and present, male and female. They are used to demonstrate, first, the ideal conditions for creation as perceived by the writers themselves, and second, almost every imaginable impediment to that creation. The financial and cultural pressures that gagged Melville, the religious agonies of Hopkins, the bitterness of Thomas Hardy after the vicious reception of "Jude the Obscure," Willa Cather's feeling of nullity in the face of the suave Eastern establishment; political, cultural, sexist and sexual censorship; the denial of a voice to a race, a class, a sex, by the denial of its access to literature; breakdowns,

[*] Reprinted from *New York Times Book Review* 30 July 1978: 1, 27.

abdications, addictions; all are cited. Reading this section may be hazardous if you are actually writing a book. It's like walking along a sidewalk only to be shown suddenly that your sidewalk isn't a sidewalk but a tightrope over Niagara Falls. How have you managed to do it at all? "Chancy luck," Tillie Olsen replies, and in view of the evidence she musters, she's probably—for all writers not white, male, rich and from a dominant culture—quite right.

Tillie Olsen's special concern is with how her general observations on silencings apply, more heavily and with additions, to women. Here, the obstacles may seem to be internal: the crippling effects of upbringing, the burdens of motherhood, the lack of confidence that may prevent women from writing at all; and, if they do write, their own male-determined view of women, the fear of competing, the fear of success. We've heard a lot of this before, but it's invigorating to see its first expressions by women coming new to the problems: Virginia Woolf worrying about her childlessness, Katherine Mansfield having to cope with all the domestic arrangements while John Middleton Murray nagged her about tea. And, in contrast, quotations from men whose wives dedicated their lives to sharpening pencils and filling the inkwell for them. As Tillie Olsen points out, almost all of the women in the 19th century who wrote were childless or had servants. Her study of Rebecca Harding Davis, author of the remarkable "Life in the Iron Mills," is a telling example of what happened to one writer who made the switch from solitude to child-rearing.

In construction, "Silences" is a scrapbook, a patchwork quilt: bits and pieces joined to form a powerful whole. And, despite the condensed and fragmentary quality of this book, the whole is powerful. Even the stylistic breathlessness—the elliptical prose, the footnotes blooming on every page as if the author, reading her own manuscript, belatedly thought of a dozen other things too important to leave out—is reminiscent of a biblical messenger, sole survivor of a relentless and obliterating catastrophe, a witness: "I only am escaped alone to tell thee." The tone is right: The catastrophes do occur, daily though they may not be seen as such. What Tillie Olsen has to say about them is of primary importance to those who want to understand how art is generated or subverted and to those trying to create it themselves.

The true measure of a book's success, for the reader, is the number of people she wants to give it to. My own list is already long.

Review of *Silences* by Tillie Olsen[*]

Nolan Miller

Most of the reviews of this book at best have been grumpy. It has been called a "hodge-podge," a "scrapbook." All have expressed disappointment that Mrs. Olsen, whose short stories appearing in such publications as *New Campus Writing* and *New World Writing* in the early 60s hit literary consciousness like thunderbolts, has not offered more of her highly charged, highly original fiction. In 1974 she offered only *Yonnondio*, a novel lost to the public for forty years.

There is a good reason for this writer's low production. For more than forty years she has been a wife and mother, a family wage-earner at dull and time-sapping menial jobs. She has been, like multitudes of other talents, frustratingly "silent"—silent because, most of all, of the necessities of earning a living and keeping a family together.

Silences, her third book, tells us all this—tells us why, and how arduous and obstructed her life, a woman's life, has been. She has not been alone. Her abundant quotations from others who have endured silently, both men and women, may seem abundant only to those unacquainted with or indifferent to society's waste of individual talents.

If categories are wanted, call this a highly personal commonplace book. Call it a case-book, a text. Above all, it bears the stamp of a passionate and reasonably angry voice. What is said here needed to be said, however it is said. Value the book as one values the person, the talent. One can only return to a reading of "Tell Me a Riddle" and "Hey Sailor, What Ship?" marveling the more. The experience of these stories can only be deepened by our knowledge of how they managed, eventually, to struggle into lasting significance.

[*] Reprinted from *Antioch Review* 36.4 (Fall 1978): 513.

Books: Tillie Olsen. *Silences*[*]

I read Tillie Olsen's *Silences* in high excitement, as I'm sure did all who love her stories. The coming of a book of hers—or an essay, or a story—is rare and portentous; this book is about why it has been so rare: an examination of creativity in hobbles. She says she has undertaken "to expand the too sparse evidence on the relationship between circumstances and creation." She herself has been one of "the rarest of all [artists], the worker-mother-writer."

Silences is not the kind of polemic that relaxes its reader into gratified agreement. After the title essay it is hard going. It is full of agitated reflection, on either side of a long essay about another book and the life of its author. It is angry, resentful, plaintive, repetitive—one could pile on the adjectives of vehemence. Sometimes it reads like a lawsuit, but in its distressed rhythm and integrity of emotion it is more a poem than an argument. As lawsuit it convinces; you no more contend with her thesis—that many artists, women in particular, are grossly thwarted by their societies—than you contend with Dickens about trapped children. The documentation alone, from diaries and letters, of the struggle of dozens of writers to reach their full capacities, is a gold mine.

Does the question of the hindered artist seem passé? Read the table of contents in a contemporary anthology of poetry, counting the women in the canon.

This is a radical book, concerned with work. As work, art requires sacrifice from the attempter just as going to an office or a sawmill does, but requires also time, place, and some assurance that, if not society, then some part of it—even one "enabler," her excellent term—concurs wholly in what you are doing. So the book takes up the question of all the "diminished, excluded, foundered, silenced" who lack enabling circumstances and enablers, and whose voices stop.

The second half of Part I is Olsen's long afterword to the reissue of Rebecca Harding Davis' 1861 novel *Life in the Iron Mills*. It is a loving study of the woman who wrote "that fiction which incorporates social and economic problems directly, *and in terms of their effects on human beings,*" who was accused by critics of writing "sentimental propaganda for the negro" and being "the poet of the poor people," who began to devalue herself and broke off in her development as a novelist. (*Silences* ends with an excerpt from her extraordinary novel.)

[*] Reprinted from *American Poetry Review* May-June 1978: 18-19.

Part II (with the grueling subtitle, "Acerbs, Asides, Amulets, Exhumations, Sources, Deepenings, Roundings, Expansions") contains all the paraphernalia of private notetaking: quotation without comment, or with comment abbreviated and jerky; hurried jampacked soliloquy; italics; parentheses; cryptic remarks. Nouns-as-adjectives, giving it the flavor at times of a self-help text: "profound (woman) life comprehensions." Odd strained high language: "Trespass vision cannot make circumference." At first I found myself quibbling with the book on these grounds and wondering why Tillie Olsen would use any part of the language of pop therapy, or leave on the page the sighs and exclamations that follow some of the quotations—"Amen" for instance.

But as I came under the spell of the book I reread her fiction, where the accumulation of detail is similar, very rapid and explosive. In *Silences* she has created the form to make her case, a language of sweeping, insistent, repetitive movement. It amasses, marshals evidence. A voice persuades, decries, weaves—a story. For she is a story-writer, and has told the story of Rebecca Harding Davis and of herself, and of Rilke, Hardy, Baudelaire, Cather, Dickinson, George Eliot and others, some with the odds for them and some with the odds against them as artists.

She talks as a mother about the family: " . . . and remember, in our society, the family must often try to be the center for love and health the outside world is not." Not a popular idea, the solemn obligation of family life. Yet she does not evade the conclusion that for the female artist, as for the male, family life will not substitute for art. Nor does she pretend the feeling of truancy that the woman writer has, with or without children (for not having them is a contrariness in itself, worse in many eyes than taking poor care of them), is eased by theories.

Once the evidence is in, what is to be done? No use to fall back on the old proposition "this book should be required reading" for editors, publishers; certainly for women who write, and their families, and their readers; and for those who don't bother to read them, like Norman Mailer who says he doesn't like the sniffs he gets from their ink. It's comical to think of what he might say about this book, exciting (in a pathetic way) to conjure up political solutions to the problem of the artist, sad to think of our own equivalents of Hardy's giving up fiction when *Jude the Obscure* was not understood.

Tillie Olsen extends to those writing now an unusual generosity, taking them seriously. Hers is the generosity of contemporaries, missing for so many writers—an enabling circumstance indeed.

Lessons in Killing Wonder

Carol Lauhon

In 1983, Tillie Olsen landed in our Iowa-Illinois town to devote herself fully to us for seven days. She enchanted audiences in five colleges, lovingly authorized all of us who gathered around her to believe in our own creativity, and then she flew away.

"Tillie Olsen Week in the Quad-Cities" was a celebration. Feminism in the United States had crested once again. We were inspired by the visiting woman writer who had miraculously overcome demands of time and circumstance to write and publish. We viewed her as the icon of the survivor: damaged potential in triumphant protest.

They're mostly a blur now, all those passionate panels, papers, manuscript critiques, readings, film screenings, and long discussions. A decade has passed, and it's the woman herself I remember and love, as familiar and close-up as breath.

She is not tall. She's simply the only size she could be, like one's mother. Her hair is not young. It's thick. The natural gray waves have been trimmed and brushed back. Wisps escape in a halo of distraction. The folds of her soft cheeks are deep. Her nose is hawklike, not prominent, but a useful size. Her eyes when they find me shine at me as if I were her only child. I memorize that look, the wrinkled lids, the darkening sockets. Someday she will have to leave and I will stay behind.

Day after day, her sense of urgency outlasts her exhaustion. At the end of a long evening, when I ask for just an autograph on the inside cover of *Tell Me a Riddle*, I watch her struggle against ebbing accuracy:

For Carol -

> Exhaustedly -
>> all we we [sic] shared this weeek [sic]
>> when I came to know and love
>> you - beginning of [first?] -
> You <u>must</u> keep on writing - <u>publish</u> -
>> we will not lose each other.

Tillie

Her awareness of her waning strength increases her resolve to encourage me.

At the manuscript critique, Tillie drinks me in: me, my work, my love for her. She reads deeply and laughs. She removes her glasses and wipes her eyes. This moment is the only moment ever. Then, reminded that it's late and the room assigned will be locked up, she bursts out angrily against the messenger. She wants to stay! I learn that I am to defy time. Defy circumstance. I am never, ever, to relinquish the moment.

At the panel discussion, I'm billed as a "writing student." Already three times a mother, I tell stories of women's power to create in all of our womanly roles, especially as artists and mothers. The audience laughs, nods agreement, is moved to loud and long applause even after I have exceeded my humble ten-minute allotment outrageously. They turn expectantly to Tillie Olsen. She says, "With Carol Lauhon, who needs Tillie Olsen?"

It's an accolade in every new and old sense: praise, duty, embrace, collar. This tired, mothering woman has collared me all right. Tillie's dreams were deferred. Others' are, too. Her fame is a miracle. The fame of others is, too. I must promise to remember and outdo her. I am to write. And I am to be the nurturer-in-residence, genius divining genius. She is counting on me.

In the wake of Tillie Olsen's visit, I was handed *Killing Wonder*, a mystery novel by Dorothy Bryant published in 1981 by Ata Books. The central figure is an aging Bay Area writer named India Wonder, an activist and autodidact famous for her one and only book written two decades before. India Wonder's book, *Emma Pride's Journal*, is an autobiographical novel about a woman's struggle to write.

India Wonder may as well be Tillie Olsen. Both have thick gray hair and bright eyes. Both blossom in public gatherings, singing out lovingly the names of those present. Both speak in fragments, appositives. Both are celebrating writing careers that did not bloom until they were in middle age. Both engage in voluminous correspondence with aspiring writers. Both go on tour.

In the opening scene, the great writer dies from a poisoned drink. Her writer friends are suspects. The reader eventually discovers that no one murdered Wonder but everyone is to blame for her death. She killed herself.

Maybe I have to be from California to enjoy this entertainment: borrowing heavily from the life of a living woman, showing her death, proving how it was that she could come to kill herself. A decade has passed, and *Killing Wonder* still seems a perverse biography, a too-playful take on a passionate life.

We are shown that India Wonder killed herself because of enormous pressure to produce another book. Although she had money and a room of her own, she was depressed. Her husband was dying and her hypertension was affecting her memory. Because she was unable to refuse requests for attention from literary audiences and aspiring writers, she spent all of her time on letters and lectures. Yet she desperately felt the need to produce another book in order to deserve the love and adoration of her friends and followers.

Unfortunately, her friends and followers were only human. Each had reason to be grateful to her but to resent her as well. Yolanda Dolores, for example, credits India with early support in developing writing workshops for children at a community center in the Mission District. "When I wrote to [India] ten years ago, about my work here, she came right out," Yolanda says. "Those kids had never seen anything like her. She hugged them. She cried. She set those wild gray eyes on them and told them they were all pure divine fire inside, burning to get out. Have you ever seen her do that number?"[1]

Yolanda is speaking to Jessie Posey, the young writer who has turned detective to hunt for India's killer. Jessie learns that although India helped Yolanda in developing the workshops as well as in getting her writing published and her publishing company started, she withdrew her support after Yolanda wrote an article criticizing her.

Yolanda's article is critical of the famous India for keeping for herself a "virtual monopoly on attention and support which might be spread among other worthy writers" (122). India is in a false position, writes Yolanda, since she has continued to speak out against conditions adverse to writing, yet, free of those conditions, has not produced a new book in twenty years. India has allowed herself to remain the symbol of "the thwarted woman artist," instead of taking her chances at falling off her pedestal by publishing a second manuscript. Yolanda reminds readers that India Wonder has much more to say than what is evident from the first novel. "[T]hose of us who know India Wonder personally know that beyond the yearning 'Emma Pride' identity there is a complex, witty, assertive even contradictory person, capable of writing books very different from *Emma Pride's Journal*" (125).

Yolanda is the eighth writer interviewed by the writer-detective Jessie Posey, the eighth woman to show Jessie that India Wonder was not a symbol but a woman, who was capable of being offended and acting vindictively. As a recent graduate of the creative writing program at San Francisco State whose reading of *Emma Pride's Journal* had turned her into a writer at age sixteen, Jessie has idolized India Wonder, calling her "the greatest of them all" (2). In the party scene which opens the book, Jessie thinks India is "the only one who looked like a writer, the way I imagined a writer should look" (3). India stands for "everything I ever wanted to be" (17).

Jessie has continued to believe her hero can do no wrong in spite of the evidence of the interviews. But coming upon Yolanda's article, Jessie is finally disillusioned. She decides that India Wonder was "the biggest phony of them all" (138). Only with the memorial service, which eulogizes India as not just a writer but an activist, a mother and a nurturer of other writers, does Jessie come to appreciate that the creative genius of India's life extended beyond literary manuscripts. This claim is most clearly represented in the announcement by India's daughter Georgie (named for George Sand) that India's voluminous correspondence will be published in a book called *Letters to my Daughter*.

The book *Killing Wonder* shows that in order to become a real writer and not just a poseur, Jessie Posey must stop gazing in wonder at her idol and look around her. There are not just, in Jessie's terms, "great writers" and "nobodies." Real writers are writing, and they are everywhere. She can be one, too. Dorothy Bryant herself, the author of *Killing Wonder*, while less well-known than Tillie Olsen, has to her credit six titles, including one called *Ella Price's Journal*, listed on the inside cover of the book.

On the outside cover is a collage of photos of women. They appear to be talking to one another and posing for photographs at parties. A photo of Tillie Olsen is centered and just beneath the title—the title which refers to the fictional writer who has killed herself, while everyone around her is to blame.

In a recent essay in *Clues* magazine, Marty Knepper points out how India's sudden and lasting fame caused her to be isolated from other writers.[2] She is the token woman writer, proof that women can make it against the odds. Knepper points out that younger writers could make her their hero, while writers who have been struggling longer could resent her success. No one around her could see that just like everyone else she needed support and encouragement. Knepper agrees with India's husband that what India needed from Yolanda and the others was understanding and forgiveness, not resentment.

Knepper also agrees with India's daughter Georgie that Jessie's naive adoration of India at the party precipitated the suicide. India was about to announce that she had writer's block, that there was no second manuscript. When she saw Jessie's worship of her, she killed herself to avoid seeing Jessie's disillusionment.

Another way to understand India's torment is as a crisis of identity. Without a new manuscript, she is not who the other writers think she is, not a real writer. She sees her identity—"writer"—in its narrowest sense, thus judging herself a failure, her life without value. Her chances of producing another book as successful as her first are waning as she ages.

Her voluminous correspondence and frequent lecturing must have drained India more than sustained her. She needed to see the creative value in all of her womanly roles, not only as artist but also as "mother" to other writers. Instead, she felt, in Jessie's words, "trapped by choices," rather than embraced by them. When a woman chooses to respond to demands on her, there is the danger of suicide. She can consume herself in support of others unless she understands what nurtures her. She can call her work "writing," and feel reduced by any other activity, or she can claim that her genius is (also) of the older sort—the tutelary spirit of a place, the nurturer-in-residence. And she can surround herself with what nurtures her.

Why is the fictional writer a suicide, and the real writer a survivor? Because Tillie Olsen knows what she needs.

I remember picking her up to drive her to our evening manuscript critique. She moved from the uptown hotel assigned her to a modest motel where she could watch the barges work the Mississippi River. As she sank into the front seat, she sighed. She wanted Macintosh apples, she said, and some lettuce. A moment later she was straining eagerly toward me when I mentioned that something Jim said in *Yonnondio* meant a great deal to me. She waited in insistent silence until I could tell her precisely which sentence it was.

In the car I saw that this woman knew what she needed to sustain herself—a view of the river, Midwestern apples, California lettuce, readers who cared. In the wake of her visit, I understood that she needed writers who welcomed everything she had to give, even to the lending of her life as a prompt for their fiction.

Tillie Olsen must have agreed to be photographed for the cover of *Killing Wonder*. Lending her prominent image is akin to approval. She helps Dorothy Bryant make the point that even writers who have achieved renown need friends and forgiveness to continue believing in their own worth. Iconoclasm is healthy for aspiring writers as well. Seen up close writers are, as Alix Kates Shulman says, "fallible and ordinary folk."[3] Discovering this gives aspiring writers the courage to write. And many writers can be seen, on the cover of the book and around Tillie Olsen, if aspiring writers leave off fixing their gaze on "the greatest of them all."

Despite surface similarities, Tillie Olsen must not see herself as India Wonder: "You see, I am a survivor," she tells a 1974 gathering at Panjandrum Press in San Francisco. "Any woman who writes is a survivor."[4] Calling herself a survivor is to insist on life in the face of death. She wants to stay.

Tillie Olsen left the Quad Cities as she will leave us all someday. She will be survived by many "children" like me. She will be remembered not only for her exquisite fiction and her unrelenting activism on behalf of genius. She will be remembered by those lucky enough to have felt her real-life embrace, as a living passionate presence to whom caring meant doing.

I memorize that person as did Sandy Boucher, herself a "daughter" in the 1974 Panjandrum gathering (and a "writer" at the party in the opening scene of *Killing Wonder*), almost two decades ago. First testifying about Tillie Olsen the writer, whose work is "for me, all that is most living in literature," Boucher commemorates the woman as well: "dear, struggling and flawed, profound and trivial, inarticulate much of the time, harried almost always, amused, joyful, sometimes eloquent, deeply caring . . . always intensely and immediately loved."

Sandy Boucher and Alix Kates Shulman and Dorothy Bryant, but for differences in time and circumstance, were with me in the audiences a decade ago in the Quad-Cities of Iowa-Illinois. Marty Knepper was actually in those audiences, and on the panel, and not only the professor of the seminar in which I first read *Silences,* but the friend who lent me *Killing Wonder.* All "daughters," survivors of Tillie Olsen, we have come to believe in genius as the spirit of a place. Even after our mother leaves, we must continue to nurture one another.

NOTES

1. Subsequent page references to Dorothy Bryant's *Killing Wonder* from the 1981 Ata Books paperback edition, will be placed in the body of the essay.

2. Marty S. Knepper, "Who Killed Janet Mandelbaum and India Wonder?: A Look at the Suicides of the Token Women in Amanda Cross's *Death in a Tenured Position* and Dorothy Bryant's *Killing Wonder,*" *Clues* 13.1 (Spring/Summer 1992): 57.

3. Alix Kates Shulman, "Overcoming Silences: Teaching Writing for Women," *Harvard Educational Review* 49.4 (November 1979): 530.

4. Sandy Boucher, "Tillie Olsen: The Weight of Things Unsaid," *Ms.* 3 (September 1974): 30.

Bibliography

Works by Tillie Olsen

1930s

"I Want You Women Up North to Know" [Tillie Lerner]. *Partisan* 1 (Mar. 1934): 4. Rpt. in *Feminist Studies* 7.3 (Fall 1981): 367-69.

"There Is a Lesson" [Tillie Lerner]. *Partisan* 1 (Apr. 1934): 4. Rpt. in Burkom and Williams.

"The Iron Throat" [Tillie Lerner]. *Partisan Review* 1.2 (Apr.-May 1934): 3-9. Reappears as Chapter One in *Yonnondio: From the Thirties.*

"Thousand-Dollar Vagrant" [Tillie Lerner]. *New Republic* 80 (29 Aug. 1934): 67-69.

"The Strike" [Tillie Lerner]. *Partisan Review* 1.4 (Sept.-Oct. 1934): 3-9. Rpt. in *Years of Protest: A Collection of American Writings of the 1930s.* Ed. Jack Salzman. New York: Pegasus, 1967. 138-44.

1950s

Tell Me a Riddle. Philadelphia: Lippincott, 1961. Rpt. New York: Delta 1989. This collection includes "I Stand Here Ironing" which first appeared under the title "Help Her to Believe" in *Pacific Spectator* 10 (Winter 1956): 55-63; "Hey Sailor, What Ship?" which first appeared in *New Campus Writing* 2. Ed. Nolan Miller. New York: Putnam, 1957. 199-213; "O Yes" which first appeared under the title "Baptism" in *Prairie Schooner* 31 (Spring 1957): 70-80; and "Tell Me a Riddle" which first appeared in *New World Writing* 16. Eds. Stewart Richardson and Corlies M. Smith. Philadelphia: Lippincott, 1960. 11-57.

1970s

"Requa." *Iowa Review* 1 (Summer 1970): 54-74. Reprinted as "Requa-I." *Granta:*
  New American Writing Sept. 1979: 111-32, and later as "Requa I" in *The Best*
  American Short Stories, 1971. Eds. Martha Foley and David Burnett. Boston:
  Houghton, 1971. 237-65.
Yonnondio: From the Thirties. New York: Delacorte, 1974. Rpt. Delta, 1981.
Silences. New York: Delacorte, 1978. Rpt. Delta, 1989. Includes early talks and
  essays: "Silences in Literature," first published in *Harper's* 231 (Oct. 1965): 153-
  61; "One Out of Twelve: Women Who are Writers in Our Century" first
  published in *College English* 34 (Oct. 1972): 6-17; and "Rebecca Harding Davis:
  Her Life and Times," which first appeared as "A Biographical Interpretation,"
  an Afterword for *Life in the Iron Mills* by Rebecca Harding Davis. Old
  Westbury: Feminist, 1972. 67-174.

1980s

"Dream-Vision." *Mother to Daughter: Daughter to Mother: Mothers on Mothering:*
  A Daybook and Reader. Selected and Shaped by Tillie Olsen. Westbury:
  Feminist, 1984. 261-64.
Foreword. *Black Women Writers at Work.* Ed. Claudia Tate. New York:
  Continuum, 1986. ix-xi.
"Mothers and Daughters" [Tillie Olsen with Julie Olsen Edwards]. *Mothers and*
  Daughters: That Special Quality: An Exploration in Photography. Eds. Tillie
  Olsen, Julie Olsen Edwards and Estelle Jussim. New York: Aperture, 1987. 14-
  17.
Introduction. *Allegra Maud Goldman.* By Edith Konecky. New York: Feminist,
  1987. ix-xi.

Filmed or Recorded Works by Tillie Olsen

Tillie Olsen Reads "I Stand Here Ironing" and Excerpts from Yonnondio and "O
  Yes." Audiotape. Rec. San Francisco 1981. American Audio Prose Library.
  AAPL 1131. 1986. 77 min.
Tell Me A Riddle. Videorecording. Media Home Entertainment. 1988. 94 min.

Interviews with Tillie Olsen

"Breaking Silence." With Kenneth Turan. *New West* 28 Aug. 1978: 56, 59.

[Tillie Olsen] Reading: Selected Passages from the Novel Yonnondio: From the Thirties, "I Stand Here Ironing," "Tell Me a Riddle"; and Interview with Tillie Olsen. Audiotape. Clinton, NY: Hamilton College, 1979.

"Tillie Olsen: From a Public Dialogue Between Olsen and Marilyn Yalom, Stanford Center for Research on Women, Nov. 5, 1980 and Subsequently." *Women Writers of the West Coast: Speaking of Their Lives and Careers.* Ed. Marilyn Yalom. Santa Barbara, CA: Capra, 1983. 57-66.

Tillie Olsen: A Profile. With Susan Stamberg. *All Things Considered.* Audiotape. National Public Radio. AT800303.01/01-C. 1980. 29 min.

"'Surviving Is Not Enough': A Conversation with Tillie Olsen." With Kay Mills. *Los Angeles Times* 26 Aug. 1981: 3.

Tillie Olsen Interview with Kay Bonetti. Audiotape. American Audio Prose Library. AAPL 1132. 1981. 51 min.

"An Interview with Tillie Olsen." With Linda Park-Fuller. *Literature in Performance: A Journal of Literary and Performing Art* 4.1 (Nov. 1983): 75-77.

"A Riddle of History for the Future." With Naomi Rubin. *Sojourner* July 1983: 4, 18.

See, Lisa. "Tillie Olsen." PW Interview on *Mother to Daughter, Daughter to Mother. Publishers Weekly* 226 (23 Nov. 1984): 76, 79.

Works about Tillie Olsen

Ackroyd, Peter. "The Living Image." Review of *Yonnondio: From the Thirties.* Spectator 14 Dec. 1974: 767-68.

Adams, Phoebe-Lou. Review of *Silences. Atlantic Monthly* Sept. 1978: 96.

Atwood, Margaret. "Obstacle Course." Review of *Silences. New York Times Book Review* 30 July 1978: 1, 27.

Avant, John Alfred. Review of *Yonnondio: From the Thirties. New Republic* 30 Mar. 1974: 28-29. Rpt. in Vol. 4 of *Contemporary Literary Criticism.* Detroit: Gale, 1975. 385.

Banks, Joanne Trautman. "Death Labors." *Literature and Medicine* 9 (1990): 162-71.

Barr, Marleen. "Tillie Olsen." Vol. 28 of *Dictionary of Literary Biography.* Detroit: Gale, 1984. 196-203.

Bauer, Helen Pike. "'A child of anxious, not proud, love': Mother and Daughter in Tillie Olsen's 'I Stand Here Ironing.'" *Mother Puzzles: Daughters and Mothers in Contemporary American Literature.* Ed. Mickey Pearlman. Westport: Greenwood, 1989. 35-39.

Blustein, Bryna Lee. "Beyond the Stereotype: A Study of Representative Short Stories of Selected Contemporary Jewish American Female Writers [Yezierska, Olsen, Paley, Darwin, Ozick]." Diss. St. Louis U, 1986.

Boucher, Sandy. "Tillie Olsen: The Weight of Things Unsaid." *MS* Sept. 1974: 26-30.

Buford, Bill. "Leave of Absence." Review of *Tell Me a Riddle, Yonnondio: From the Thirties,* and *Silences. New Statesman* 31 Oct. 1980: 23-24.

Burkom, Selma, and Margaret Williams. "De-Riddling Tillie Olsen's Writings." *San Jose Studies* 2 (Feb. 1976): 64-83.

Cantwell, Robert. "The Little Magazines." Review note on "The Iron Throat." *New Republic* 25 July 1934: 295-97.

———. "The Literary Life in California." *New Republic* 22 Aug. 1934: 49.

Chevigny, Bell Gale. Review of *Yonnondio: From the Thirties. Village Voice* 23 May 1974: 38-39. Rpt. in Vol. 4 of *Contemporary Literary Criticism.* Detroit: Gale, 1975. 387.

Clapp, Susannah. "Deep Depression." Review of *Yonnondio: From the Thirties. Times Literary Supplement* 10 Jan. 1975: 29.

Clayton, John. "Grace Paley and Tillie Olsen: Radical Jewish Humanists." *Response: A Contemporary Jewish Review* 46 (1984): 37-52.

Coiner, Constance. "'No One's Private Ground': A Bakhtinian Reading of Tillie Olsen's *Tell Me a Riddle. Feminist Studies* 18.2 (Summer 1992): 257-81.

———. "Literature of Resistance: The Intersection of Feminism and the Communist Left in Meridal LeSueur and Tillie Olsen." *Left Politics and the Literary Profession.* Eds. Lennard J. Davis and M. Bella Mirabella. New York: Columbia UP, 1990. 162-85.

———. *Better Red: Tillie Olsen and Meridel LeSueur's Writing and Resistance* (Working Title). New York: Oxford UP, 1995.

Coles, Robert. *The Call of Stories: Teaching and the Moral Imagination.* Boston: Houghton, 1989. 49.

———. "Reconsideration." Review of *Tell Me a Riddle. New Republic* 6 Dec. 1975: 29-39. Rpt. as "Tillie Olsen: The Iron and the Riddle." *That Red Wheelbarrow: Selected Literary Essays by Robert Coles.* Iowa City: U of Iowa P, 1988. 122-27.

Connelly, Julia E. "The Whole Story." *Literature and Medicine* 9 (1990): 150-61.

Culver, Sara. "Extending the Boundaries of the Ego: Eva in 'Tell Me a Riddle.'" *Midwestern Miscellany* 10 (1982): 38-48.

Cunneen, Sally. "Tillie Olsen: Storyteller of Working America." *Christian Century* 21 May 1980: 570-74.

Dillon, David. "Art and Daily Life in Conflict." Review of *Silences. Southwest Review* 64.1 (Winter 1979): 105-07.

Doherty, Gail and Paul Doherty. "Paperback Harvest." Review of *Yonnondio: From the Thirties. America* 18 Oct. 1975: 236-37.

"Dressed to Kill." Review of *Tell Me a Riddle. Times Literary Supplement* 6 Feb. 1964: 101.

Duncan, Erika. "Coming of Age in the Thirties: A Portrait of Tillie Olsen." *Book Forum* 6.2 (1982): 207-22. Rpt. as "Tillie Olsen." *Unless Soul Clap Its Hands: Portraits and Passages.* New York: Schocken, 1984. 31-57.

Elman, Richard M. "The Many Forms Which Loss Can Take." Review of *Tell Me a Riddle. Commonweal* 8 Dec. 1961: 295-96.

Faulkner, Mara. *Protest and Possibility in the Writing of Tillie Olsen.* Charlottesville: UP of Virginia, 1993.

Fisher, Elizabeth. "The Passion of Tillie Olsen." *Nation* 10 Apr. 1972: 472-74.

Fishkin, Shelley Fisher. "The Borderlands of Culture: Writing by W.E.B. DuBois, James Agee, Tillie Olsen, and Gloria Anzaldúa." *Literary Journalism in the Twentieth Century.* Ed. Norman Sims. New York: Oxford U P, 1990. 133-82.

Fishkin, Shelley Fisher, and Elaine Hedges, eds. *Listening to "Silences": New Essays in Feminist Criticism.* New York: Oxford U P, (In Progress).

Frye, Joanne S. "'I Stand Here Ironing': Motherhood as Experience and Metaphor." *Studies in Short Fiction* 18.3 (Summer 1981): 287-92.

Gardiner, Judith Kegan. "A Wake for Mother: The Maternal Deathbed in Women's Fiction." *Feminist Studies* 4 (June 1978): 145-65.

Gelfant, Blanche H. "After Long Silence: Tillie Olsen's 'Requa.'" *Studies in American Fiction* 12.1 (Spring 1984): 61-69. Rpt. in Blanche H. Gelfant. *Women Writing in America.* Hanover, NH: U P of New England, 1984. 59-70.

———. "Chronicles and Chroniclers: Some Contemporary Fictions." Review of *Yonnondio: From the Thirties. Massachusetts Review* 16 (Winter 1975): 127-43.

Glastonbury, Marion. "The Best Kept Secret—How Working-Class Women Live and What They Know." *Women's Studies International Quarterly* 2 (1979): 171-81.

Glendinning, Victoria. "Cold Comfort." Review of *Yonnondio: From the Thirties. New Statesman* 20 Dec. 1974: 907.

Gottlieb, Annie. "Feminists Look at Motherhood." *Mother Jones* 1 (Nov. 1976): 51-53.

———. "A Writer's Sounds and Silences." Review of *Yonnondio: From the Thirties. New York Times Book Review* 31 Mar. 1974: 5. Excerpt rpt. in Vol. 4 *Contemporary Literary Criticism.* Detroit: Gale, 1975. 386.

Graulich, Melody. "Violence Against Women in Literature of the Western Family." *Frontiers: A Journal of Women's Studies* 7.3 (1984): 14-20. Rpt. in Susan H. Armitage and Elizabeth Jameson, eds. *The Women's West.* Norman: U of Oklahoma P, 1987. 111-25.

Grumbach, Doris. "Tillie Olsen's Scrapbook." Review of *Silences. Washington Post* 6 Aug. 1978: F1, F4.

Halischak, Kathleen. "Recent Voices in American Feminist Literature." Diss. U of Notre Dame. 1982. ProQuest DA: AAC 822 5814.

Hedges, Elaine. "Women Writing and Teaching." *College English* 34 (Oct. 1972): 1-5.

Hill, Iris Tillman. Review of *Silences. Georgia Review* 33.4 (Winter 1979): 958-61.

Howe, Florence. "Literacy and Literature." *PMLA* 89 (May 1974): 433-41.

Howe, Irving. "Stories: New, Old and Sometimes Good." Review of *Tell Me a Riddle. New Republic* 13 Nov. 1961: 22.

Jacobs, Naomi. "Earth, Air, Fire and Water in 'Tell Me a Riddle.'" *Studies in Short Fiction* 23.4 (Fall 1986): 401-06.

———. "Olsen's 'O Yes': Alva's Vision as Childbirth Account." *Notes on Contemporary Literature* 16.1 (Jan. 1986): 7-8.

Jacobsen, Janet L. *Study Guide for Tell Me a Riddle by Tillie Olsen.* Angle of Vision: Interpreting Contemporary Western Fiction. n.p.: Arizona State University, 1986.

Jones, Beverly. "The Dynamics of Marriage and Motherhood." *Sisterhood Is Powerful.* Ed. Robin Morgan. New York: Vintage, 1970. 49-67.

Kamel, Rose. "Riddles and Silences: Tillie Olsen's Autobiographical Fiction." *Aggravating the Conscience: Jewish-American Literary Mothers in the Promised Land.* New York: Peter Lang, 1988. 81-114.

———. "Literary Foremothers and Writers' Silences: Tillie Olsen's Autobiographical Fiction." *MELUS: The Journal of the Society for the Study of the Multi-Ethnic Literature of the United States* 12.3 (Fall 1985): 55-72.

Kapp, Isa. "A Literary Life." Review of *Silences. New Leader* 22 May 1978: 5-6.

Kirschner, Linda Heinlein. "I Stand Here Ironing." *English Journal* 65 (Jan. 1976): 58-59.

Lester, Elenore. "The Riddle of Tillie Olsen." *Midstream* Jan 1975: 75-79.

Levin, Eric. Review of *Mothers and Daughters, That Special Quality. People Weekly* 13 July 1987: 16.

Lyons, Bonnie. "Tillie Olsen: The Writer as a Jewish Woman." *Studies in American Jewish Literature* 5 (1986): 89-102.

Malpezzi, Frances M. "Sisters in Protest: Rebecca Harding Davis and Tillie Olsen." *Artes Liberales* 12.2 (Spring 1986): 1-9.

Manning, Gerald F. "Fiction and Aging: 'Ripeness is All.'" *Canadian Journal on Aging/La Revue Canadienne de Vieillissement* 8.2 (Summer 1989): 157-63.

Marcus, Jane. "Still Practice, A/Wrested Alphabet: Toward a Feminist Aesthetic." *Feminist Issues in Literary Scholarship.* Ed. Shari Benstock. Bloomington: Indiana U P, 1987. 79-97.

Martin, Abigail. *Tillie Olsen.* Boise State University Western Writers Series Number 65. Boise: Boise State U, 1984.

McElhiney, Annette Bennington. "Alternative Responses to Life in Tillie Olsen's Work." *Frontiers* 11.1 (Spring 1977): 76-91.

McNeil, Helen. "Speaking for the Speechless." Review of *Silences, Yonnondio: From the Thirties,* and *Tell Me a Riddle. Times Literary Supplement* 14 November 1980: 1294.

Meese, Elizabeth A. "Deconstructing the Sexual Politic: Virginia Woolf and Tillie Olsen." *Crossing the Double Cross.* Chapel Hill: U of North Carolina P, 1986. 89-113.

Miller, Lynn Christine. "The Subjective Camera and Staging Psychological Fiction." *Literature in Performance: A Journal of Literary and Performing Art* 2 (Apr. 1982): 35-42.

Miller, Nolan. Review of *Silences. Antioch Review* 36 (Fall 1978): 513.

Mintz, Jacqueline A. "The Myth of the Jewish Mother in Three Jewish, American, Female Writers." *Centennial Review* 22 (1978): 346-55.

Morris, Victoria E. "Tillie Olsen on the Privilege to Create." *Radcliffe Centennial News* 1.3 (July 1979): 9.

Moss, Ruth J. "Generations of Images." Review of *Mothers & Daughters: That Special Quality. Psychology Today* Nov. 1987: 80.

Nelson, Kay Hoyle. "Tillie Olsen." *Jewish American Women Writers*. Ed. Ann R. Shapiro. Westport, CT: Greenwood, [1994].

Newman, Mordecai. "Do Jewish Filmmakers Have Enough To Say? Review of film version of *Tell Me a Riddle. Present Tense* 9 (Winter 1982): 19-20.

Niehus, Edward L., and Teresa Jackson. "Polar Stars, Pyramids, and 'Tell Me a Riddle.'" *American Notes and Queries* 24. 5-6 (Jan-Feb. 1986): 77-83.

Nilsen, Helge Normann. "Tillie Olsens's [sic] 'Tell Me a Riddle': The Political Theme." *Etudes Anglaises: Grande-Bretagne, Etats-Unis* 37.2 (Apr.-June 1984): 163-69.

Oates, Joyce Carol. Review of *Silences. New Republic* 29 July 1978: 32-34.

O'Connor, William Van. "The Short Stories of Tillie Olsen." *Studies in Short Fiction* 1 (Fall 1963): 21-25.

Orr, Elaine Neil. *Tillie Olsen and a Feminist Spiritual Vision*. Jackson: U P of Mississippi, 1987.

Owen, Carolyn Sutton. "Tillie Olsen: A Comparative Study of Two Works of Fiction and their Film Adaptations." M.A. Thesis. Texas Women's University, 1988. ProQuest Dissertation Abstract: AC 1336295.

Pace, Stephanie. "Lungfish, or Acts of Survival in Contemporary Female Writing." *Frontiers* 10.1 (1988): 29-33.

Park-Fuller, Linda M., and Tillie Olsen. "Understanding What We Know: *Yonnondio: From the Thirties." Literature in Performance: A Journal of Literary and Performing Art* 4.1 (Nov. 1983): 65-74.

———. "Voices: Bakhtin's Heteroglossia and Polyphony, and the Performance of Narrative Literature. *Literature in Performance: A Journal of Literary and Performing Art* 7.1 (Nov. 1986): 1-12.

Parker, Dorothy. "Book Reviews." Review of *Tell Me A Riddle. Esquire* June 1962: 64, 66.

Pearlman, Mickey, and Abby H. P. Werlock. *Tillie Olsen*. Boston: Twayne, 1991.

Peden, William. "Dilemmas of Day-to-Day Living." Review of *Tell Me a Riddle. New York Times Book Review* 12 Nov. 1961: 54.

Peters, Joan. "The Lament for Lost Art." Review of *Silences. Nation* 23 Sept. 1978: 281-82.

Pratt, Linda Ray. "Tillie Olsen's Omaha Heritage: A History Becomes Literature." *Memories of the Jewish Midwest* 5 (Fall 1989): 1-16.

———. "Tillie Olsen: Author, Organizer, Feminist." *Perspectives: Women in Nebraska History* June 1984: 42-60.

Rhodes, Carolyn. "'Beedo' in Olsen's *Yonnondio:* Charles E. Bedaux." *American Notes and Queries* 14 (Oct. 1976): 23-25.

Rhodes, Carolyn, and Ernest Rhodes. "Tillie Olsen." *Dictionary of Literary Biography Yearbook:* 1980. Detroit: Gale, 1981. 290-97.

Rose, Ellen Cronan. "Limning: Or Why Tillie Writes." *Hollins Critic* 13.2 (Apr. 1976): 1-13.

Rosenfelt, Deborah. "Divided against Herself: The Life Lived and the Life Suppressed." *Moving On* Apr.-May 1980: 15, 23.

————. "From the Thirties: Tillie Olsen and the Radical Tradition." *Feminist Studies* 7.3 (Fall 1981): 370-406.

Samuelson, Joan Wood. Patterns of Survival: Four American Women Writers and the Proletarian Novel. DAI 43 (1983): 2607A.

Salzman, Jack. "Fragment of Time Lost." Review of *Yonnondio: From the Thirties. Washington Post-Book World* 7 Apr. 1984: 1. Rpt. in Vol. 4 *Contemporary Literary Criticism.* Detroit: Gale, 1975. 386-87.

Schultz, Lydia Agnes. "Perceptions from the Periphery: Fictional Form and Twentieth Century American Women Novelists. (Olsen, Erdrich, Wharton)." Diss. U of Minnesota, 1990. ProQuest DA: AAC 9109208.

Schwartz, Helen J. "Tillie Olsen." Vol. 3 of *American Women Writers.* New York: Ungar, 1981. 303-05.

Shulman, Alix Kates. "Overcoming Silences: Teaching Writing for Women." Review of *Silences. Harvard Education Review* 49.4 (Nov. 1979): 527-33.

Staub, Michael. "The Struggle for 'Selfness' through Speech in Olsen's *Yonnondio: From the Thirties." Studies in American Fiction* 16.2 (Autumn 1988): 131-39.

————. "Tillie Olsen and the Communist Press: Giving the People Voice." *Voices of Persuasion: Politics of Representation in 1930s America.* New York: Cambridge UP, [1994].

Stimpson, Catharine R. "Three Women Work It Out." Review of *Yonnondio: From the Thirties. Nation* 30 Nov. 1974: 565-68.

————. "Tillie Olsen: Witness as Servant." *Polit: A Journal for Literature and Politics* 1.2 (Fall 1977): 1-12.

Stone, Elizabeth. "Olsen on the Depression, Roth on the Couch." Review of *Yonnondio: From the Thirties. Crawdaddy* Sept. 1974: 88-89.

"Tillie Olsen." *Contemporary Literary Criticism.* Detroit: Gale, 1975, 385-87.

"Tillie Olsen." *Jewish American Fiction Writers: An Annotated Bibliography.* Eds. Gloria L. Cronin, Blaine H. Hall, and Connie Lamb. New York: Garland, 1991.

"Tillie Olsen Week: The Writer and Society." Symposium sponsored by The Visiting Artists Series of Davenport, IA; St. Ambrose College, Davenport, IA; Augustana College, Rock Island, IL; Marycrest College, Davenport, IA; Scott Community College, Bettendorf, IA; and Black Hawk College, Moline, IL. 21-26 Mar. 1983. Publication, under the direction of The Visiting Artists Series, includes the following essays: Winifred Farrant Bevilacqua's, "Women Writers and Society in 1930 America: Tillie Olsen, Meridel LeSueur, and Josephine Herbst," pp. 1-19; Mary K. DeShazer's "'In the Wind of the Singing': The Language of Tillie Olsen's 'Tell Me a Riddle,'" pp. 20-31; Sally H. Johnson's "Silence and Song: The Structure and Imagery of Tillie Olsen's 'Tell Me a

Riddle,'" pp. 33-44; Sara McAlpin's "Mothers in Tillie Olsen's Stories," pp. 46-58; Kathleen McCormack's "Song as Transcendence in the Works of Tillie Olsen," pp. 59-69; Violet Olsen's "The Writer and Society," pp. 70-74; Vicki L. Sommer's "The Writings of Tillie Olsen: A Social Work Perspective," pp. 75-87.

Trensky, Anne. "The Unnatural Silences of Tillie Olsen." *Studies in Short Fiction* 27.4 (Fall 1990): 509-16.

Trueblood, Valerie. Review of *Silences. American Poetry Review* May-June 1979: 18-19.

Turan, Kenneth. "A Riddle Wrapped in Mystery." *New West* 14 July 1980: 17-19.

Turow, Scott. Review of *Yonnondio: From the Thirties. Ploughshares* 2.2 (1974): 113-17.

Wade, Gerald. "Mari Sandoz Award Recipient Tillie Olsen Speaks from the Heart." *Omaha World-Herald* 5 Nov. 1991, sunrise ed.: 29.

Wiegand, William. "Tormented Alienation Dramas." *New Leader* 5 Feb. 1962: 29-30.

Yeager, Patricia. "Writing as Action: A Vindication of the Rights of Women: Silences." *Honey-Mad Women: Emancipatory Strategies in Women's Writings.* New York: Columbia U P, 1988. 153-59.

Index

Aaron, Daniel, 56, 59, 87n.7
Ackroyd, Peter, 6, 26-27
Adams, J. Donald, 22
Adaptation of works, 9, 19n.13, 19n.14
Aesthetic, Olsen's: balance activism and art, 14, 24, 42, 64, 67-68, 82; and change with critical perspective, 196; and concept of creativity, 47; as debt to Hawthorne, 10, 125; as debt to Whitman, 10, 125-27; with didactic ends, 71, 73-74, 76; to distinguish insight vs. observation, 120-27; with feminism, 10; vs. formalism, 7-8, 91; and reliance on conventions, 161, 167n.13; as in visually fragmented texts, 15, 159, 206, 213, 219; and use of polemics, 25, 37-40 passim, 50, 62, 71, 122, 149, 176, 247, 253; as voice for working class, 24, 30-31, 76, 93-100, 209, 214n.8
Africanism, 198
Alcott, Bronson, 121
Algren, Nelson, 69, 88n.19
Aliases, Olsen's use of, 231, 236, 241

Allen, "Red," 60
Alvarez, Anthony, 247
American Depression of the 1930s, 26, 27, 100, 206-07, 211, 230. *See also* Thirties, the
American Jewish literature, 146
American Left, 56. *See also* Left, the
American Writers Congress, 69, 77, 242n.12. *See also* Congress of American Writers
Anti-semitism, 235
The Anvil, 42
Atlantic Monthly, 32n.1, 59
Atwood, Margaret, 14, 250-51
Auden, W. H., 247
Autobiographical writing, Olsen's: and subject matter, 13, 19n.19, 117, 229-30, 240. *See also* "O Yes," 238-39; "Tell Me a Riddle," 113, 177, 239-40; *Yonnondio*, 237-38; *Silences*, 246-47, 250; "Requa," 227n.15; Jewish heritage

Babel, Isaac, 247
Bakhtin, Mikhail, 90-95 passim, 100, 101, 169-71 passim, 183, 186

Kübler-Ross, Elizabeth, 162, 163

Labor Defender, 67
Labor Lyceum Journal, 242n.11
Lacanian analysis, 217
Landale, Teresa (pseud. Olsen), 22, 41, 236
Langer, Elinor, 63, 79, 87n.9, 88n.29
Larimore, Theta (pseud. Olsen), 236
LaTorriente, Lola de, 18n.1
Lauhon, Carol, 17, 255-60
Lawrence, D.H., 58, 159
League of American Writers, 1, 18n.1
Left, the, 54-86 passim. *See also* American Left; New Left, the; Old Left, the
Lerner, Gene, 235
Lerner, Harry, 237
Lerner, Ida, 34, 57, 176, 177, 231, 232, 233, 234, 237, 239
Lerner, Samuel, 34, 57, 231, 232, 233, 234, 237, 239
Lerner, Tillie (Olsen), 1-6, 21-22, 28, 42-43, 57, 58, 78, 216, 229, 231, 237. *See also* Olsen, Tillie
Lessing, Doris, 9, 50, 248
Lester, Elenore, 9, 148
LeSueur, Meridel, 7, 18n.6, 56, 73, 77, 78
Liberator, The, 58, 59, 68
Life in the Iron Mills (Davis), 3-4, 10, 19n.19, 32n.1, 39, 47, 49, 59, 120-22, 152, 246, 251, 253
Literary foremothers, 19n.19
Literature and Medicine, 10
Lockyer, Joseph N., 140
Lu Hsun, 68
Lumpkin, Grace, 56
Lyons, Bonnie, 12-13, 144-57

McCarthy, Mary, 54, 248
McCarthy era, 28, 86

MacDowell Colony, 29, 46
McElhiney, Annette Bennington, 214n.7
McKenney, Ruth, 56
Mailer, Norman, 31, 247, 254
Malamud, Bernard, 111
Malpezzi, Frances M., 19n.19
Mann, Thomas, 121
Manning, Gerald F., 19n.20
Mansfield, Katherine, 58, 251
Margaret Howth: A Story of Today (Davis), 10, 120
Martin, Abigail, 16
Marx, Karl, 7, 28, 37, 85
Marxist, Marxian perspective, and Olsen: in character speech, 97; and literary resolutions, 76, 80, 81; for message in fiction 40; for narrative design, 91; as theoretical base, 28, 37, 70-71, 86; in view of society, 7, 56; in views of family, 85
Meese, Elizabeth A., 169, 170, 172, 187
Melville, Herman, 47, 48, 119, 246, 250
Mentoring, Olsen's, 3-4, 14, 32, 50, 255-56
Middlebrook, Diane Wood, 20n.32
Midstream, 9
Millay, Edna St. Vincent, 54, 58, 60
Miller, Nolan, 15, 252
Mintz, Jacqueline, 12
Misreading, as interpretative strategy, 197-201
Modern Quarterly, 59, 68
Moers, Ellen, 56
Monroe, Harriet, 87n.8
Moore, Marianne, 248
Morrison, Toni, 183, 198, 201, 203, 204
Mortimer, Penelope, 248
Motherhood/maternal as symbolic structure: "common female

About the Editors

Kay Hoyle Nelson is Assistant Professor of English and Humanities at Aurora University's School of Nursing at Illinois Masonic Medical Center in Chicago, Illinois. She teaches courses in writing, literature, and communications. Her research interests include contemporary writers and early women writers.

Nancy Huse is Professor of English and Director of Women's Studies at Augustana College (Illinois), where she teaches American literature, feminist criticism, and other courses in literature and culture. She has research interest in the field of children's literature.

The Critical response to
Tillie Olsen